Photographic Composition

Albrecht Rissler

Photographic Composition

Principles of Image Design

rockynook

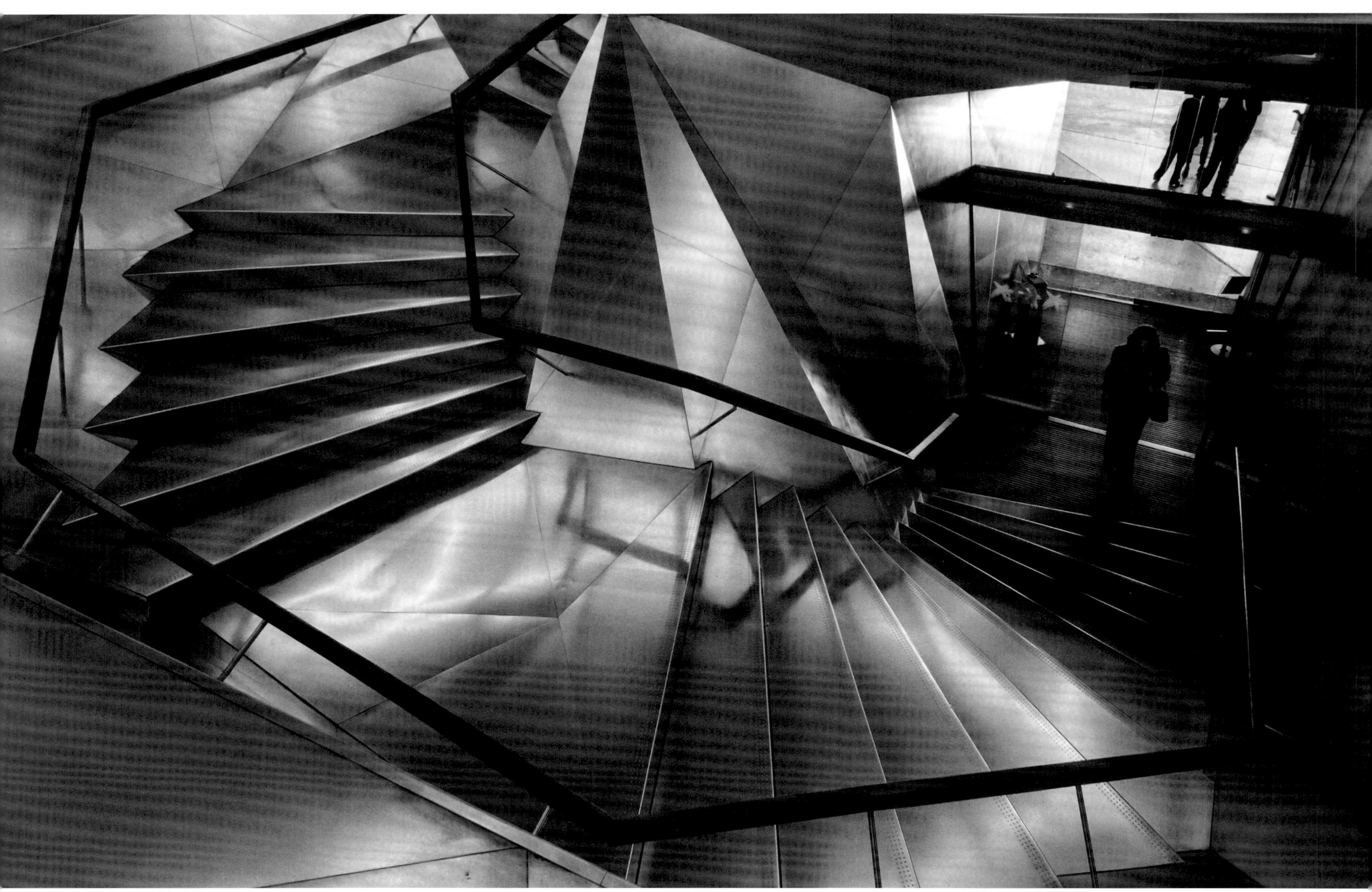

Contents

Foreword vi

Why compose? 2
The Playing Field 4
Value Added 6

The Image Area 8
Serene, Neutral, Charged, Proud 10
Harmony 12
Up or Down? 14

Diagonals 16
Squared Away 18
Heavenly Beaches 20
A Touch of Drama 22
Death of a Giant 24
Coming or Going? 26
Surfers and Insects 28
Star Shapes 30
Forked 32
Breaking the Rules 34

Perspectives 36
Central 38
Field Practice 40
Finding a View 42
Atmospheric Perspective 44
Eye Level 46
Hit the Deck! 48
A Change of Perspectives 50
A Question of Standpoint 52
Pars Pro Toto 54
Changing Places 56

Lattices 58
Obstructing the View 60
Onlookers 62
Look Through! 66
Themes 68
Before and Behind 70

Cropping 72
Extreme Crops 74
Fascination Tree 82
Beyond the Picture 84
Busting Out 86
Symmetry 88
Asymmetry 90
A Comparison 92
Figure/Ground 94
Positive/Negative 96

Contrast 100
The Big Picture 102
Opposites 104
Contrasting Shapes 106
Conspicious Contrast 108
Bull's Eye 112
Walkway 114

Light and Shadow 116
Let the Light In 118
Ice-Cold Warmth 120
Shadow Begets Light 122
Backlight 124
A Subtle Difference 126
Light Spaces 128
Early Birds 130
All Weather 132
Multiplicity 134
Nighthawks 136
The Dark Side of Light 138
Reflections 142

Sharpness and Blur 144
Chance and Intention 146
Stillness and Movement 148
Static and Dynamic 150
Options 152
Experiments 154

Texture 156
A Universe 158
Moving and Stationary 162
Closeup 164
Macrocosm 166

The Right Moment 168
On the Lookout 170
Windfall 172
Reflexes 174
Dialogue 176
Pairs 178
Eyes Peeled 180

Thanks 182
The Author 184

Foreword

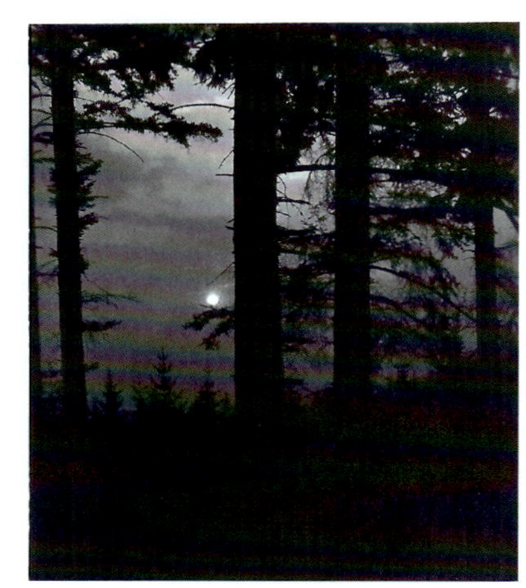

Photographers, painters, and other visual artists are united in their purpose: to reflect and reveal the world around them. Making sense of the world through pictures is a process that begins in the earliest stages of childhood. As soon as I could hold a pen, I started to draw. The habit stuck, and eventually became my career.

Photography first became a part of my life when my parents entrusted me with a folding camera, which I took on a bicycling tour of southern Germany. At the time, I could afford only two rolls of film—16 exposures, which needed to last me 14 days. The very first photograph I took is shown here. I printed it on baryta-coated paper. Today keeping a camera at my side is just as natural as keeping a drawing pad or a sketchbook handy.

Drawing forces you to be attentive and teaches you how to see. Developing my ability to draw has improved my work with the camera significantly. The inverse is true, too: I owe many of the important artistic inspirations I've had while drawing to my photography.

The ability to produce good drawings and impressive pictures does not happen overnight. A wide array of experiences is needed to acquire these skills. Artistry and a broad education in the visual arts are the building blocks for a successful artist and they must be complemented by an aptitude for visual composition and design techniques. Viewers will intuitively be able to tell if these skills are being utilized successfully in the image.

Painting, photography, and graphic arts involve composing elements within fixed dimensions. How can a composition use surrounding elements to support and enhance the main subject? Where should the subject be positioned within the visual field? Where should the horizon be placed? How will the viewer navigate through an image? In what direction should a diagonal line point? To what extent does light contribute to the overall effect of a picture? These are critical questions related to visual composition. I address these questions in my lectures on visual design at the University of Mainz. I use examples from all branches of the visual arts, including photography. In many instances, I've taken pictures for the express purpose of exploring these ideas.

You may lament the gradual disappearance of film photography, but digital cameras offer substantial advantages that are of real use to artists interested in composition. For instance, the framed display screen is a tremendously helpful tool when trying to create an ideal composition. The display instantly reveals your results, which allows you to decide which shots in your series are the most successful. Another advantage of digital photography is that the concerns about the physical equipment required for shooting film are eliminated, allowing you to use your digital camera like a sketchbook. You can keep the good photos and delete the rest.

The original spark for creating this book was the realization that photography is an ideal medium for illustrating the broad possibilities of visual composition. The photographs in these pages are reproduced in black-and-white, or grayscale, so that the main compositional elements are front and center while any potential distractions from colors are kept at bay.

I dedicate this book to my former students. I wrote it for them as well as for the participants in my courses; for beginning and advanced drawers; for graphic designers, painters, and illustrators; and, of course, for artists who work exclusively in photography. This book will also be a valuable tool for readers who would like to view and evaluate images—regardless of the specific medium—with greater expertise.

Albrecht Rissler, July 2014

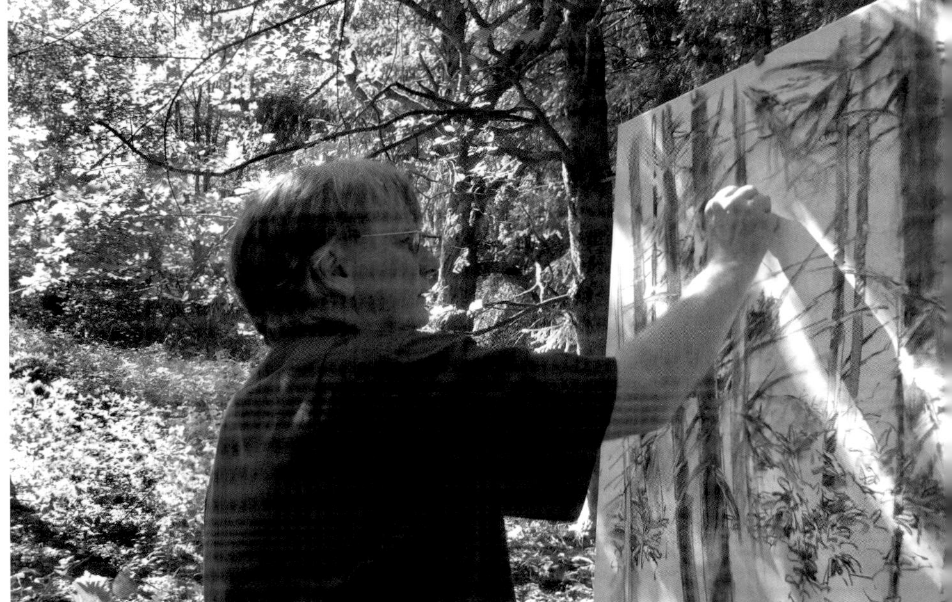

2 Why Compose?

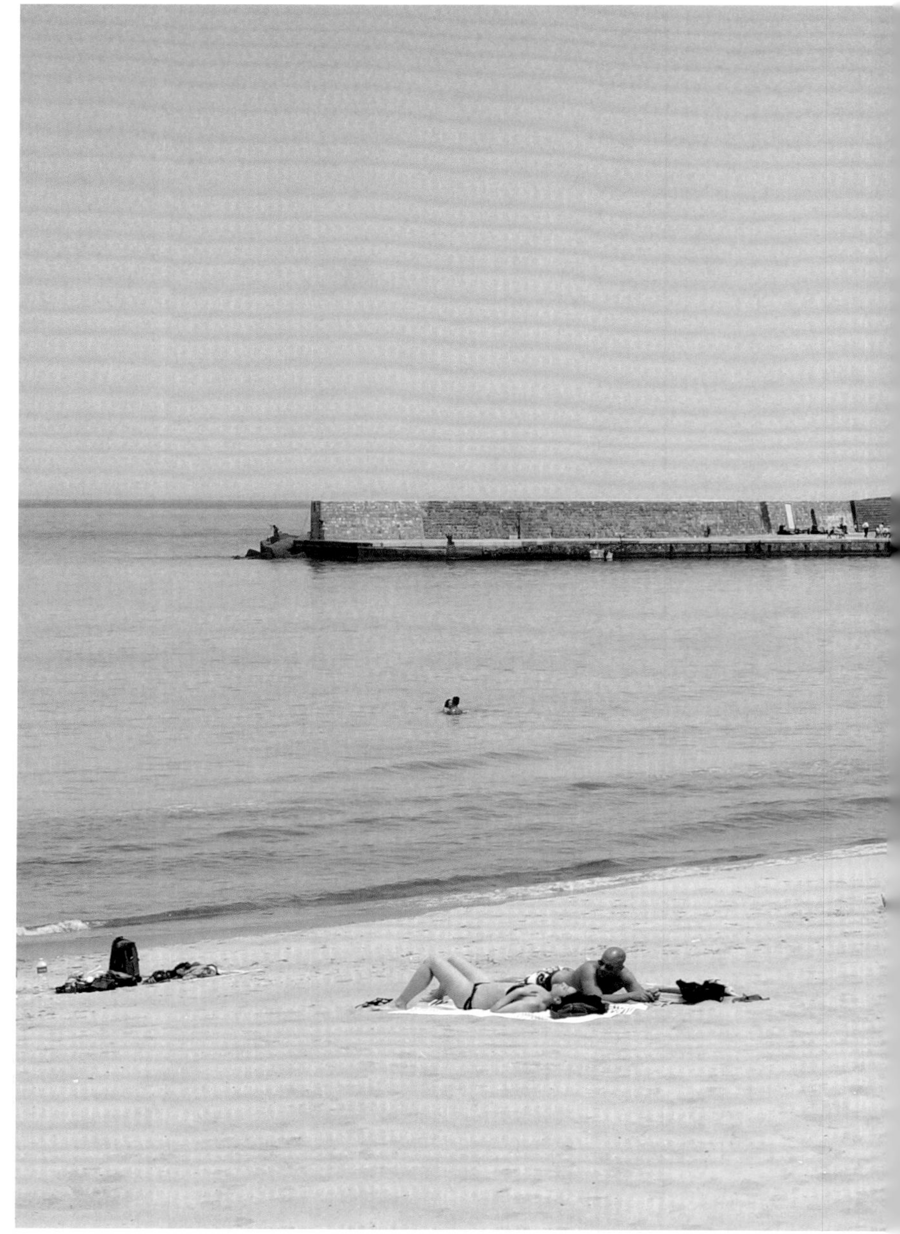

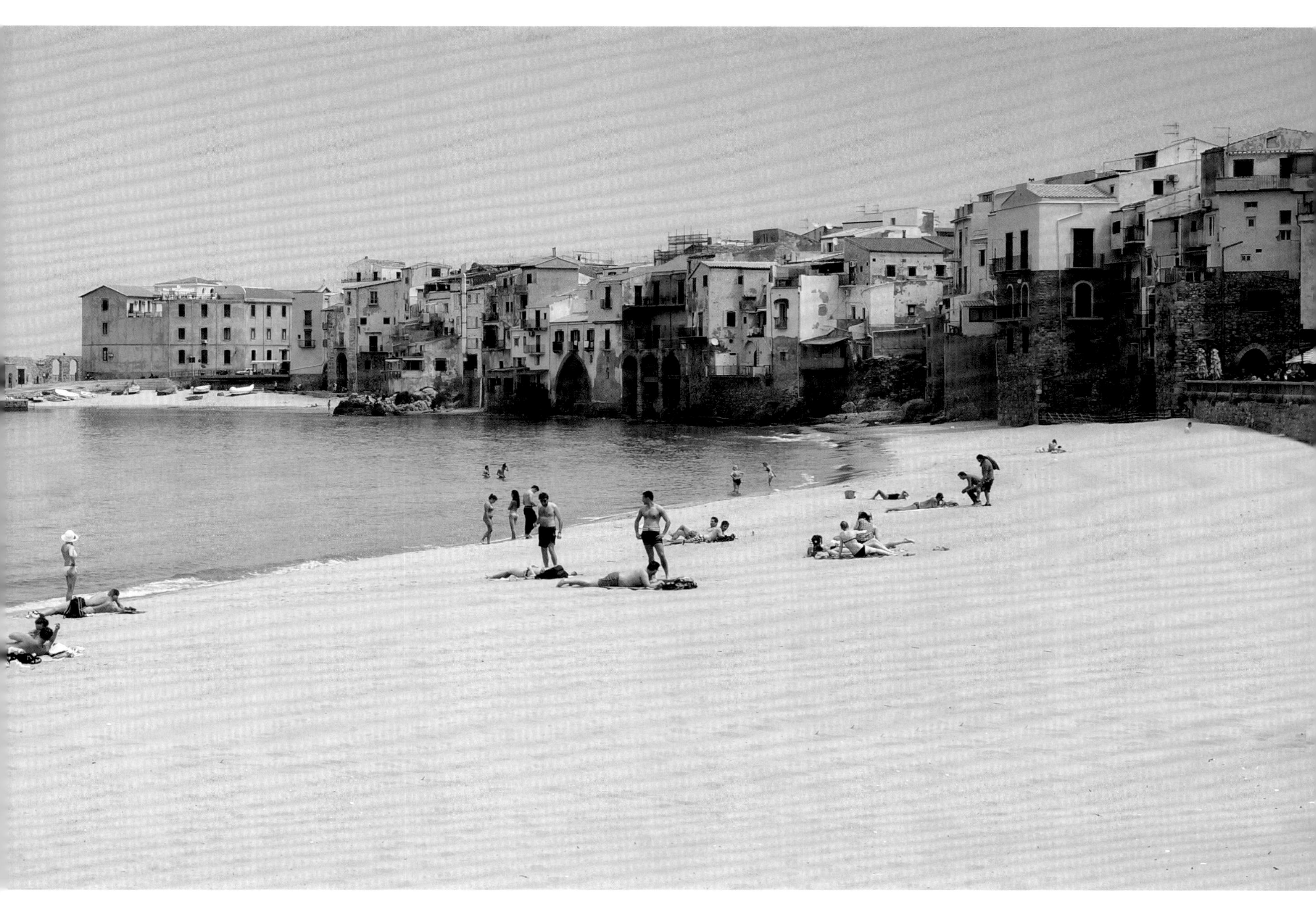

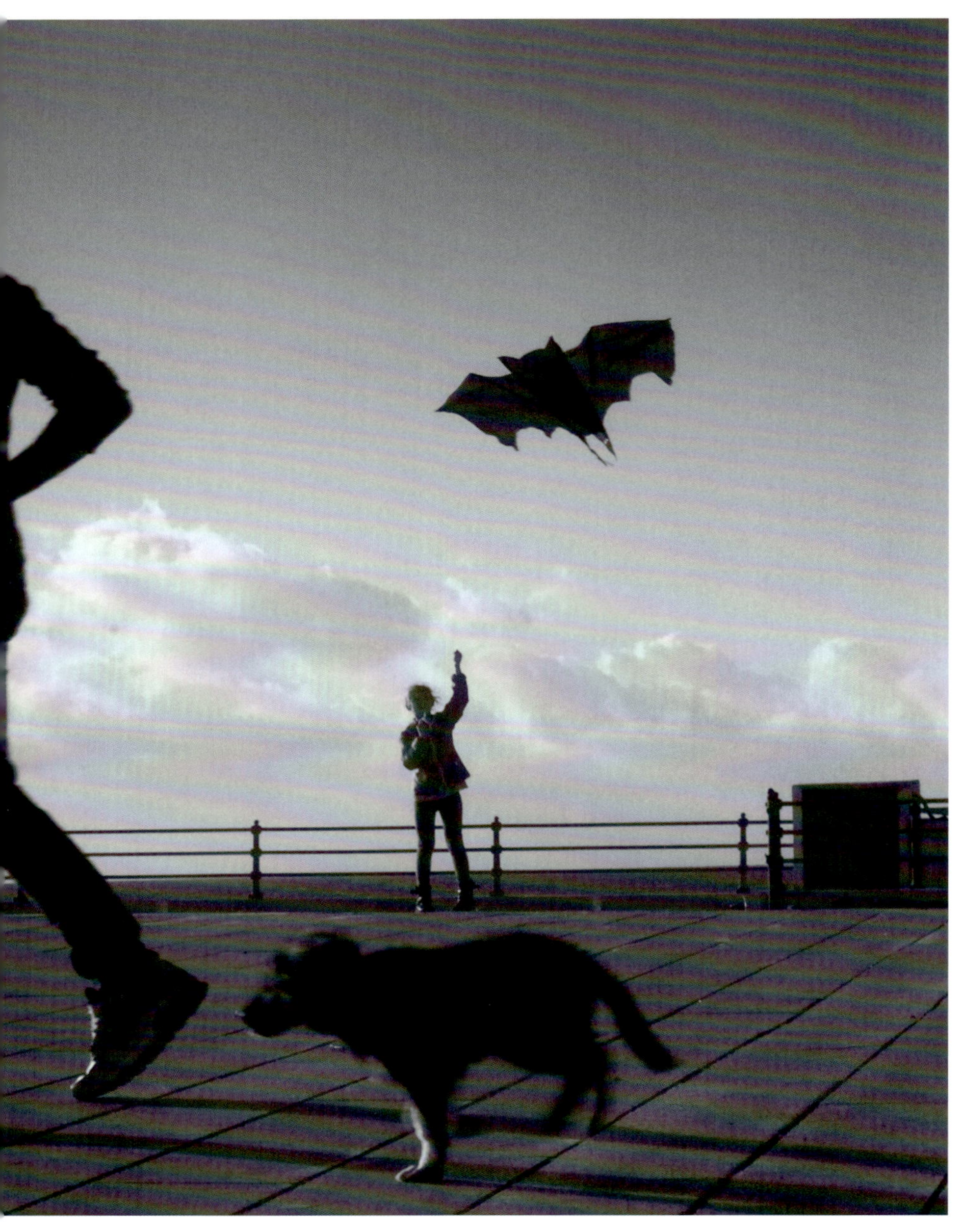

The Playing Field Composition means bringing together individual elements into a cohesive whole. Music emerges from the assembly of notes, rhythm, and the interplay of instruments. Individual graphic elements interact in a similar way in the visual arts. Sculptors work with three-dimensional components, as do architects and city planners.

When it comes to painting, drawing, graphic design, and photography, composition pertains to the organization of two-dimensional elements within a predefined image area. In most cases, the image area is a rectangle. It is in this area that all of the visual subject matter is conveyed.

When a viewer observes an image, his or her eye immediately responds to the overall effect of the image, even if it is difficult to initially grasp the elements at play. The fundamental effectiveness of an image is its composition, its formal organization. Even a well-selected subject that has been immaculately reproduced in a technical sense will usually fail to impress viewers when not supported by a compelling visual design: a picture's content and composition should merge into one cohesive image.

An image's composition consists of various individual elements that exhibit unique qualities. Individual elements may strike dramatic contrasts with one another or they may play harmoniously off one another. Anything appearing within an image is always seen in relation to its outer boundaries. How a subject is positioned within the image area determines its effect. Keep in mind that different results will be produced depending on the size and shape of the image area you use. The dimensions of the image area and the relative positioning of the objects that appear within it should always be considered when composing an image.

The photos here show scenes from the town of Aspra on the island of Sicily.

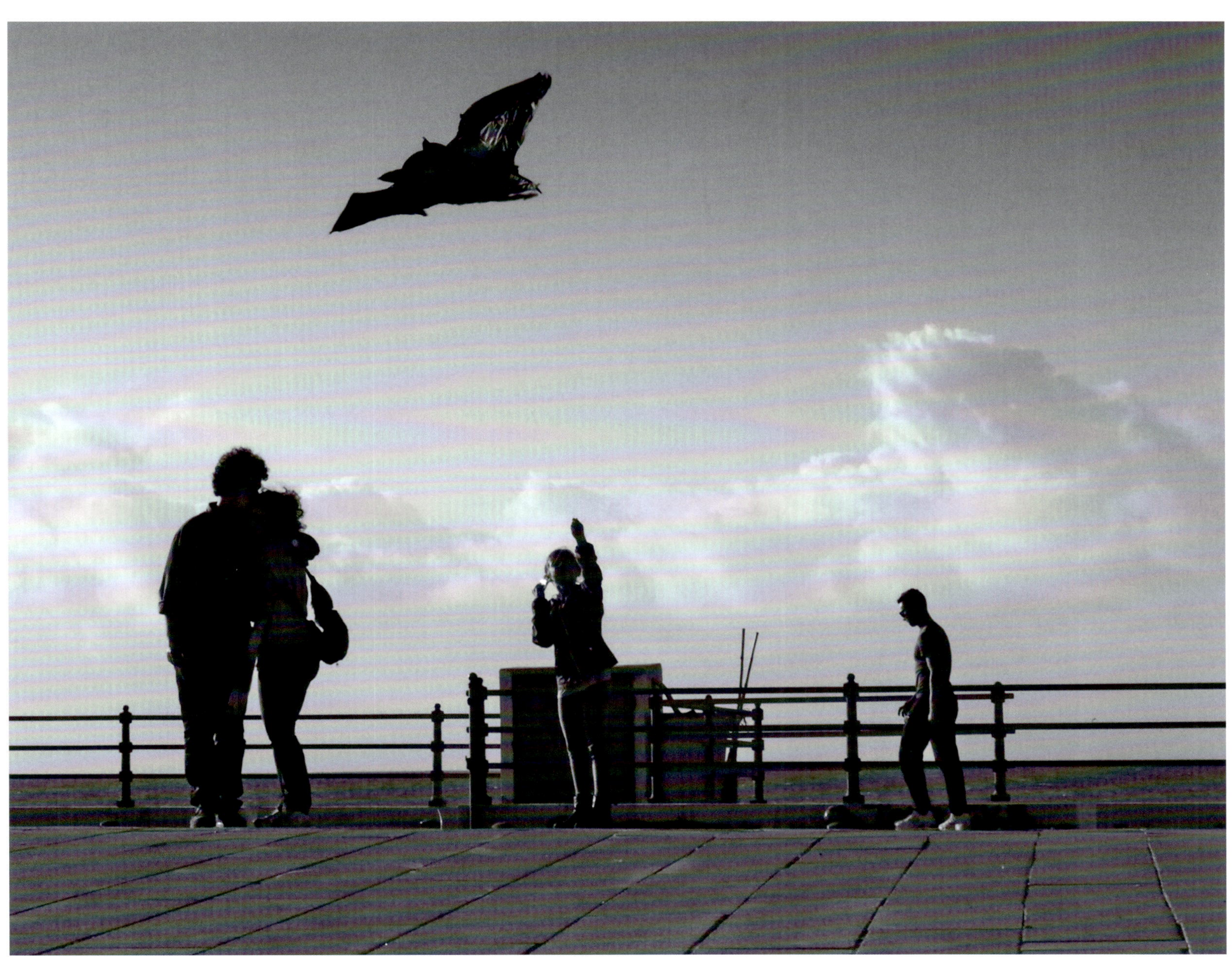

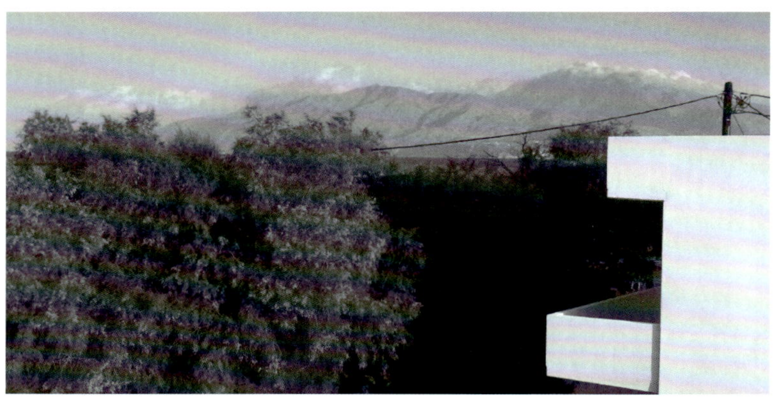

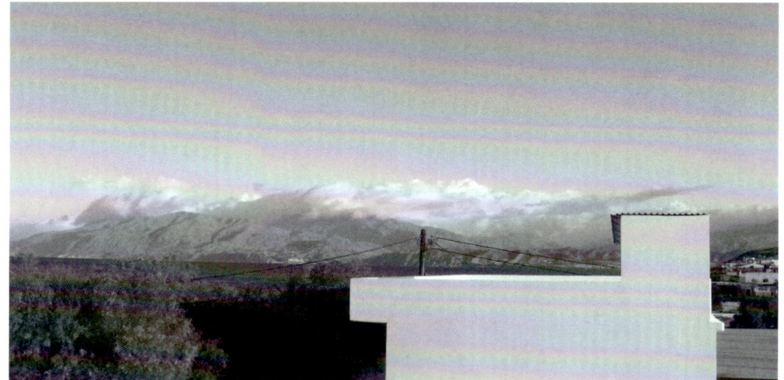

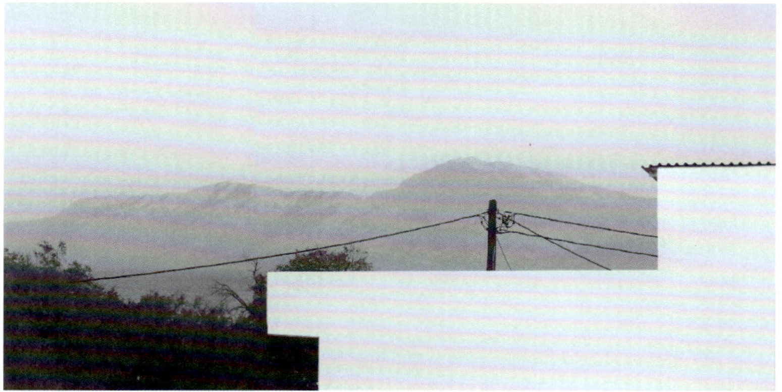

Value Added A familiar experience: the view from a hotel room. There isn't much to see here—just trees and a white chunk of a building blocking the view. Tough luck! This view doesn't make for a worthwhile vacation photo. Time to give up? No!

Turning the camera to find the same view at a different angle causes a few interesting things to happen. By zooming in a little, a picture starts to emerge within the bordered camera display that reveals something more interesting than a hurried memento snapshot. Examining the viewfinder image or the image within the borders of the camera's display screen is really helpful to discover that the subtle curved contour of the mountains creates an interesting contrast with the angular building in the foreground. Gradually the appeal of the subject starts to increase.

Zooming in even more causes the pole and the electrical lines to gain prominence. The large, monochromatic area of the building contrasts with the delicate lines of the wires. Furthermore, the wires' dark silhouettes produce a sharp contrast between darkness and light. Now all that's left is to avoid central positioning of the horizontal top edge of the house's wall. A slight adjustment to the perspective results in the inclusion of the edge of the roof, which slants into the picture's spatial depth.

This example demonstrates that a successful photo requires both a photographic vision and an effective visual design. The more you are aware of the compositional possibilities for a photo, the better you will be able to satisfy both requirements. Having a fundamental knowledge about visual design in conjunction with a proficiency in the technical operation of a camera greatly improves the number of your photos that will be successful. This series also illustrates that a patient, deliberate engagement with your subject matter is often necessary to produce memorable results.

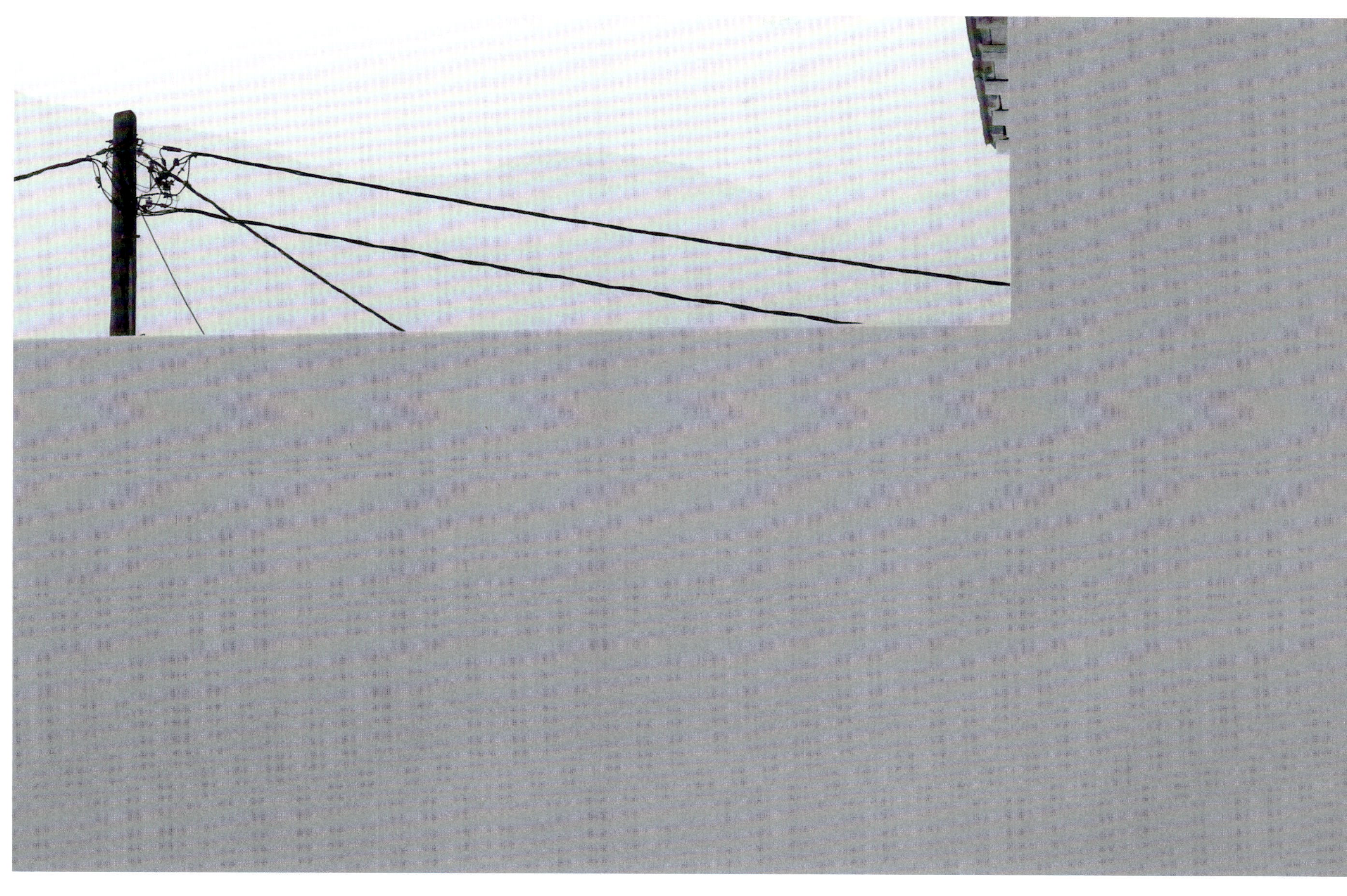

8 The Image Area

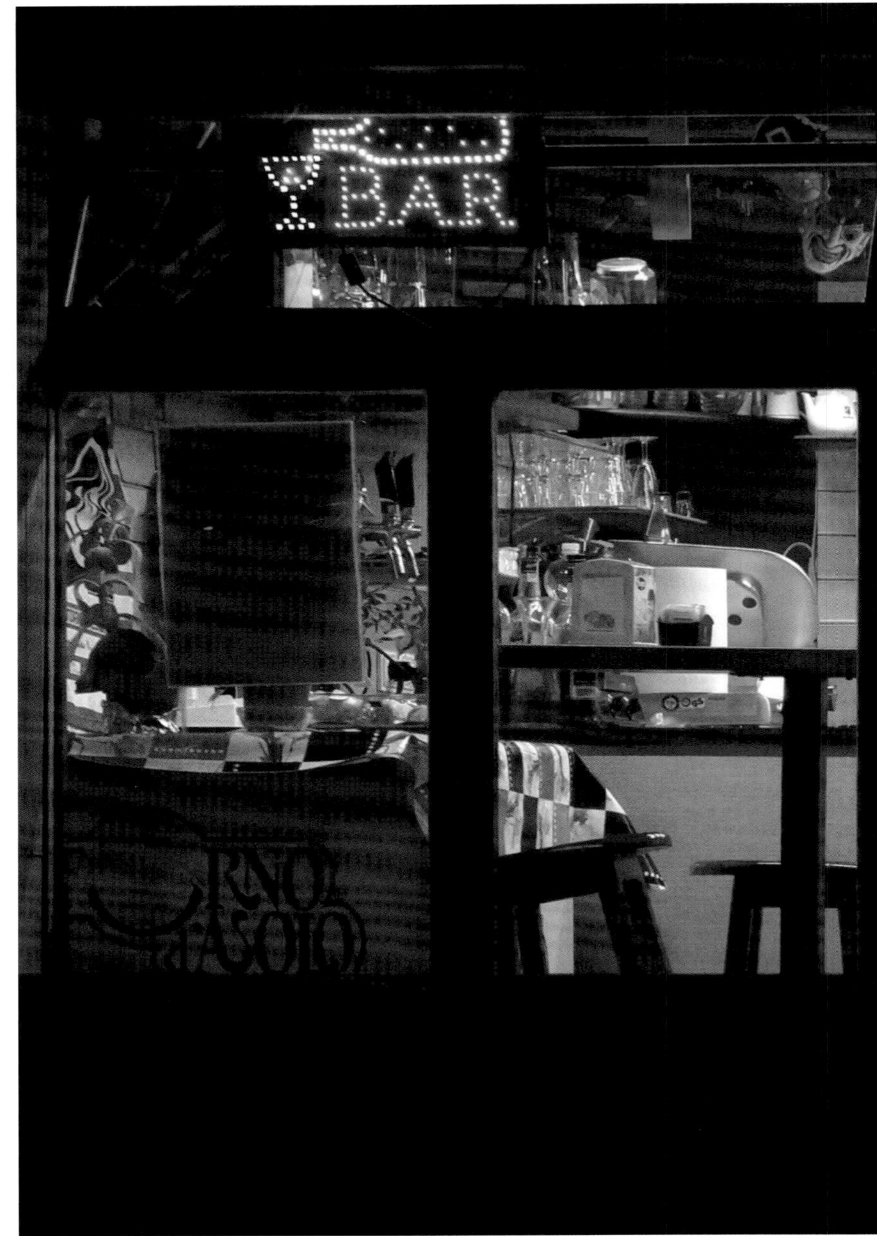

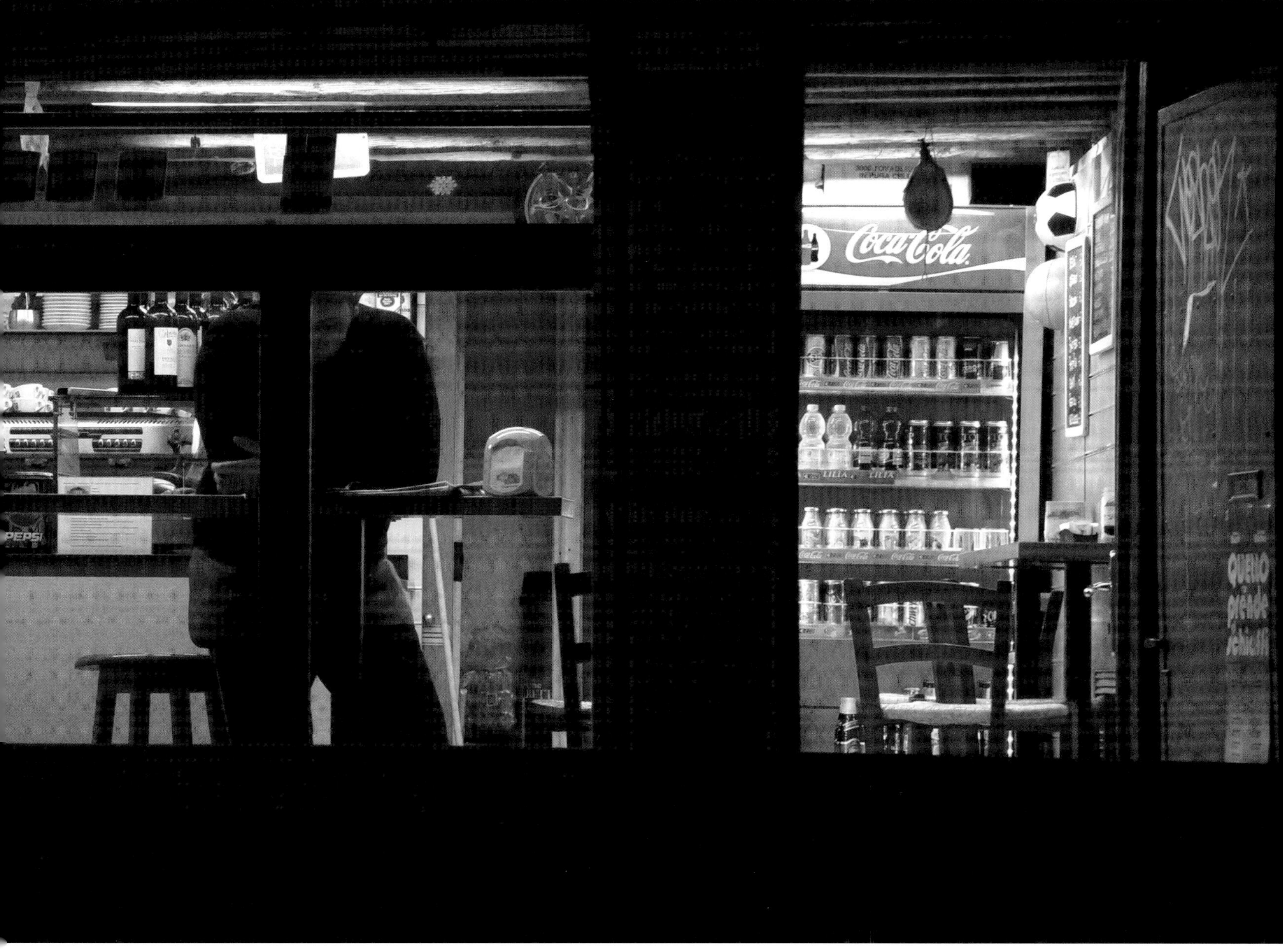
Coca-Cola
PEPSI
LILIA

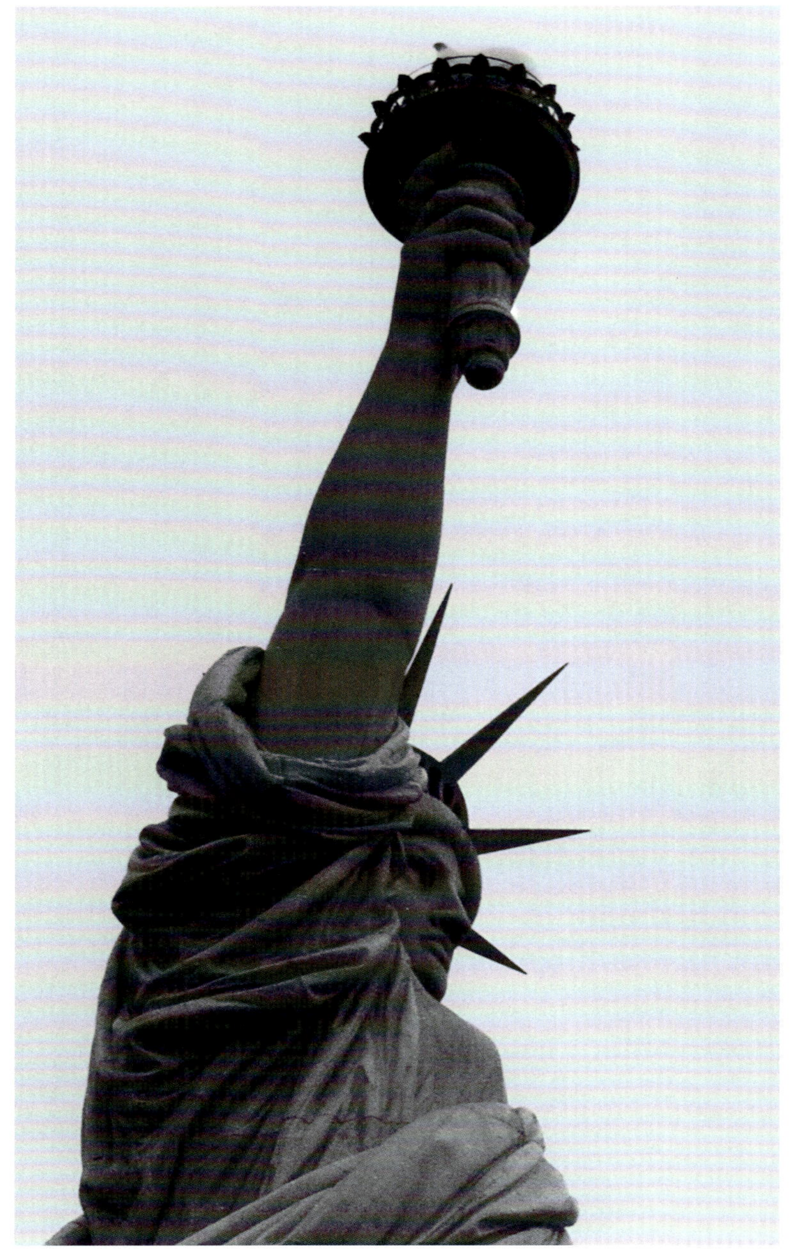

Serene, Neutral, Charged, Proud There are many variables that determine whether a photograph enchants or underwhelms a viewer. Key among them in determining the quality of a photo is the ratio of an image's proportions. Every format, or aspect ratio, produces a unique effect. Visual formats have the potential to accentuate or undercut the subject of an image.

The 16:9 aspect ratio better approximates the natural human perspective. When employed horizontally, this format is well grounded and often ideal for revealing broad-angled views of sweeping landscapes. When employed vertically, such as this image of the Statue of Liberty, this format can exude proud or even toplofty undertones.

In painting and graphic arts, the image area or canvas dimensions can be even longer and narrower than the 16:9 format, resulting in thin strips of artistic space. The precursors for such works of art can be traced to nineteenth-century woodcuts from Japan. Kitagawa Utamaro and other artists inspired many Western artists to experiment with such extreme visual formats. *Japanese Lilies* by Impressionist Claude Monet and *Judith II* by the Viennese painter Gustav Klimt are famous examples of images with particularly slender aspect ratios.

In contrast to the 16:9 format, images in a square format are highly relaxed. Their proportions do not pull the viewer's gaze toward any particular side or area of the image. The photograph on the right-hand page of the rocking chair on the porch and the nearly square snippet of the background landscape achieves the placidity intended by the photographer. The photograph is far from dull, however, because the right-leaning perspective of the image and the resulting contrast of visual areas subtly work against the otherwise sedate qualities of the square aspect ratio.

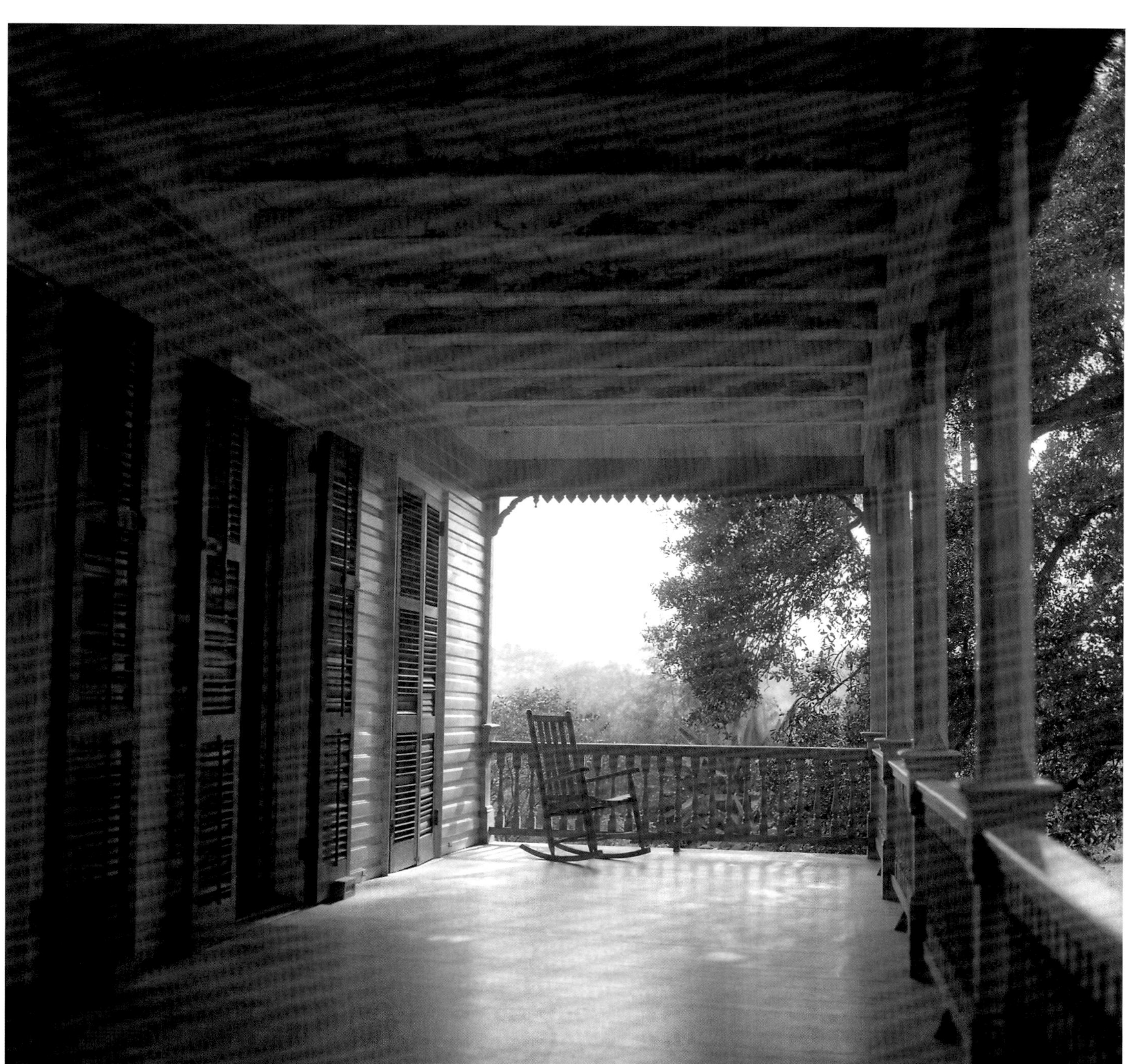

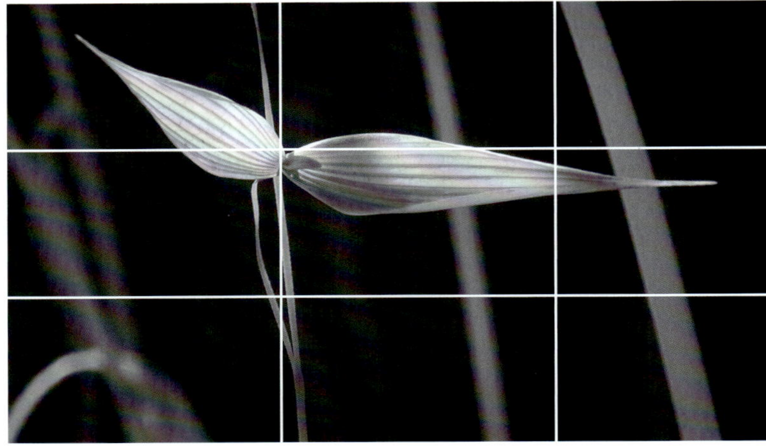

Tip *Many cameras allow you to superimpose gridlines in the viewfinder or on the camera's display screen to help with your composition efforts when previewing a photograph. The intersection points of the horizontal and vertical lines, which create a grid with nine fields, roughly correspond to the golden ratio. Photographers can use this rule of thirds to quickly arrange the image's key elements and achieve a harmonious visual balance.*

Harmony A physicist named Theodor Fechner (1801–1887), from Leipzig, Germany, conducted an experiment in which he offered study participants 10 rectangles with different aspect ratios and asked them to select the rectangle that was the most pleasing to them. The data showed a clear preference (approximately a 35 percent approval) for the proportion of 21:34, often referred to as the golden ratio. The least popular ratio—nearly a square—had a ratio of 5:6. It received only 0.27 percent approval. The study was conducted to demonstrate that the golden ratio satisfied a human proclivity for harmonious proportions.

A striking number of examp es of the golden ratio can be found in the natural world—especially in the growth patterns of plants and animals. The nautilus—related to a squid—and the daisy are often cited as examples of this phenomenon. The nautilus's hard shell and the daisy's inflorescence grow in logarithmic spirals that correspond to the proportions of the golden ratio. It's no wonder that visual artists, including photographers, as inveterate observers of nature, orient their work with these proportions.

The aspect ratio of 2:3, which is offered as a shooting option by many modern cameras, comes close to matching the golden ratio. This format offers a rich array of possibilities for creating particularly harmonious compositions. When using the golden ratio, the composition of the outside dimensions of the image area, the positioning of the subject within the image area, and the relative proportion of the subject within the image area create a natural harmony.

The photo of the oat glumes nearly achieves this standard. With a format of 2:3, the axis of the object is approximately positioned at an intersection point of the golden ratio. The difference in length between the two glumes also roughly corresponds to the golden ratio.

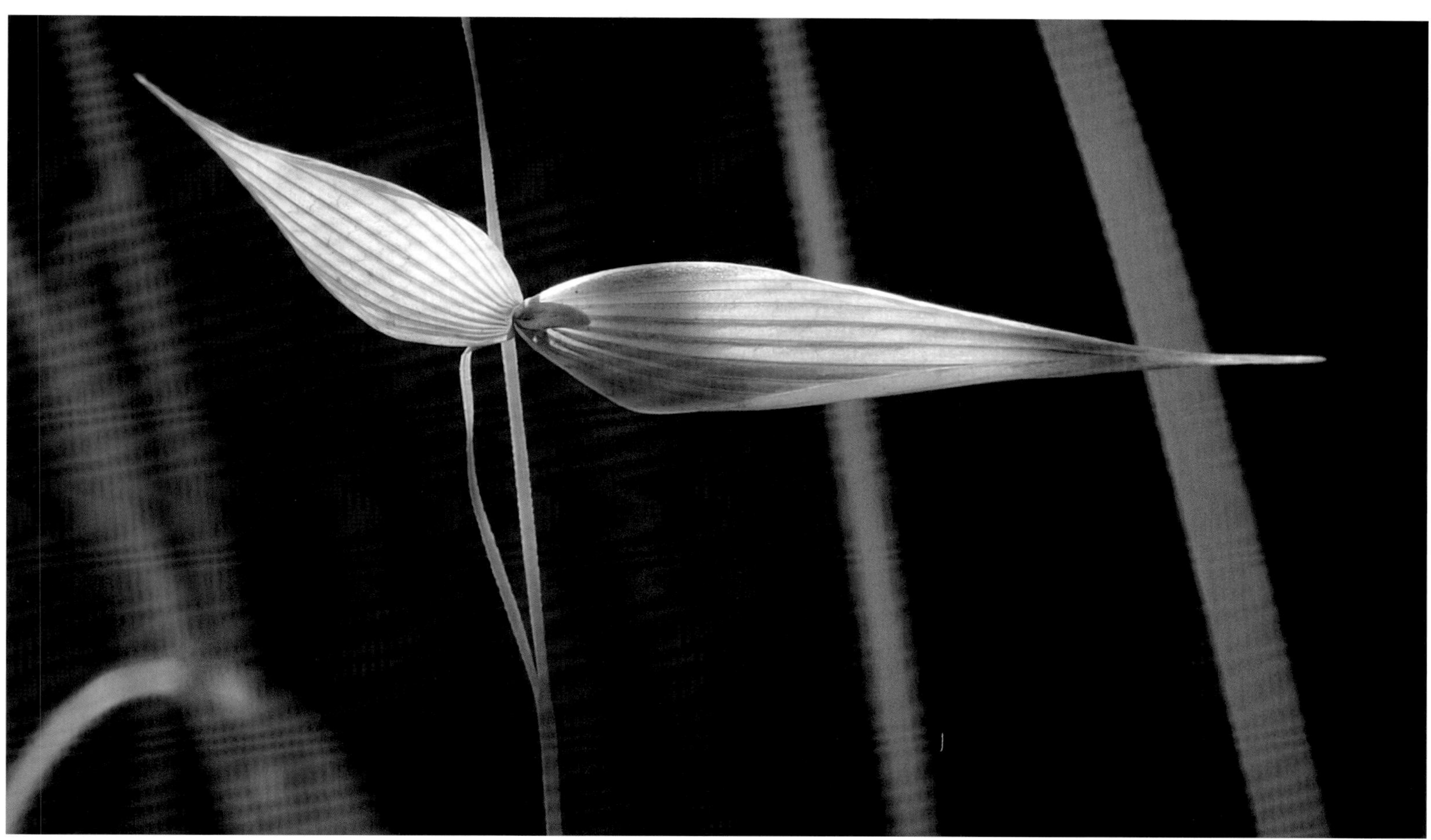

Up or Down? Horizon lines and other horizontal visual elements divide photographs into two halves. In deciding where to position such lines, photographers can establish a distinct area of contrast. The composition of the photographs featuring the mosque at the Schwetzingen Palace offers an example of how to determine which position is the most effective. Centrally located horizon lines often result in boring photographs, but the picture below illustrates that the middle is not always easy to identify. In cases like this, it is better to consider the visual balance of the image rather than the literal, measurable location of the photo's center.

Photographs should make clear that one area of the image is the dominant section. The sky and the trees on the left make this distinction obvious in the narrow portrait-format shot of this scene (right).

If the top portion of the image is too short, the mosque will be pushed up against the upper boundary of the image area. If you want to avoid central divisions, you should opt for the version on the right-hand page. The mosque, the sky, the lake, and the opposing groups of trees bring an effective balance to the photograph.

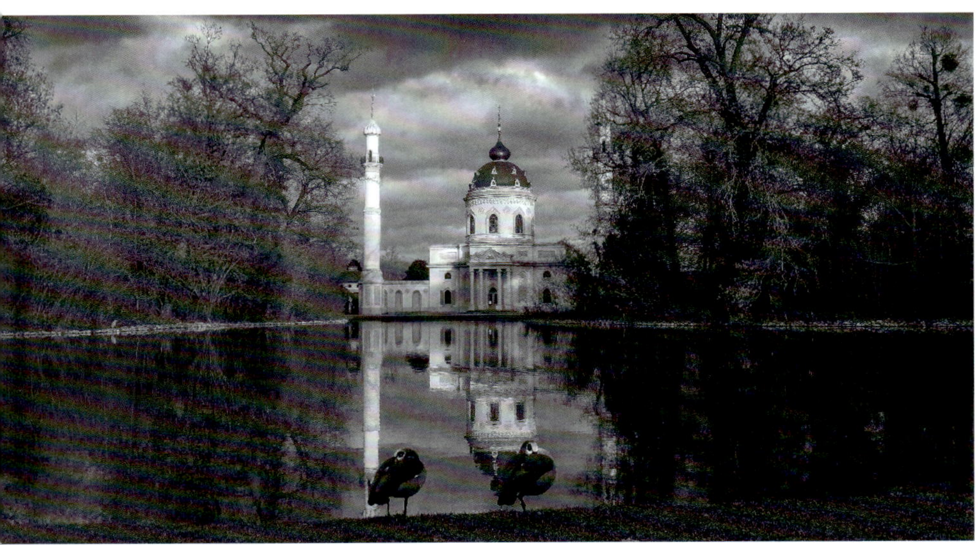

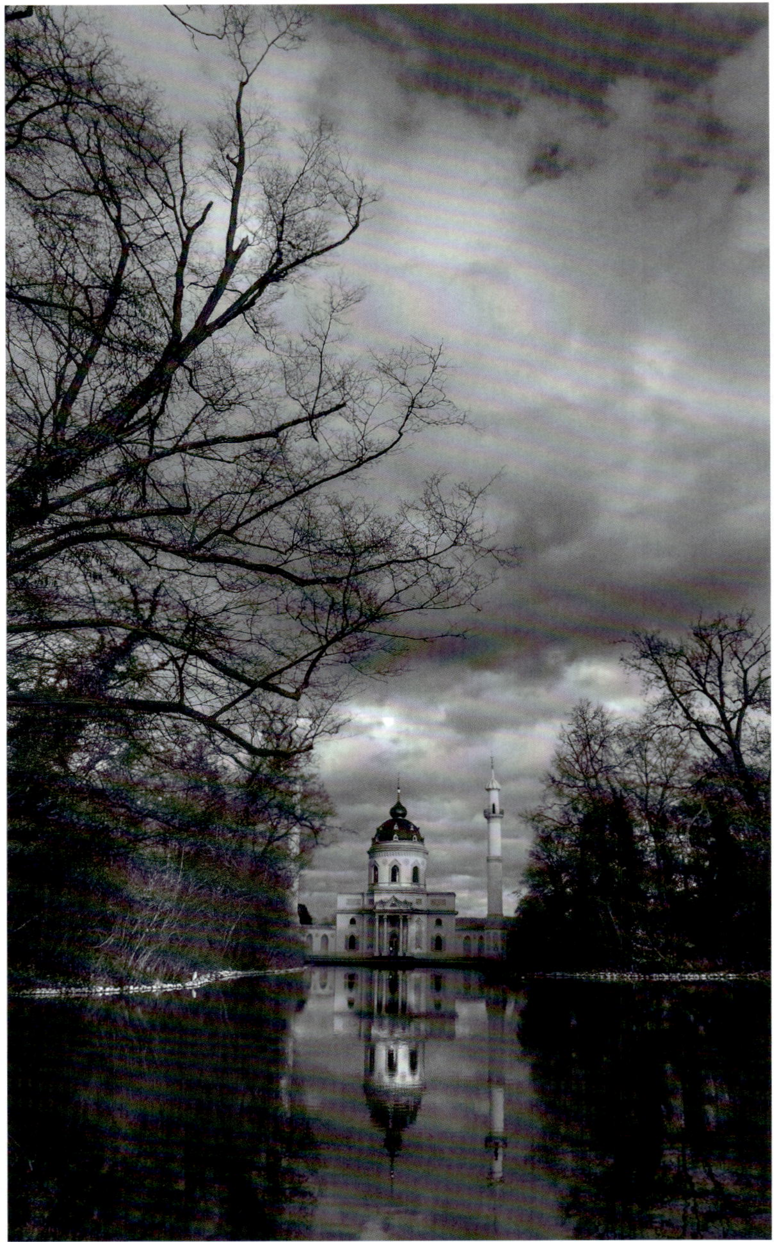

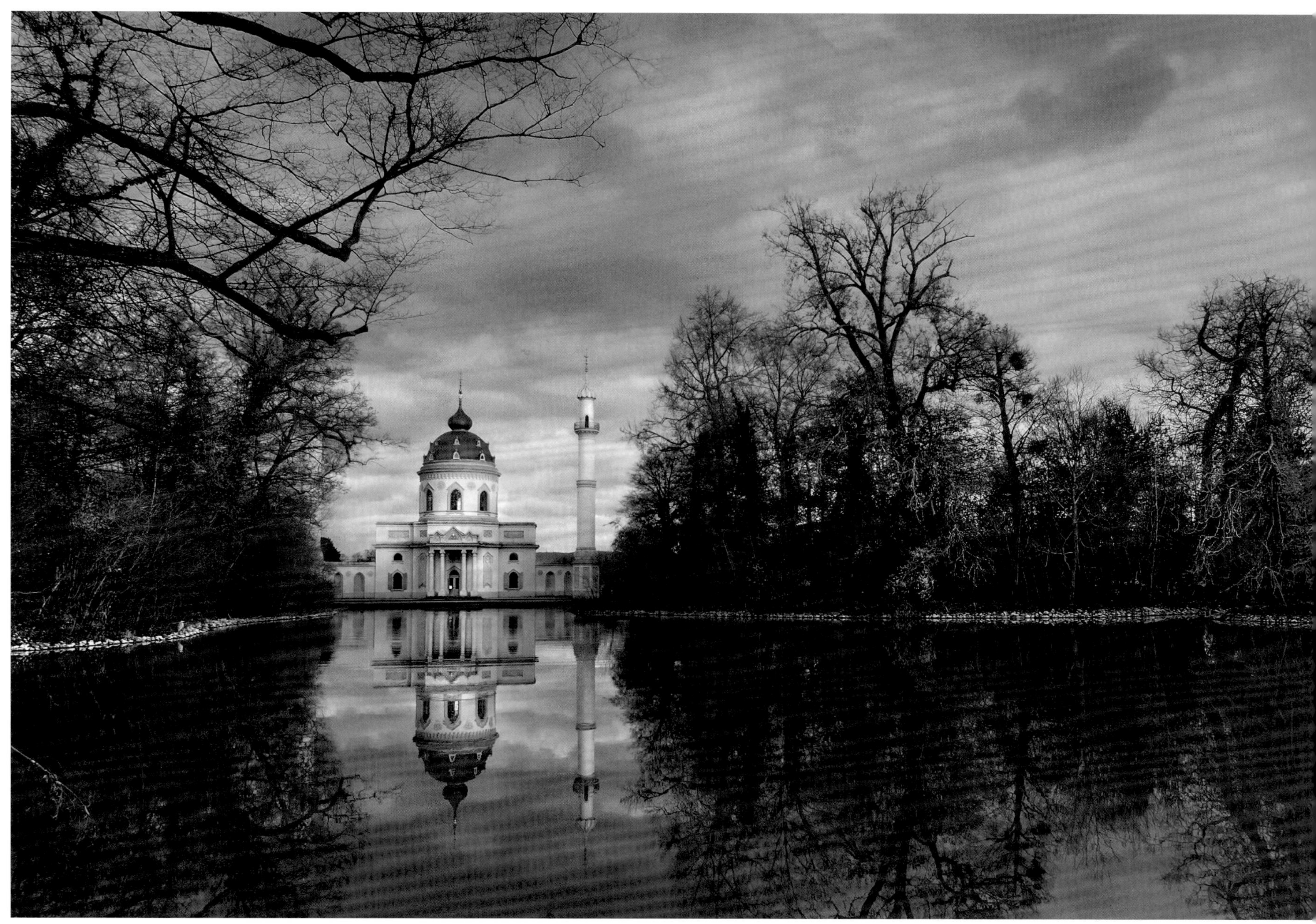

16 Diagonals

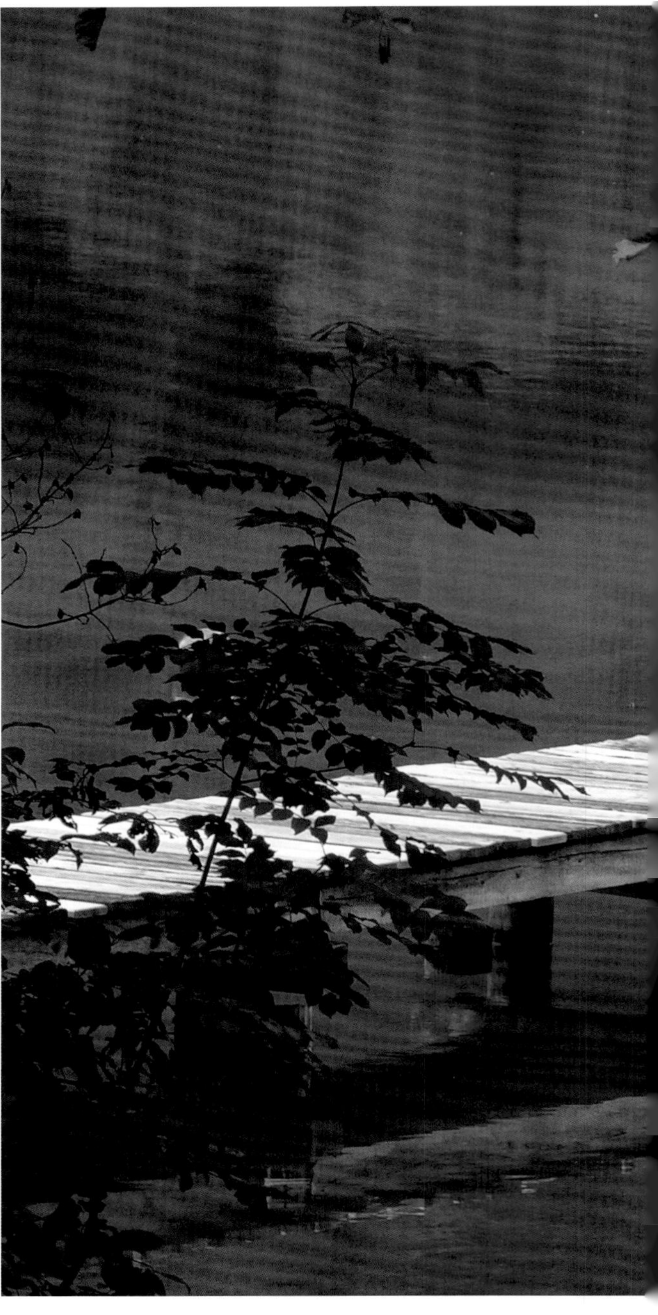

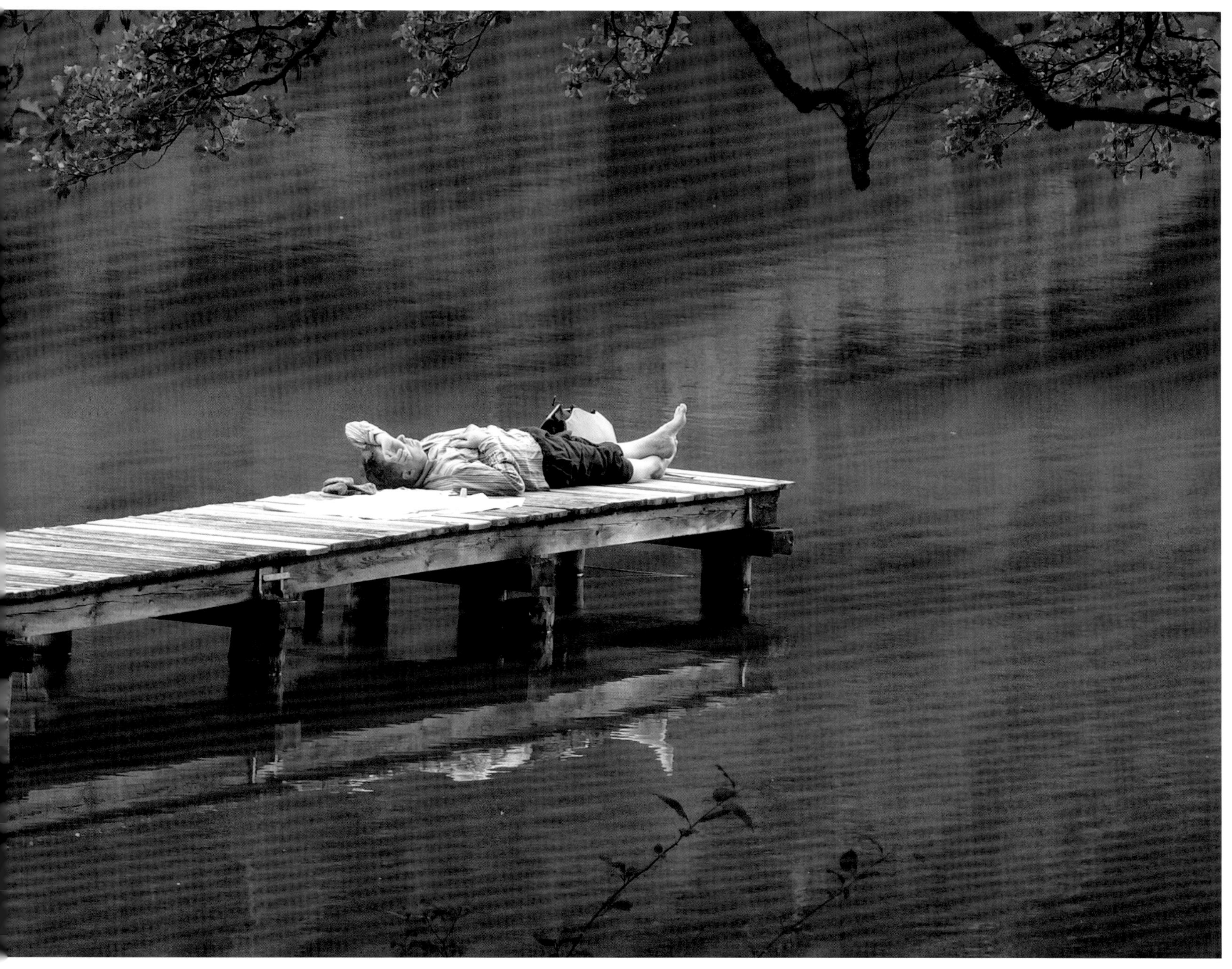

Squared Away Photographers can use diagonal lines when composing photographs to establish a sharp contrast with the right-angled outside border of the image area. This photo (top) showing a diagonal dividing line between the sand and the water at La Calete de Famara on the island of Lanzarote illustrates this effect. The predominant diagonal line is broken up by many smaller slanted lines running in opposing directions.

The visual effect of the diagonal lines in this photo of a fisherman at the port of Cala Figuera on Mallorca is much more complex. The elaborate network of diagonals leading in varying directions is critical to the photo's composition. These lines build a palpable tension with the rectangular boundaries of the image area. The man's legs and the fishing nets surrounding him establish the primary diagonal lines, which zigzag up to the top border of the image area, creating a sense of spatial depth. The shorter diagonal lines direct the viewer's attention to the man's hands in the center of the picture.

Tip *Try to avoid aligning a subject's prominent contours in parallel with the vertical and horizontal borders of a picture. For example, the composition of a photo depicting a house from a corner perspective is much more engaging than that of a photo taken from a head-on perspective. It's often worthwhile to adjust your standpoint so that the most important contours of your subject run diagonal to the rectangular image border.*

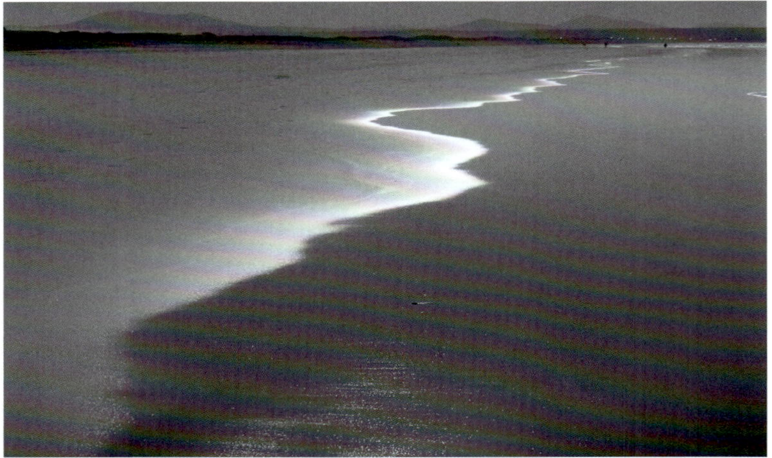

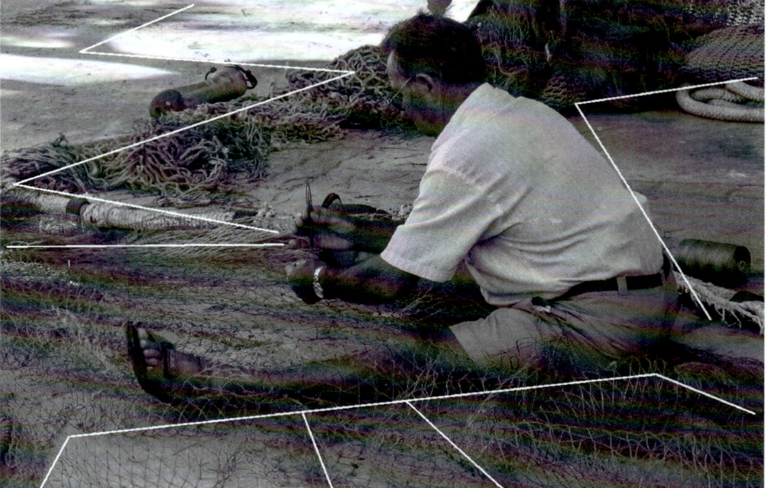

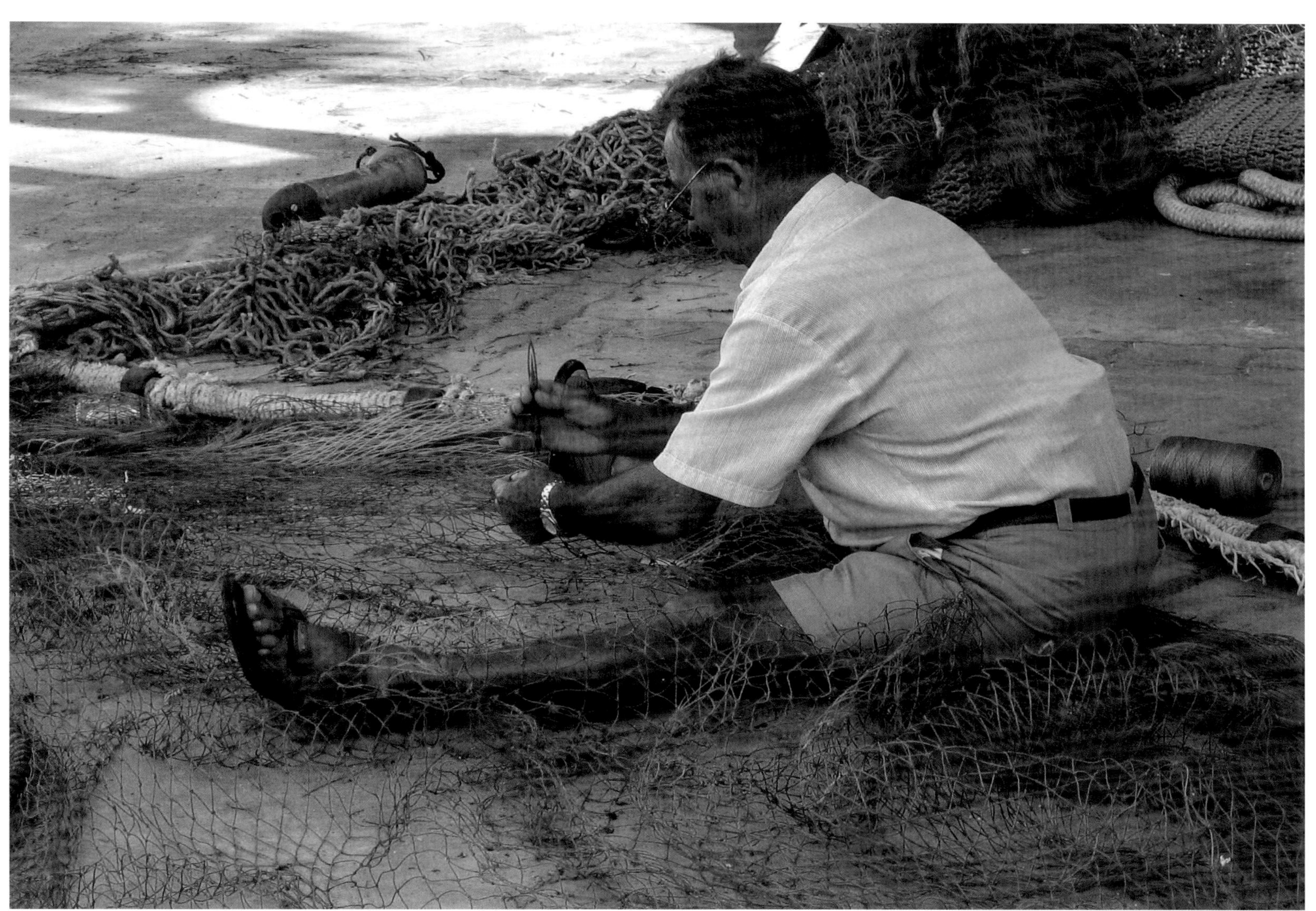

Heavenly Beaches It's lovely to walk along beaches that appear to be endless. Backlighting makes the waves look particularly attractive—the water almost takes on the appearance of boiling lead. The light of the early morning and late evening are ideal for shooting photos, in part because this light makes the contrast between the water, the sky, and the sand the most discernable. The diagonals created by these elements are also especially prominent during dawn and twilight.

Diagonal lines contribute to a sense of depth in this (top) photo of an Andalusian beach on the Atlantic. Significant diagonal contours are created by the waves pointing up to the horizon, the series of fishing poles, and the human figures that appear small due to their distance from the camera.

The back and forth of the diagonal lines visible in the surface of the water at a beach near the San Francisco Bay (bottom) is much more understated. Capturing a photo such as this one requires an attentive eye and the courage to work with a less-than-conspicuous subject.

The image of the beach in Andalusia (right-hand page) shows how the human figures integrated into the picture contribute to the photo's composition. The diagonal line of the shoreline is quite subtle, but the positioning of the people in relation to one another creates an additional effect. There's a certain charm arising from the contrast of the men in the background resolutely leaning forward and the tentative pose of the woman in the foreground. Her position and the horizon line are located roughly at a harmonious intersection point based on the golden ratio.

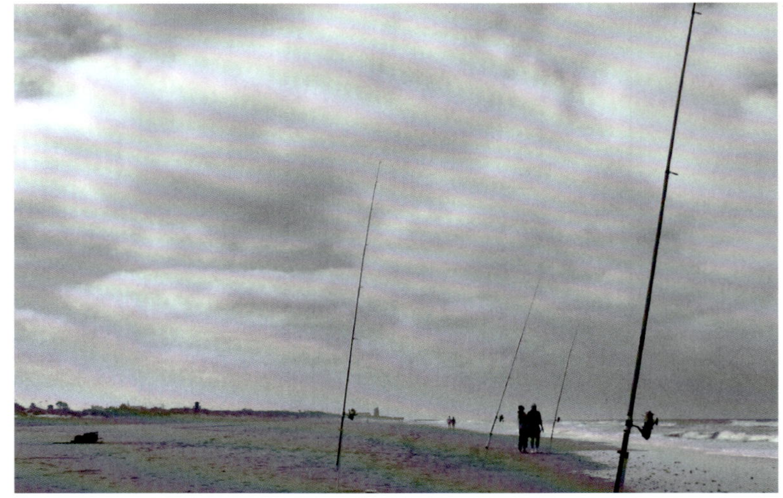

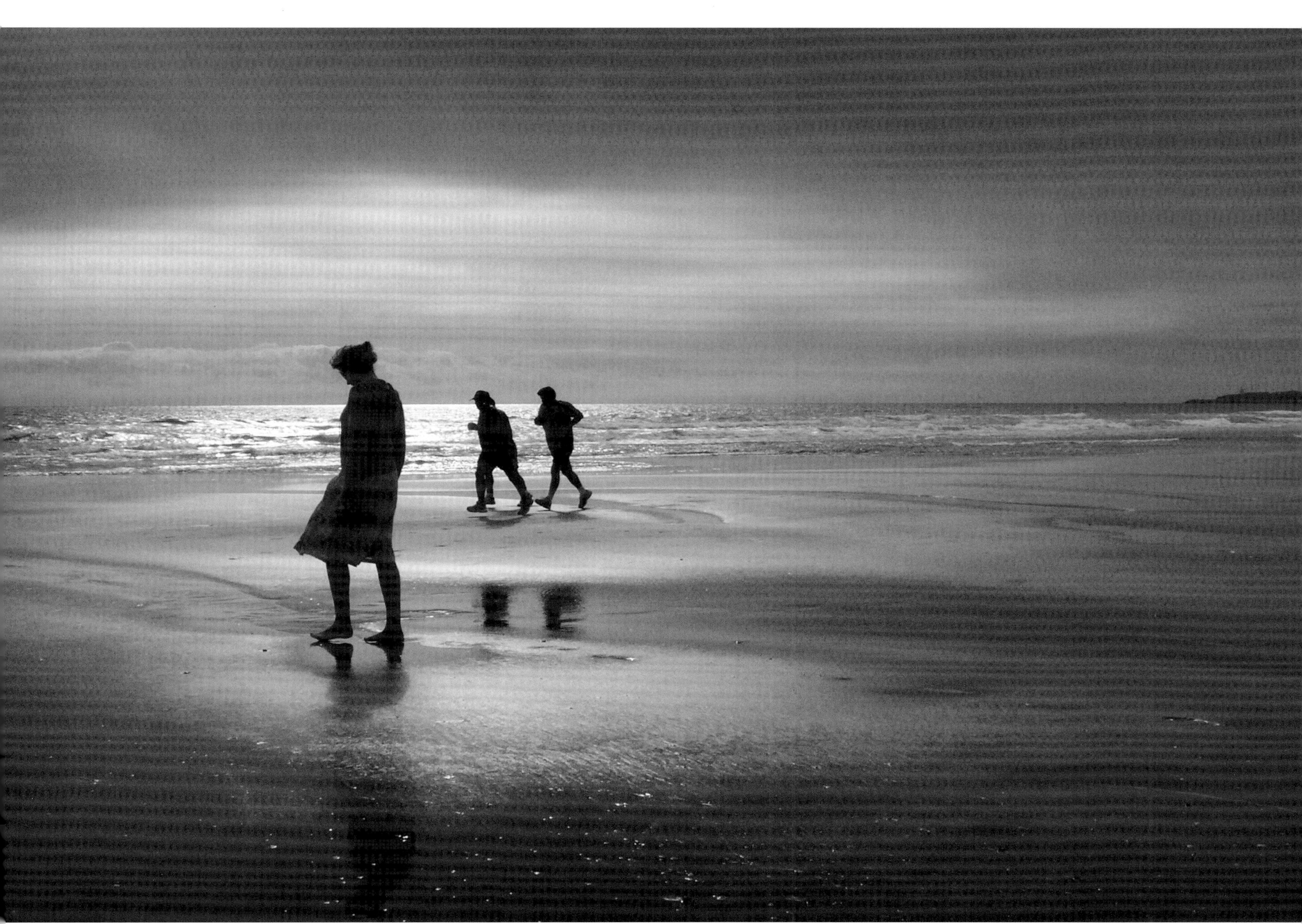

A Touch of Drama Pure white pillow-like clouds float across a deep blue sky above the silhouette of an alpine mountain ridge. This majestic subject might be found in any number of places around the world. Both photographs here are similar, but they differ in one key way. The top photo relies on two dominant diagonal lines that run in opposite directions. They seem to want to continue beyond the edges of the photograph. The composition of the photo is easy to recognize.

Moving just a few meters away from where the top photo was taken opened up the opportunity to bring something else into the picture. A bush now appears in the left foreground of the bottom photo. Now an additional short diagonal line runs against the grain of the mountain ridge and prevents the viewer's eye from following it out of the image area. The viewer's attention is isolated within the picture. In contrast to the more dramatic photo on the top, this picture feels much more self-contained.

Tip *Always pay attention to diagonal elements in your photographs. Landscape and architecture photos as well as still lifes are often ideal candidates for dynamic compositions featuring prominent diagonal lines.*

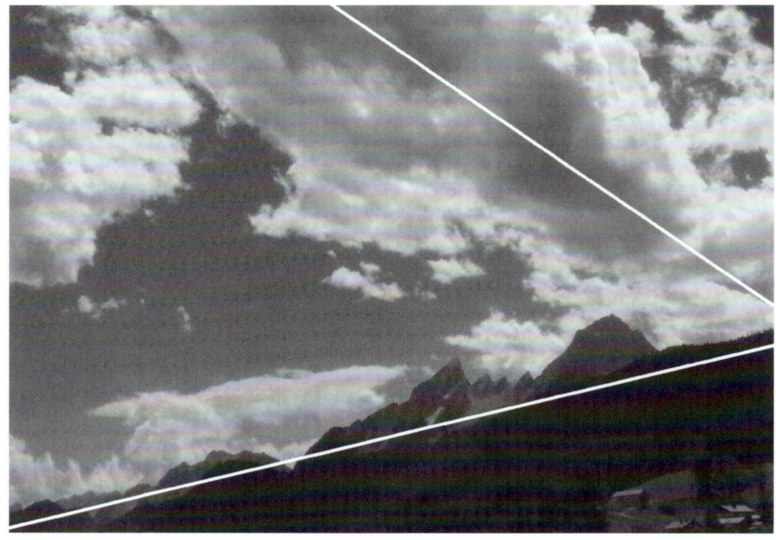

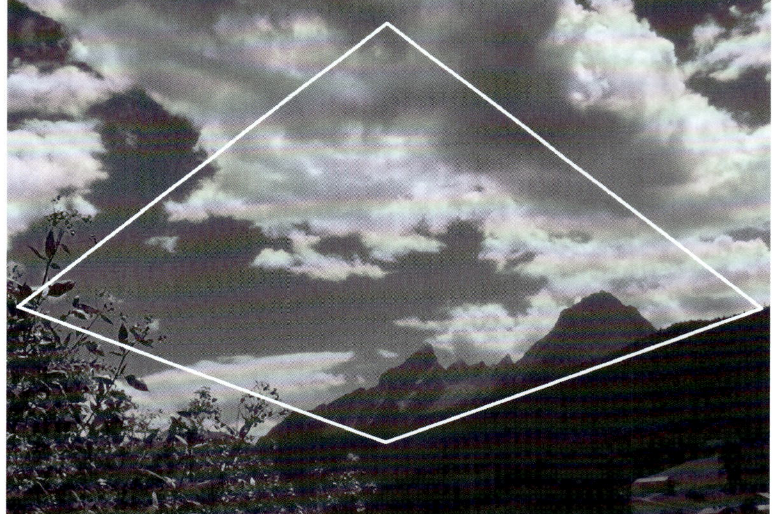

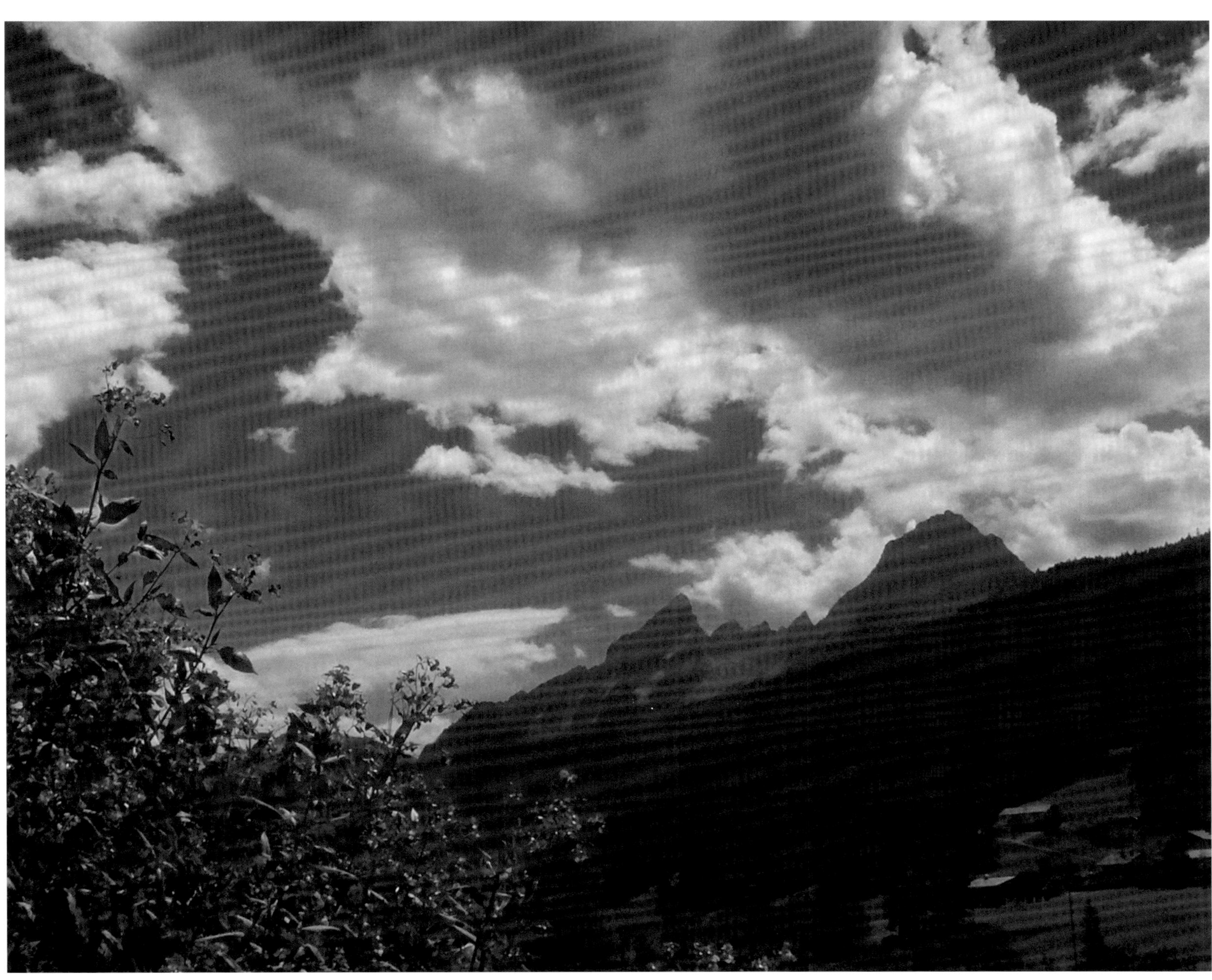

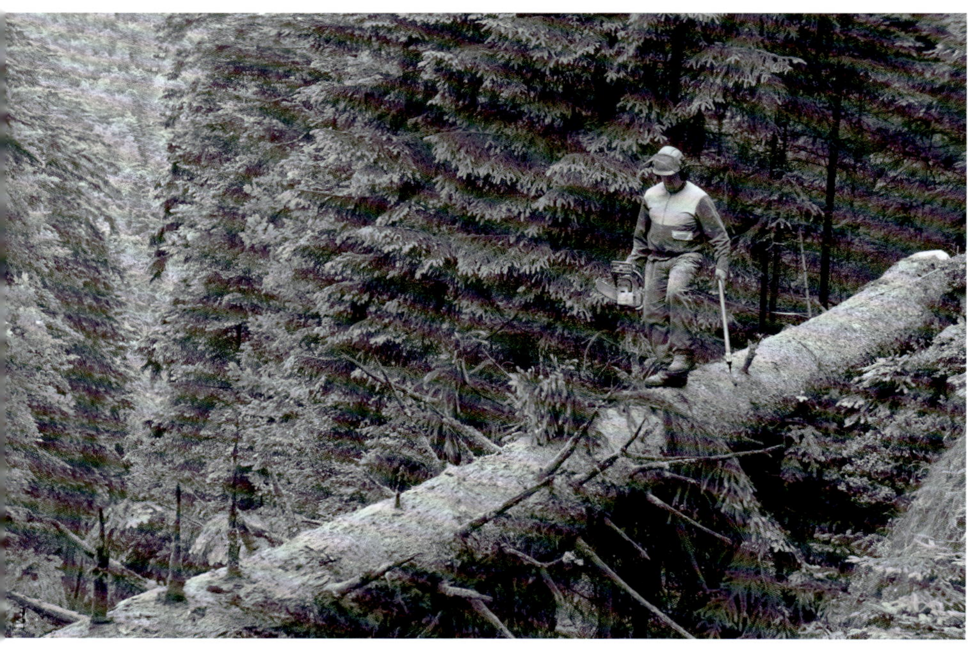

Tip *For most subjects, you can adjust your standpoint or tilt the camera's display to evaluate the effects of various descending and ascending lines.*

Death of a Giant Conventional design guidelines for incorporating diagonal lines in a photo's composition dictate that lines extending from the upper left to the lower right of a picture have negative connotations while those extending from the lower left to the upper right have positive ones. Is this always clear-cut?

In the original photo (left), the Alsatian forest worker in the Vosges Mountains can be seen walking downward to the left along a fallen fir tree. The man in the photograph described the natural process of decay as "La mort d'un geant" (the death of a giant) The composition here seems to suit the subject adequately.

The mirror image of the photograph, however, reveals that the image would have been much more powerful if the camera had been positioned on the other side of the tree. The overall effect of the photo is vastly improved with the tree and the man heading downward to the right. The practice of reading from right to left is not without relevance here. Because the eye is accustomed to gathering information from right to left, images that mirror that composition create a kind of visual comfort, provided the viewer is not from a culture that reads according to a different practice. Is this mere sophistry? Don't be deceived. Our eyes subconsciously recognize these differences. Think about the photos or illustrations on book jacket designs—if the designer wants to elicit a positive response, he or she is better off using an ascending diagonal rather than a descending one.

There is another effect of diagonals on display here. The entire length of the 60-meter-long tree trunk is not visible in the photo, but the full magnitude of the tree is still easy to imagine. Illustrators for picture books and artists who draw comics use this technique of not revealing the entire scene. What's off screen can play out in the viewer's imagination.

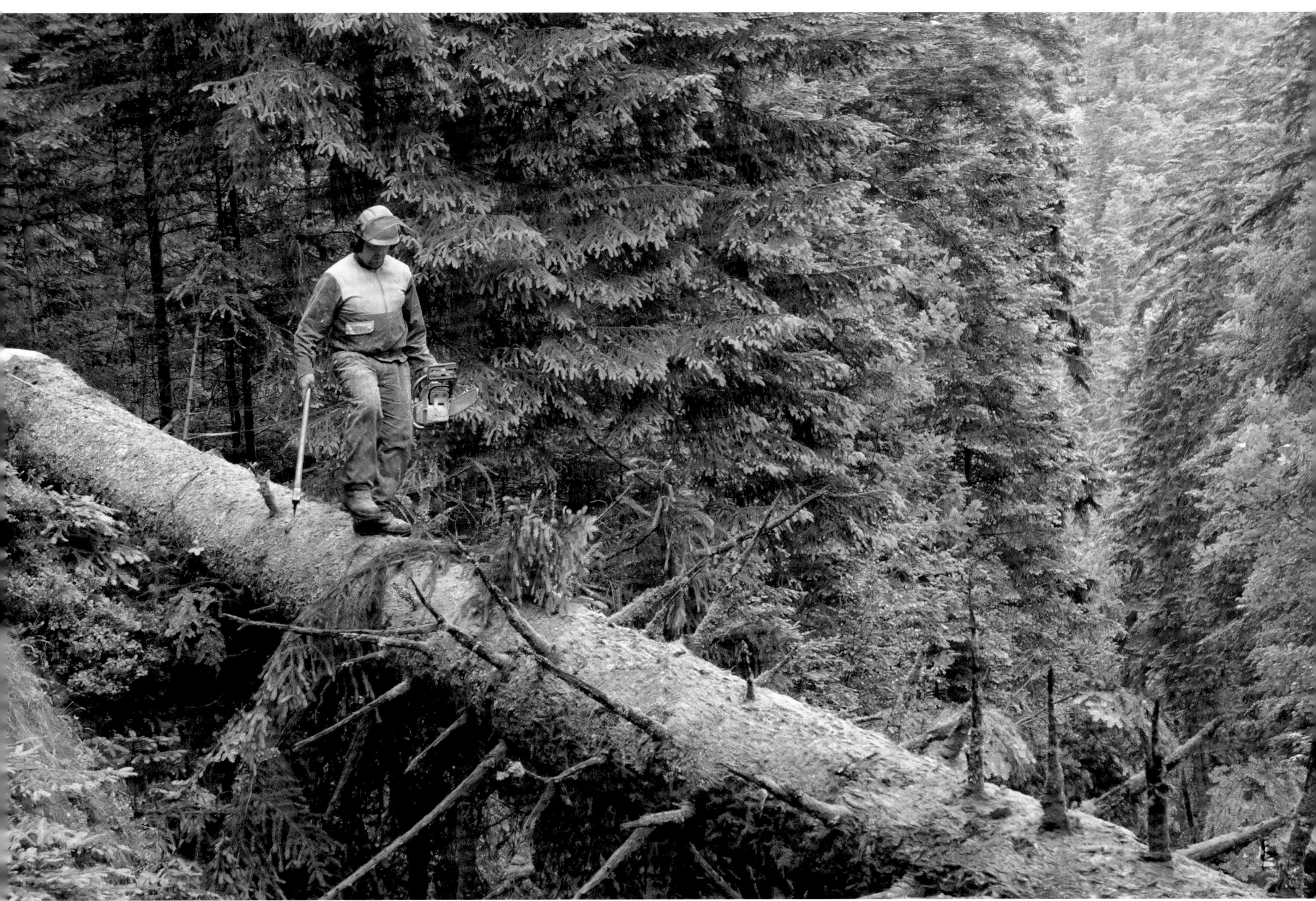

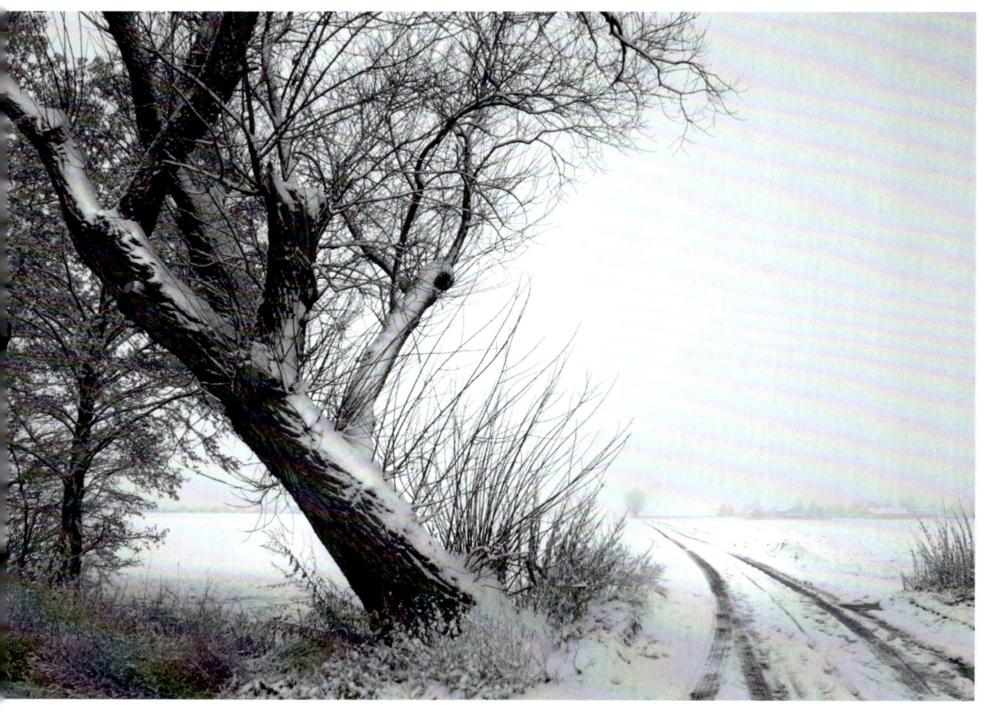

Tip *Consciously resist the temptation to default to an evenly balanced composition. Asymmetry, a deliberate lack of balance, and truncating subjects intentionally can all heighten a viewer's interest, especially when these techniques complement the intention behind the photo.*

Coming or Going? The willow tree to the left is nearly falling out of the picture. This photo is not what you would call a balanced composition, but it shows that profoundly asymmetrical compositions can succeed on their own terms if the subject matter holds up well to such a treatment. The next time you are in a bookstore, take a look at the various books on display. You may find a cover with a photo or illustration that is particularly out of balance—one that has been deliberately designed in this way to suit the title or content of the book.

The composition of the photo on the right-hand page creates a completely different effect. Here, the willow is the main subject. The delicate snow-covered branches on the left side don't serve as an equal counterweight to the strong dark trunks of the willow on the right. Neither photo presents the willow in complete repose.

Many willows—especially older specimens of the white willow variety—are visual delicacies with or without foliage. They can survive long floods without suffering any damage, and if a storm should tear a willow apart, roots can even grow from the broken branches. Because the growth pattern for each tree is so different, willows make ideal candidates for composing images with prominent diagonal lines—and not only for photographers. Willows are also among my favorite subjects to draw.

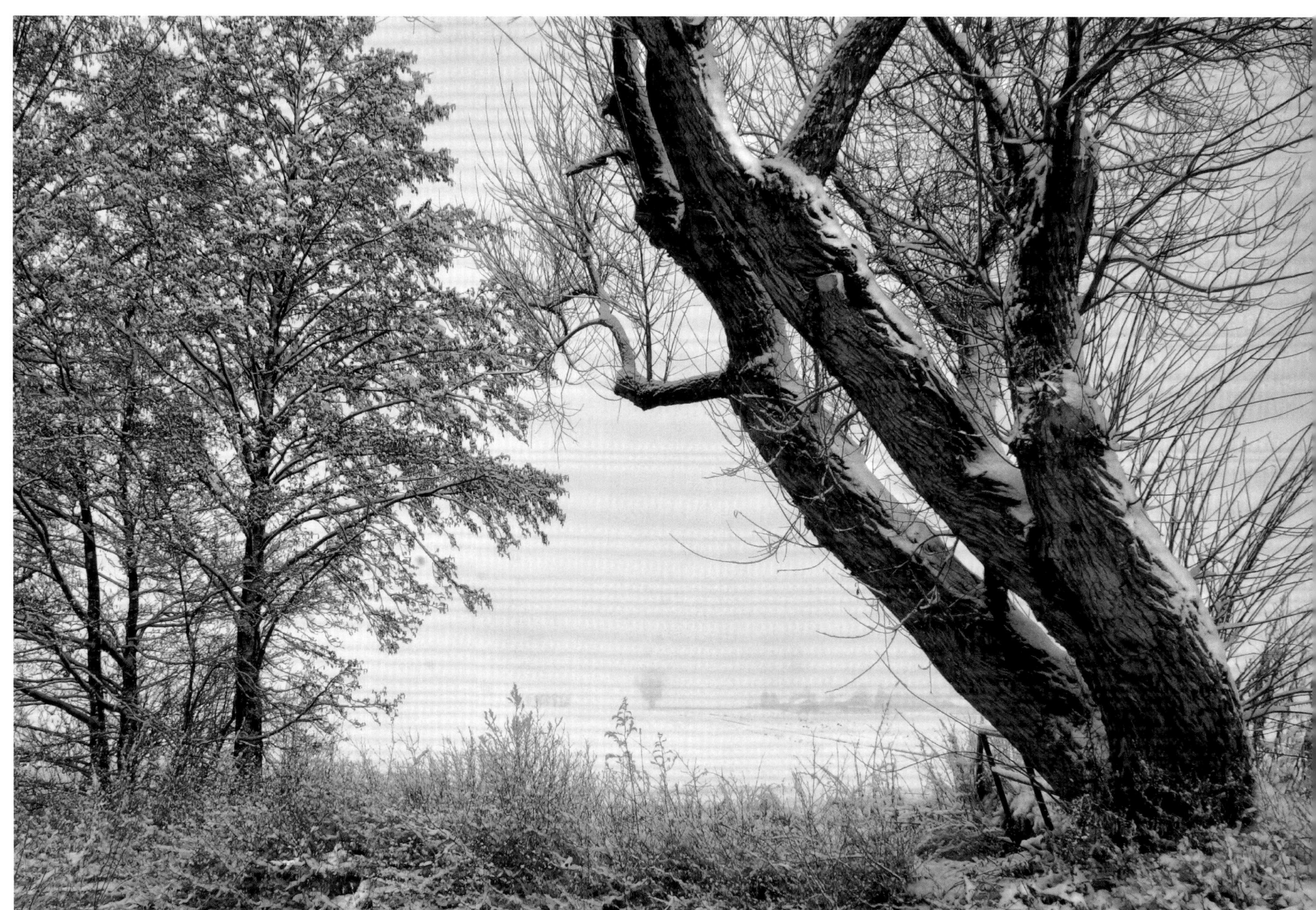

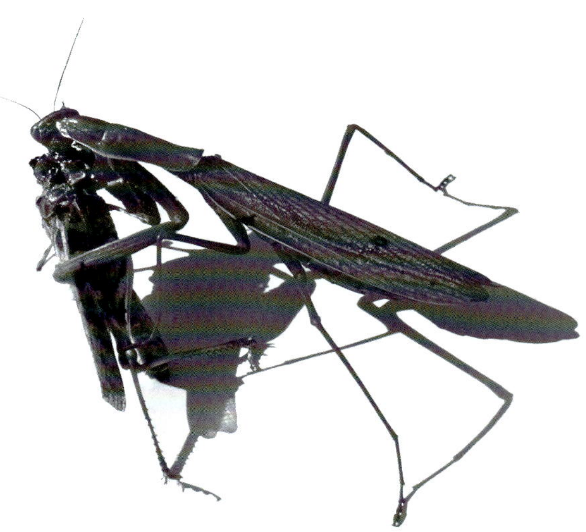

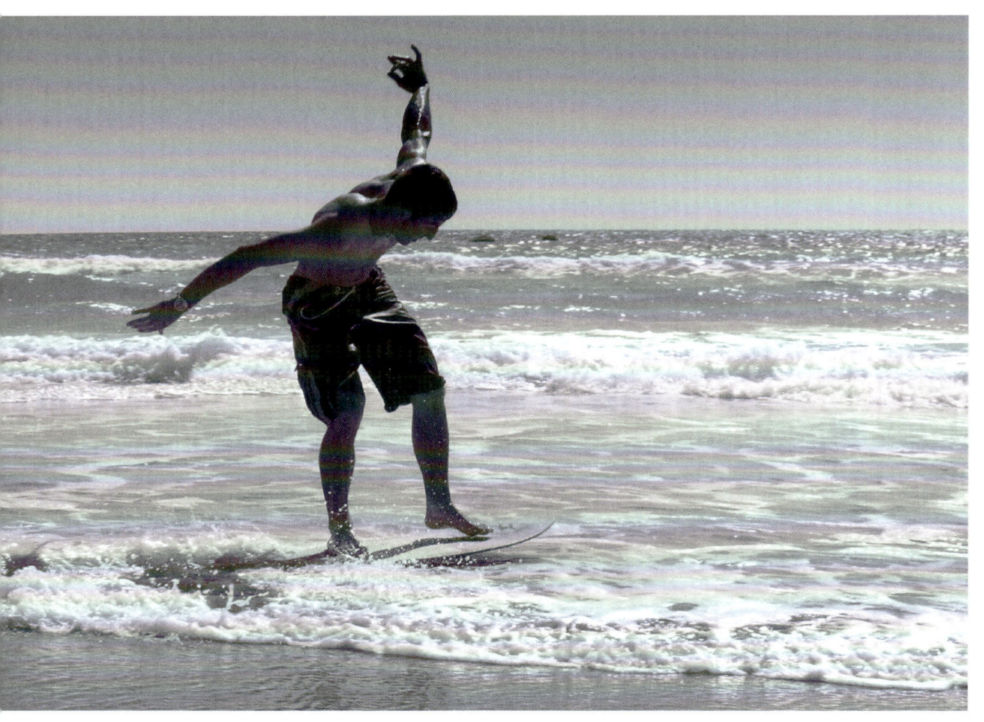

Surfers and Insects The most extreme members of the human and animal worlds make for rewarding subjects when it comes to composing images with diagonal lines. Whether stretched out or doubled over, these subjects feature limbs and appendages that create interesting contrasts with respect to one another. The fact that the sections of their bodies harmoniously correspond with each other is directly related to the principles of the golden ratio. This ratio can be found not only in the proportions of the human body, but in any number of other natural objects across the planet.

There are ample opportunities to explore the use of diagonal lines while photographing such subjects. The picture of the surfer on the left was taken on a beach in Andalusia; the one on the right-hand page was taken on the Eisbach River right in the heart of Munich.

Long-legged insects are equally gratifying for creating diagonal compositions. I have never had so much time to work with such a subject as I did when I came across a voracious praying mantis in southern France: the predator spent nearly an hour feasting on this grasshopper.

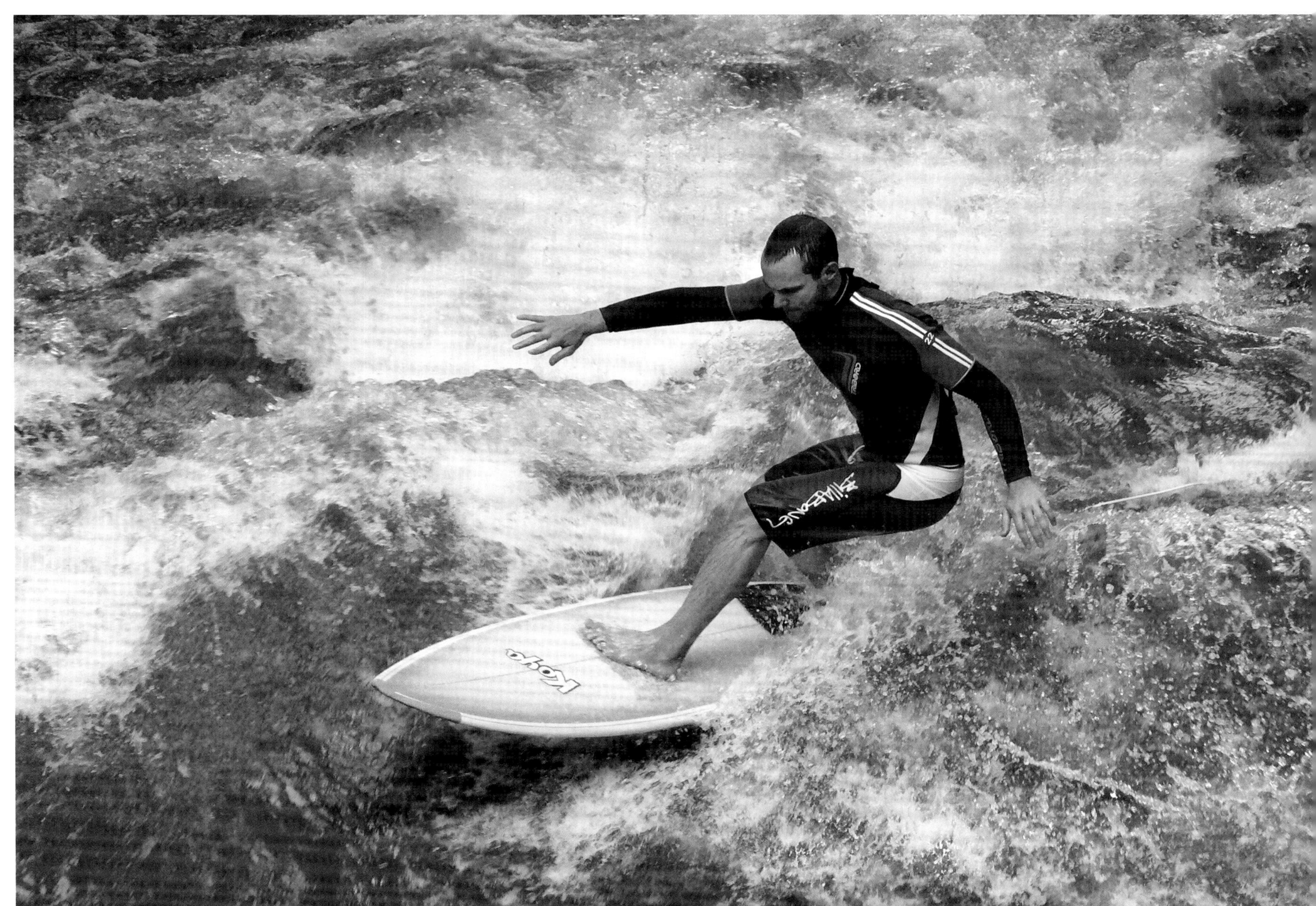

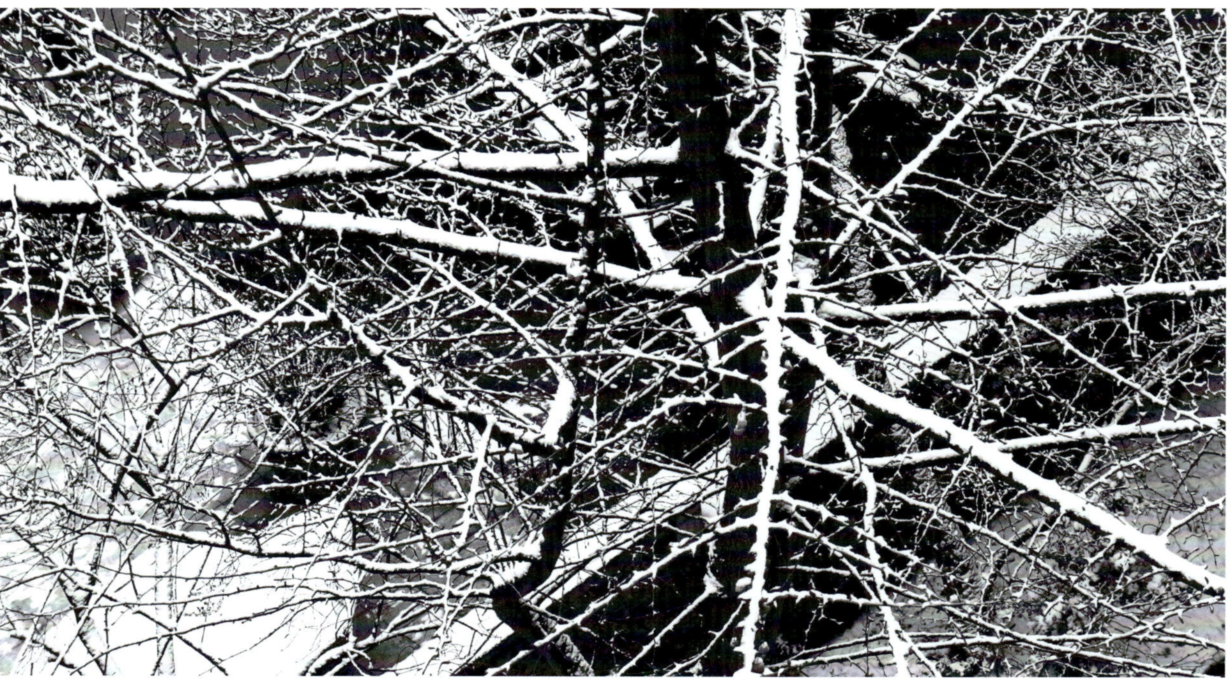

Star Shapes Yet another way for artists to incorporate diagonal lines into their images is to rely on a network of lines radiating outward to the borders of the image area. The "spokes" of such a design can be either regularly or irregularly spaced—the latter of which is often more interesting. It's usually easier to position the plexus of the diagonals at the center of the photo, but moving it away from the middle often produces more exciting results because the lengths of the individual diagonal strands will vary. A network of branches dusted with freshly fallen snow is an ideal subject for this type of composition.

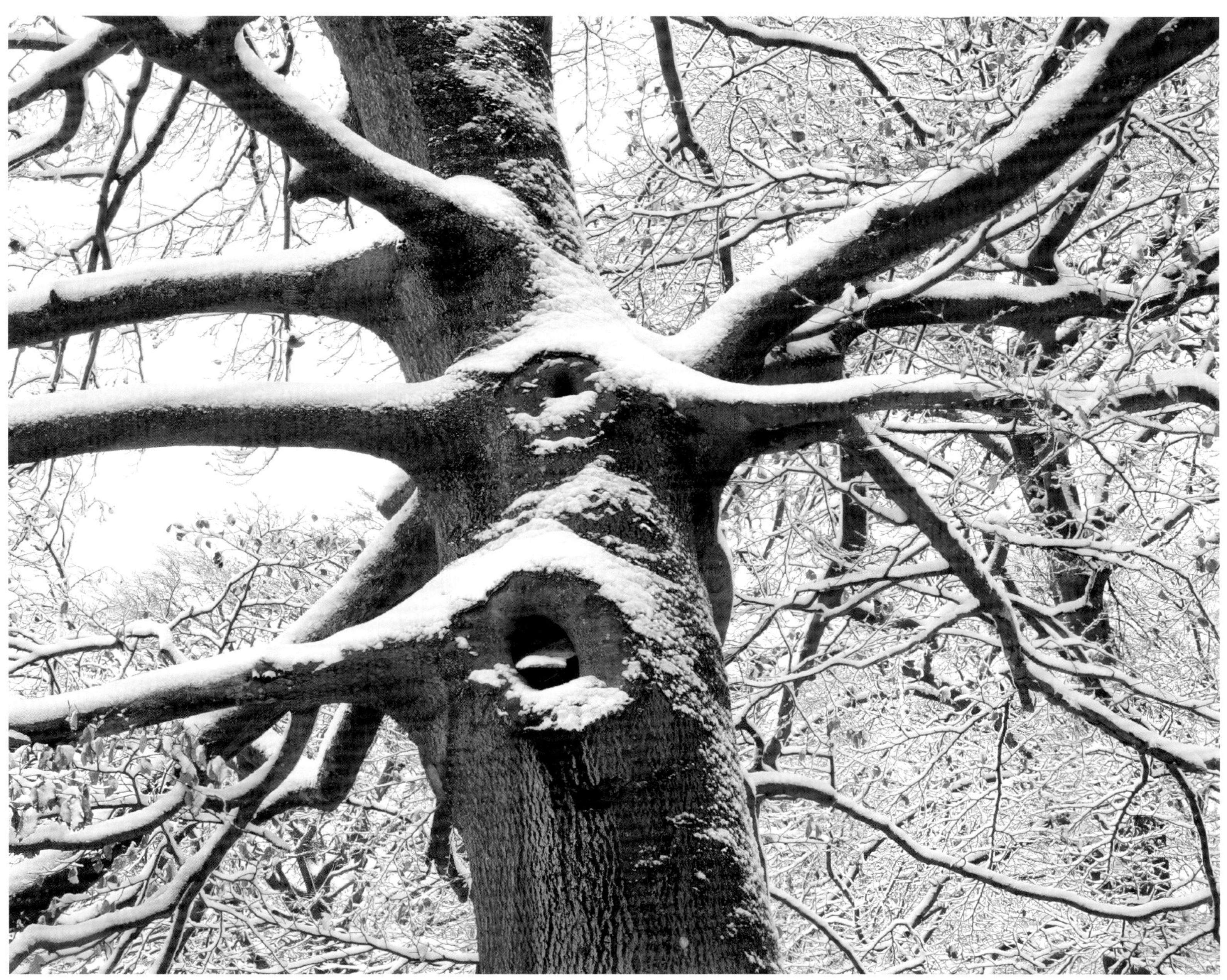

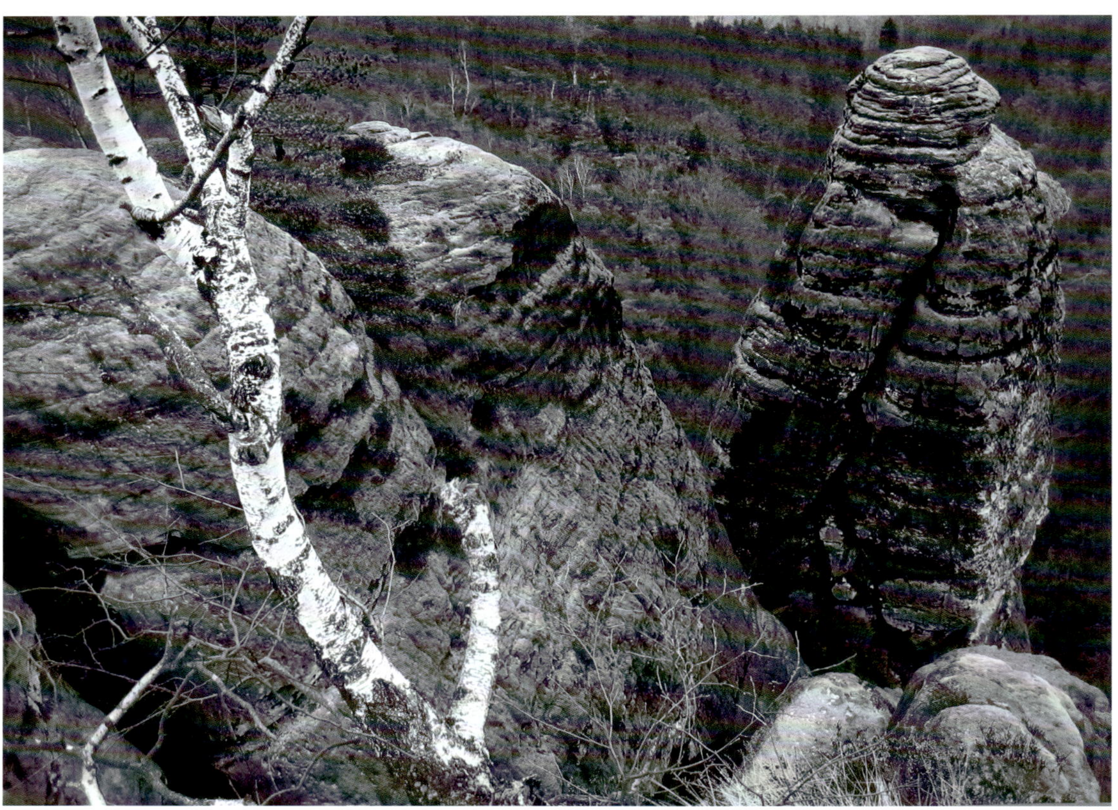

Forked Objects that fan out or split off are natural candidates for compositions relying on diagonal lines. Forked lines spread out and build tension with the rectangular photographic area. The photo of a splayed tree trunk on the facing page serves as an attractive example of this phenomenon.
The above photo of the split birch trunk has a similar-but-different effect. It is effective not because the trunk stands out as a positive element in front of white snow, but rather as a negative element in front of dark, similarly forked rock structure.

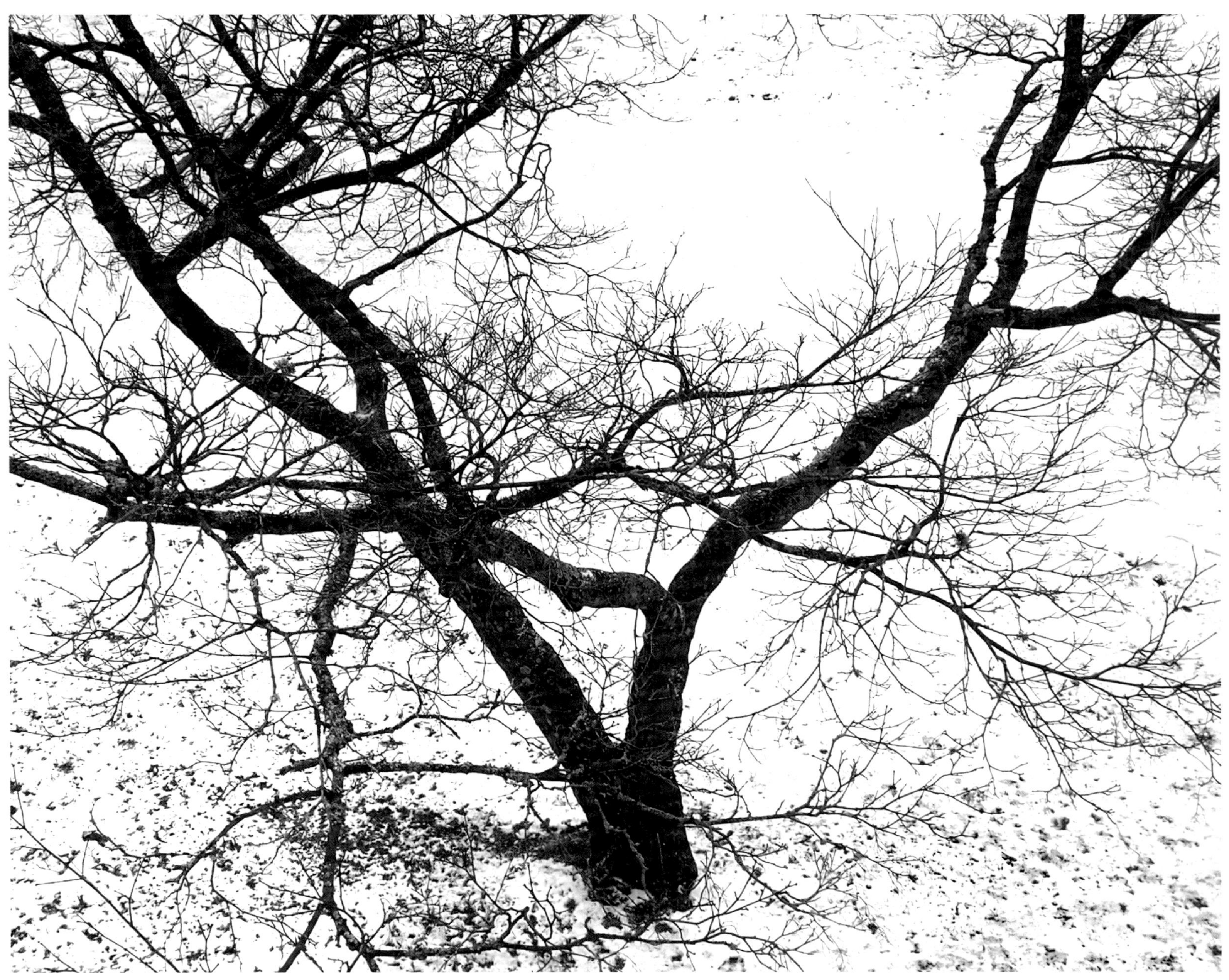

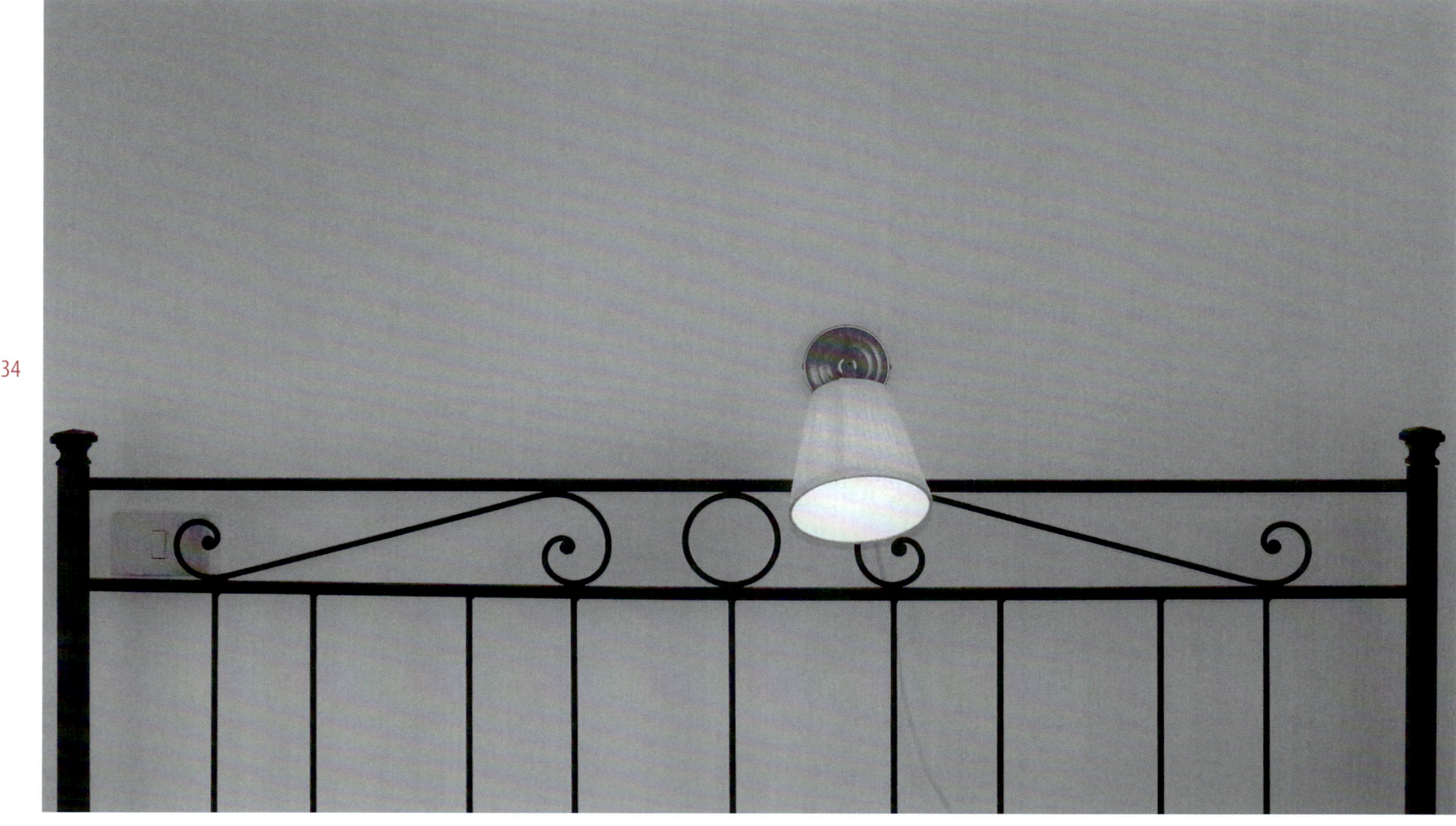

Breaking the Rules Avoiding situations in which prominent lines run parallel to the image border is one of the basic rules of image design, but these photographs show that a deliberate departure from the rules has its place when the subject matter calls for something a little different.

One could imagine a photo of a headboard with more tension, but this particular composition (above) retains an appropriate level of peace and calm. The placidity is disturbed only slightly by the off-center lamp and the wrought-iron flourishes.

It's early in the morning at Lac de la Maix in the High Vosges (right-hand page). Everything is still and the water of the lake is as smooth as glass. Nothing disturbs the enchantment of the scene. What is the best way to capture the mood of this moment? Perhaps a composition that features the lake's edge running diagonally across the entire image? Probably not—the style would not suit the subject in this case. In contrast, setting up the trees and lakeshore parallel to the boundaries of the image area is a much more relevant composition and one that captures the ambience that the photographer experienced on site.

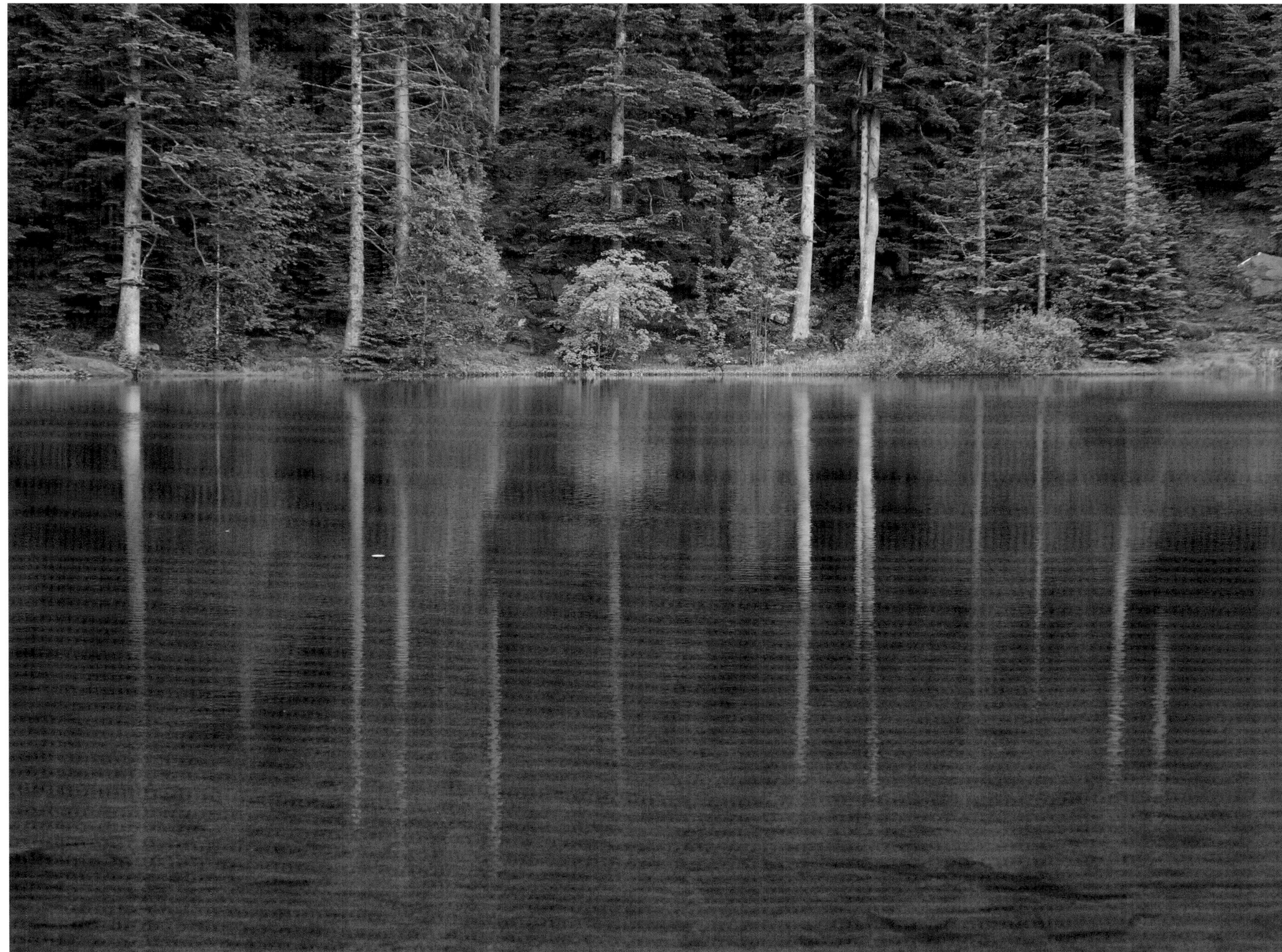

36 Perspectives

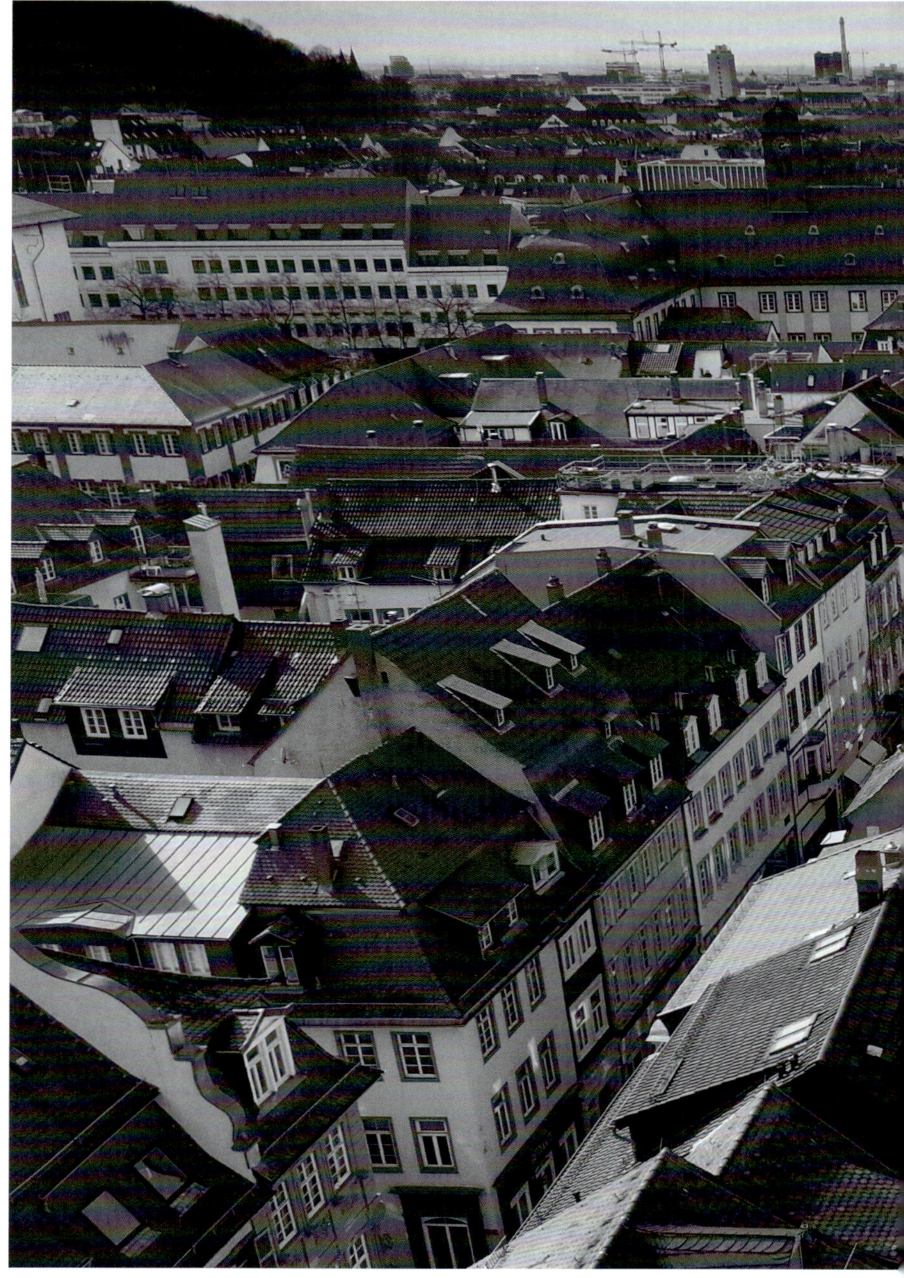

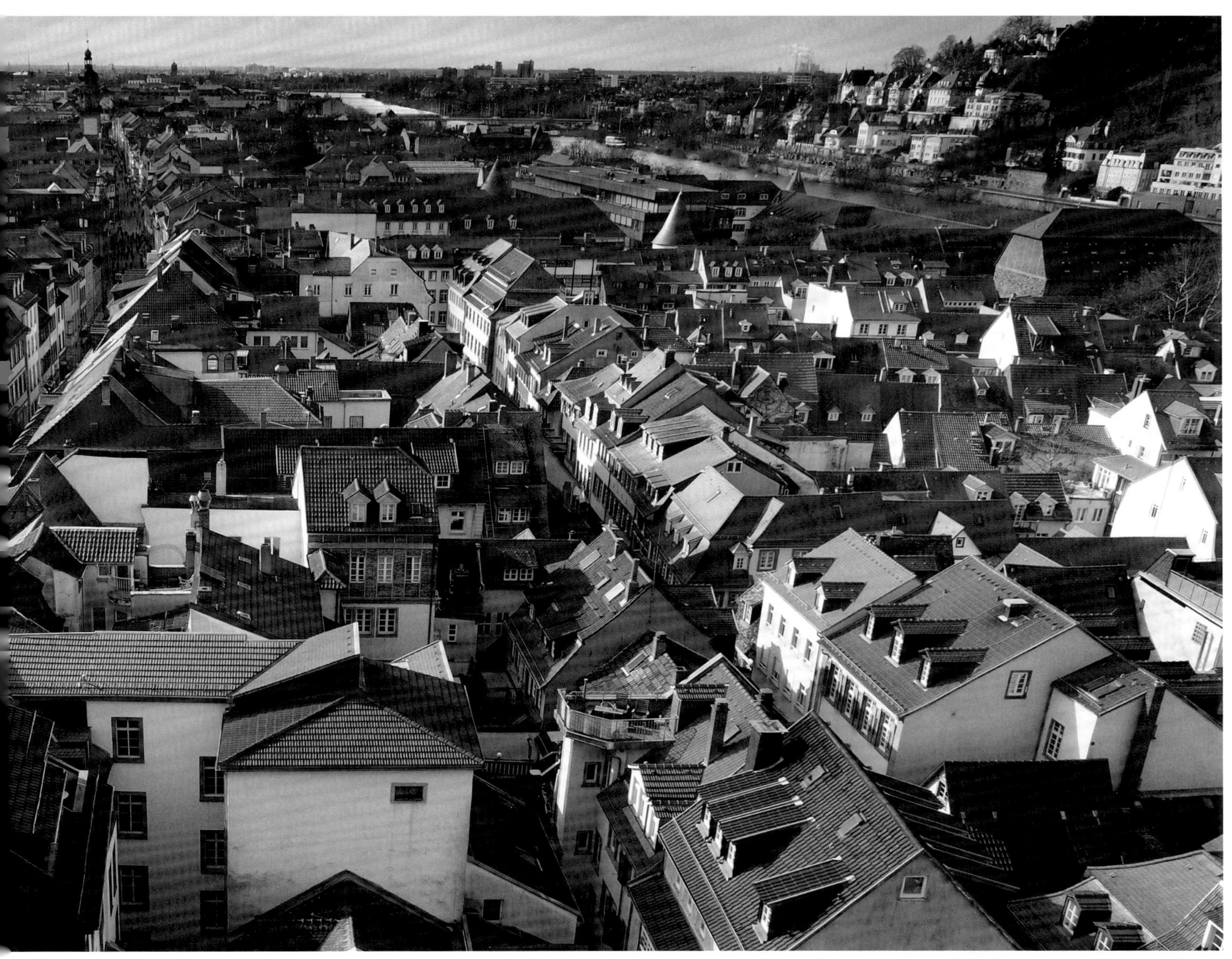

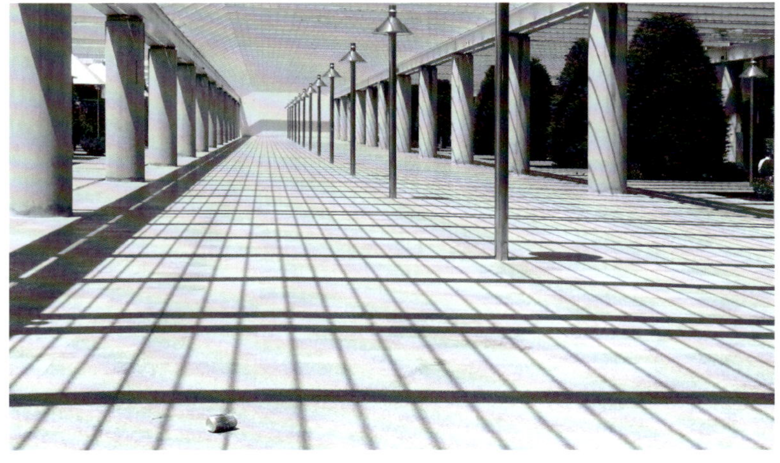

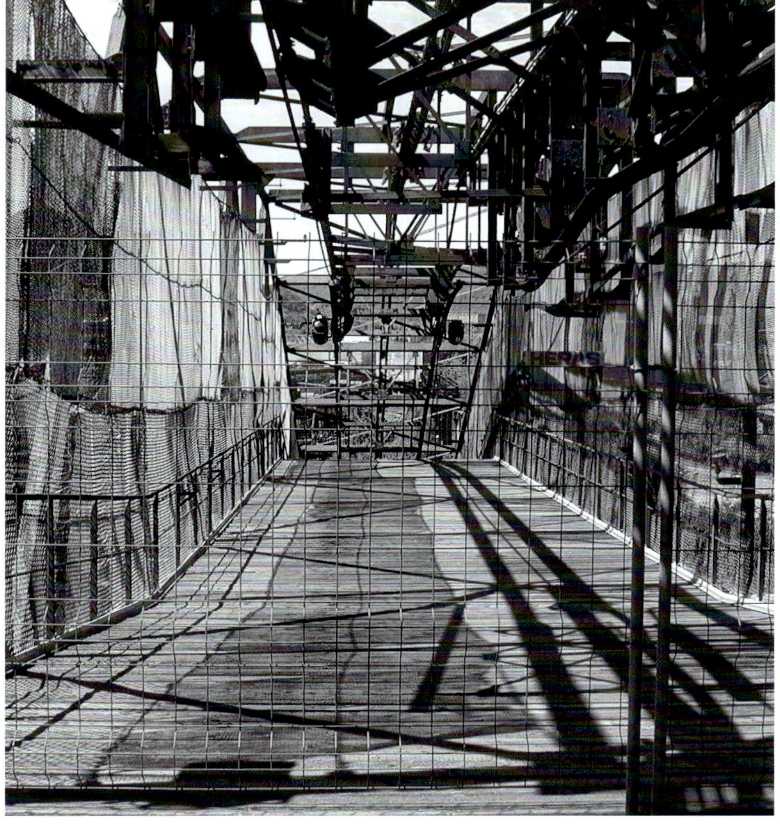

Central There are a dizzying number of methods for imitating the human sense of sight on a two-dimensional surface. Archaeological findings from the Stone Age reveal that the desire to achieve perspective in art has been around for tens of thousands of years. In antiquity, the Greeks attempted to establish a style of painting that allowed for the depiction of space. The Romans, whose achievements are impressively visible in the ruins of Pompeii and Herculaneum, further developed the visual arts. Nearly a thousand years would pass after that before architects and painters in Florence pushed to find new perspectives for depicting structures.

The central perspective played such a big role in the development of artistic style that nearly every artist thereafter experimented with it. One famous example is *The Battle of San Romano* by Paolo Uccello. From then on, every method of spatial illusion was explored. The perspectives that Venetian painter Canaletto used in his cityscapes (vedute) were early highlights of the technique. He developed these artworks with the aid of a camera obscura. This early form of the camera was a precursor to the field of photography. When photography was invented in the nineteenth century, it came to be considered a form of visual art. It remains so today.

The top photograph of a waiting room in the airport of Palma de Mallorca could have been taken from a textbook about perspective.

The Völklingen Ironworks (bottom), a World Heritage Site, offers photographers many attractive possibilities for diagonal compositions and expansive perspectives. In this particular photograph, the grid-like structure of the facilities and the resulting shadows go a long way to establish spatial depth.

The image on the right-hand page of the snowy forest flooded with light on the Königstuhl, a hill near Heidelberg, reveals that creating spatial depth in a photograph can take more than a central perspective alone. In this picture, the interplay of light and shadow establishes and embellishes the visual depth of the scene.

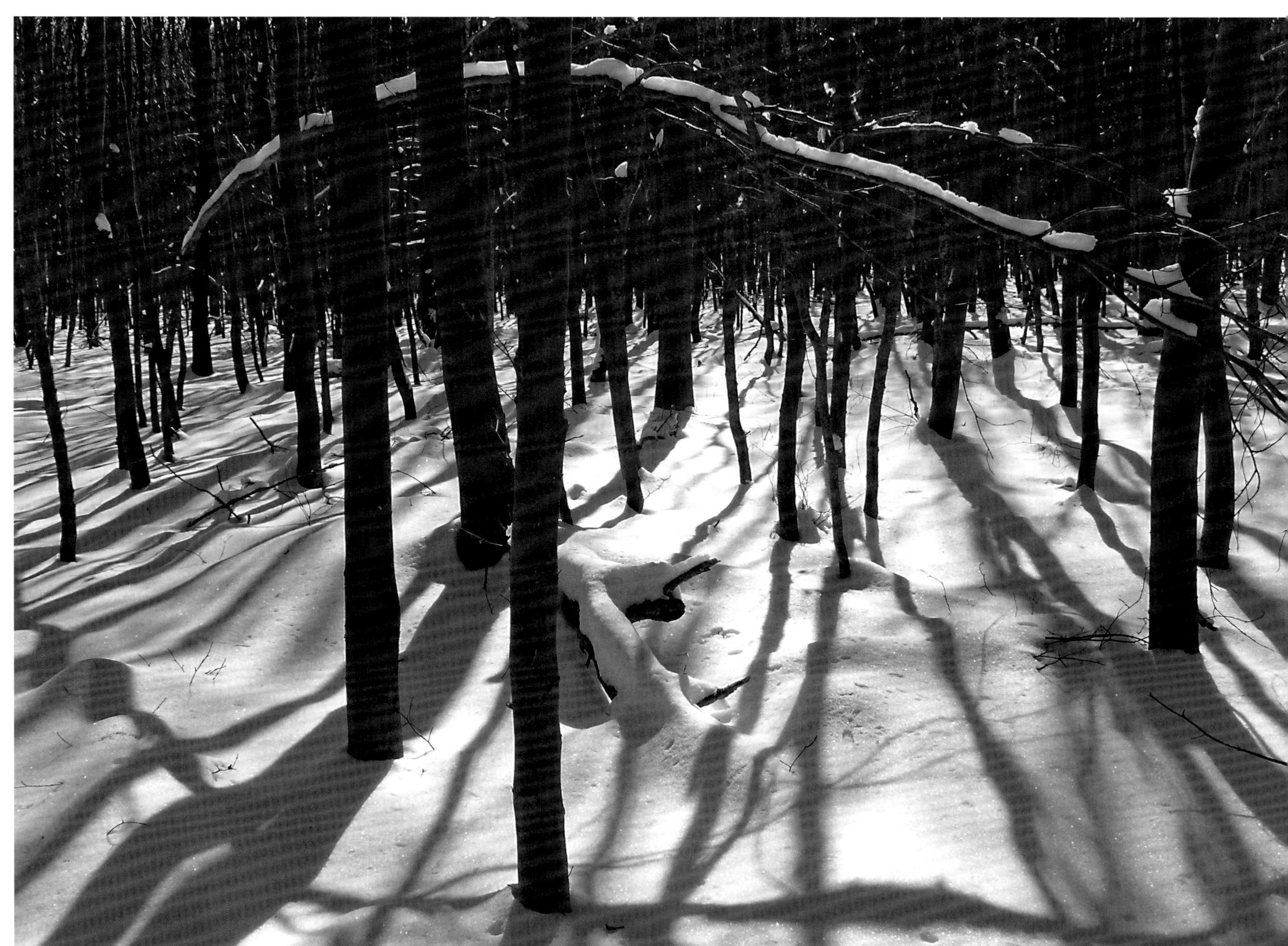

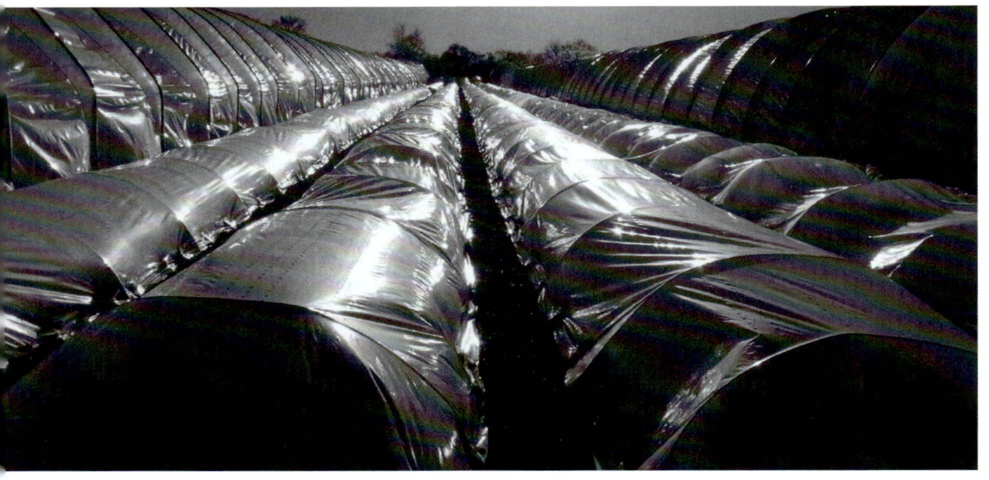

Field Practice Vegetable and fruit fields are rich with opportunities for exploring impressive perspectives. There is a produce orchard near where I live that offers worthy subjects no matter the season. In spring, giant plastic sheets protect plants from frost. An abundance of plants fill the fields in summer. Fall reveals the plow furrows that look as though they have been drawn with a ruler. And winter turns the acreage into a uniform sea of white.

Places like these are perfect for working with central perspectives as well as many other techniques for creating attractive compositions, including repeating patterns that fill up the entire image area, sequences of identical objects, diagonal lines that create visual tension, delicate gratings, branches that split in two, subtle lighting conditions, subjects that lend themselves to interesting crops, sweeping curves, and much more.

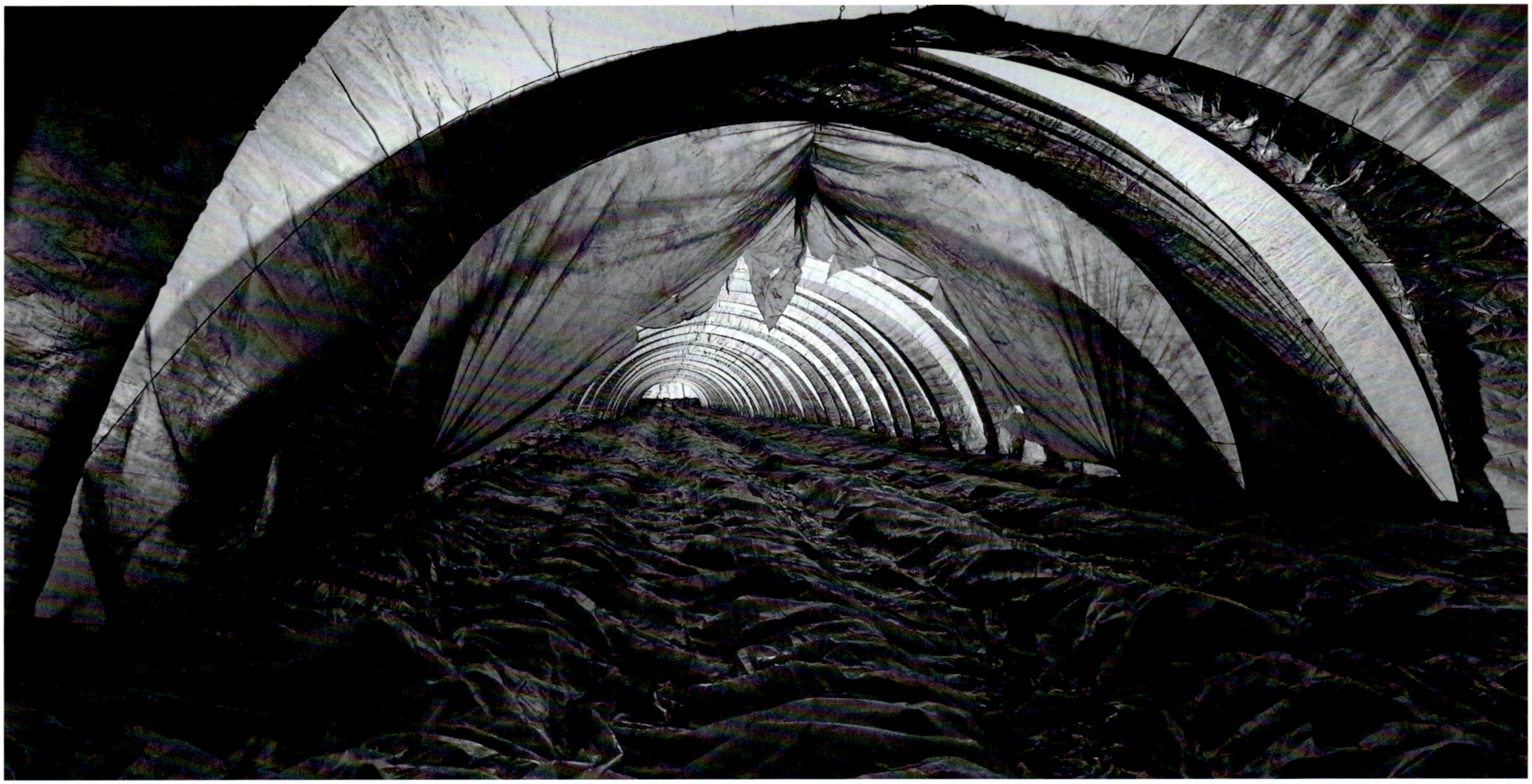

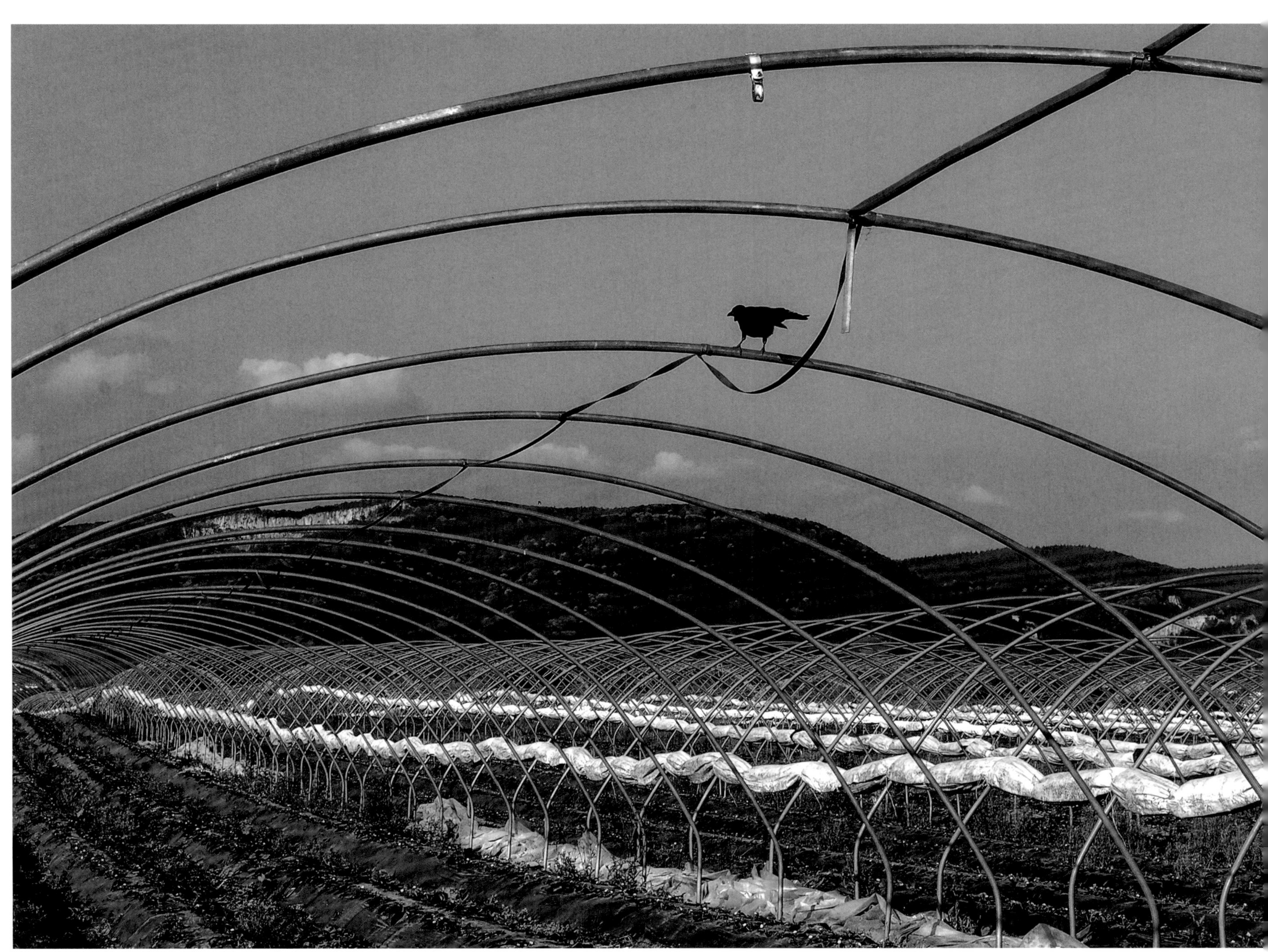

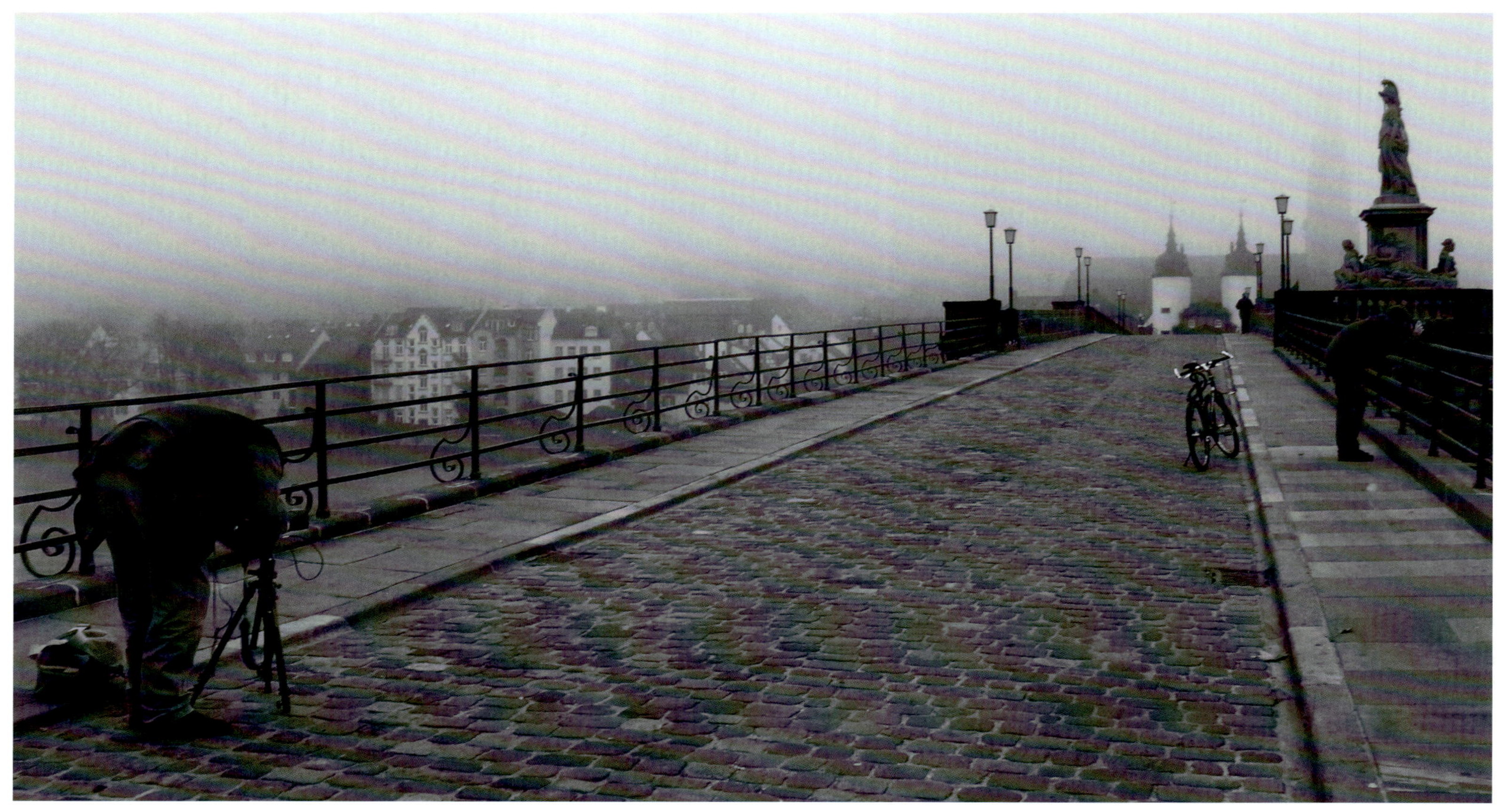

Finding a View There are places that are photographed thousands of times per day. One such spot is Heidelberg's Old Bridge, where tourists can look out at the city and the castle ruins—the epitome of German romanticism. Early in the morning and in the evening, the bridge is a little less crowded and regains some of its old-world charm. In contrast to the sweeping view of the old town (see pages 36-37), here the town fades away behind a layer of fog. The photo is interesting not only because of the off-center perspective, but also because of the anchor points in the image that guide the viewer's attention from one photographer to the other and then to the pedestrian in the top corner.

In the image on the right, a young man sits on the Old Bridge and gazes downstream toward the setting sun. The man's pensive state of mind is the subject of the photo and the inspiration for taking the picture in the first place. The overall effect of this picture relies on the fact that the camera and the subject have the same perspective. The man and the lamppost, both positioned in the foreground, support the perspective of this image.

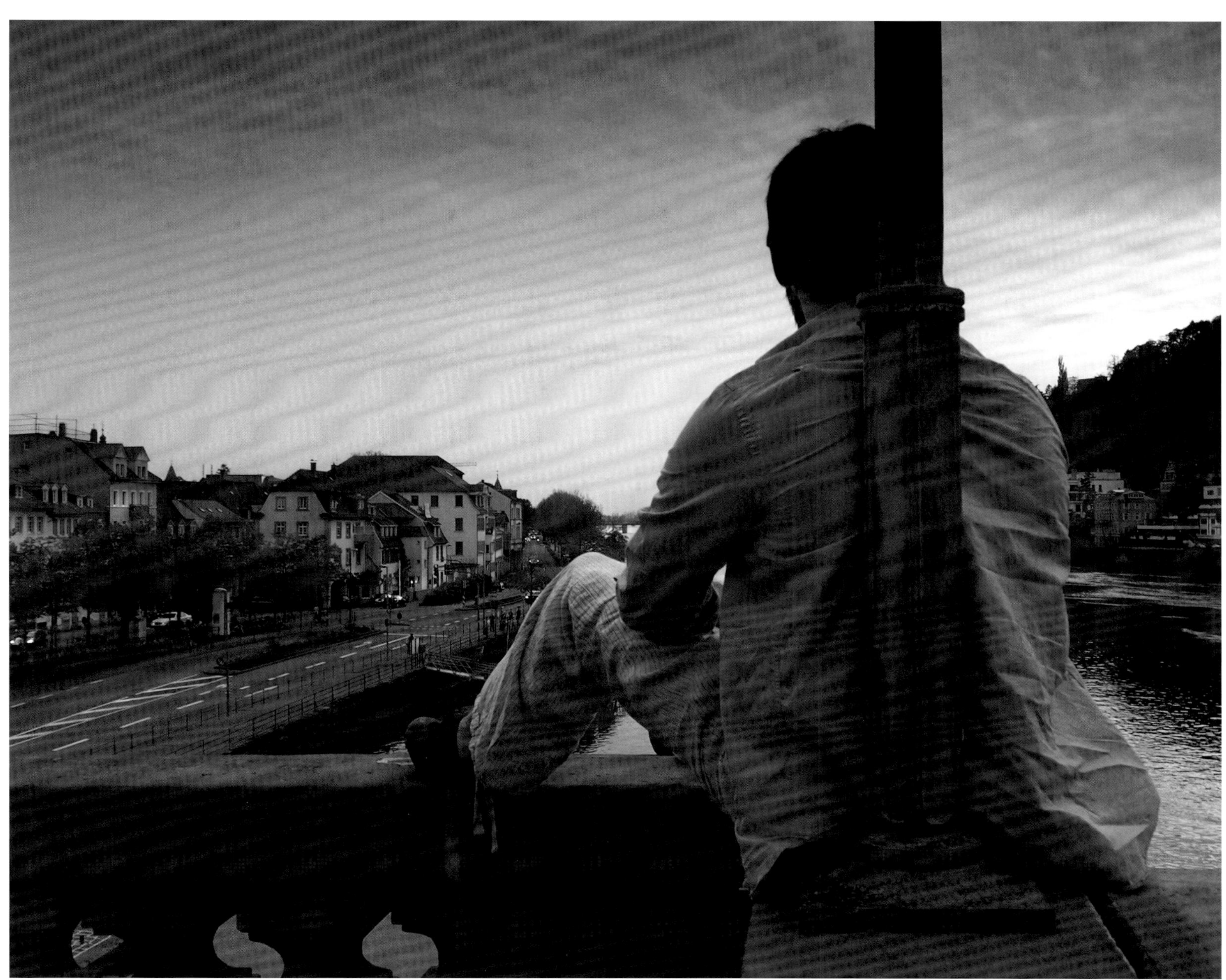

Atmospheric Perspective Atmospheric perspective refers to the effect of the atmosphere on the appearance of the subject when viewed from a distance, for example, when the colors and shapes of a landscape become more and more hazy toward the horizon, creating layers of depth. Because this photo of the Neckar River near Heidelberg is cloaked in fog and the distant horizon is invisible, atmospheric perspective does not come into play. However, this image shows that photographs can possess spatial depth even when this phenomenon cannot occur. The dense fog makes the sky and water appear extremely flat—only the contours of the riverbanks contribute any depth to the scene, and the viewer has to imagine the horizon for him or herself.

The photograph of the gardens at Schwetzingen Palace also lacks atmospheric perspective. The winter sky is uniformly gray. The wedge-like contour lines and delicate transparency of the leafless trees guide the viewer's attention to the Temple of Apollo—one of the park's attractions. The photo captures the spatial dimensions intentionally incorporated by the garden's eighteenth-century designers.

Neither photo is perfectly symmetrical. The camera's position is not directly opposite the respective vanishing points for the photos, so a central perspective is not established. The symmetry of the photos is pleasantly disrupted by the dark gray tones on the right side of the river photo and the diverse trees in the picture taken in the park.

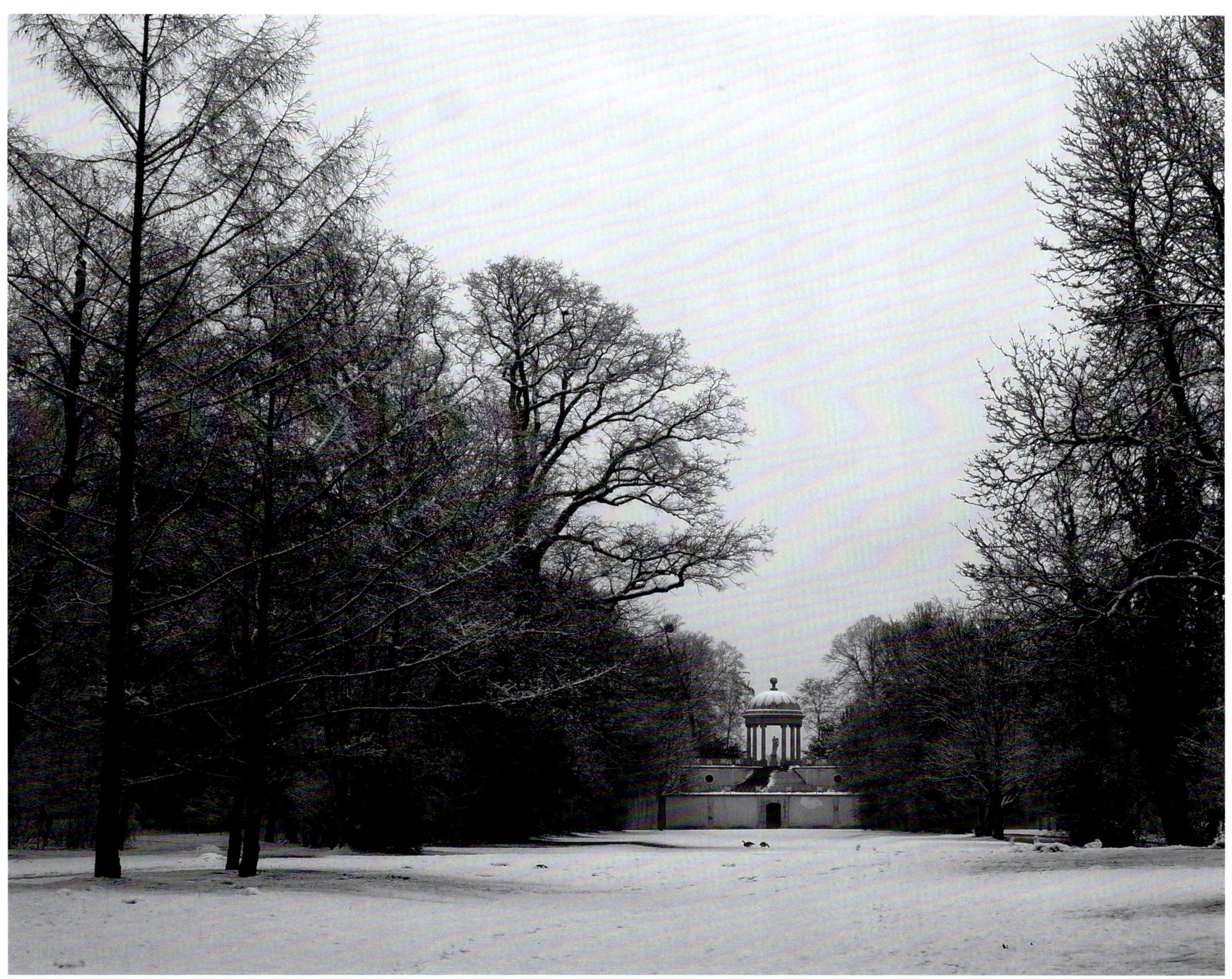

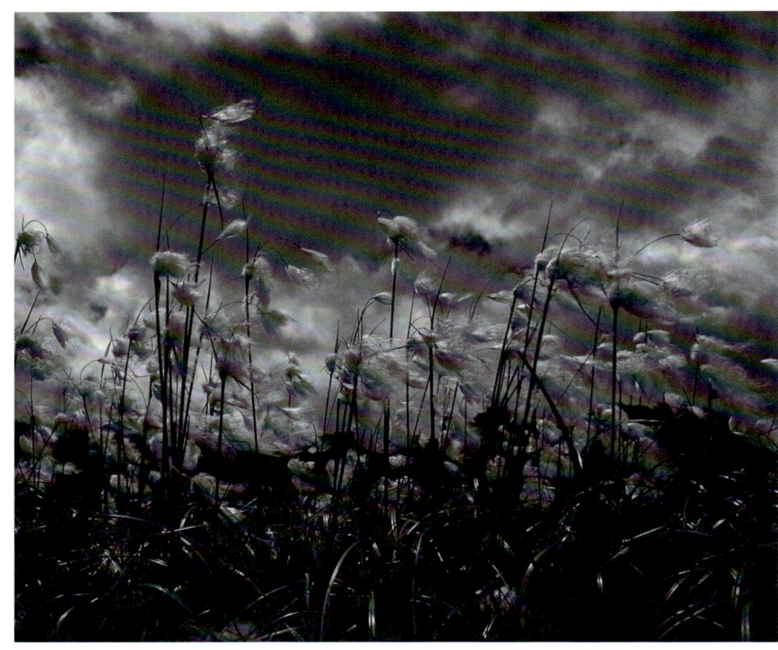

Eye Level Many of today's digital cameras have articulating LCD screens, which allow photographers to shoot from perspectives that would not be possible with a fixed display screen. Pivoting and swiveling display screens make it possible to take exacting photos above your head, at eye level, and while looking down.

Photographs of children are much more engaging when taken from eye level rather than looking downward at them. Getting up close and personal with plants or animals is also a good way to convey connection with them.

The dewy alpine cotton grass on the Aletsch Glacier in Switzerland relies on an upward perspective while the slight worm's-eye perspective gives the puffed up blackbird much more personality.

Steps define the perspective in the photo of the gulls waiting for scraps at the fish market in Venice. Being able to look down at the articulated display screen prevented the photographer from having to kneel down on the wet ground.

Tip *If you have the opportunity, I highly recommend purchasing a camera with an articulating screen. You'll be surprised how many photographic perspectives this tool will open up.*

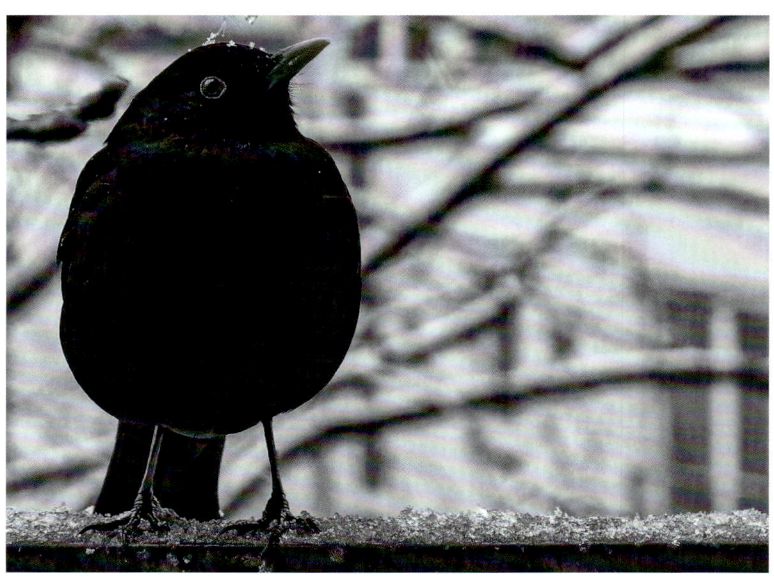

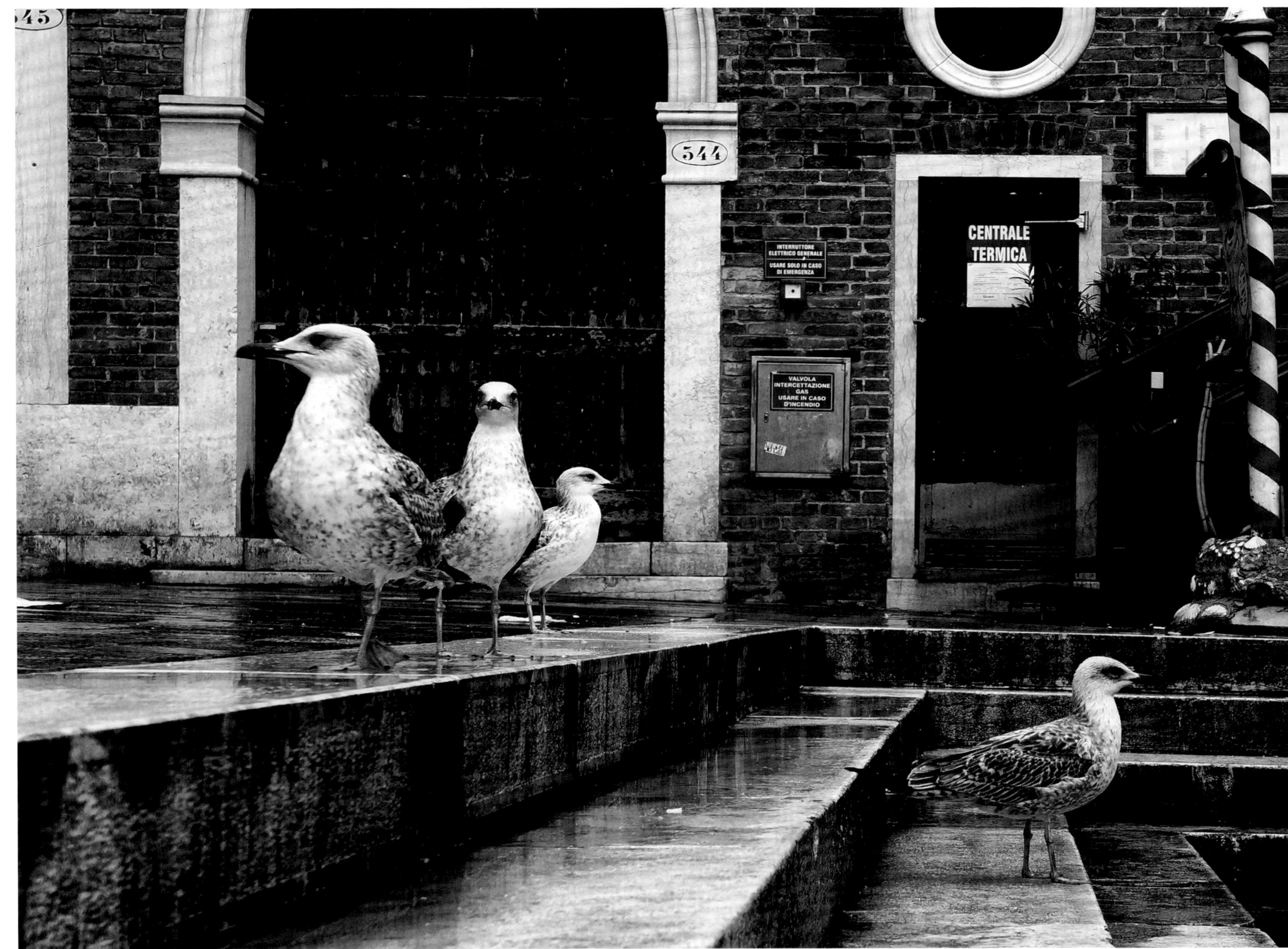
544
INTERRUTTORE
ELETTRICO GENERALE
USARE SOLO IN CASO
DI EMERGENZA
CENTRALE
TERMICA
VALVOLA
INTERCETTAZIONE
GAS
USARE IN CASO
D'INCENDIO

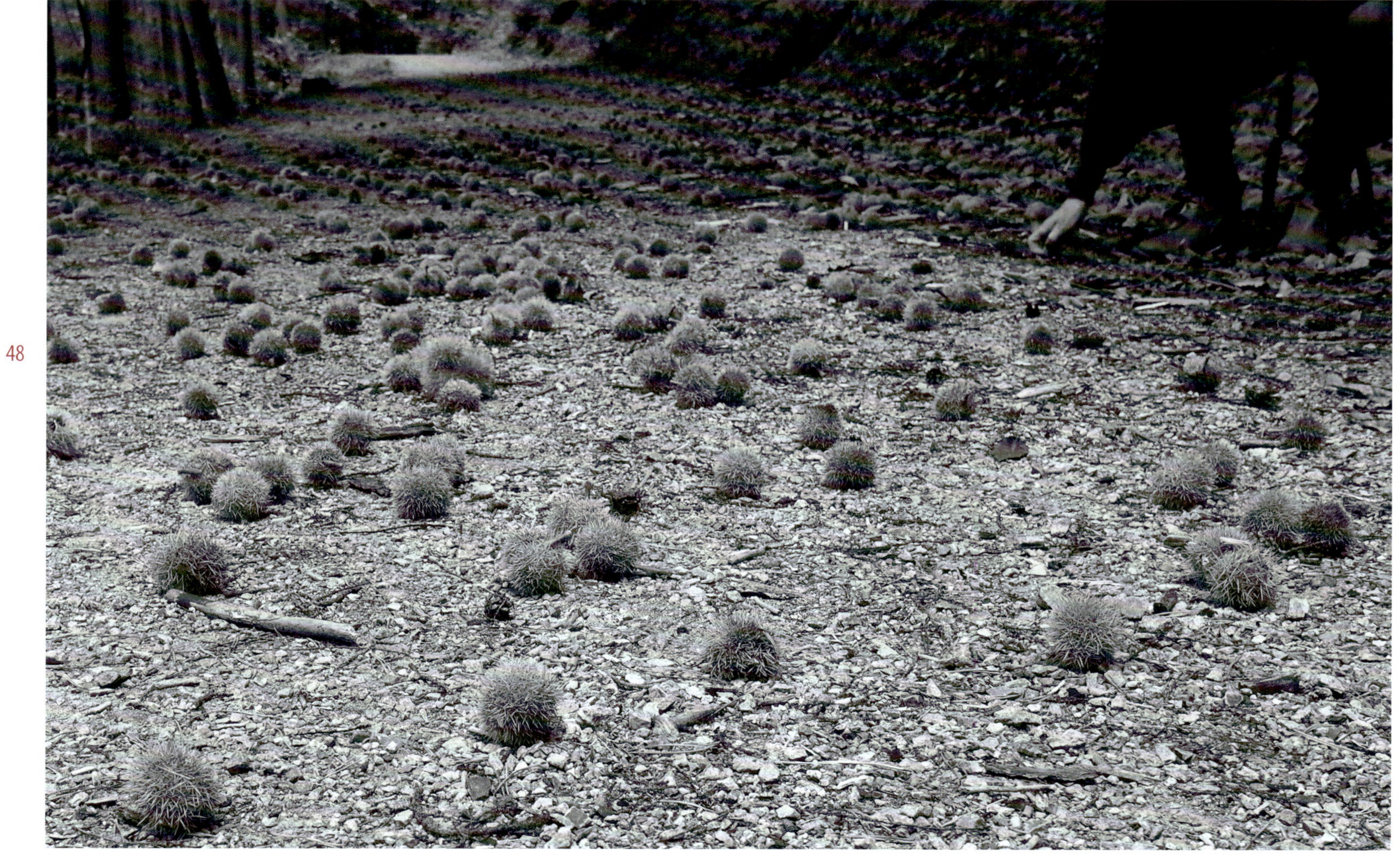

Hit the Deck! These photos also demonstrate the advantages of having a tilting LCD screen on your camera. When positioned at ground level, a camera can capture an interesting perspective or ambience that differs dramatically from when it is held at eye level.

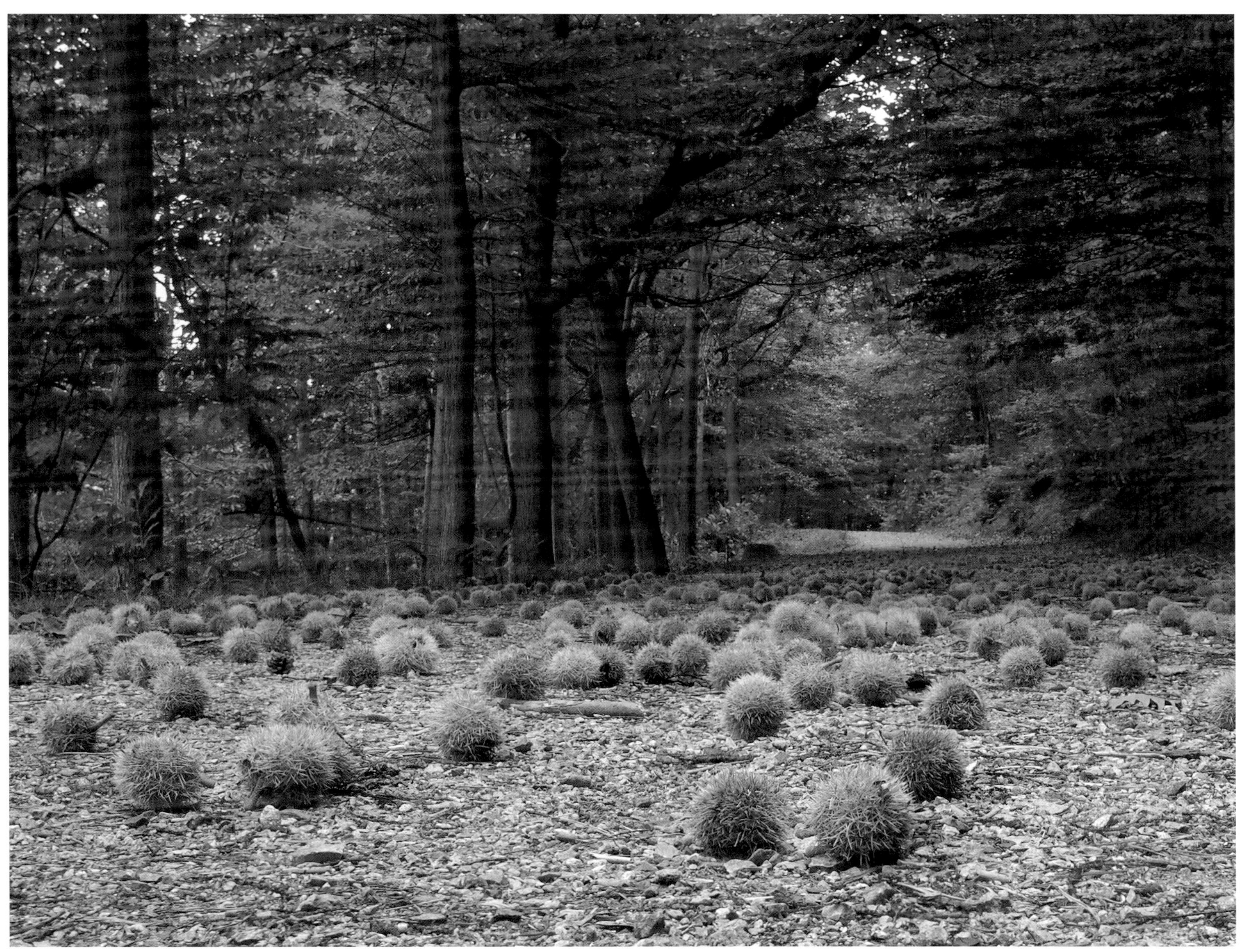

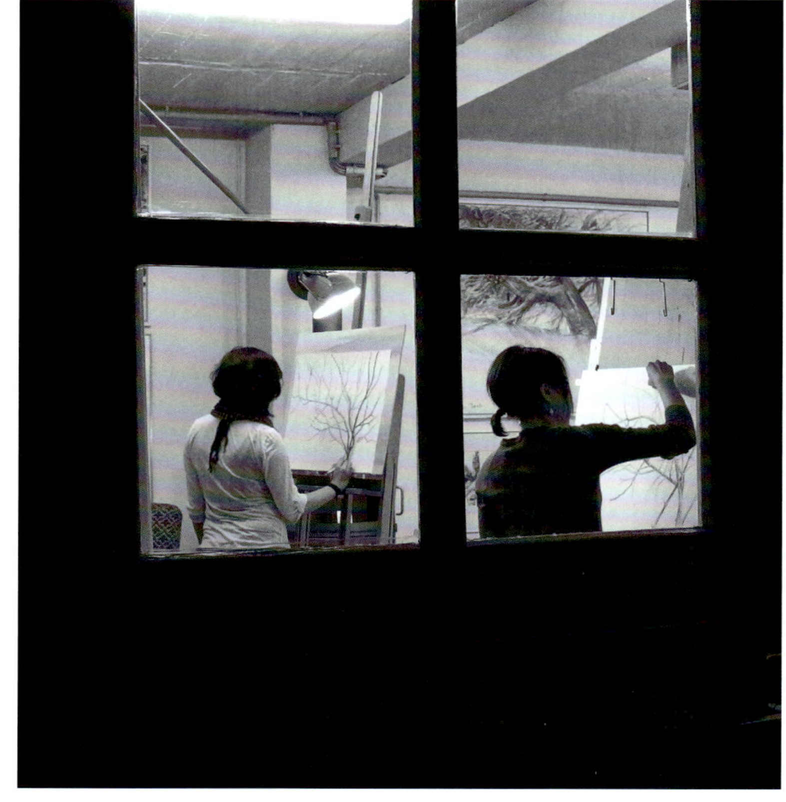

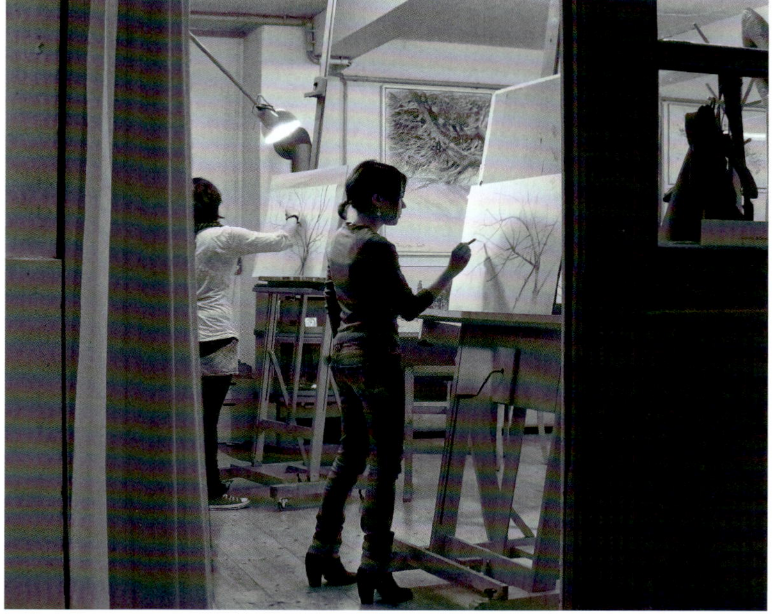

Tip *Changing your position often produces ideas for interesting compositions. Always be on the lookout for situations where formal design techniques will underscore key elements of a scene.*

A Change of Perspectives These three photos show the same subject, artists in a studio, but each image has a unique story to tell. Changing the perspective opens up new possibilities in terms of composing the elements in the scene. The closed door (top left) illustrates the grid-based design method (see page 58) in the foreground of the photo. In this case, the photographer is a discreet observer. The photograph with the open doorway (top right) seems to invite the viewer in, and has a much different feel, although there is still a noticeable distance between the subject and the viewer.

In the third version of the photograph (right-hand page), the camera appears much more involved, since the image reveals what the artist is drawing.

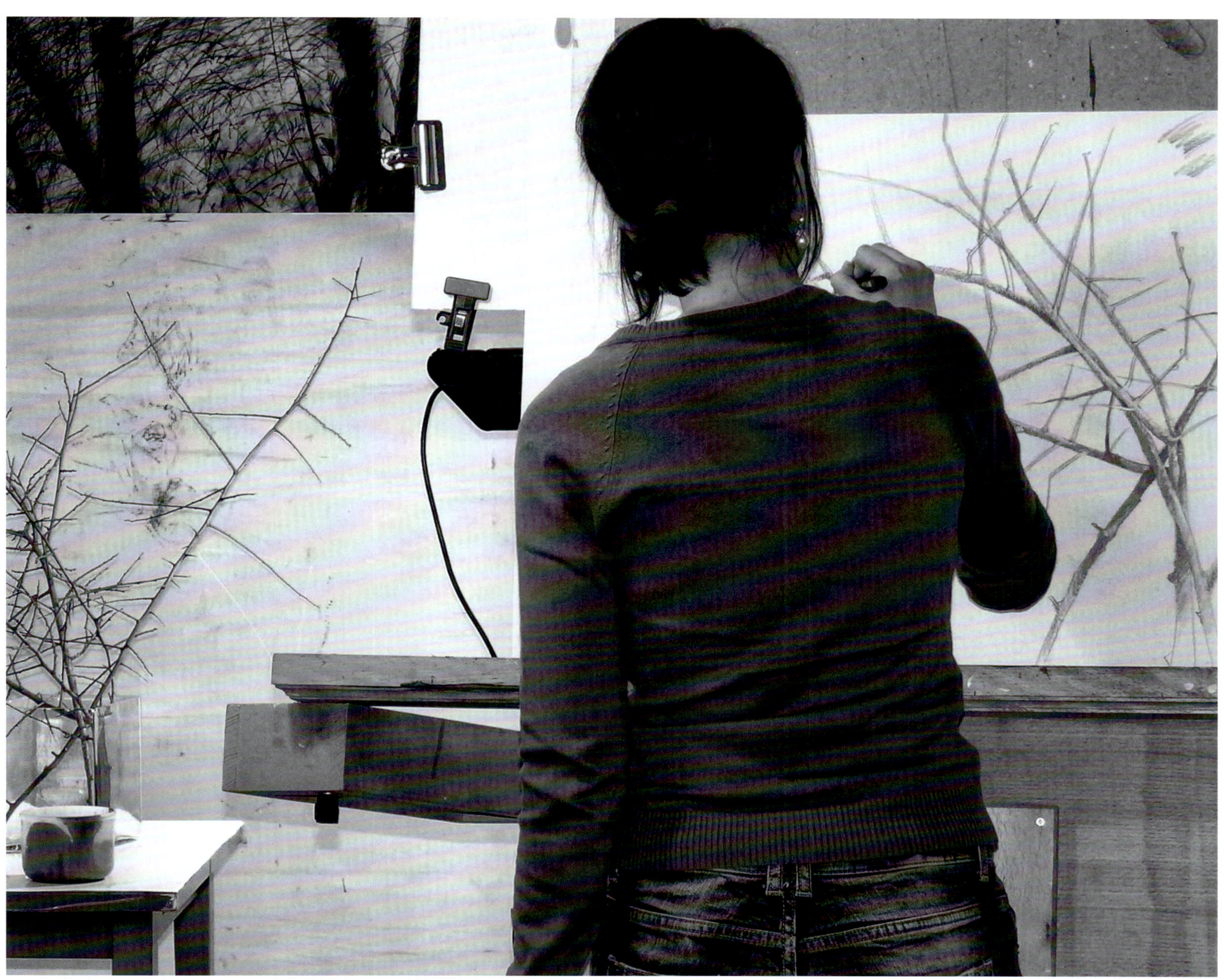

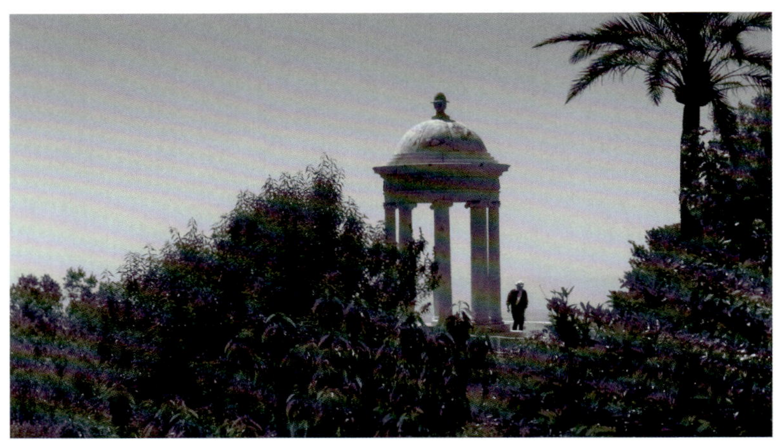

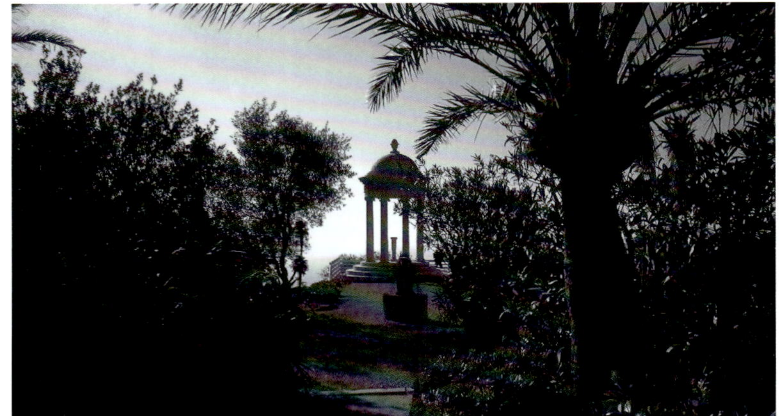

A Question of Standpoint Austrian Archduke Ludwig Salvator had this classic temple constructed in the nineteenth century at his country estate, Son Marroig, in western Mallorca. This series of pictures is an attempt to do justice to the idyllic location of the temple.

I prefer the photos that provide a sweeping view of the ocean in the background (right-hand page). These perspectives emphasize both the breathtaking location of the temple at the top of the bluff as well as the rich stillness and warmth of a late summer evening. Other visual elements—framing the temple, for example—are superfluous to achieving this desired effect.

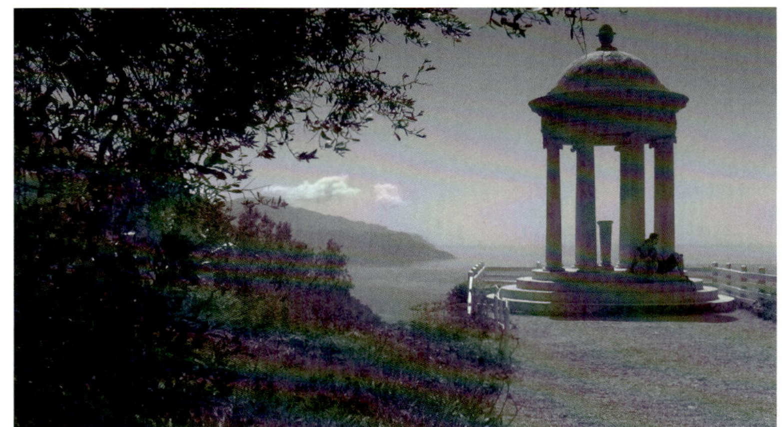

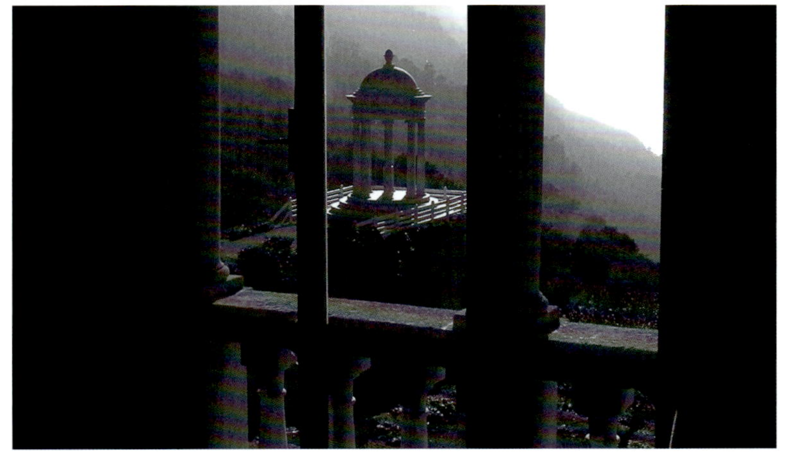

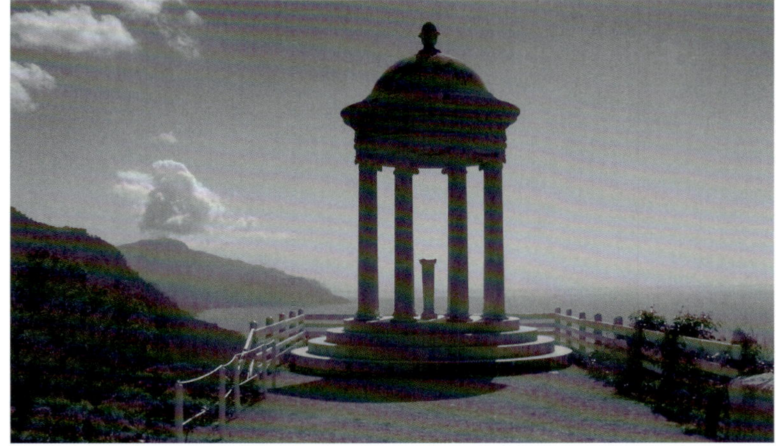

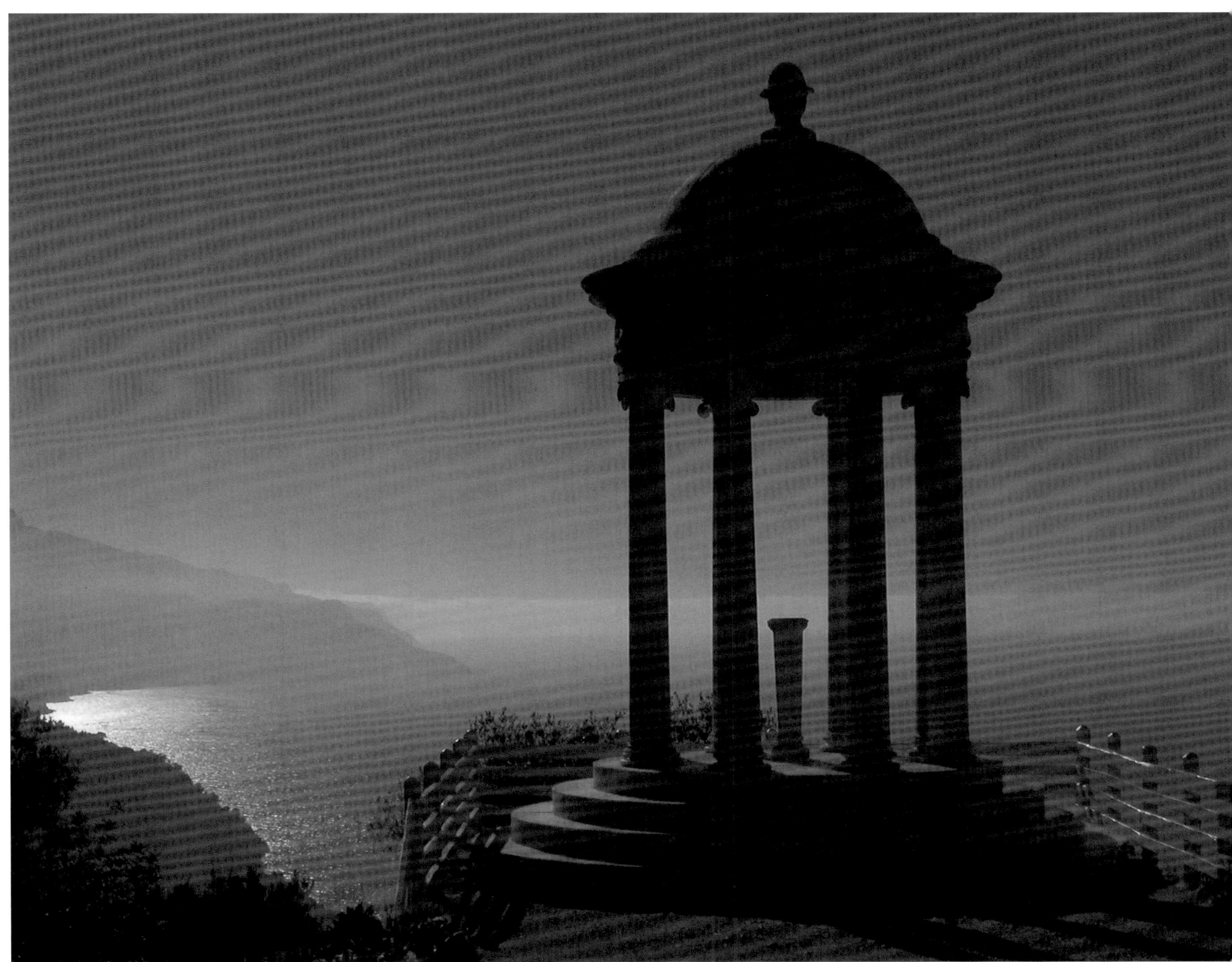

Pars Pro Toto The bay pictured here is one of the quaintest in all of Mallorca. Taking an overview shot of the area may be more appropriate for tourism marketing materials, but a photographer interested in composing images thoughtfully would do well to hone in on a single detail that can stand in for a specific memory or impression of the Mediterranean island. In this case, that detail is a partial view of a whitewashed wall that's surrounded by rocks and shaded by an Aleppo pine (right-hand page). Forgoing a comprehensive overview shot in favor of a single detail is usually the right way to go when working with a scene that has so many different aspects.

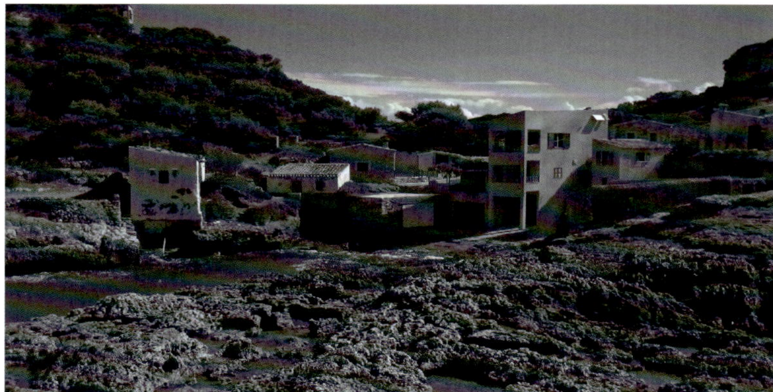

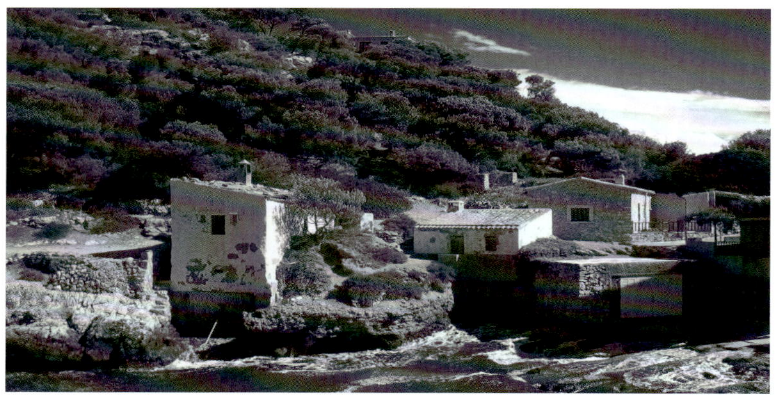

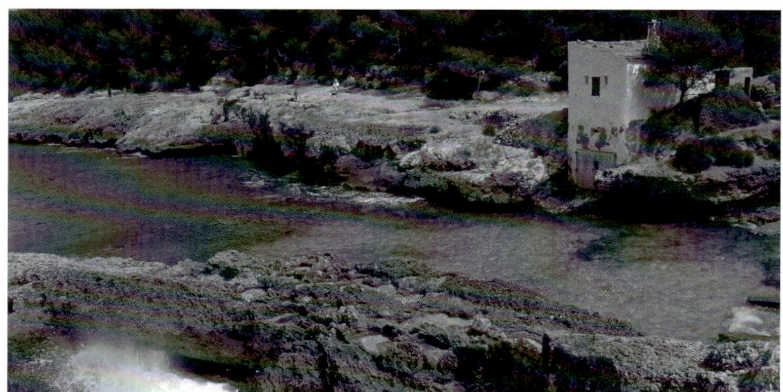

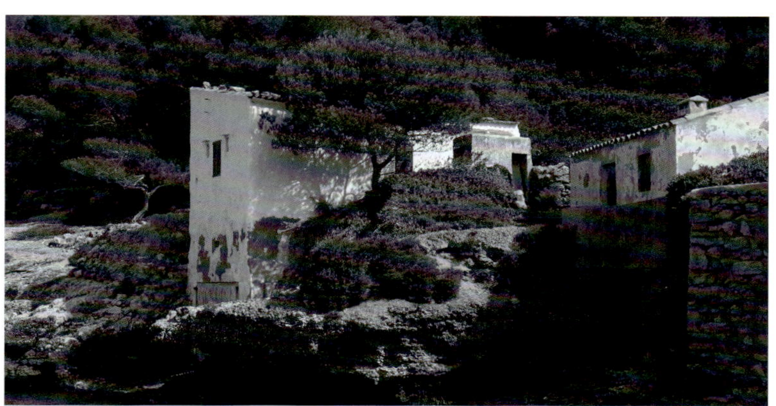

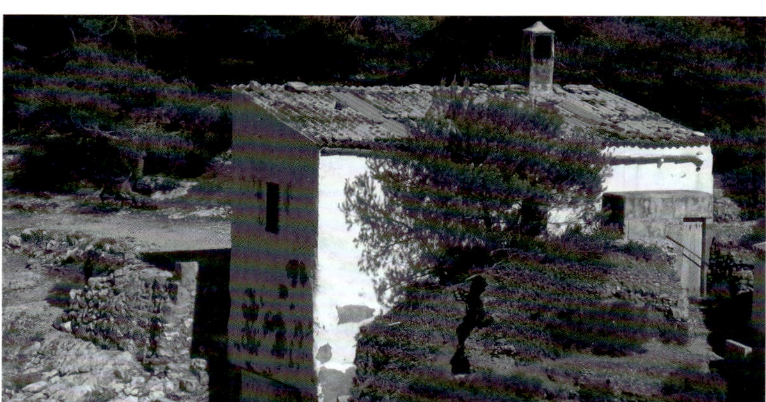

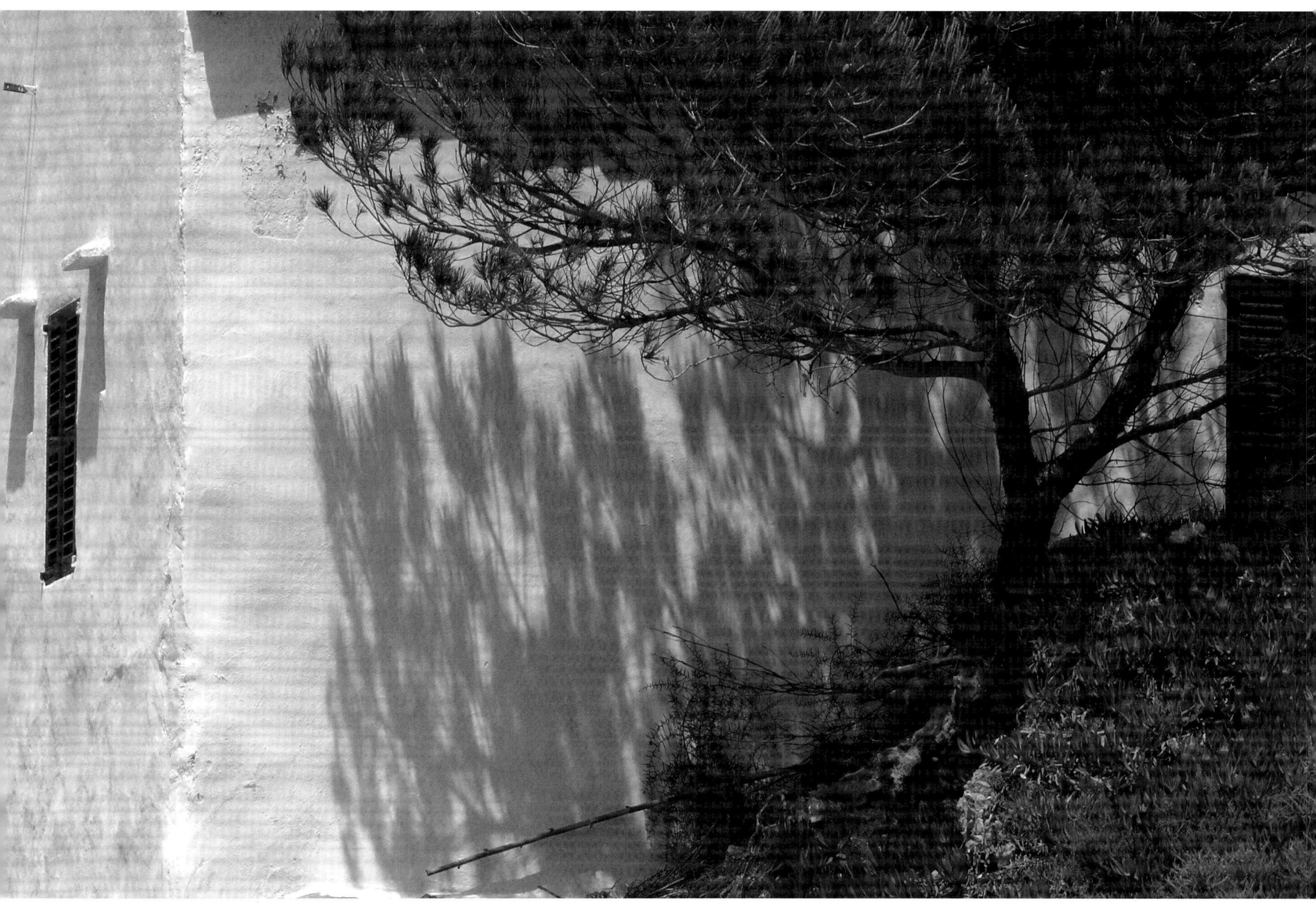

Changing Places Shifting your feet is an effective way to avoid common pitfalls when it comes to composing your images. Taking pictures in the forest, such as this one near Mannheim, often results in compositions that feature notable weaknesses: central dividing lines, uninventive perspectives, a lack of organizational coherence, ill-advised crops, and prominent lines running parallel to the image borders (top and bottom).

Creating an organizational framework, or structural lattice, for the viewer's eye develops and defines the spatial relations within an image. Diagonal lines that run opposite one another often bring tension or balance into pictures, particularly landscapes (right-hand page). Areas divided along the golden ratio also produce harmonious effects. Light and dark parts contrast with each other. Bright light and dark shadows emphasize the Mediterranean atmosphere of the inland dunes.

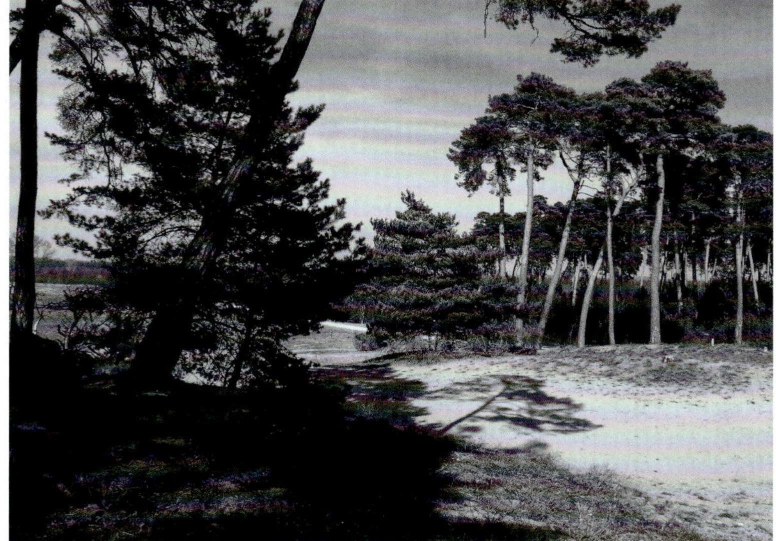

Tip *Don't give up on a subject even when it feels like there is no way to produce an interesting composition. Give yourself time! Change your standpoint and approach your image elements anew. Keeping an attentive eye on your camera's live display and honing in on the most essential elements of a scene often yield good results.*

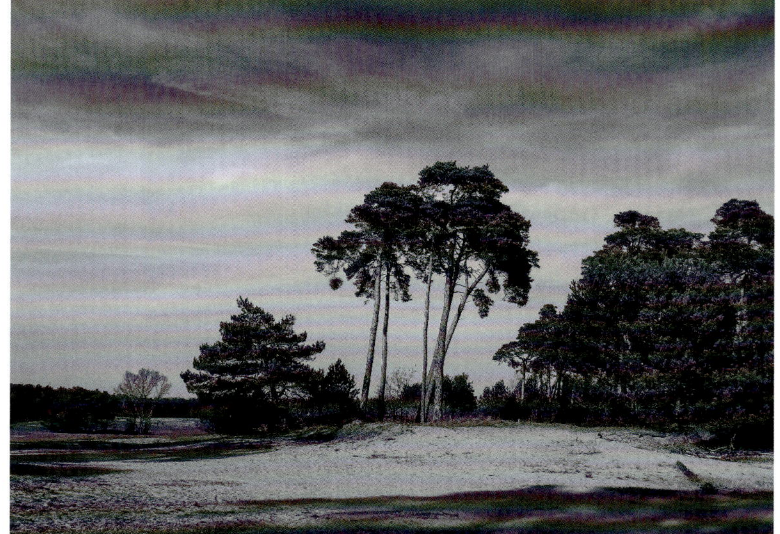

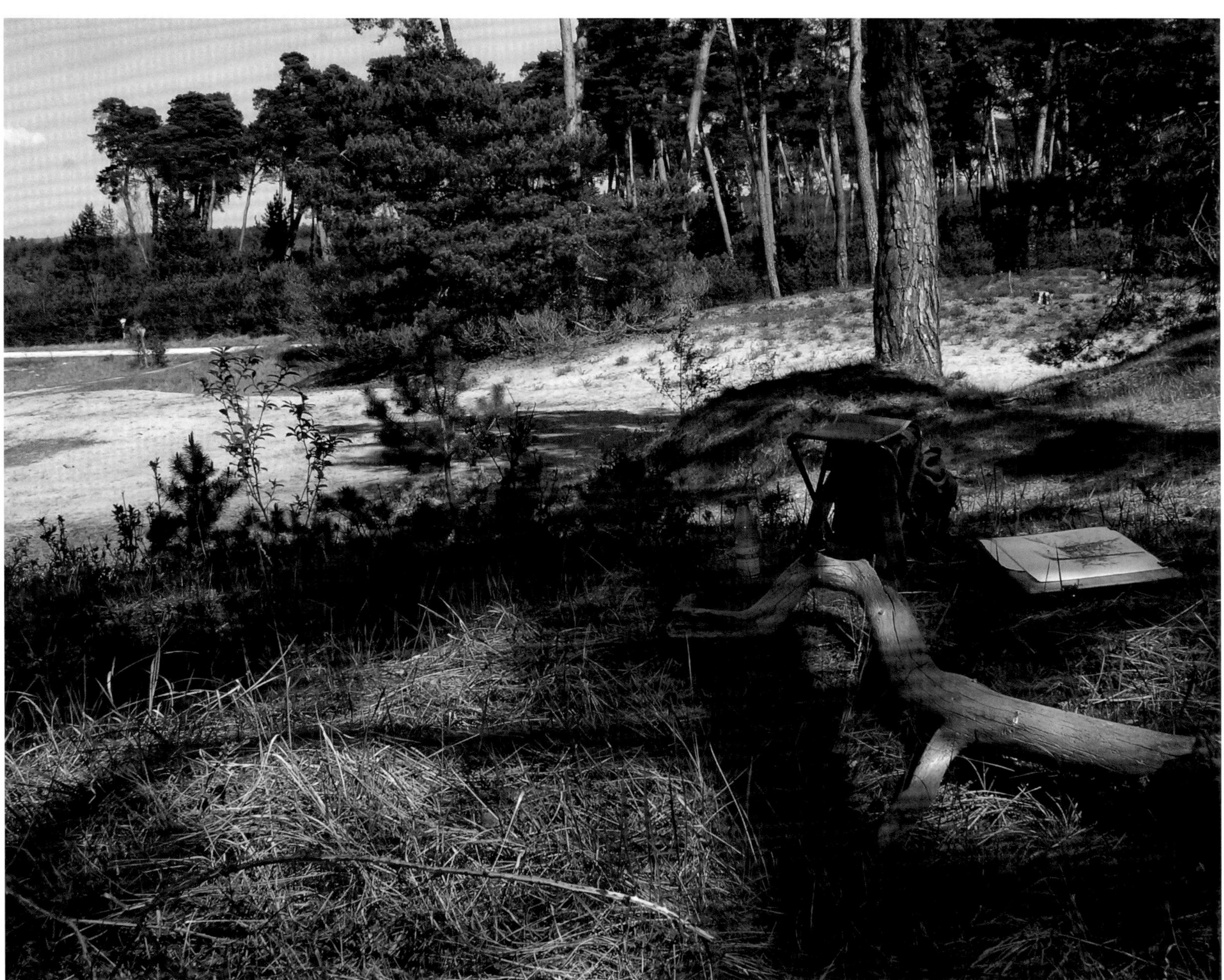

58 Lattices

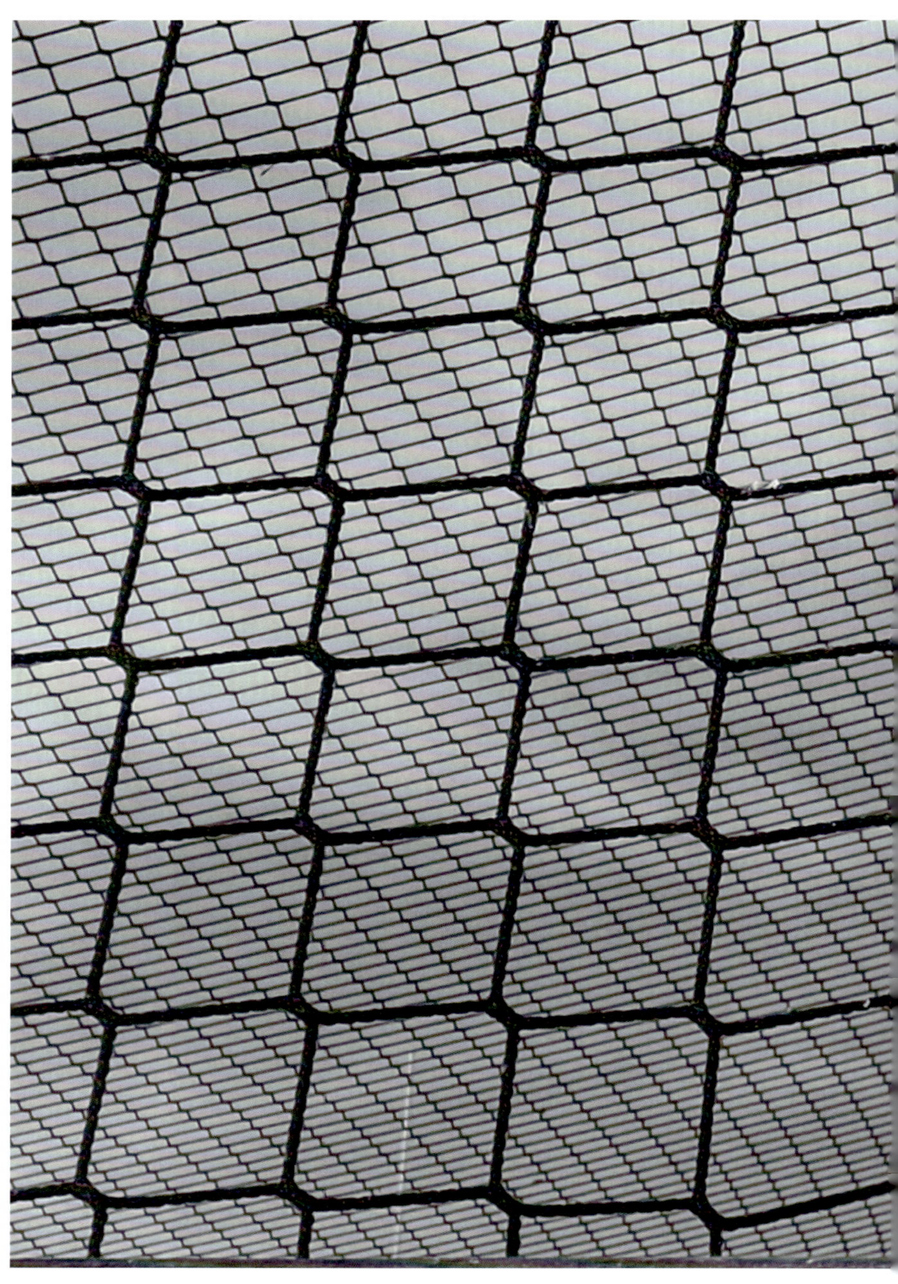

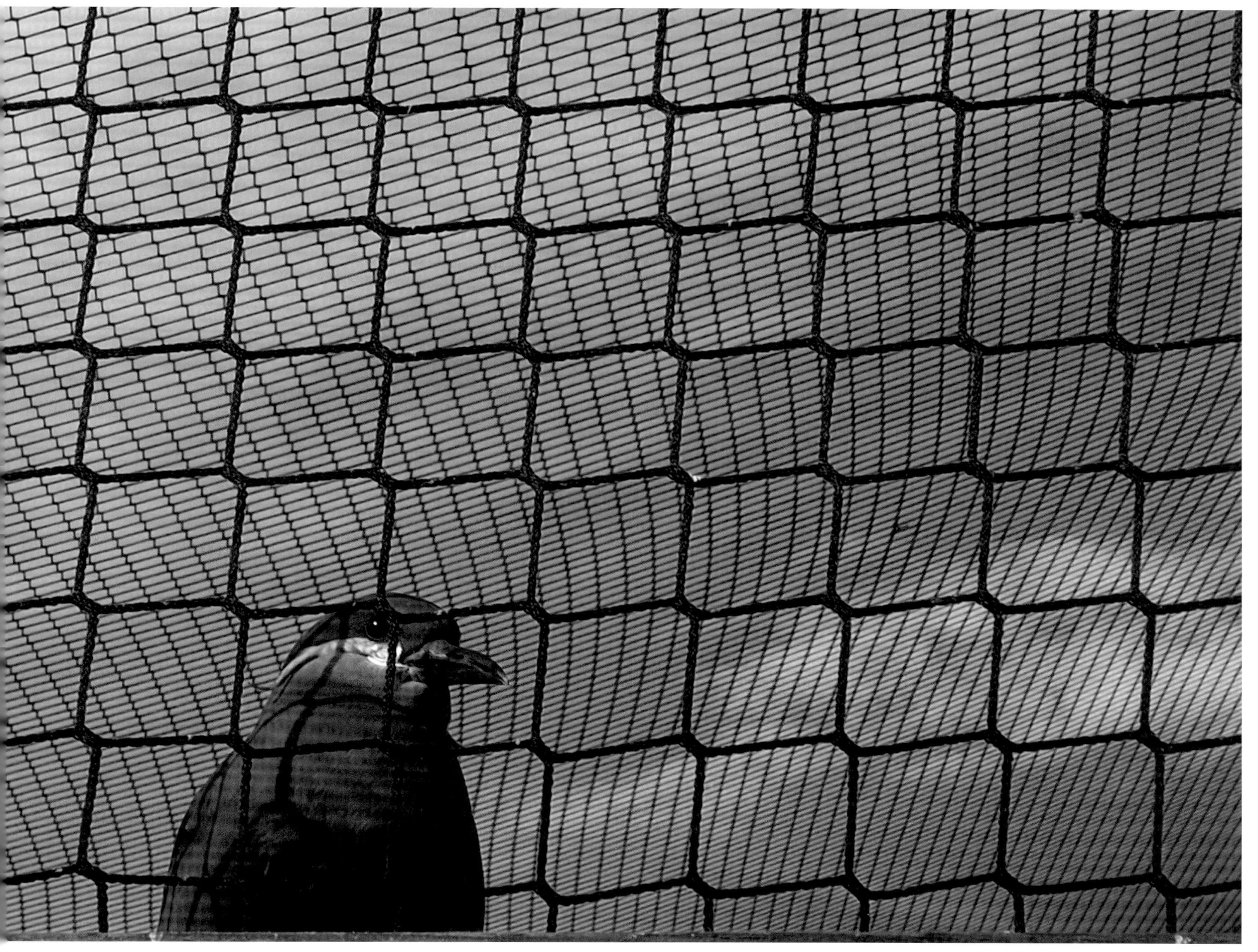

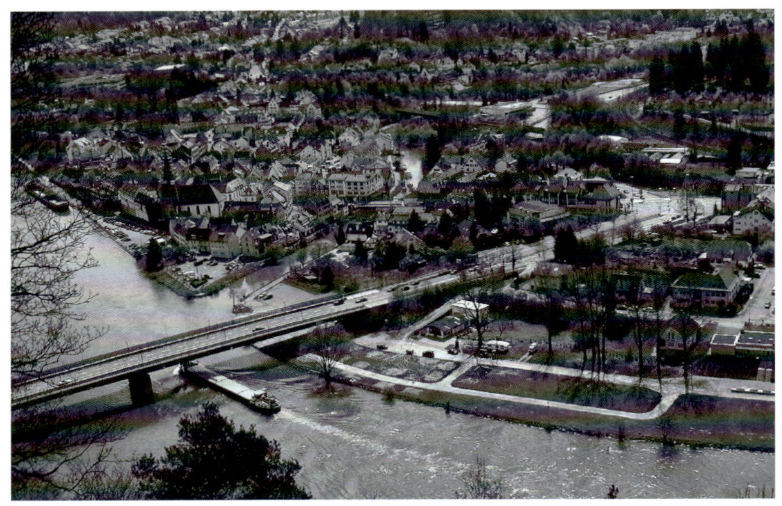

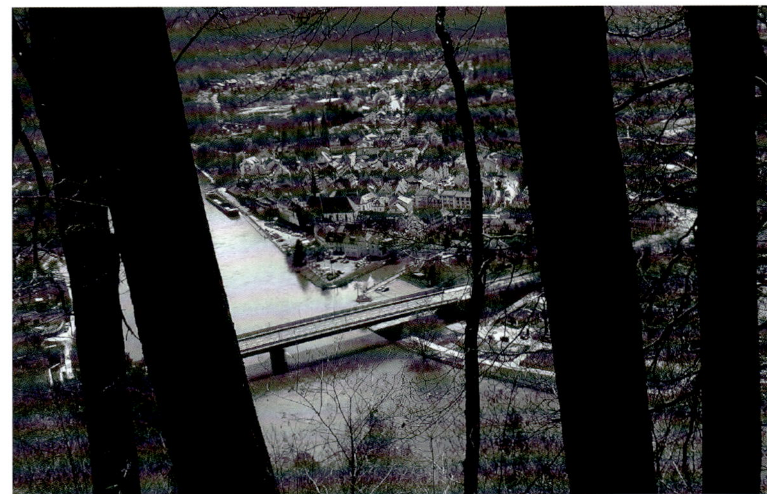

Obstructing the View In the history of the visual arts, there are few examples of images that use a lattice or grating framework as a foundation for an image's composition. One example is *The Return of the Hunters*, painted by Pieter Bruegel the Elder. The 1565 painting depicts a small forest through which hunters carrying lances march downhill in the snow with their dogs, which are partially obscured from the viewer. Many Japanese woodcuts exhibiting a similar design came to Europe after the middle of the nineteenth century, and many artists enthusiastically adopted the technique. This method, which at the time was seen as a revolutionary idea from the Far East, can be found in the works of the impressionists, including Pierre Bonnard, Claude Monet, and Edgar Degas. Vincent van Gogh reported to his brother, Theo, that man sees the world with Japanese eyes in Paris. He, himself, laid tracing paper over a famous woodcut from Utagawa Hiroshige and copied it in oil. The painting shows a fork in a branch of a plum tree in the foreground through which the viewer can see a blooming garden in the background. Katsushika Hokusai became a significant influence on the artists in Europe. His depictions of the sacred Mount Fuji featured all sorts of lattice constructions, including scaffoldings, spider webs, trees, bamboo stalks, banners, and rain, and his work continues to be a source of inspiration for today's illustrators, comic-book artists, and of course, photographers. These pictures (above) taken in the German town of Neckargemünd illustrate the effect that a formal lattice can have on an image's composition: the left photograph seems like an aerial exposure, while the one on the right is divided by trees, which defines the photographer's standpoint.

The view of the Heidelberg Castle (right-hand page) through the lattice of trees in the foreground shows that using this technique can provide structure to the main subject and support the spatial image. Here the vertical and horizontal lines (in the trees and in the architecture) that run parallel to the image borders make sense, because their position and rhythmic dividing lines are a key part of the image's composition.

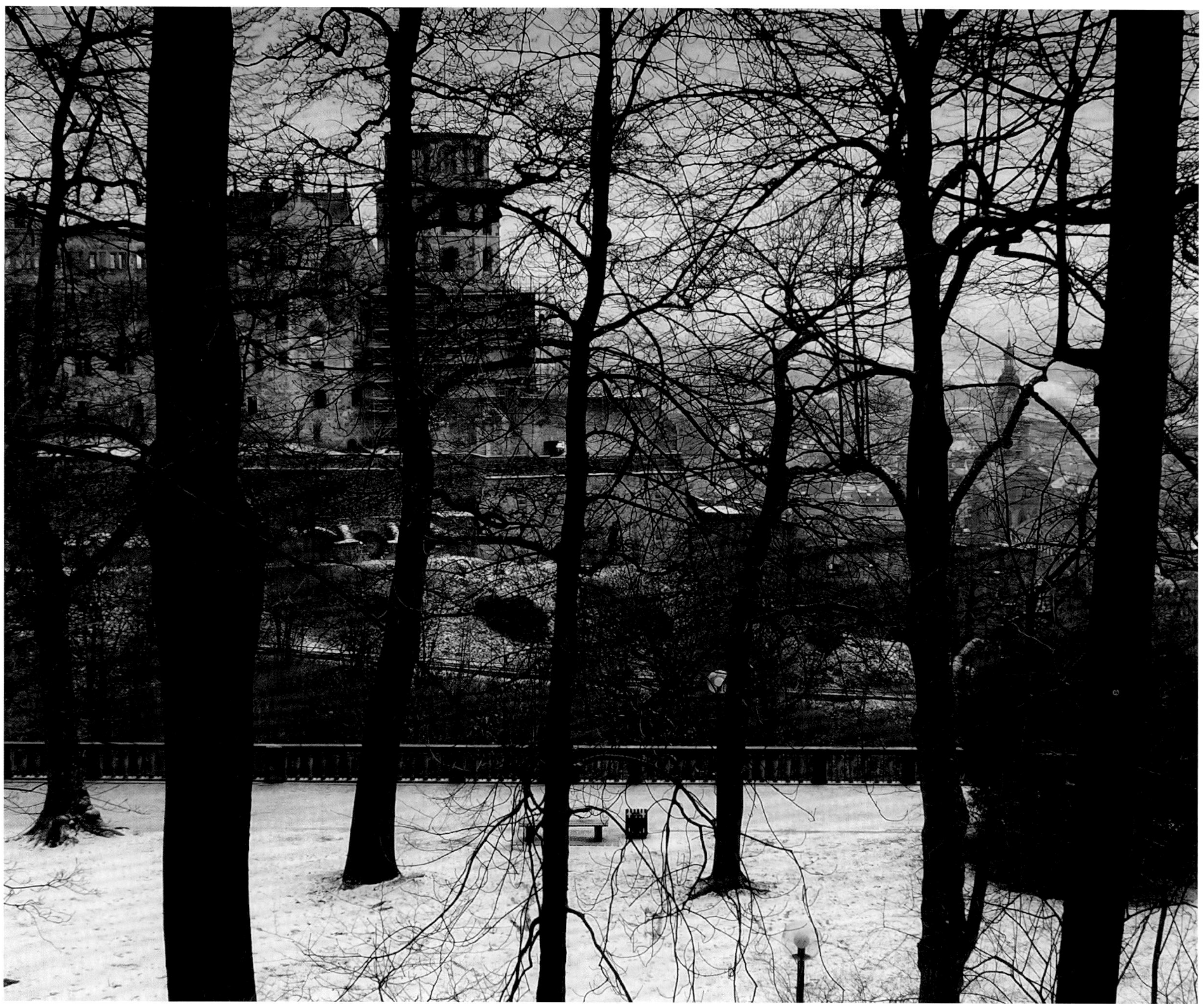

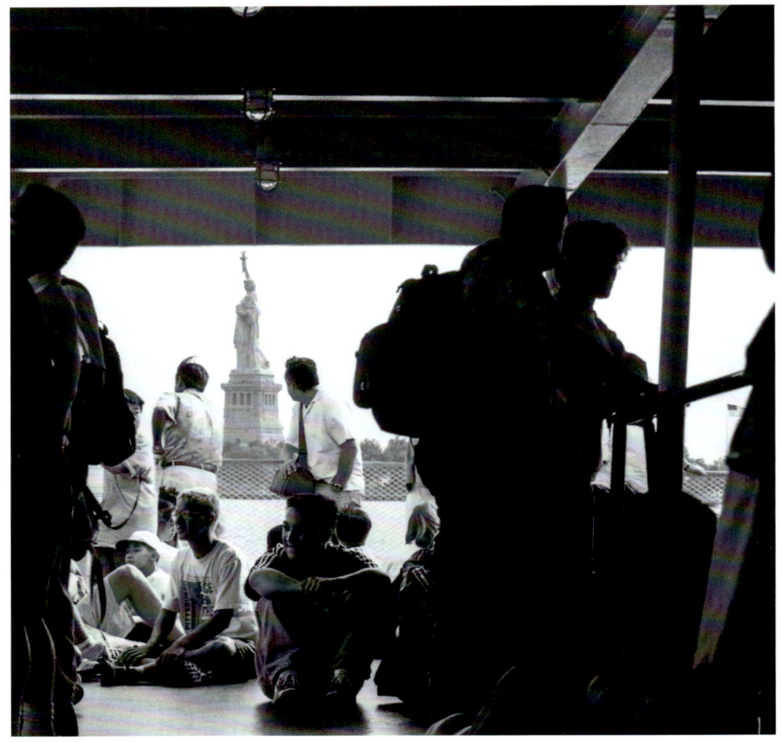

Tip *When you first hear the words* lattice *and* grate, *you might think of wood or metal. But you can execute this compositional method of forcing the viewer to look through a regular pattern of elements in the foreground with an endless variety of objects—see the examples on the next spread and experiment with your own photography.*

Onlookers Setting up a structural framework for your compositions is not the most elegant method of design, but it is one of the most evocative. Artists working in many of the visual arts use frameworks to turn viewers into curious onlookers, participants, spectators, witnesses, and even voyeurs.

A visual framing apparatus is particularly effective in film scenes, wherein the lens of the camera assumes the position of the onlooker—placing the viewer in the character's shoes. Hans Hillmann's illustrations for the book *Fly Paper* by Dashiell Hammett are construed in this way. The imagery is decidedly film noir, and one of the dark, grayscale illustrations is particularly memorable: it depicts an obscured view through a Venetian blind, giving the reader the perspective of a witness to a crime scene.

Many comics and graphic novels also make use of structural frameworks and visual lattices to connect readers to the action. The grid of panels in most comics is rich with possibilities for creative storytelling. Illustrators who work on children's books also use this composition principle to keep young readers emotionally invested in stories, page after page.

The photographs here were shot while traveling on the Staten Island Ferry from Liberty Island to Manhattan a few years before the World Trade Center attack. The photos reveal that human figures are perfectly adequate for making up the dividing lines of a compositional lattice.

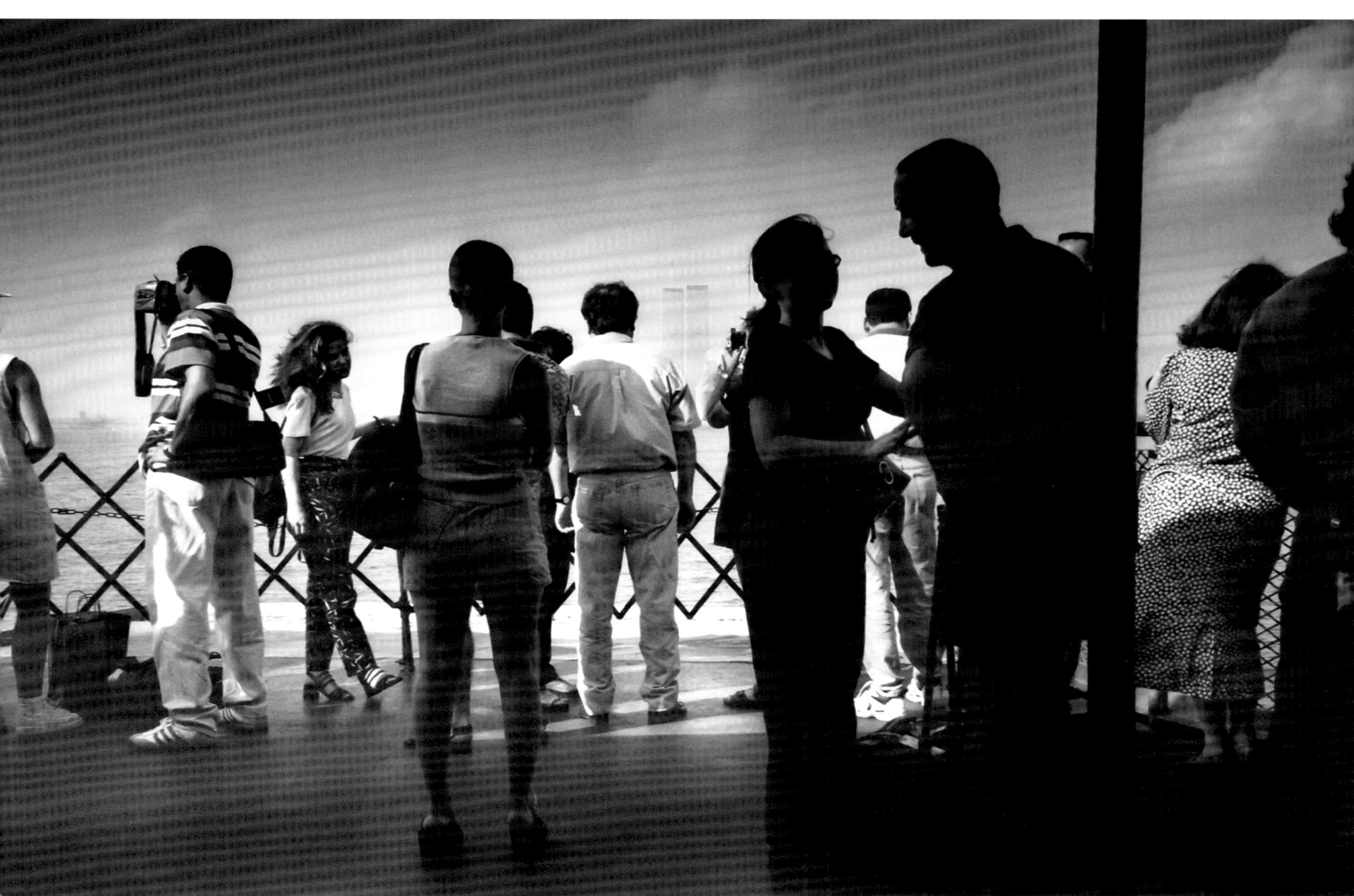

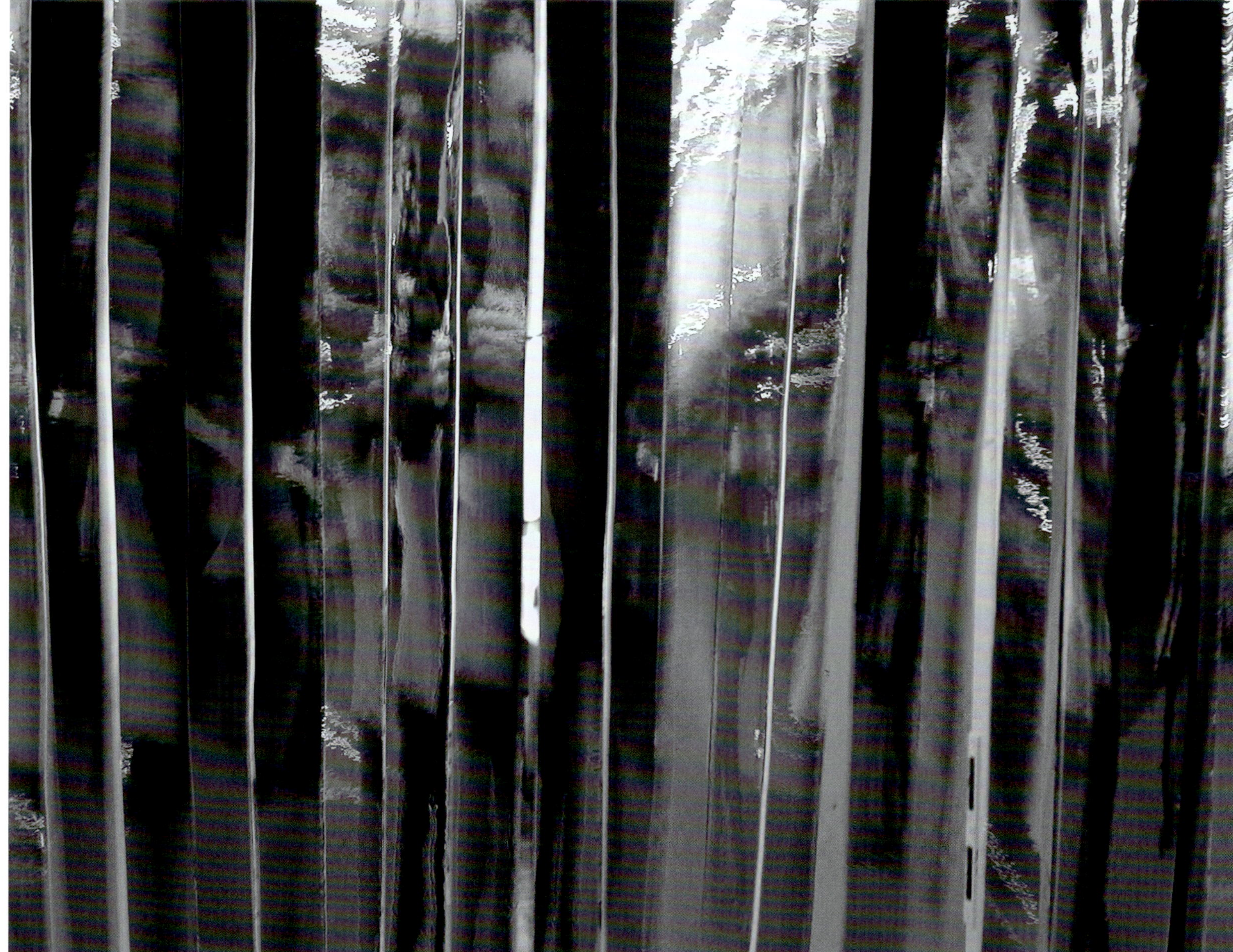

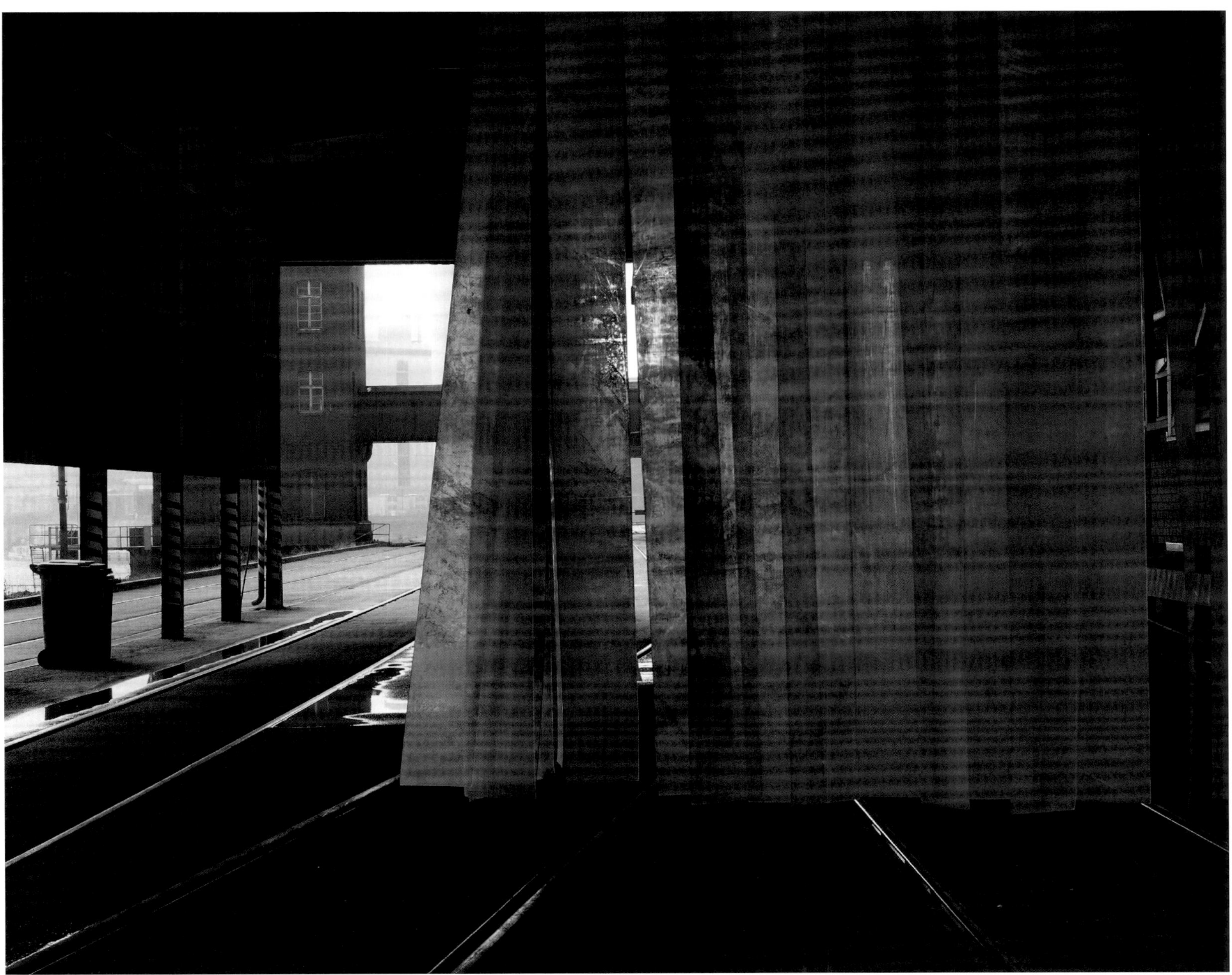

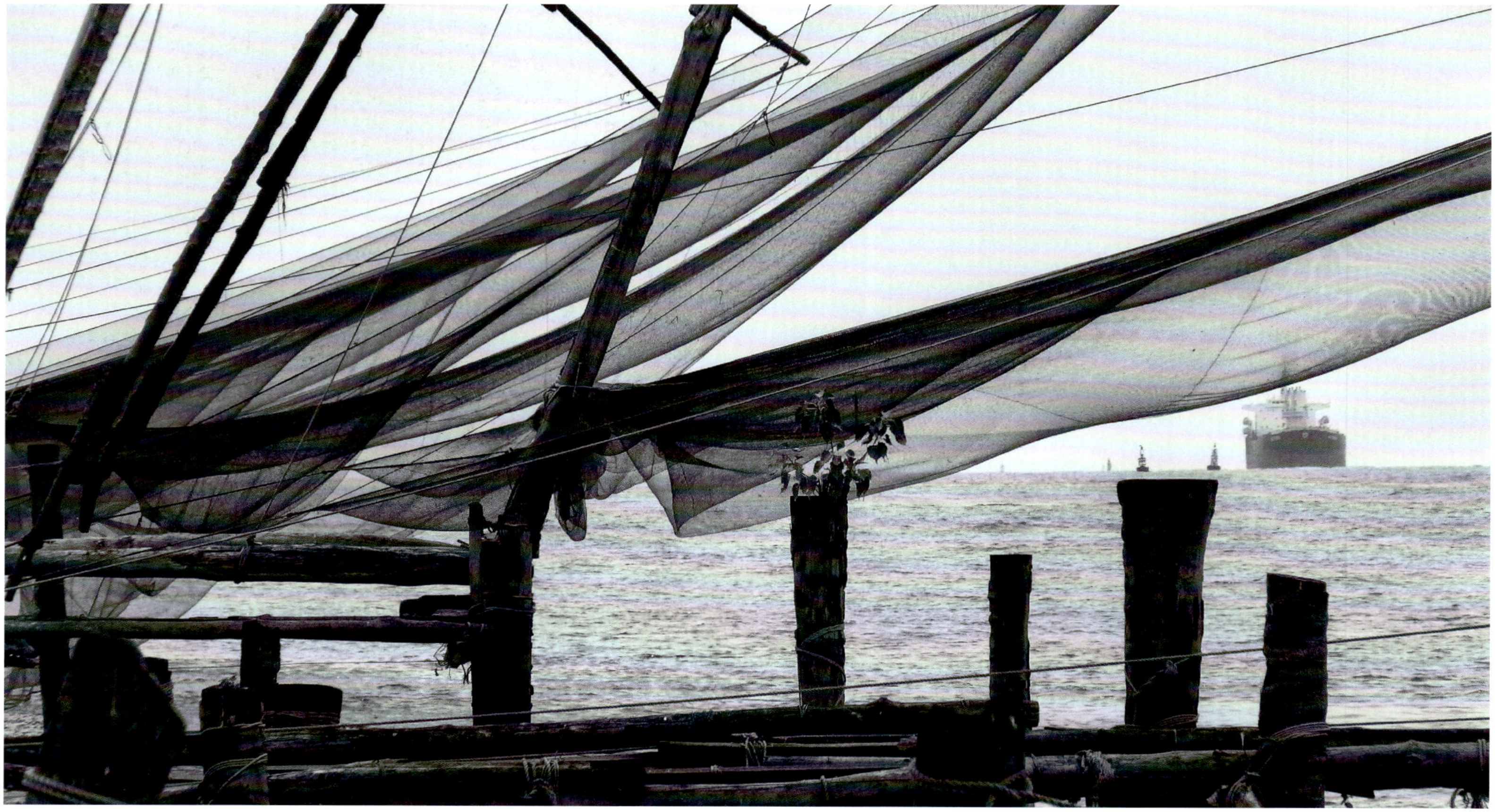

Look Through! These two photos show that various composition techniques can work harmoniously together within the same image. In the photo of the fishing nets in Kochi, India (left), the horizontal and vertical lines are key to the structure of the image, but the traversing diagonal lines of the nets, sails, and posts are the real stars of the show.

In the right image, the upright lattice formed by the breakwater in Knokke, Belgium, contrasts richly with the diagonal drift lines from the waves.

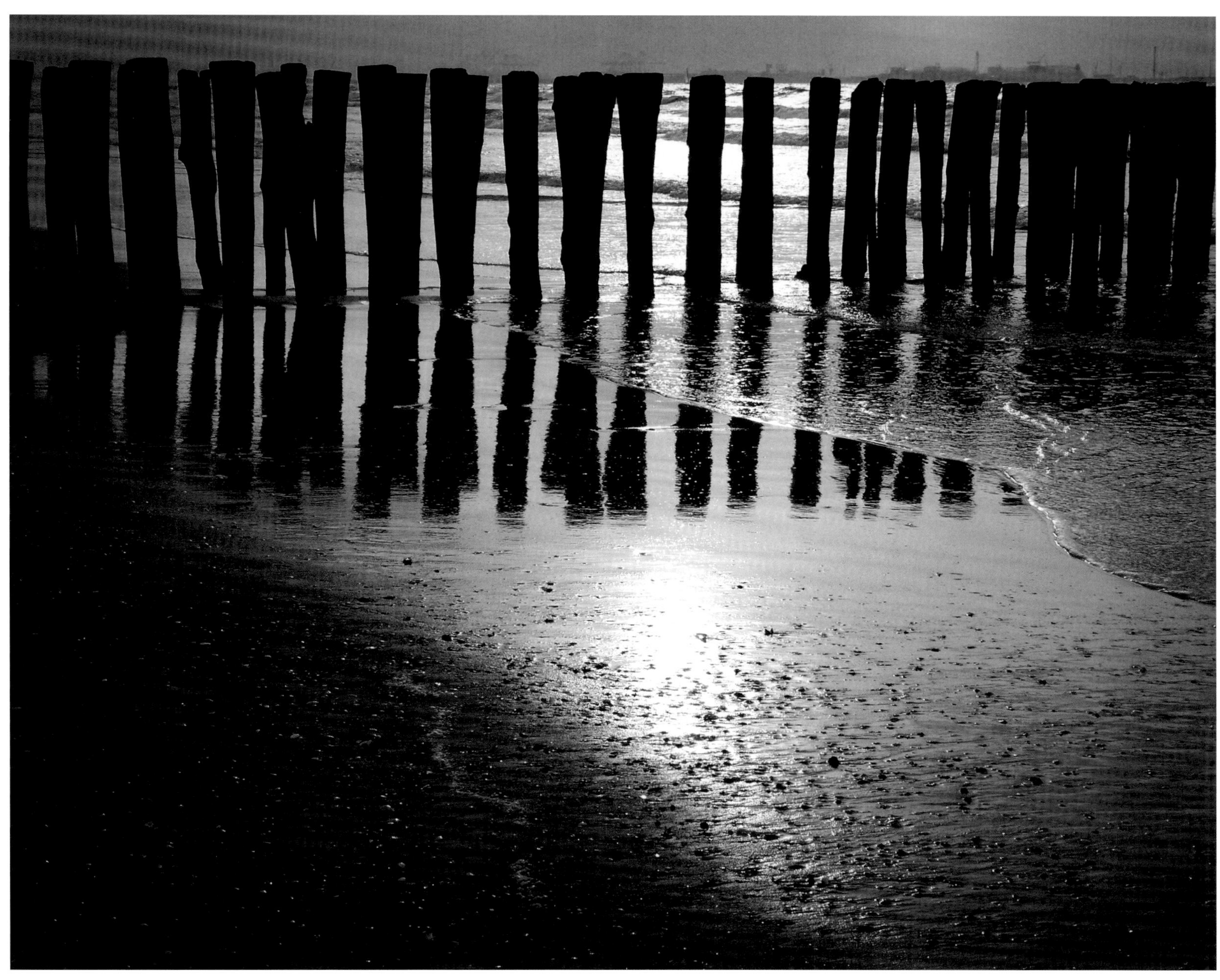

Themes Some artists have always shown an exclusive dedication to a specific theme or subject, making their images easily identifiable. When it comes to still lifes, for example, I immediately think of the Dutch masters, the French painter Jean Siméon Chardin, and the Bolognese painter Giorgio Morandi. These specialists exist in photography, as well. Among the many nature photography specialists out there, for me, Stephen Dalton opened up a whole new way of looking at the animal and plant worlds. August Sander is a good example of a photographer who dedicated himself to studying the human form and earned a significant level of mastery and success doing so.

In contrast to these artists, the Berlin artist Adolph Menzel showed an interest in nearly everything that his eyes took in and did not paint only one type of subject. There are also generalists among photographers. Andreas Feininger could be included in this category of artists who work in a variety of visual genres.

Limiting yourself to specific subjects can be addictive. Even shooting a subject as mundane-sounding as windows can develop into a full-fledged passion. Using structured frameworks in exploring this topic would be obvious, but other design elements can also play an interesting role in such a study; examples include transparency, light-dark contrasts, starkly defined areas of space, subtle plays of light and shadow, aggressive crops, proportions adhering to the golden ratio, blurriness and sharpness, as well as many other design tools.

Tip *A special tidbit of advice for students applying to universities: your portfolio should have a decisive coherence. Do not present a collection of work samples that lack an underlying consistency. Commit yourself to a specific area or theme to show that you can sustain your interest and work in a specific field for a prolonged time.*

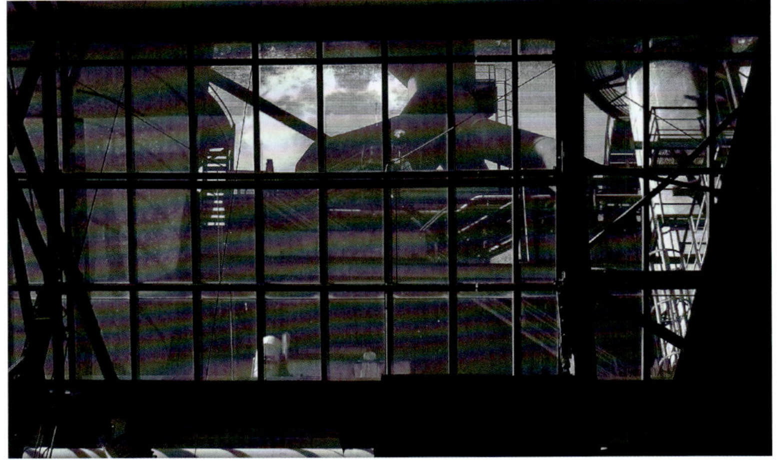

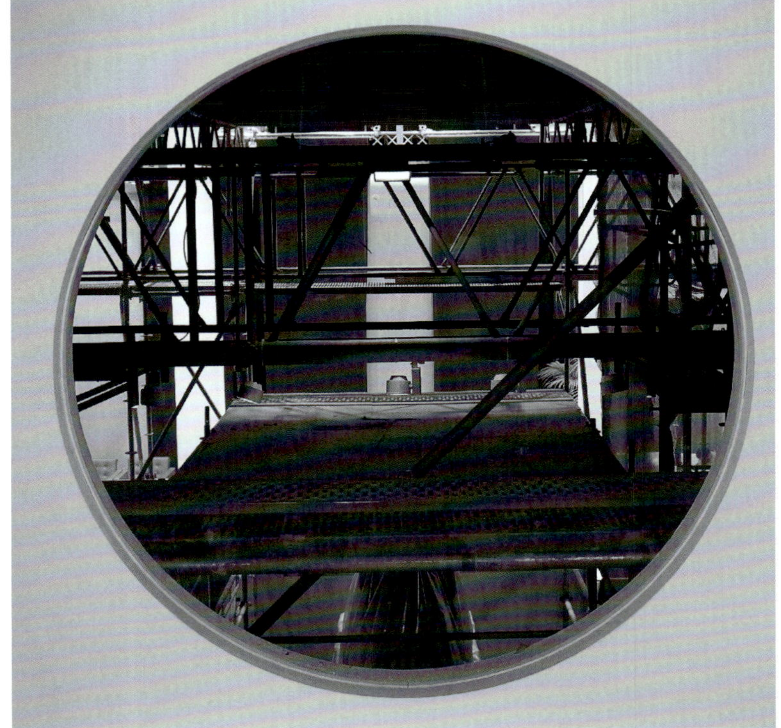

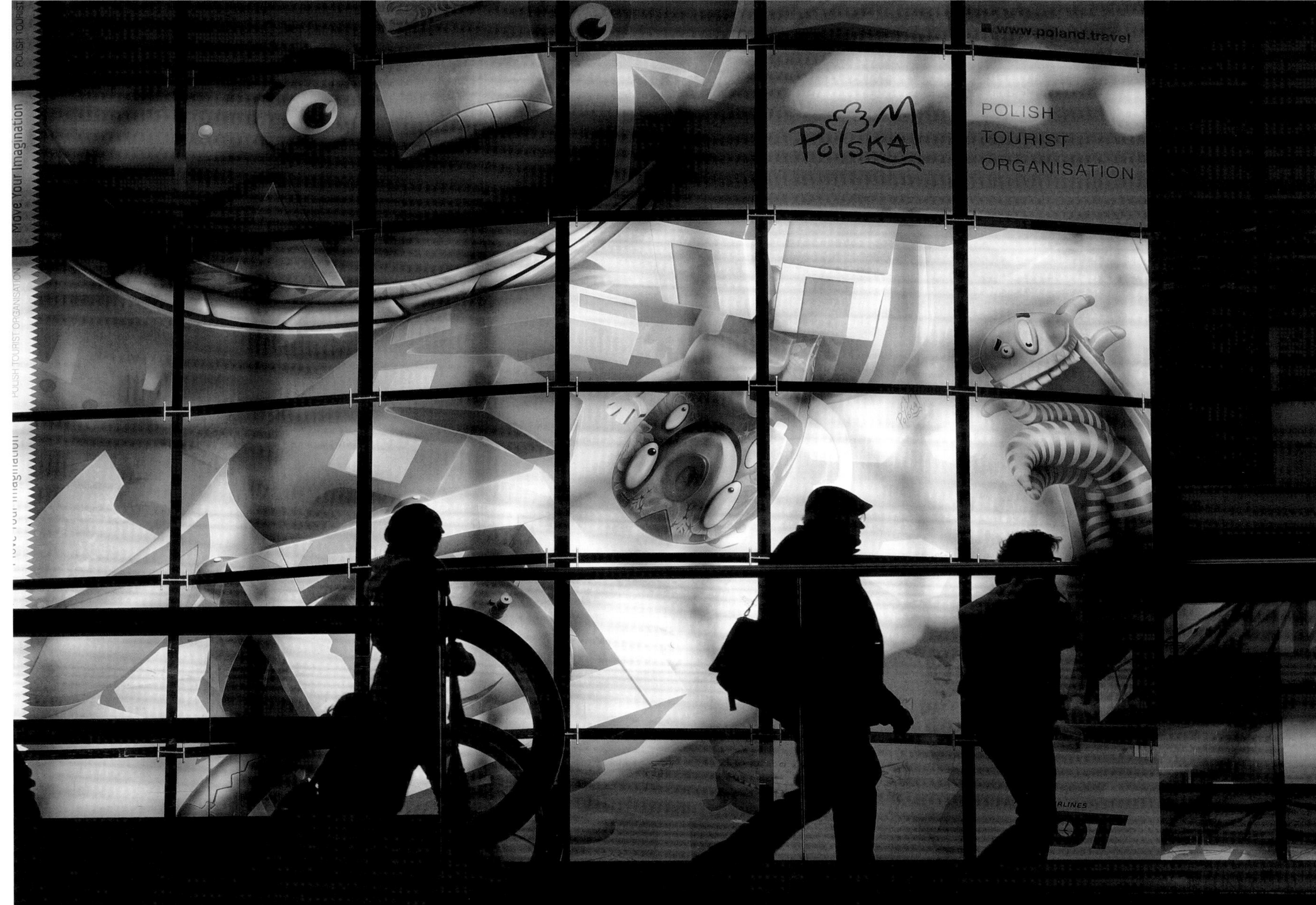

www.poland.travel
Polska
POLISH
TOURIST
ORGANISATION
Move Your Imagination
POLISH TOURIST ORGANISATION

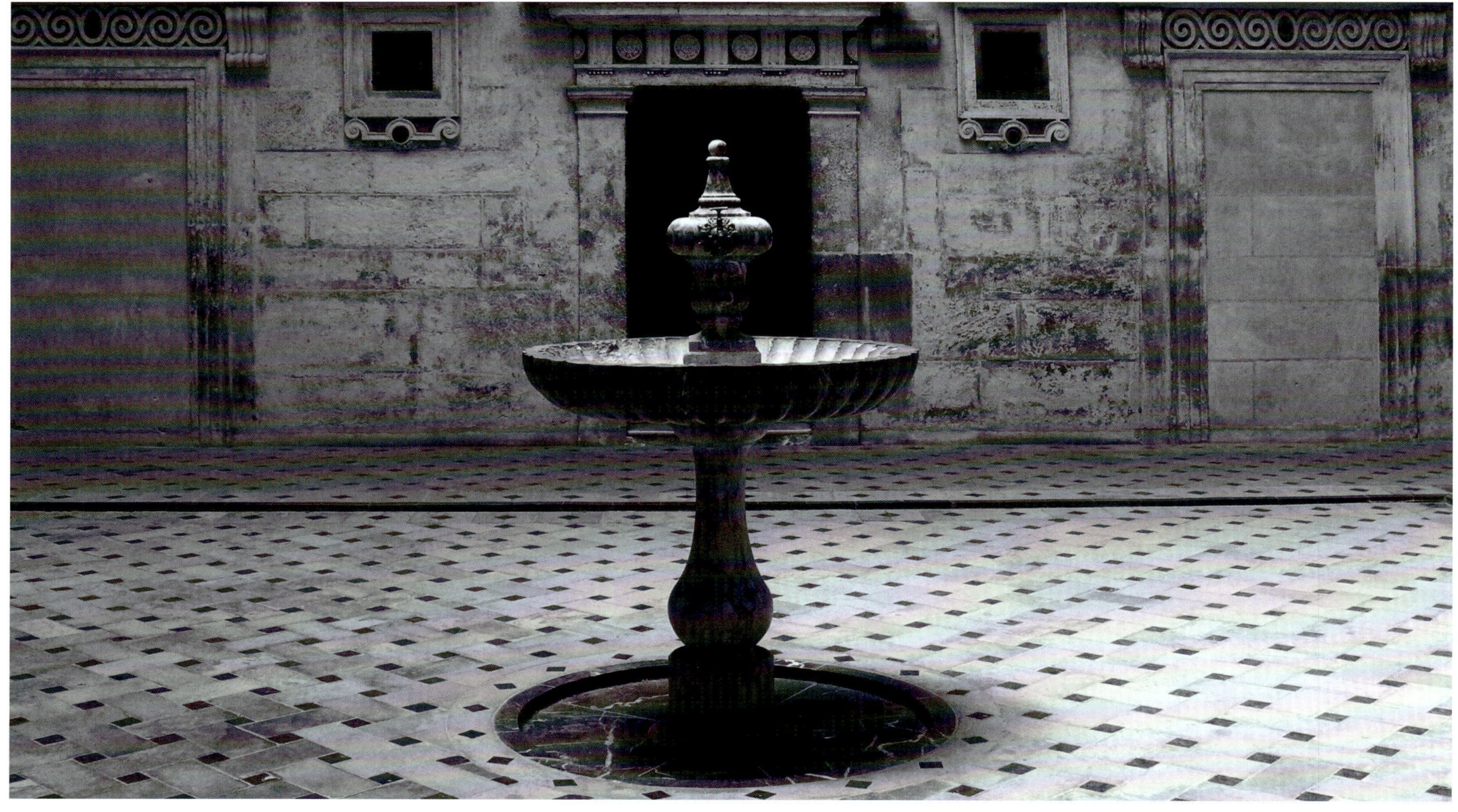

Before and Behind The two photographs of this small room in the cathedral in Seville have a completely different effect. The left image features the fountain as its main focus—the subject is centered, and further accentuated by the conspicuous backdrop of the doorway. But does this photo convey the intimacy of the small room to viewers? Without anything else to go on, a viewer might mistake the small room for a grand hall.

Taking few steps back, however, and using a doorway as a frame, creates an entirely different atmosphere (right-hand image). The viewer can see the passageway from one room to the other, where the fountain, still attractively composed, lures the viewer toward it. The outcome of the image owes its success to the principle of designing with a lattice or a frame.

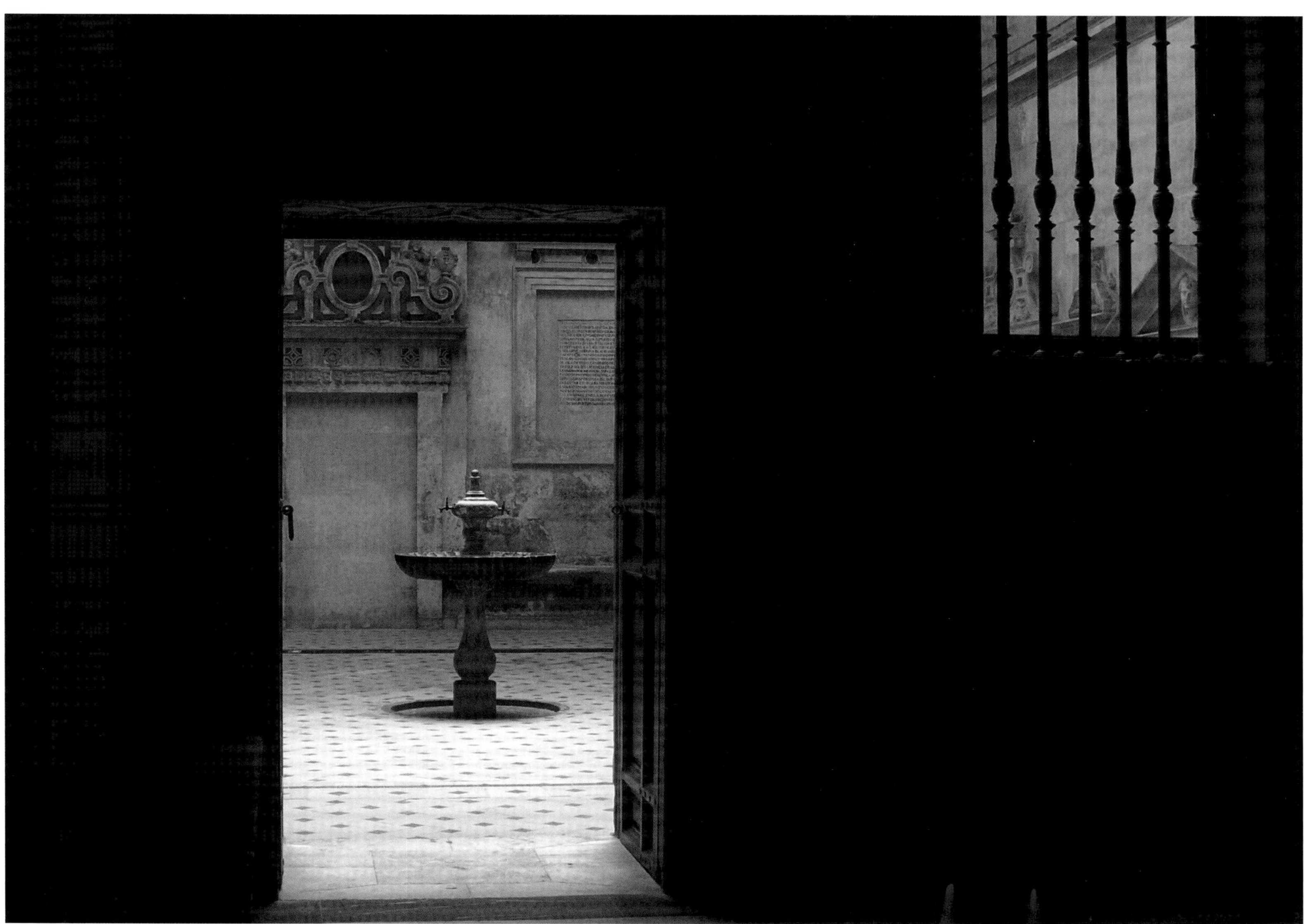

72 Cropping

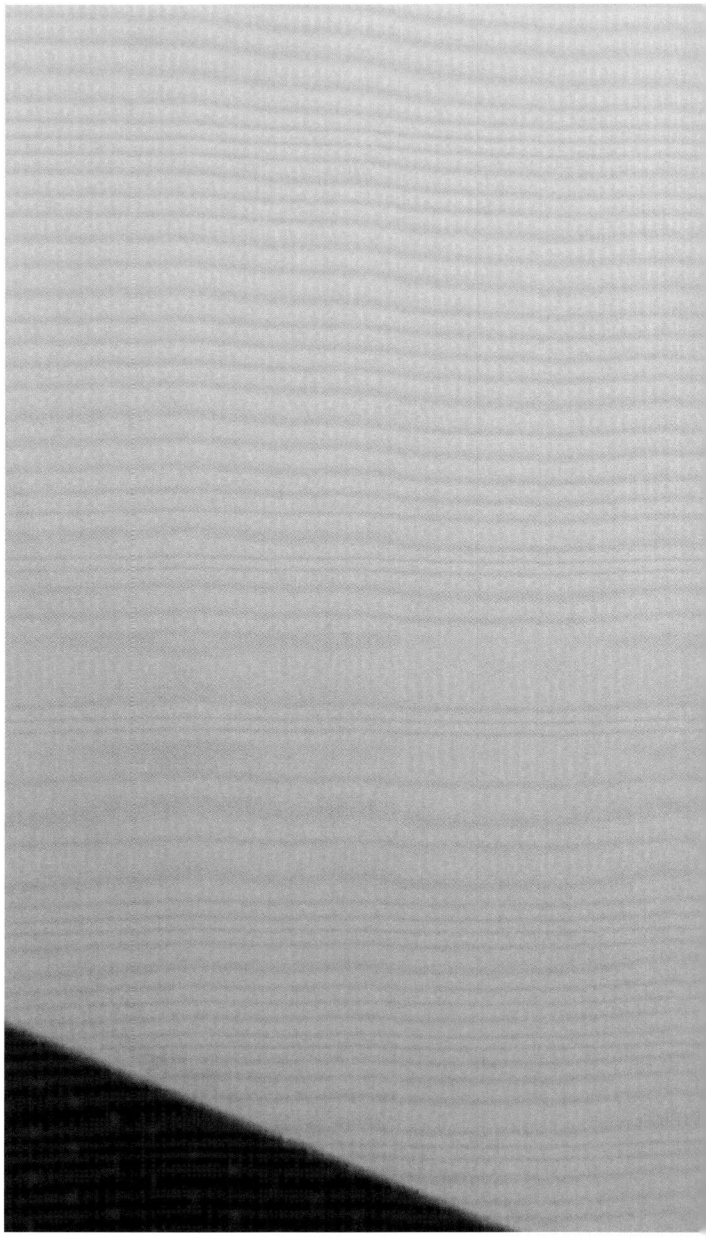

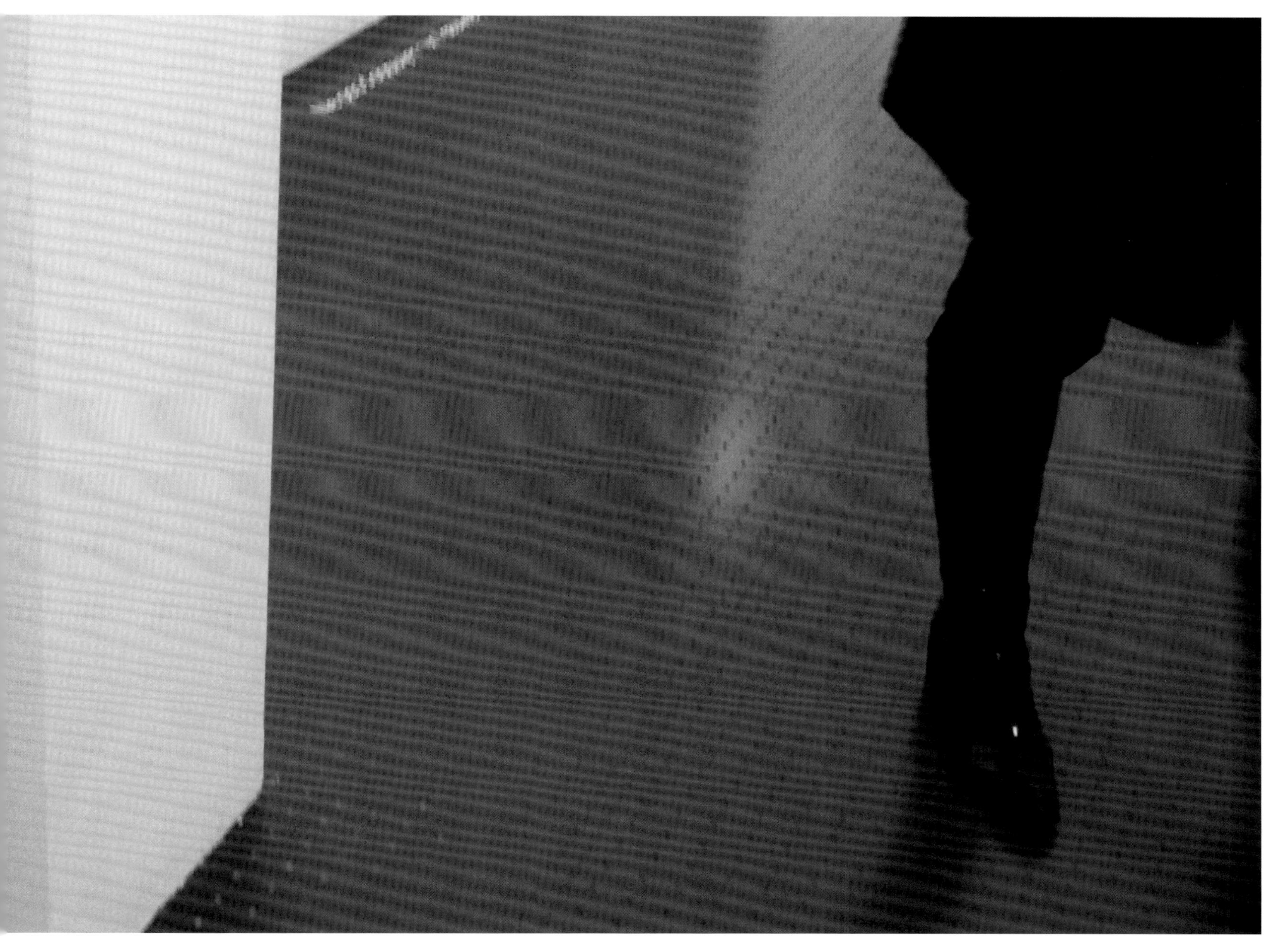

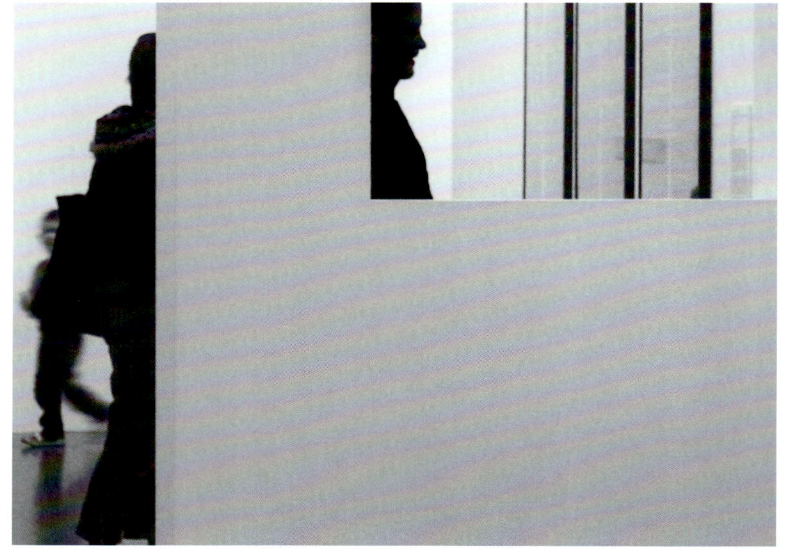

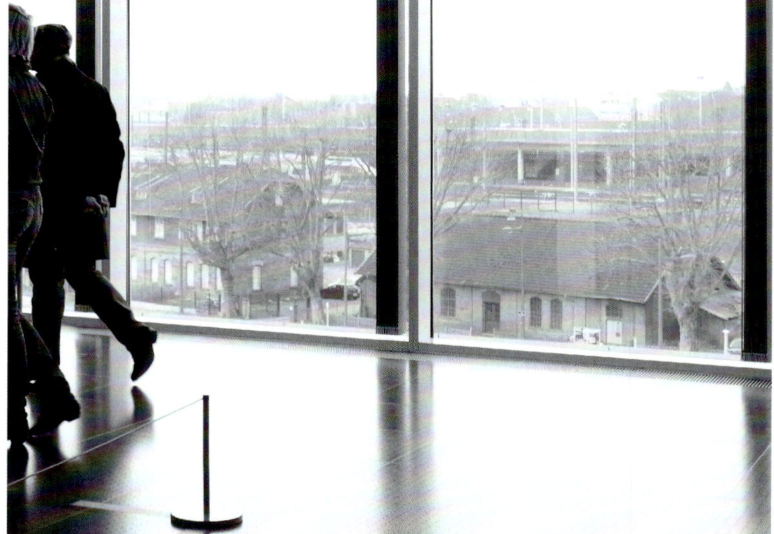

Extreme Crops Like the innovative ideas that came out of Japan, un-conventional or extreme cropping techniques are among other artistic concepts that traveled from the East to the West. Western artists have fully adopted the use of extreme crops in their repertoires. The subjects in photos treated with these extreme crops tend to be barely contained within the image area: they step out of or into the picture in what at first may seem like an arbitrary composition. Painters and graphic artists continue to use these techniques today. Comic book artists, for example, know exactly how to heighten their viewers' engagement by including an abrupt crop at the edge of a panel.

Photography is an ideal medium for this compositional technique. These photographs taken in Centre Pompidou–Metz show a variety of examples of cropping. Asymmetry, unusual vantage points, extreme close-ups in the foreground, light/dark contrasts, and the juxtaposition of unlike areas are all visual hallmarks of this method.

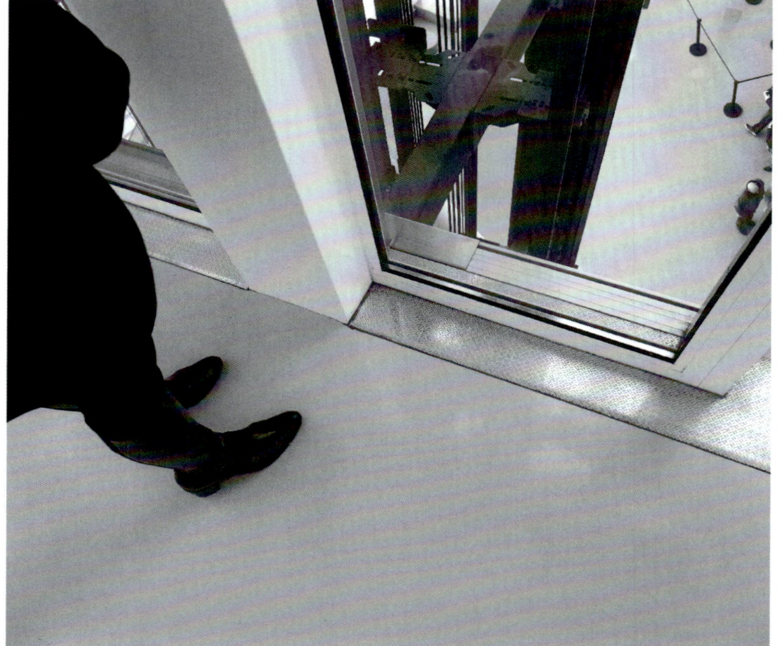

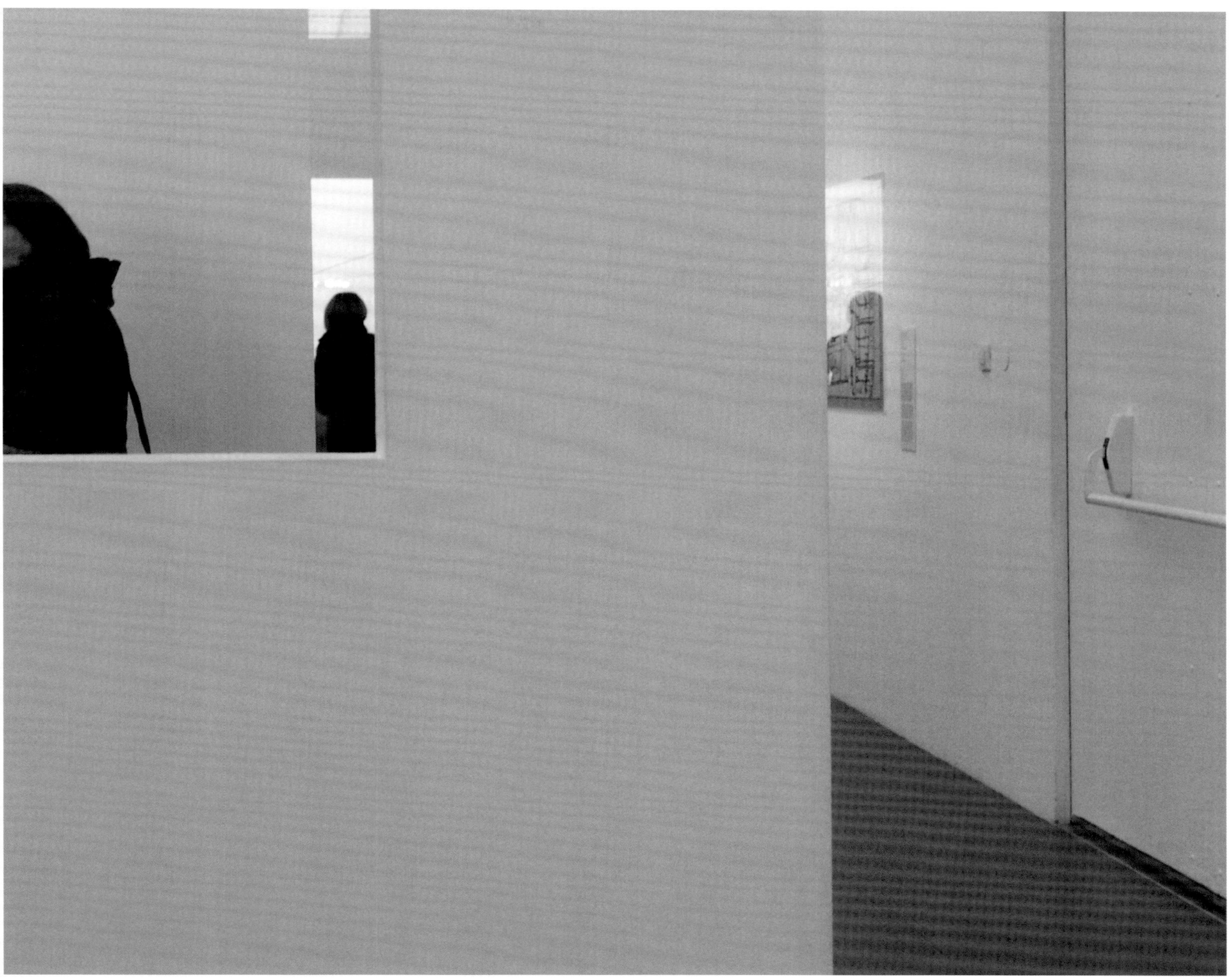

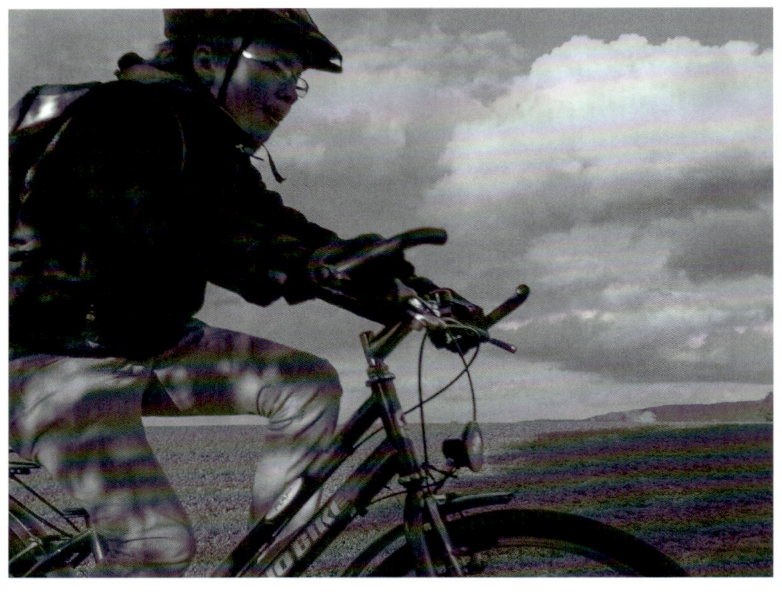

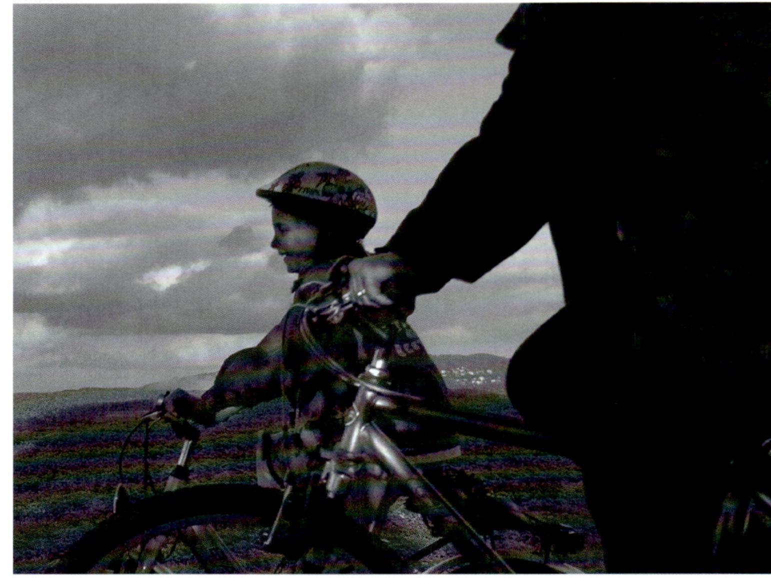

Tip *If you want to practice your ability to see and execute radical crops, find a place where lots of people pass by. All the better if the location also has a light background and good lighting. These conditions make it easier to achieve clear contrasts of positive and negative space, both of which are critical to an image's overall effectiveness. Using a camera with a burst exposure mode and a zoom lens is also to your advantage. Set your other camera settings to automatic, because blur and other technical deficiencies are a second-order concern for this experiment. The goal here is to become confident when it comes to choosing your image area in a way that deliberately truncates certain visual elements. Related to this exercise is the eventual need to crop your photos on your computer afterward—at least until you are confident that you can obtain the optimal image composition while actually exposing the image.*

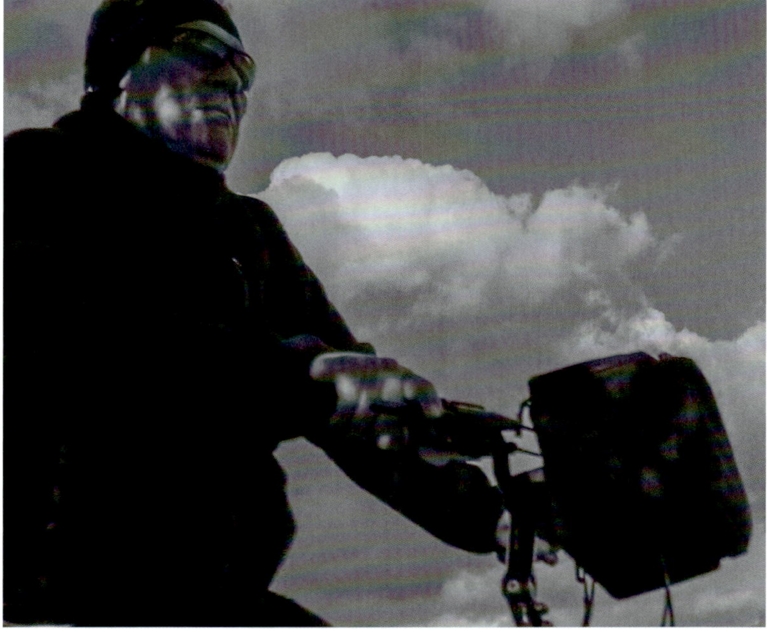

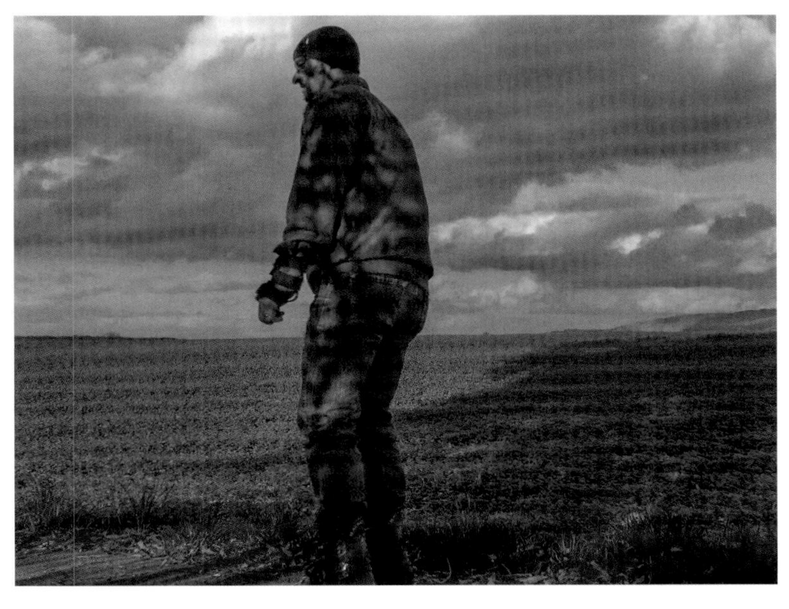

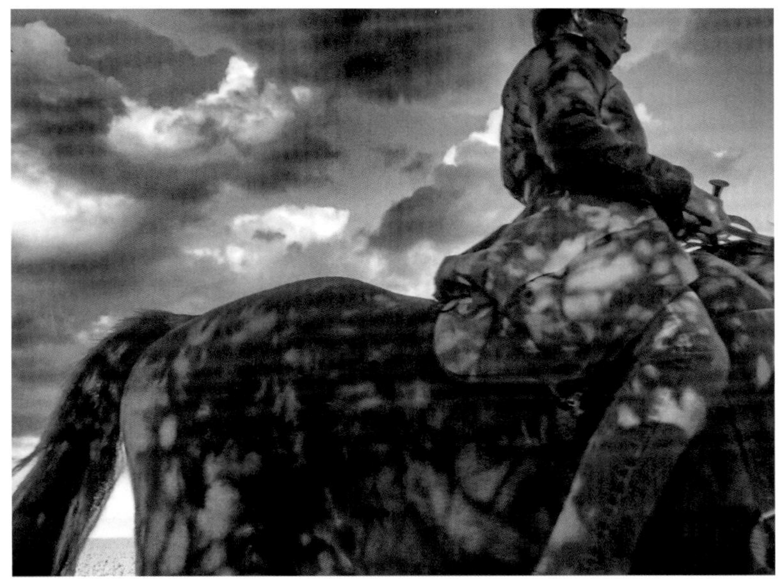

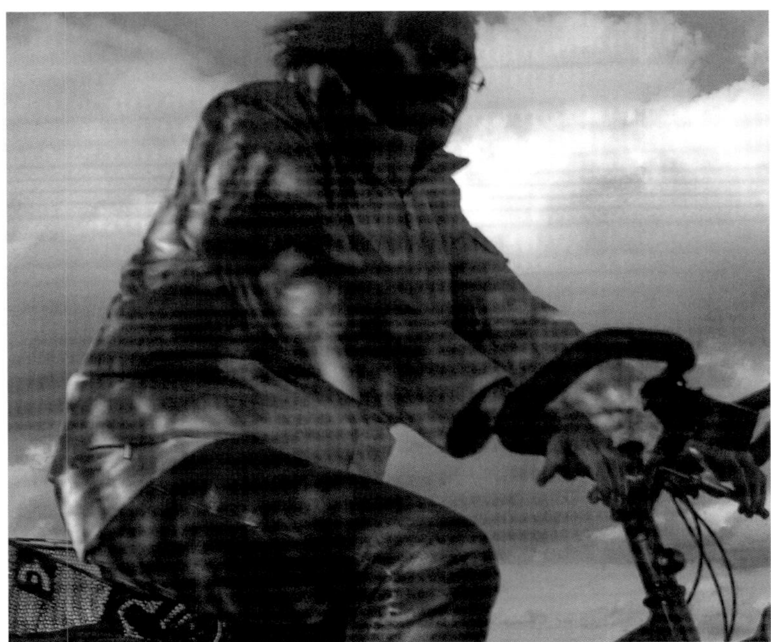

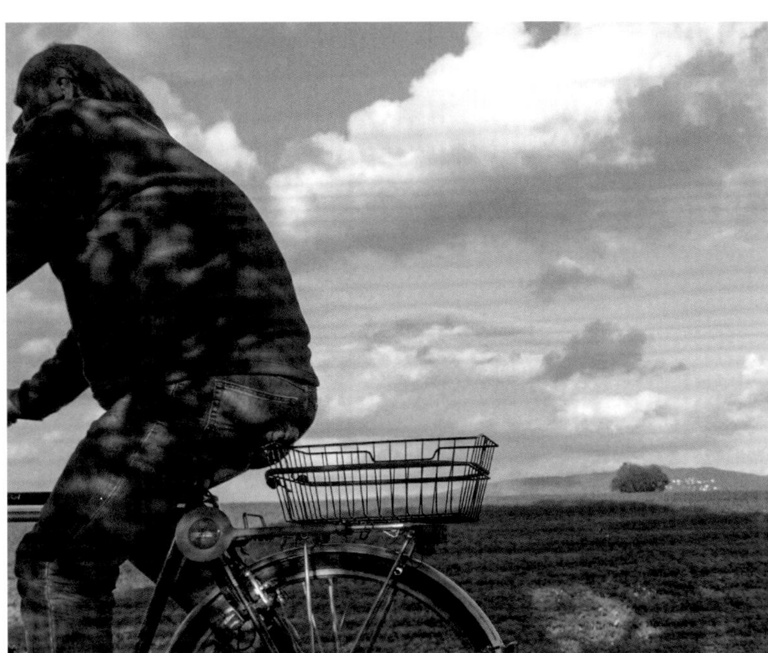

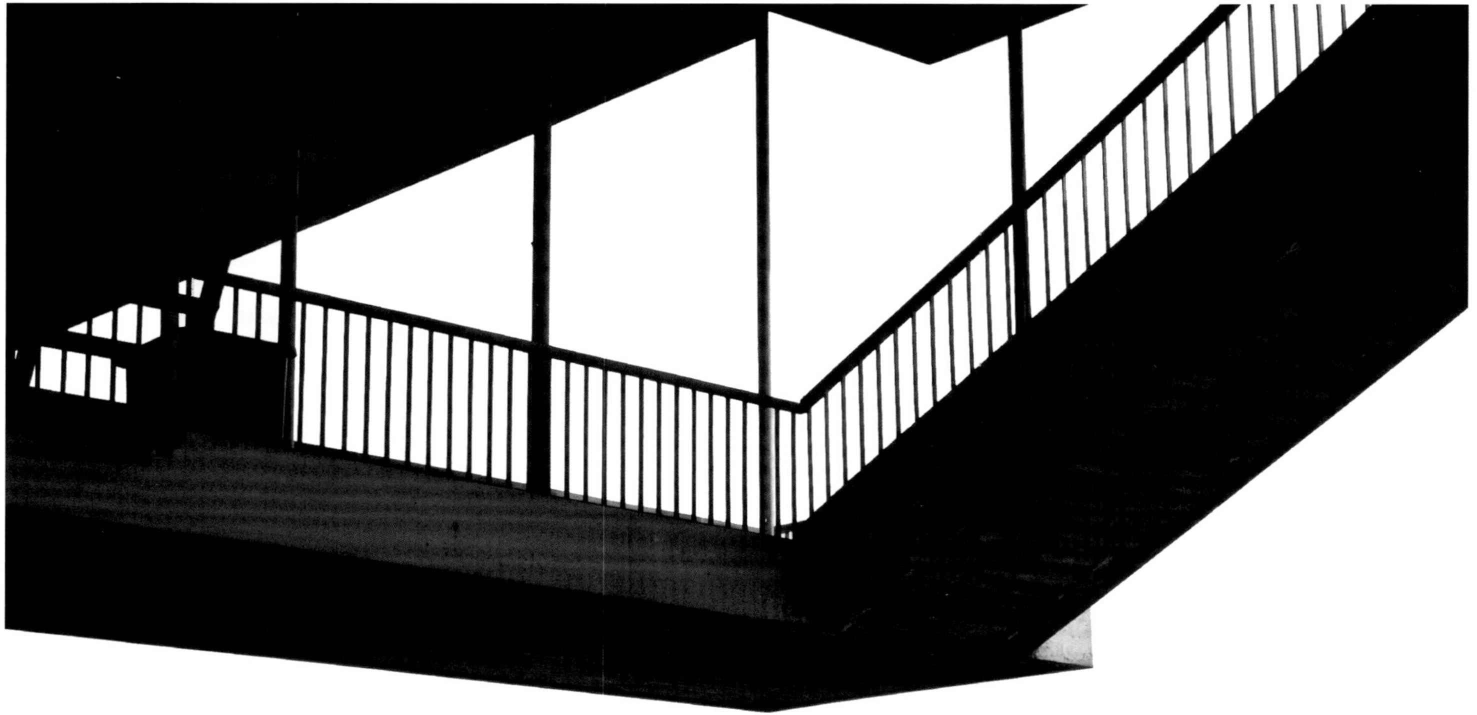

Tip *Resist the urge to always position your main subject at the center of your image area. The image area is more than just a vehicle to carry the content of the photo. The examples on this spread and the following one show that successful pictures can pull the viewer's attention to the top, to the sides, or diagonally to the corners of the image—just like this photo of the chairoplane in Salzburg (right-hand page).*
The picture of the stairs in Mannheim (left) shows that radical crops can produce exciting contrasts.
The snow-laden twig and the foot of a figurine in a fountain on the next pages were shot in the gardens of the Schwetzingen Palace.

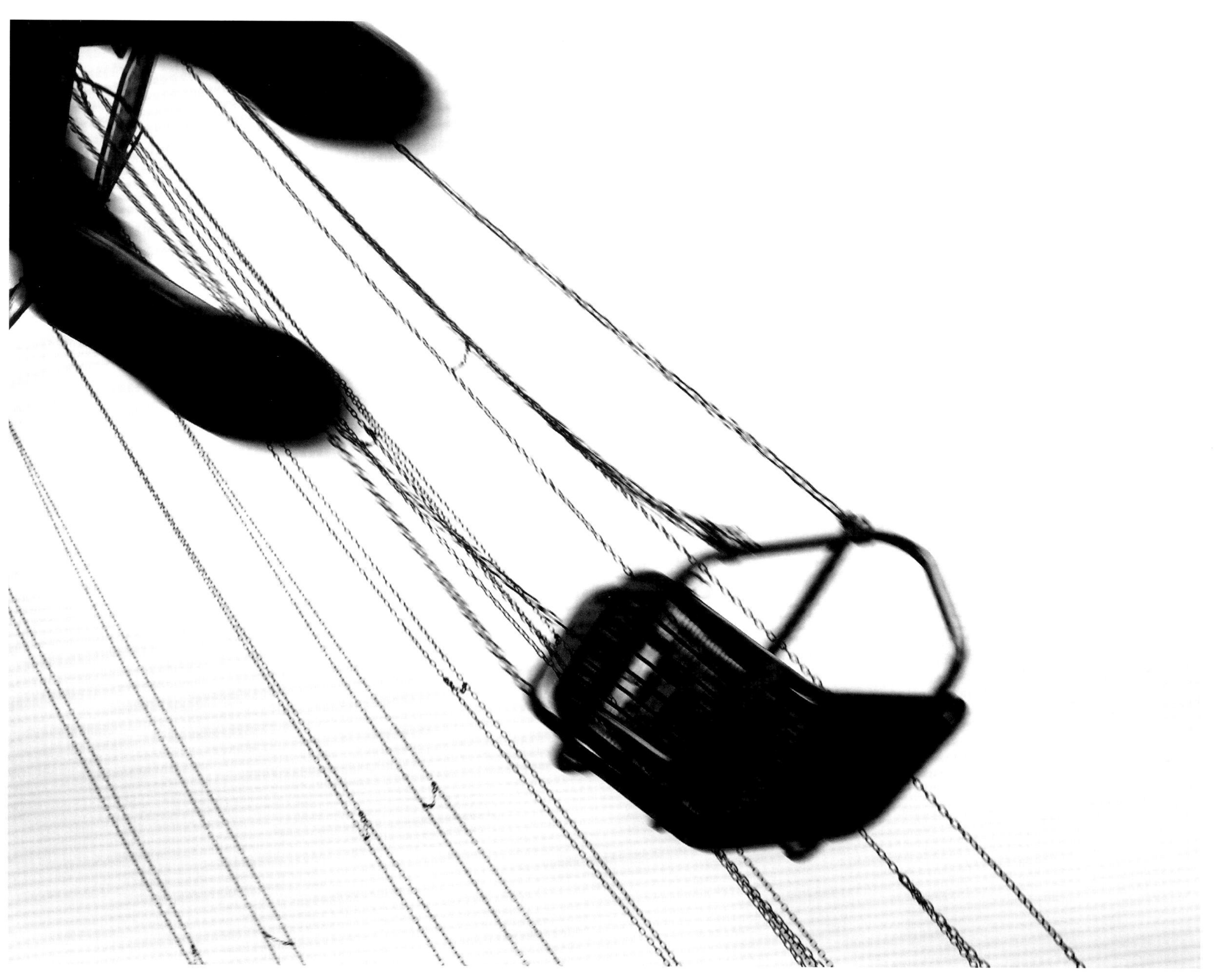

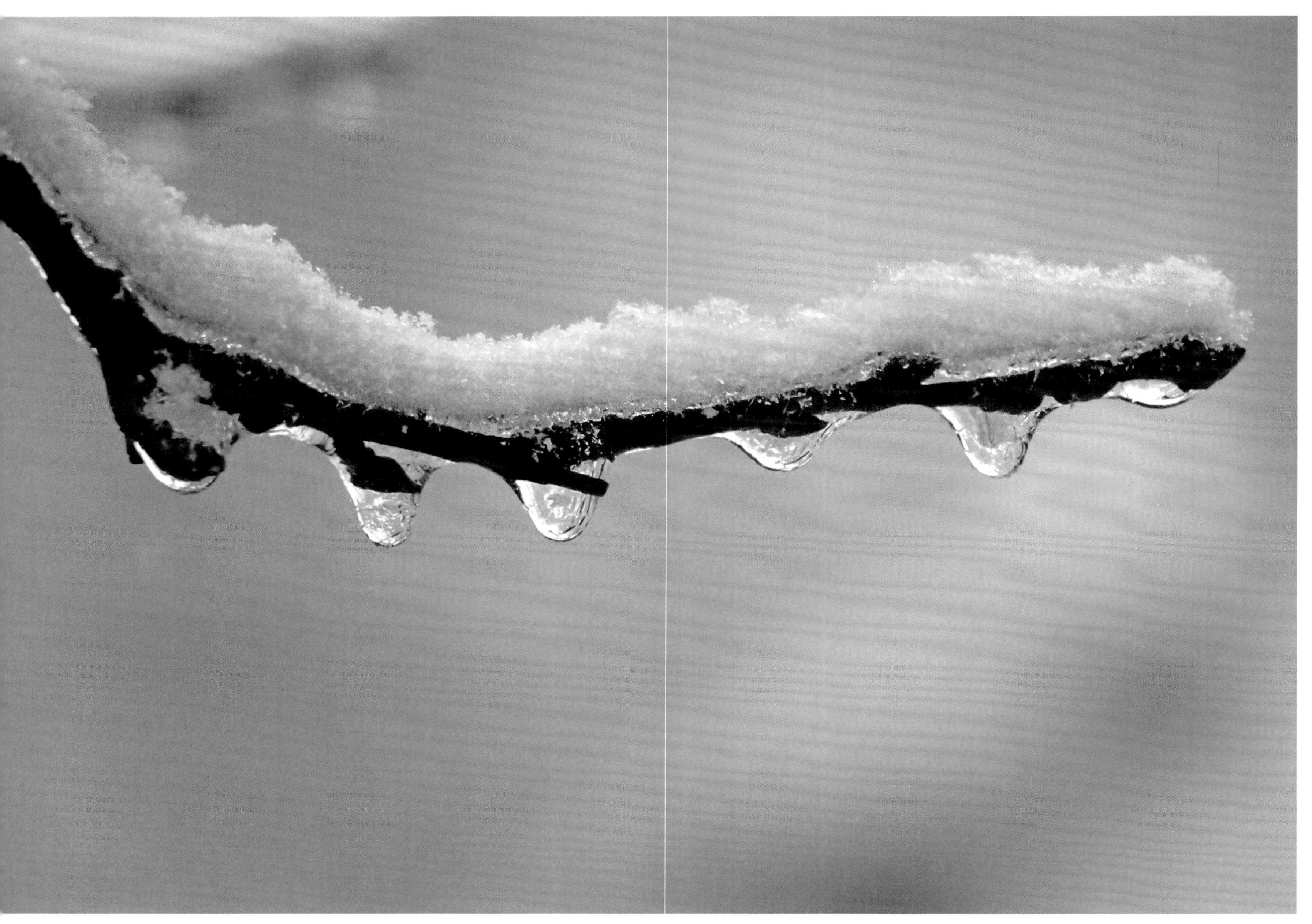

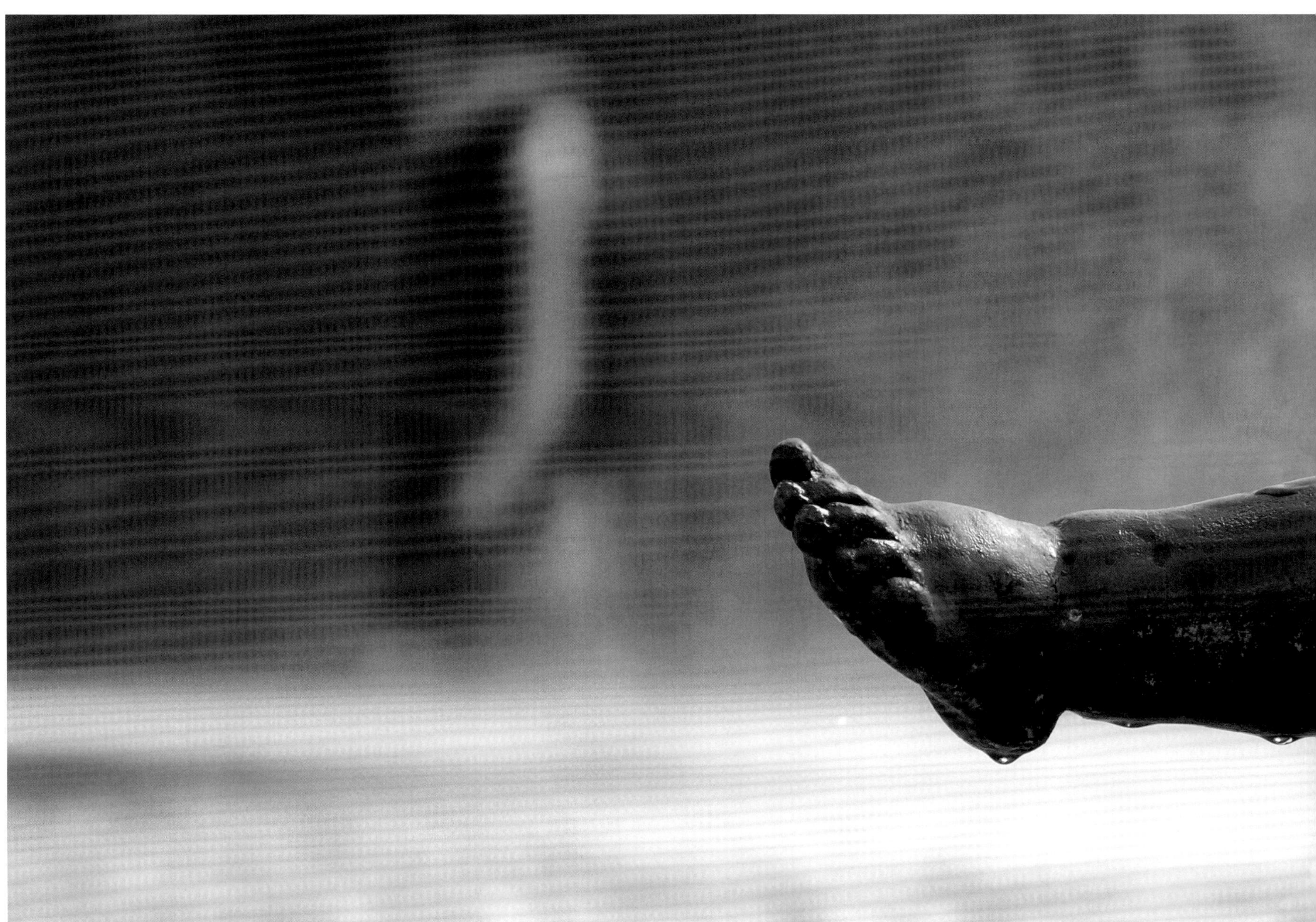

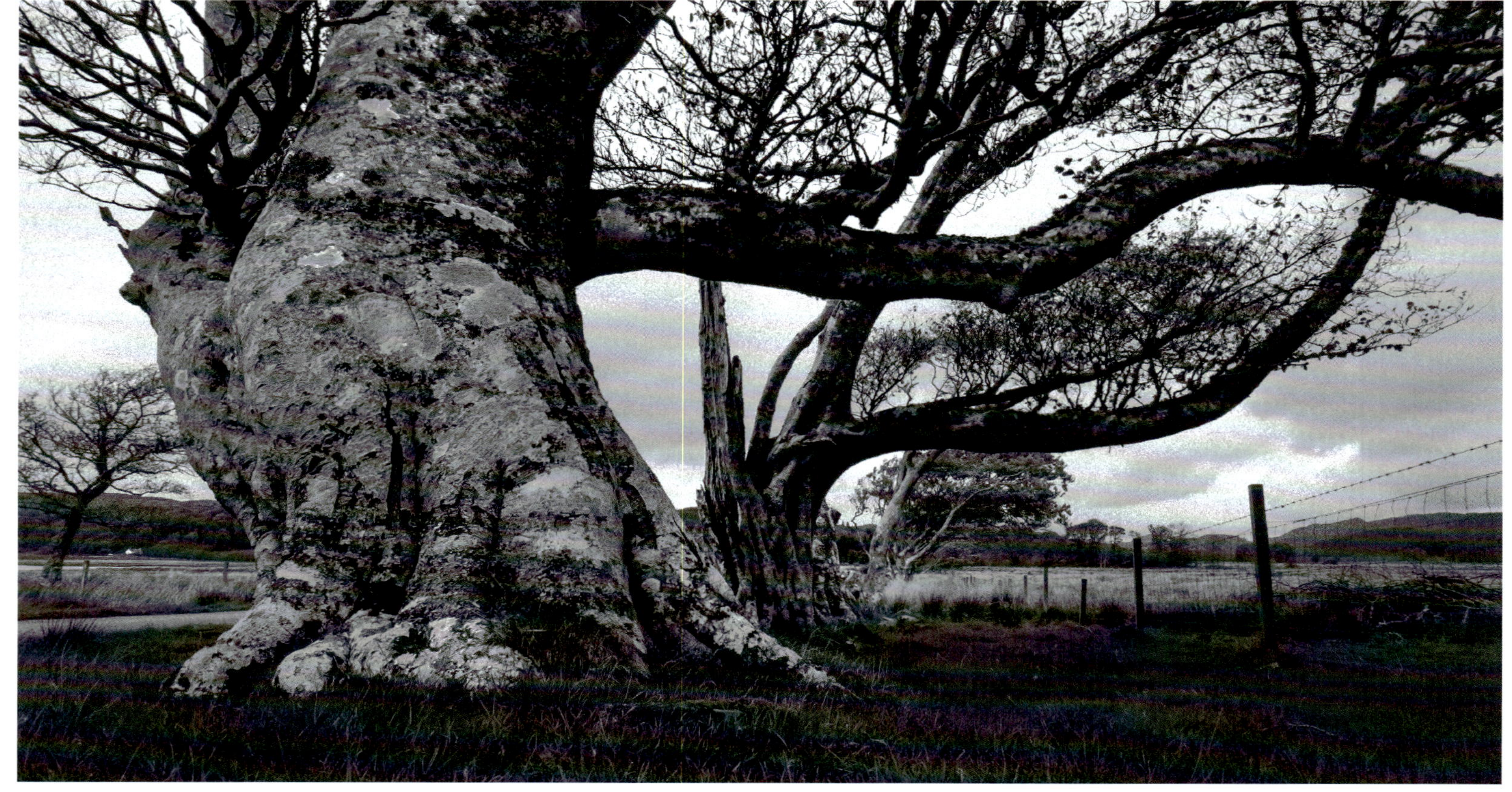

Fascination Tree The biggest and oldest plants on Earth play an important conceptual role in mankind's various creation myths. In many civilizations the tree is at the center of religious and social customs and practices, and is honored with deep adoration. For example, a Garden of Eden without trees would be unimaginable.

The tree is a symbol for the cycle of life: birth, pertinacity, prosperity, and decline, which reflects synchronicity with the human experience. It's no wonder that artists, including photographers, engage with this theme. Besides their place in our collective consciousness as a symbol of life, trees also bear some similarity in shape to the human form.

These images of trees were taken at Loch Crinan in Scotland. Their composition presents extreme close-up details, views from below, and lacing.

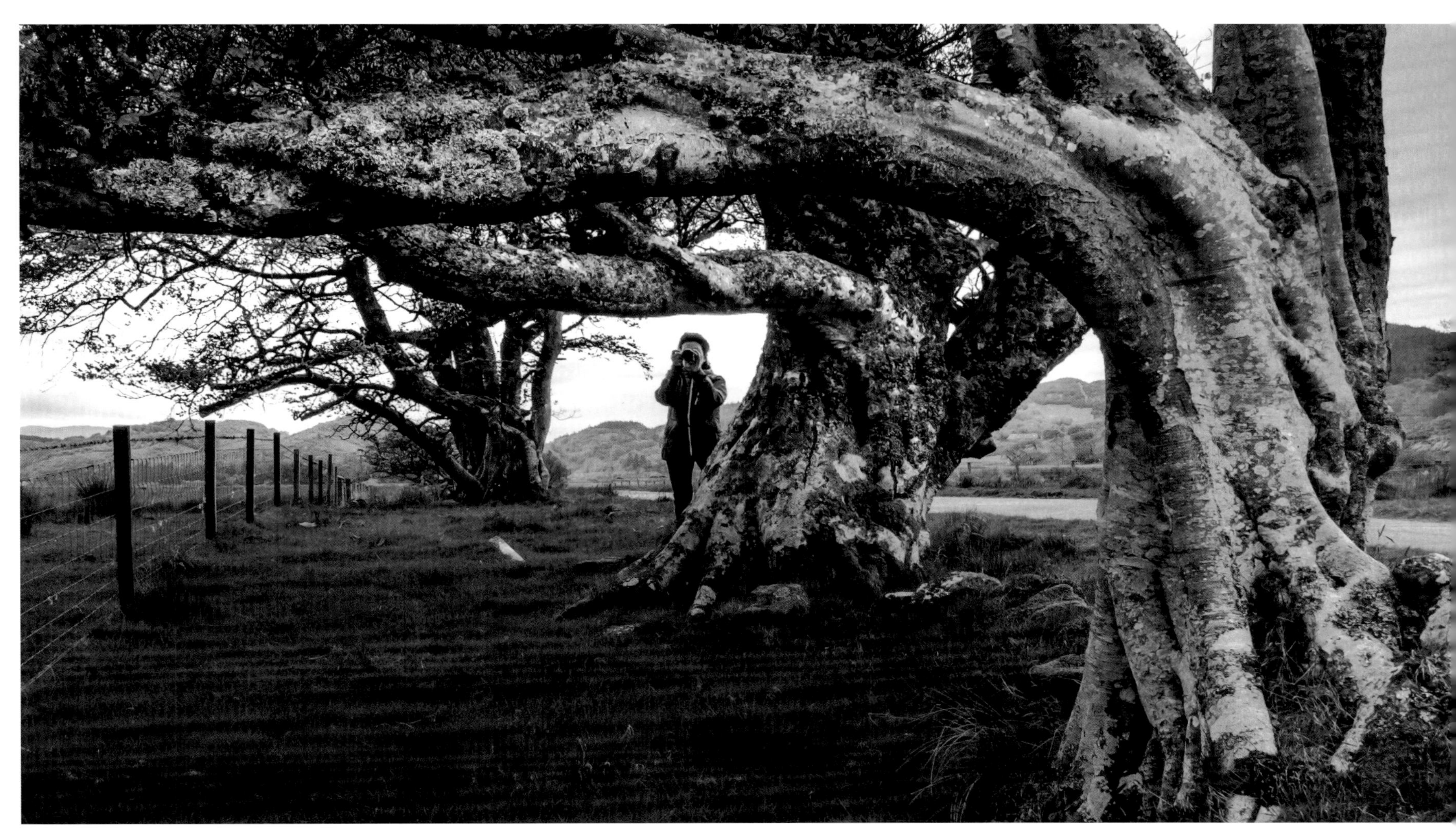

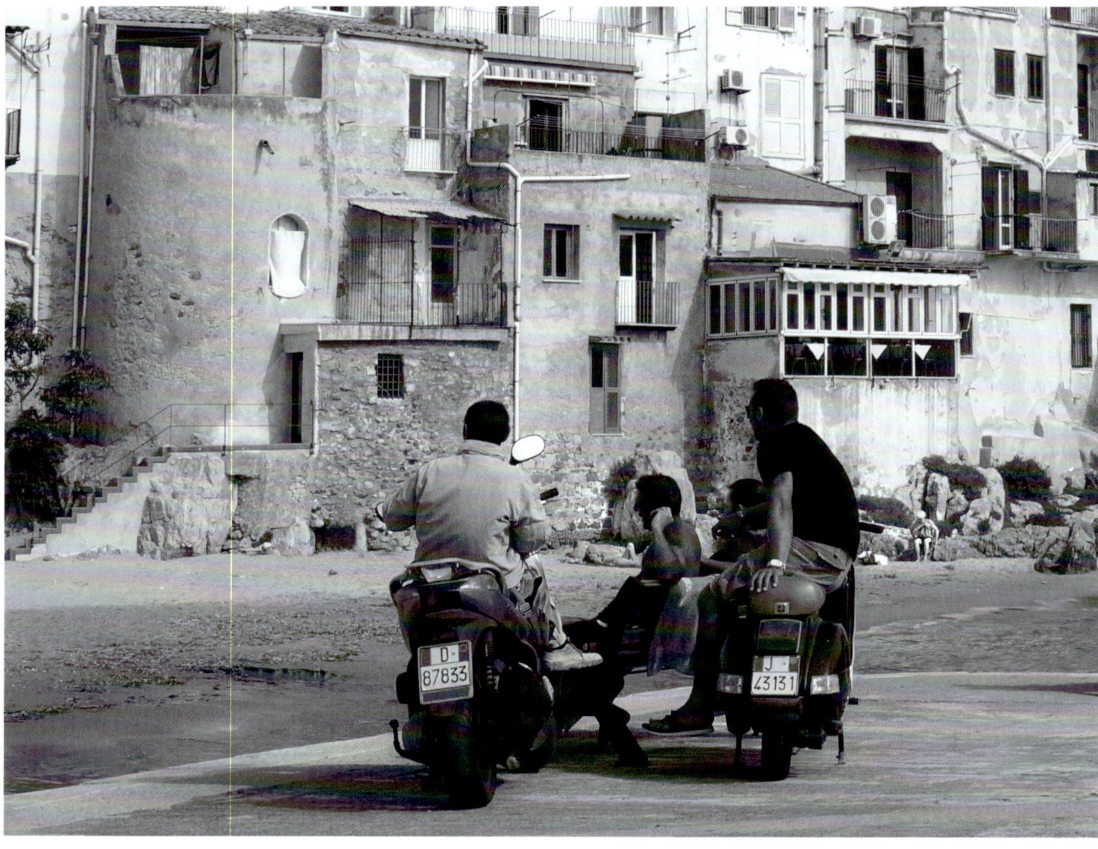

Beyond the Picture What is holding the attention of the young men in the image above? Their posture says it all, but the real action happens beyond the image area. At what is this man pointing (right-hand image)? Is he a teacher? The presence of the young people listening to him seems to justify this conclusion. What he is describing, though, and where the photo was taken is left to the viewer's imagination. Some compositions force viewers to participate in the interpretation of what's going on in an image. This is one of the tricks that picture book illustrators use to pique readers' interest until the cat is finally let out of the bag on the last page.

The photo above was taken near the beach of Cefalu, on the island of Sicily. The photo on the right-side page was taken in the Cathedral of Monreale, where a teacher directs his students' attention to amazing Byzantine iconography illustrated in mosaics from the twelfth century.

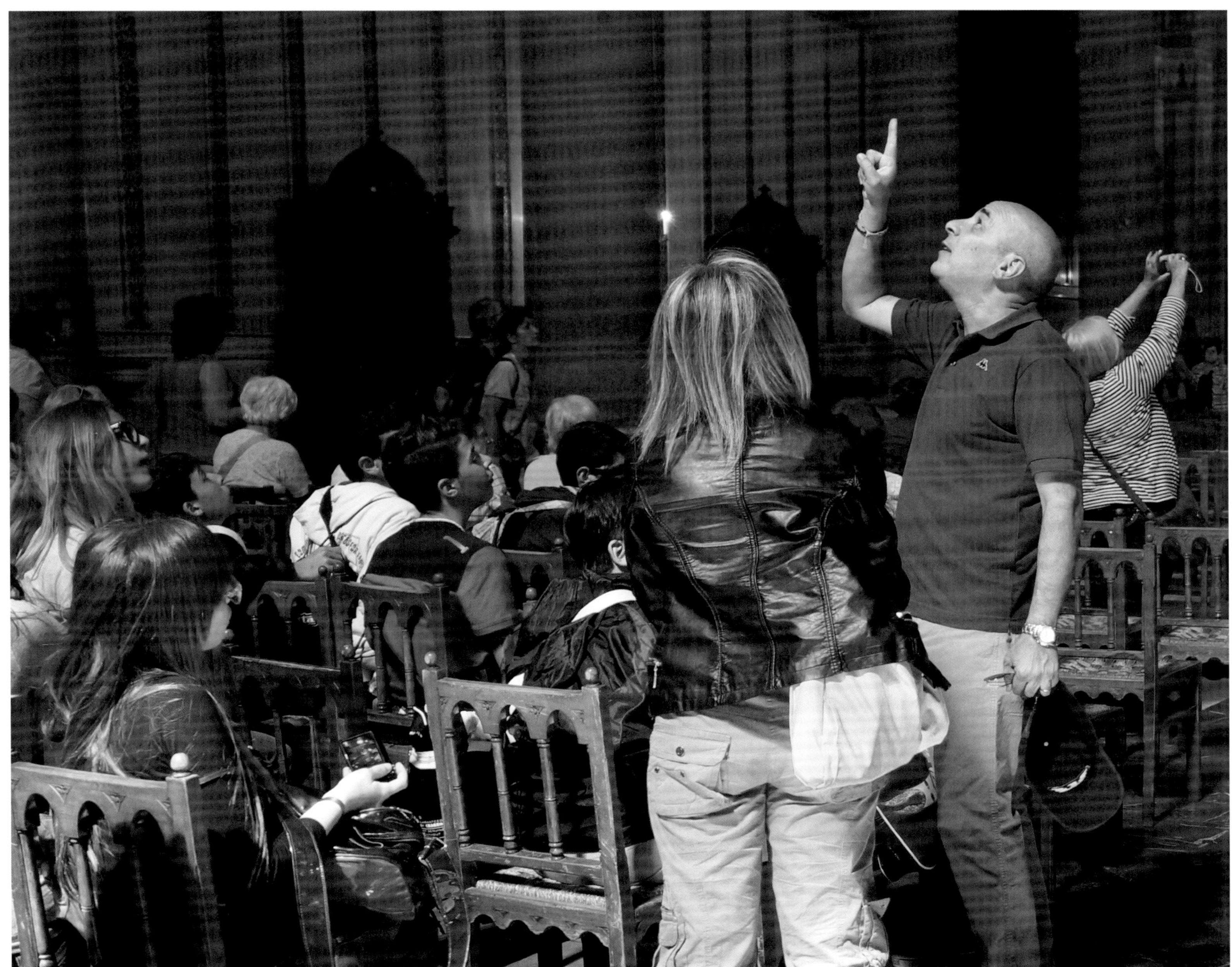

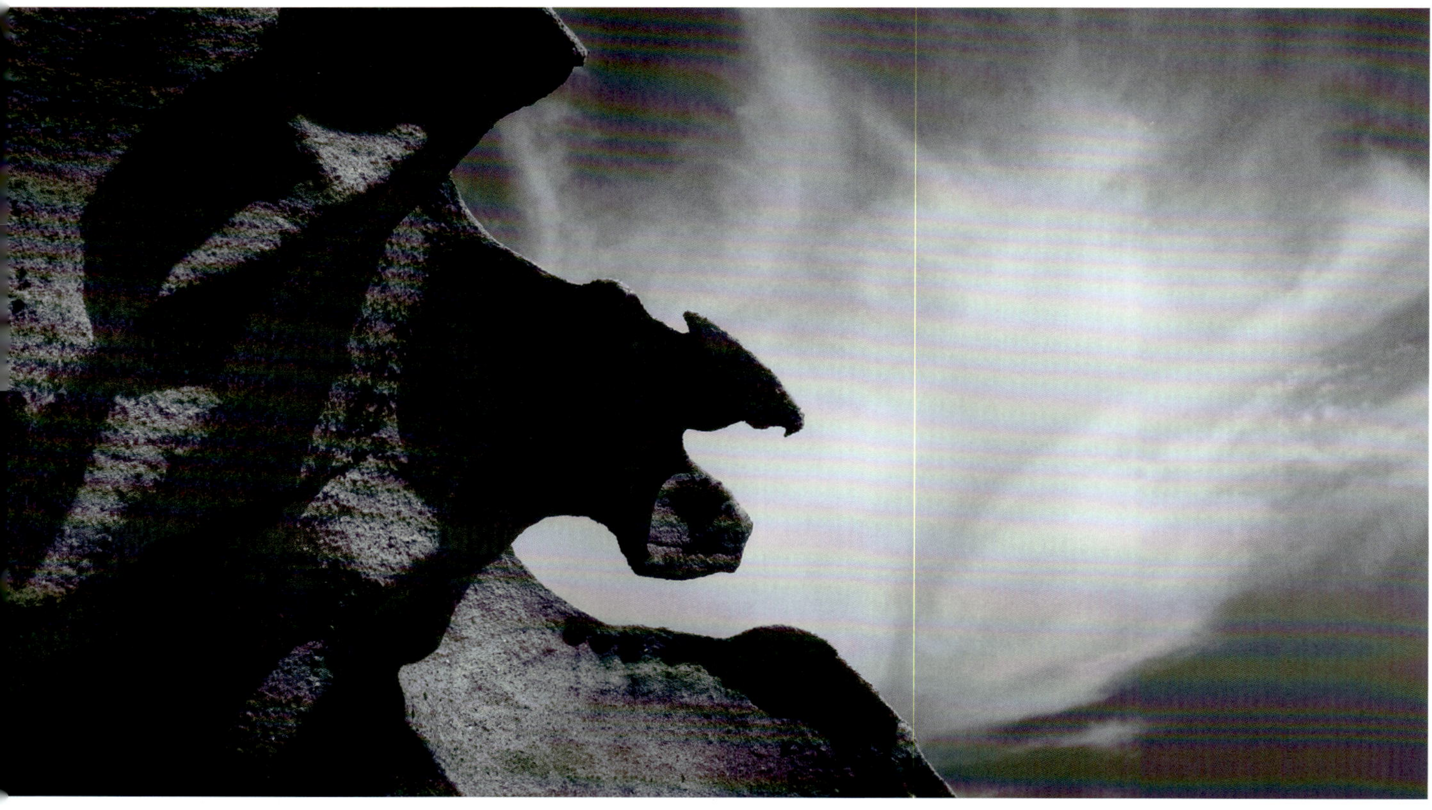

Busting Out It's no easy task to capture the granite boulders found in north Sardinia so that their hugeness comes across clearly in a photograph. One way to convey their relative size is to sever a chunk of the colossus in your frame. The monumentality of the photographed subject can be further enhanced when shot from a slightly upward-looking perspective, as with the above photo.

An alternative option is to incorporate another object as a point of reference, as with the photograph on the right.

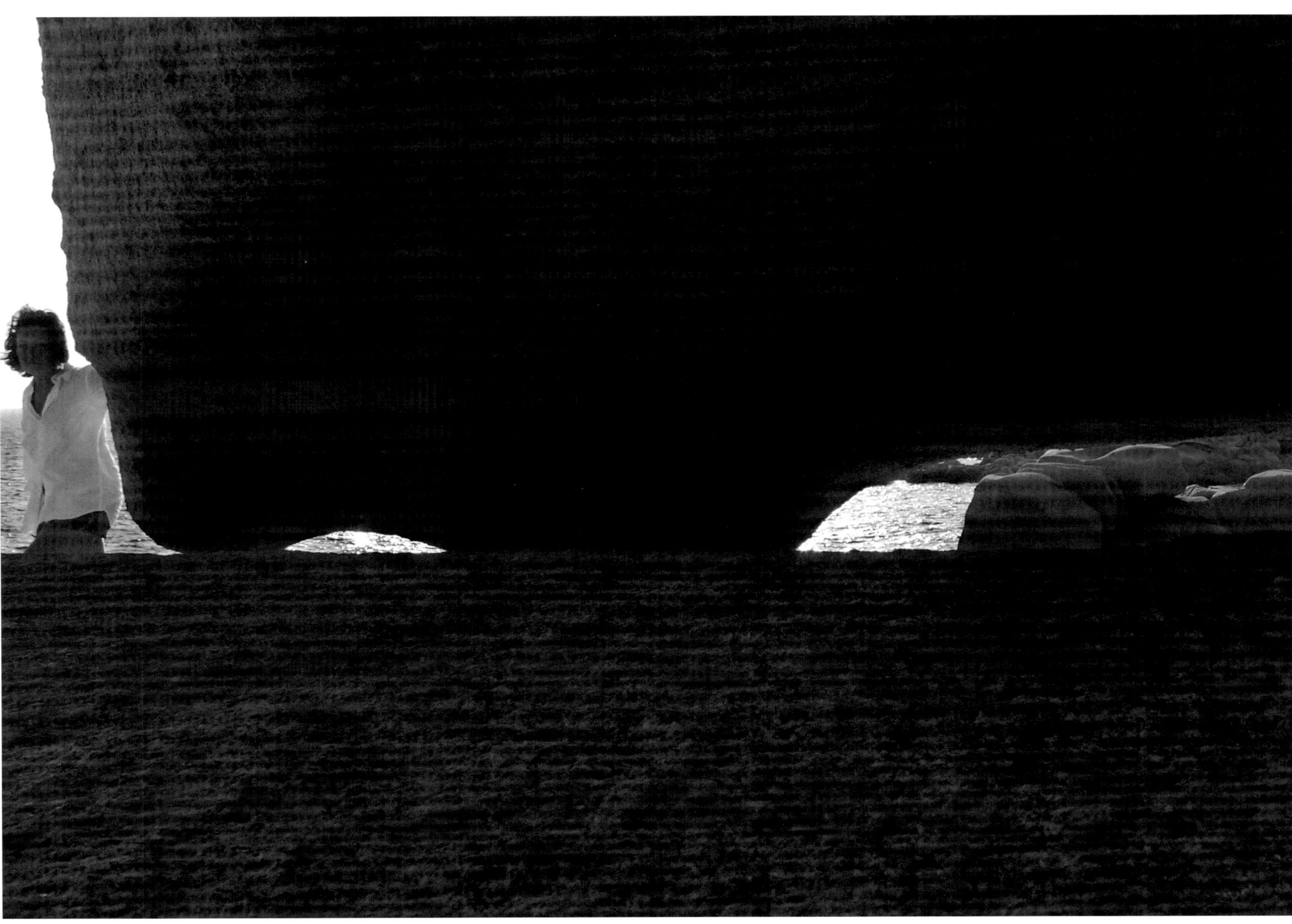

Symmetry There are many places in the world where anyone who wants to test their perspectives about symmetrical and asymmetrical designs can do so. The gardens at the Schwetzingen Palace, built in the eighteenth century, are one such place. They offer both a formal French garden, which is designed precisely according to geometrical standards, as well as an English landscape park.

The formal garden speaks to the human desire for order, harmony, and stability, but visitors likely feel closer to nature in other sections of the park. Although people have a tendency to prefer one style to the other, most enjoy both—at least to some degree.

Every photographer is familiar with the charm of shooting symmetrical subjects. But be careful! Flawless symmetry in picture after picture can quickly become boring. Photos that feature a prevailing symmetry, but that also feature details that undercut symmetrical perfection, are much more interesting. The sailboats at the South Street Seaport in Manhattan (left-hand page) are one example of this photographic design.

The symmetry of the lindens in the Palatinate garden of the Schwetzingen Palace is offset slightly by the uneven rhythm of the trunks and branches (right-hand page).

The composition in both photos relies heavily on a central perspective and a triangular wedge of light that points toward the vanishing point.

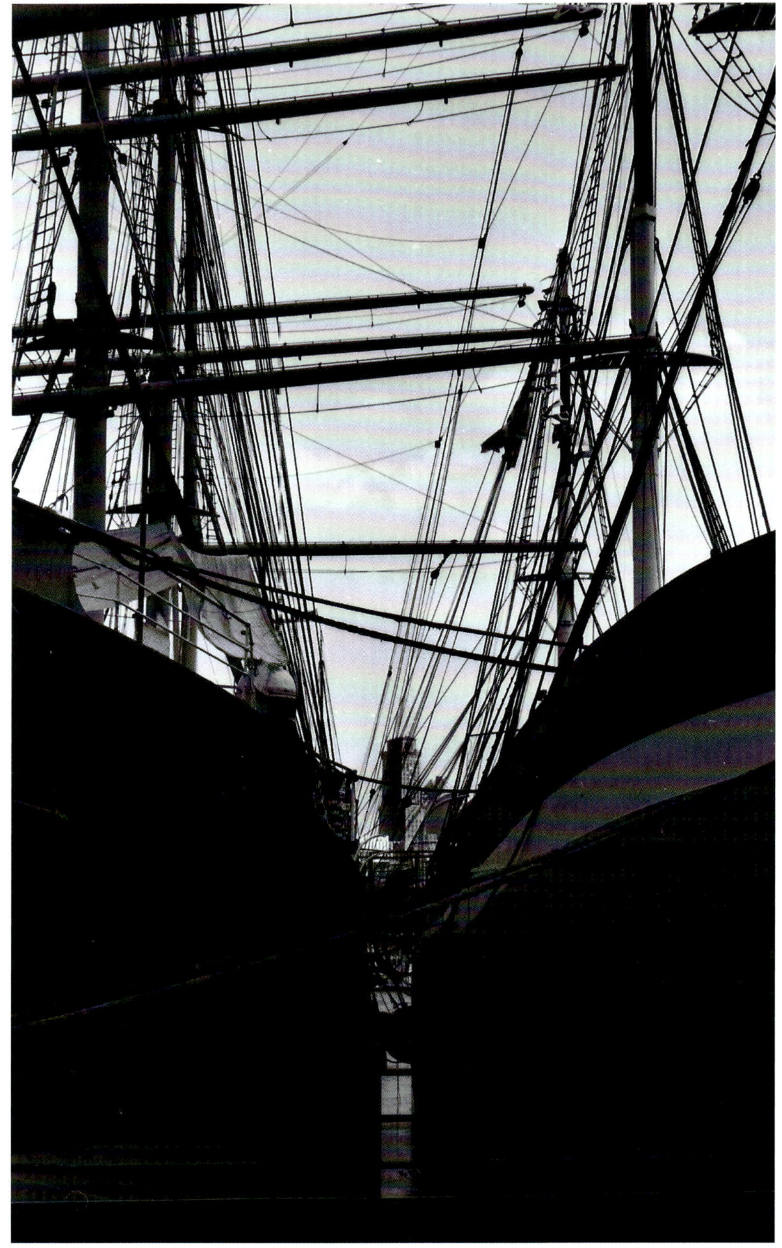

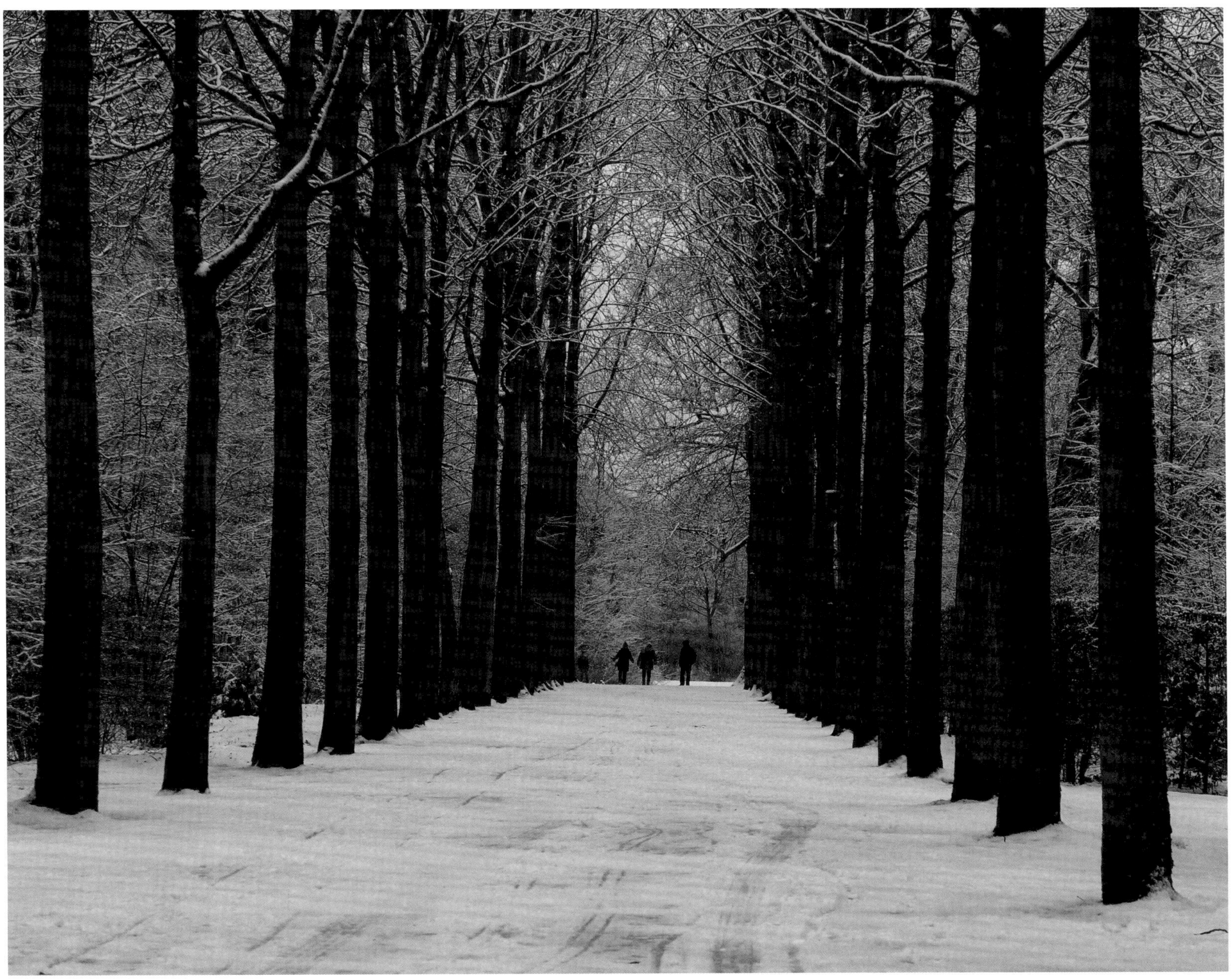

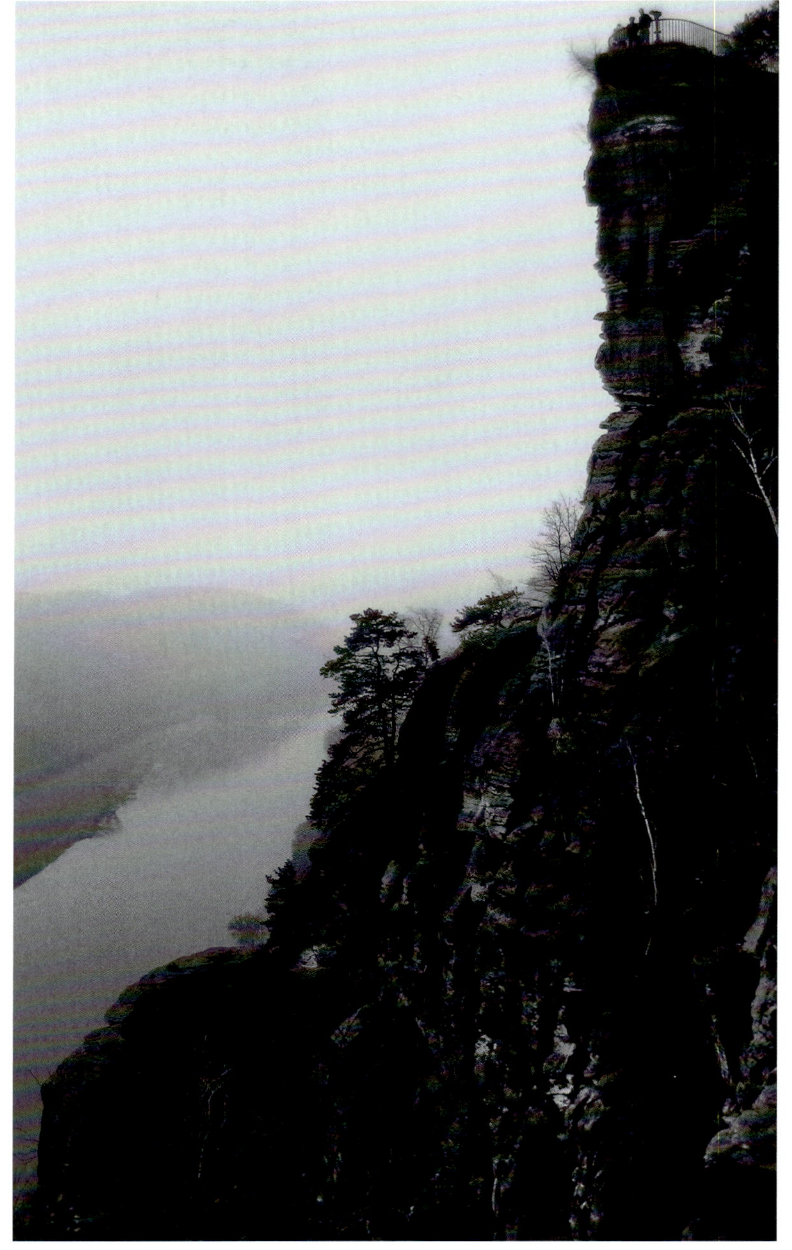

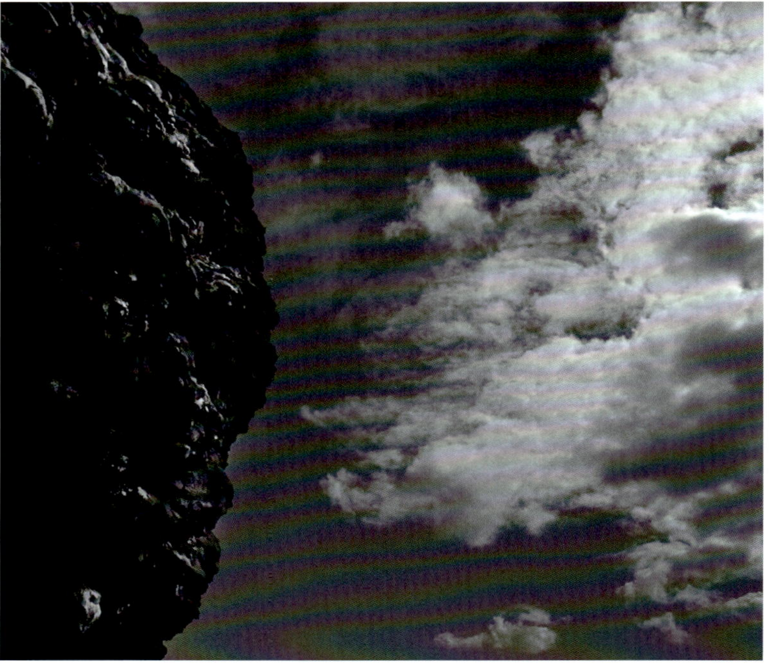

Asymmetry Asymmetry balks at the need for balance and equilibrium. This imbalance is sometimes necessary to give certain subjects an added significance.

The asymmetrical craggy cliff in Saxon Switzerland is pushed over to the side of this image to allow a clear view down to the valley of the Elbe (left). The dramatic contrast of light and dark underscores the photo's asymmetry. The lava rocks on Lanzarote positioned off to the left of the image area (top) do not feel quite so unbalanced because the opposing clouds offer something of a counterweight. The juxtaposition of these two subjects also brings interesting contrasts to the photo: black versus white and hard versus soft.

This visual effect is comparable to the photo of the birch trees on the island of Poel (right-hand page). The asymmetrically positioned birches have a tiny counterweight in the small tree on the horizon.

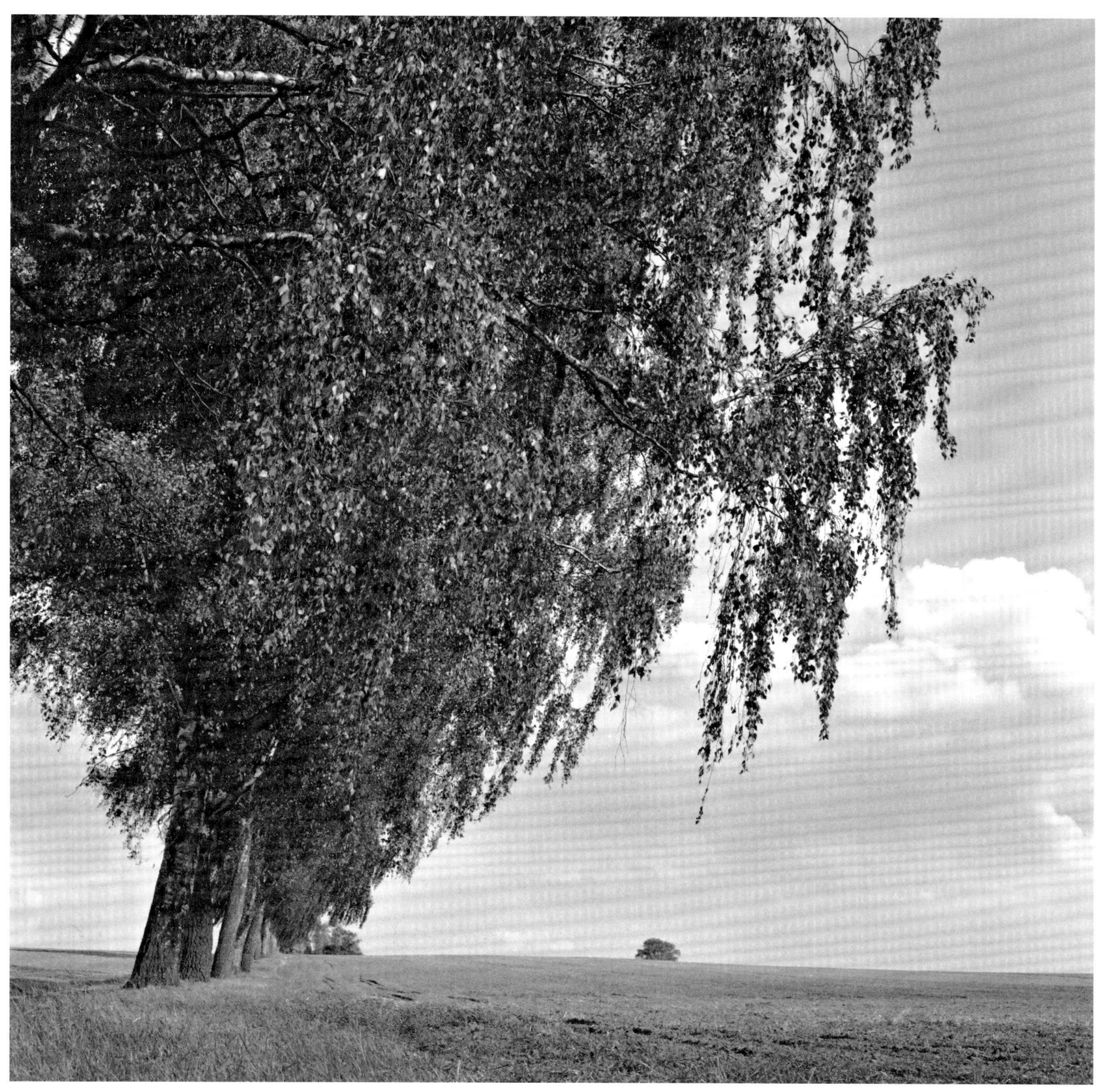

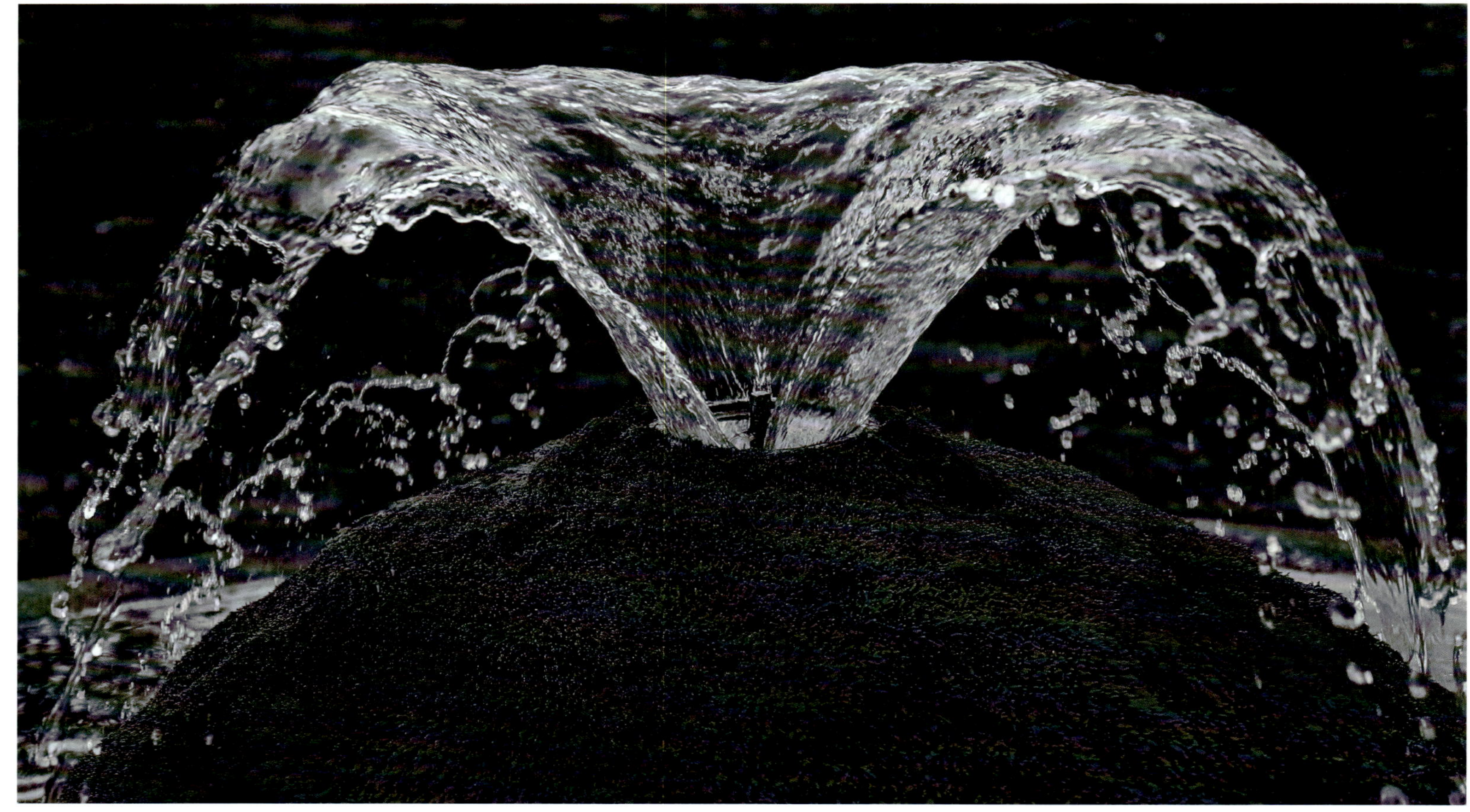

A Comparison A fountain in the gardens of the Schwetzingen Palace looks like a volcano as it spits a stream of water over a moss-covered dome. Exposed with a fast shutter speed and backlighting, this subject looks as though it were made from solid glass. The symmetrical construction encourages the viewer to look into the bowl-shaped funnel—a positive effect for this particular image. The photo is harmoniously balanced. A perfect vertical symmetry is avoided on account of the way the water drops break at the sides of the picture.

An asymmetric depiction of the same subject has its charms, too. On the right-hand page, the fountain opening is off-center and the perspective is looking upward at the fountain. The contrasts between different areas of the image are more conspicuous and the water cascading toward the camera produces a dramatic sense of depth.

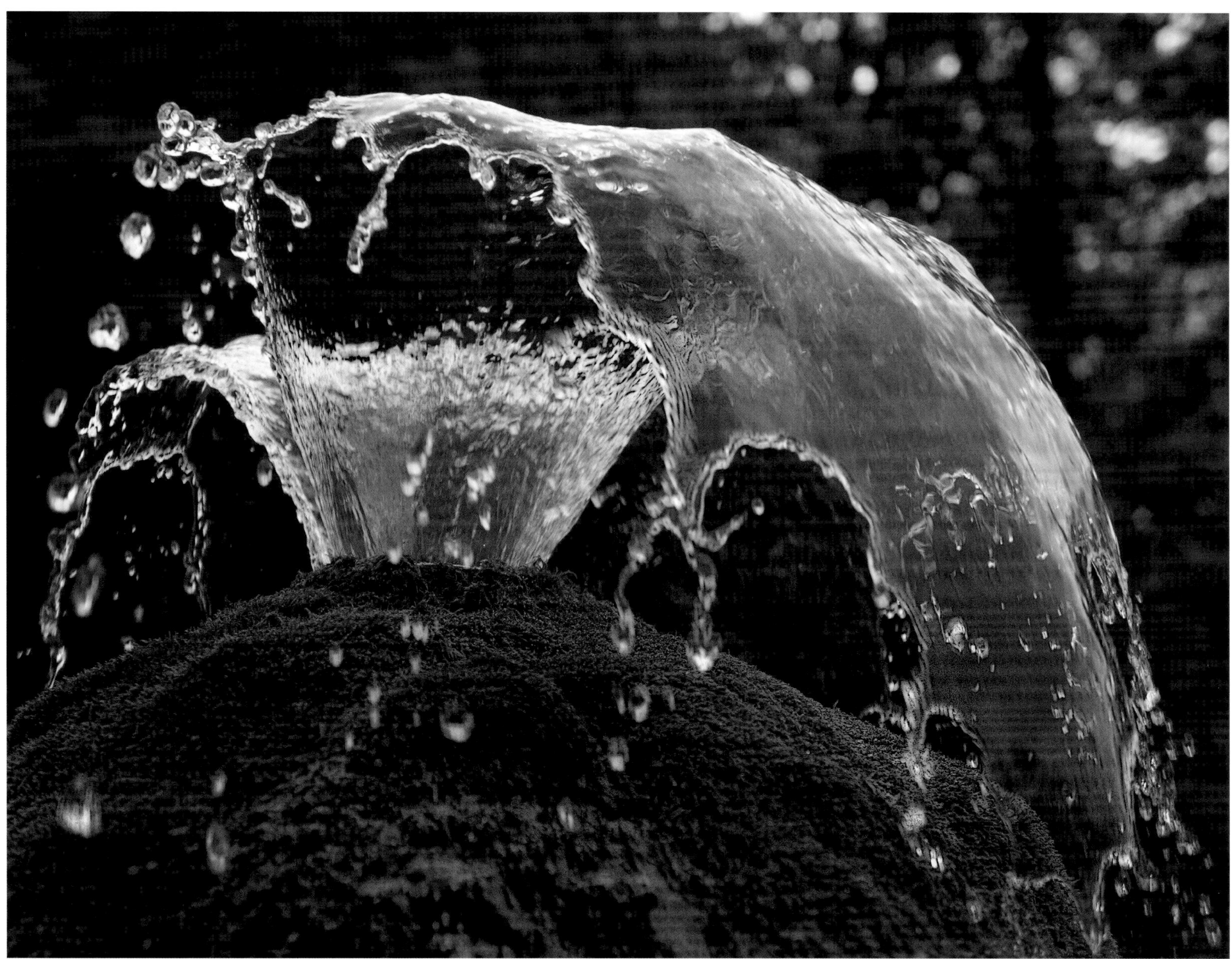

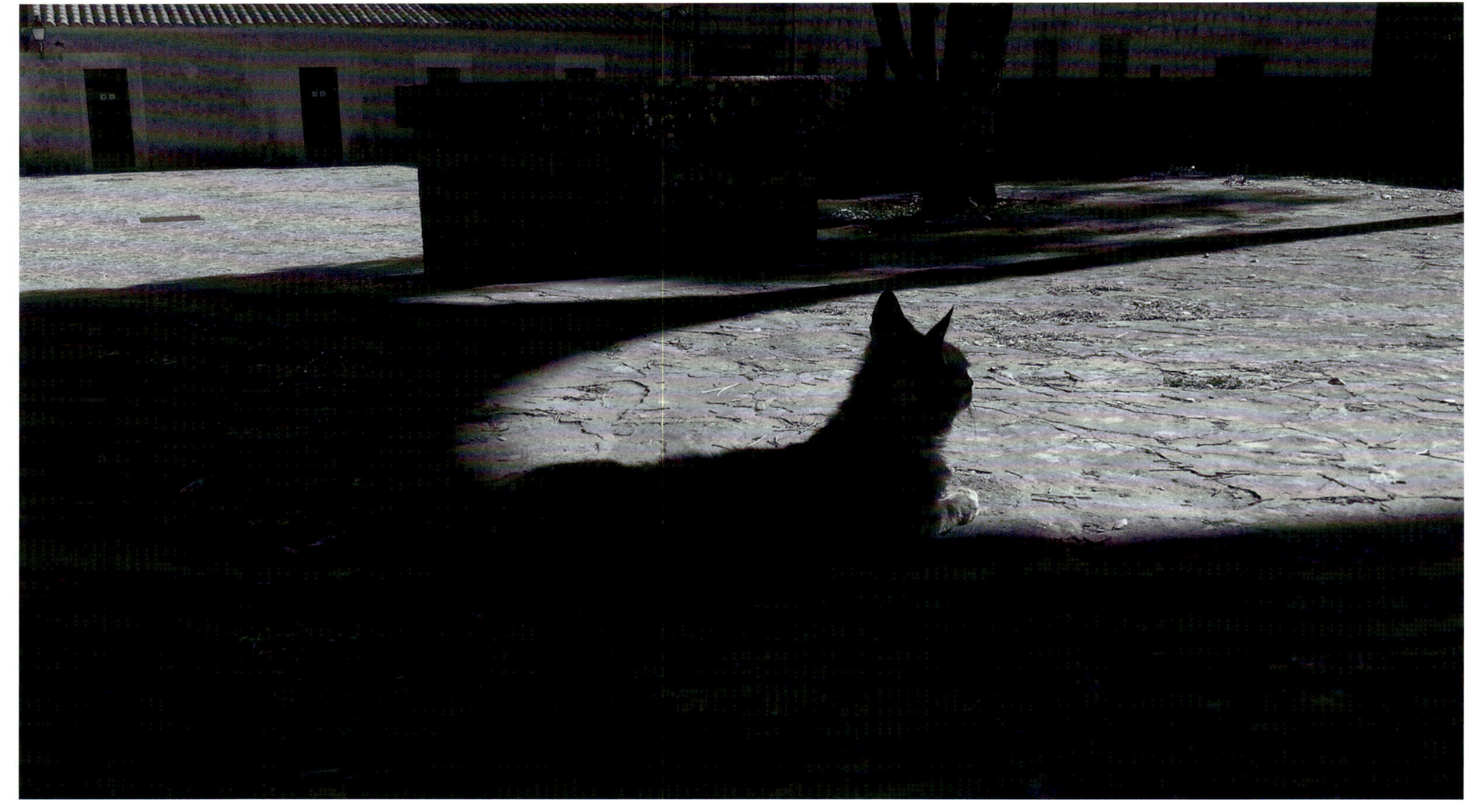

Figure/Ground One of the rules of composition and perception that comes from the teachings of psychology is that an object or a figure cannot be recognized unless it is identifiable as a different element than its background. There is a famous graphic that exemplifies this phenomenon: it shows two faces in profile looking at each other while the space between them has the shape of a vase. For photographers interested in composition, subjects with contrast-rich figure-ground relationships are especially welcome.

The photographs of the cat and the illustrator were taken in Santuari de Cura, an idyllic monastery on the island of Mallorca. The shape of the cat partially blends into the shadows in the background, making it difficult to distinguish. In contrast, the illustrator stands out against the lighter background of the wall, giving the image recognizable context.

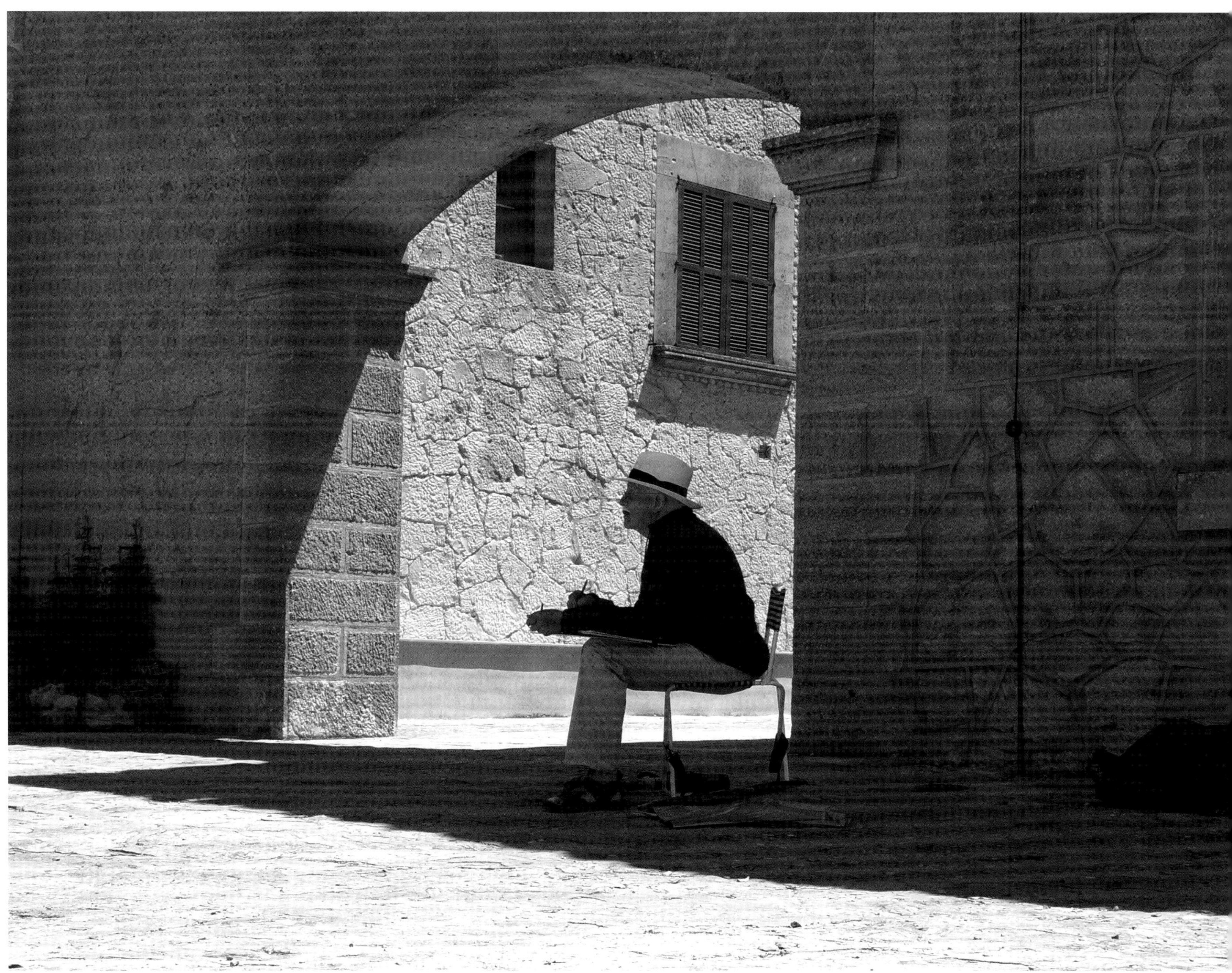

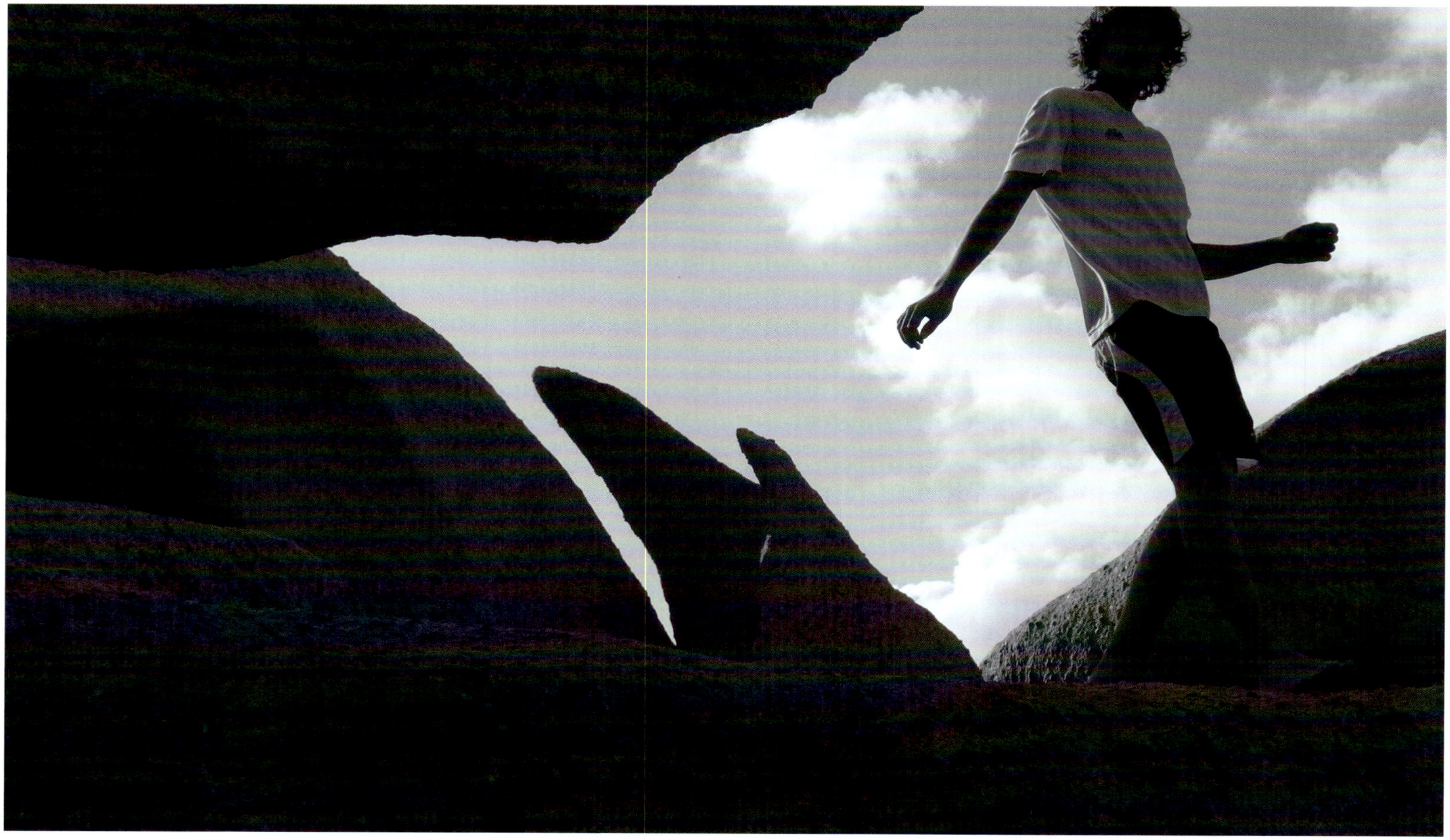

Positive/Negative The boys standing between the giant granite rocks on the north Sardinian coast provide a dramatic example of visual figure-ground relationships. These compositions owe a lot to the negative spaces between the rock formations, whose shapes and proportions in relation to the positive areas of rocks and bodies are instrumental to the overall effect of the photos.

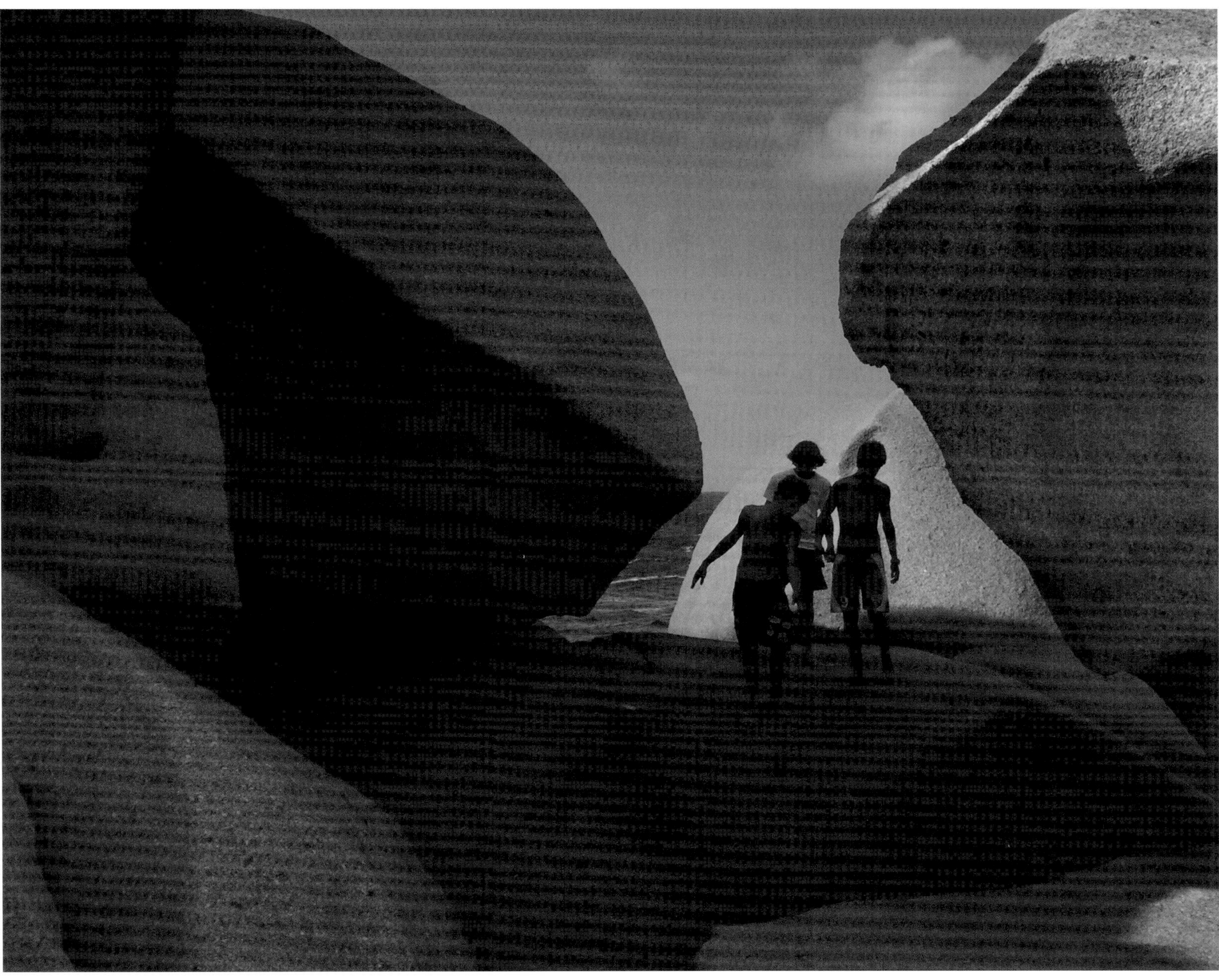

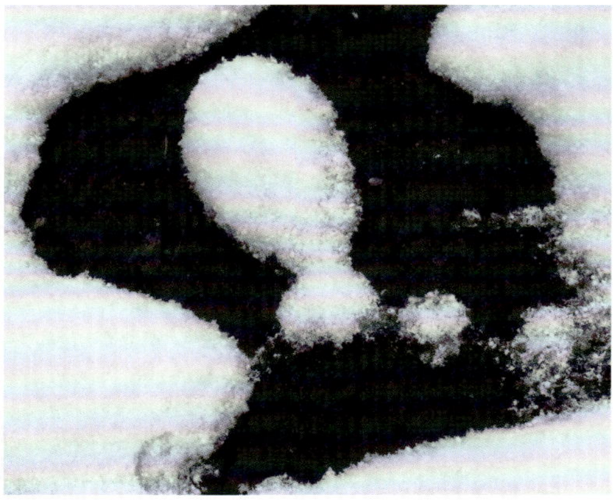

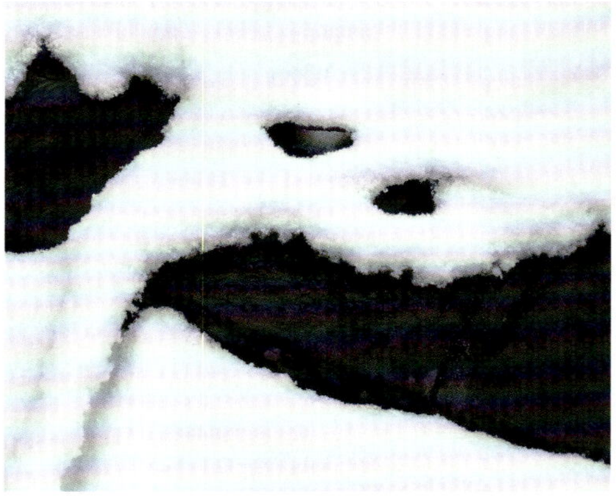

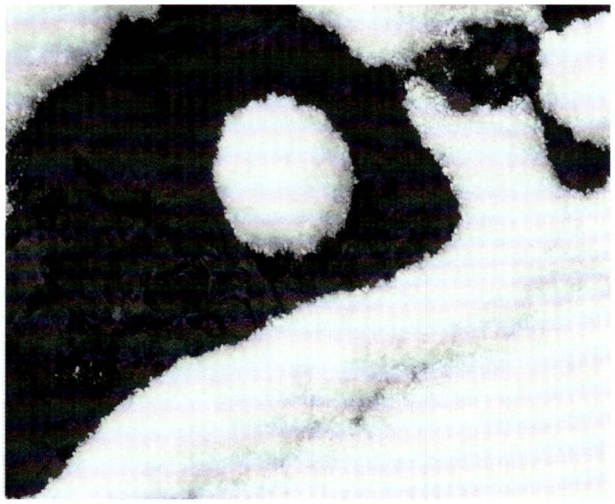

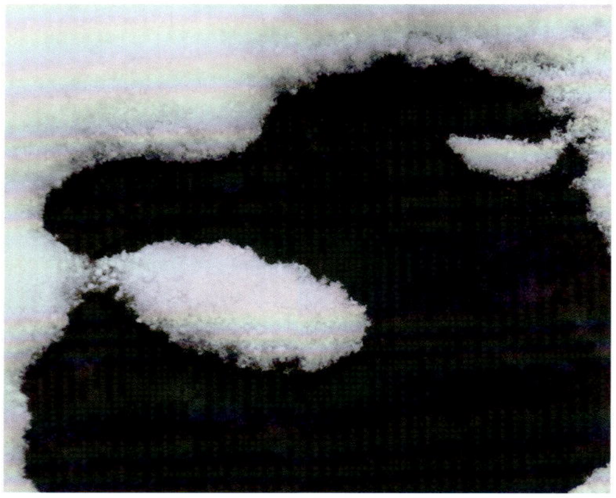

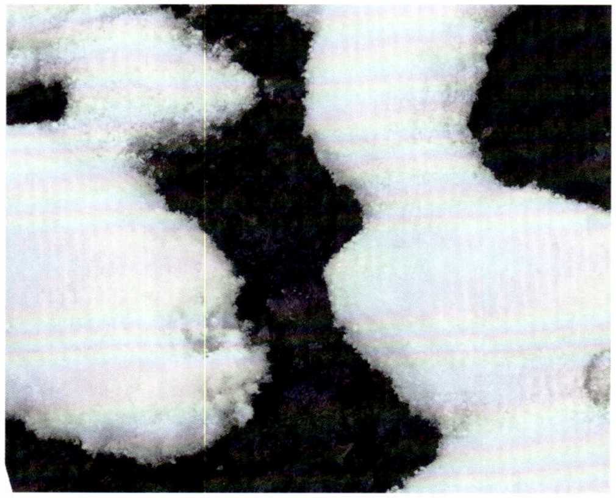

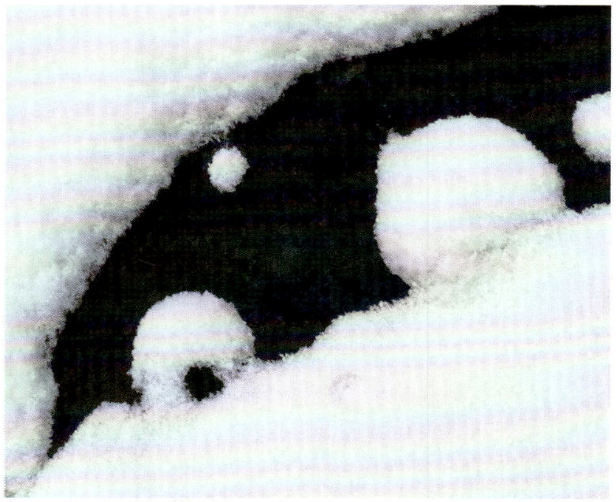

Tip *Do you also see grotesque faces, a rabbit, and a dark Viking with a white beard? Subjects like these are a playground for your eye and a training ground for learning to work with figure-ground relationships. You can find subjects like this everywhere—not just on the steps to the Thingstätte in Heidelberg... and not only in the snow.*

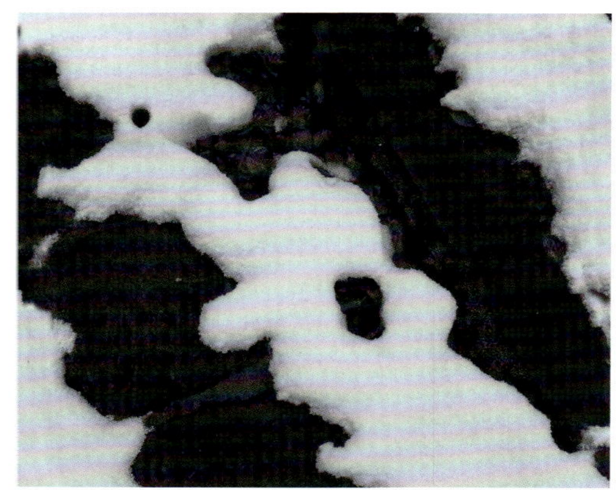

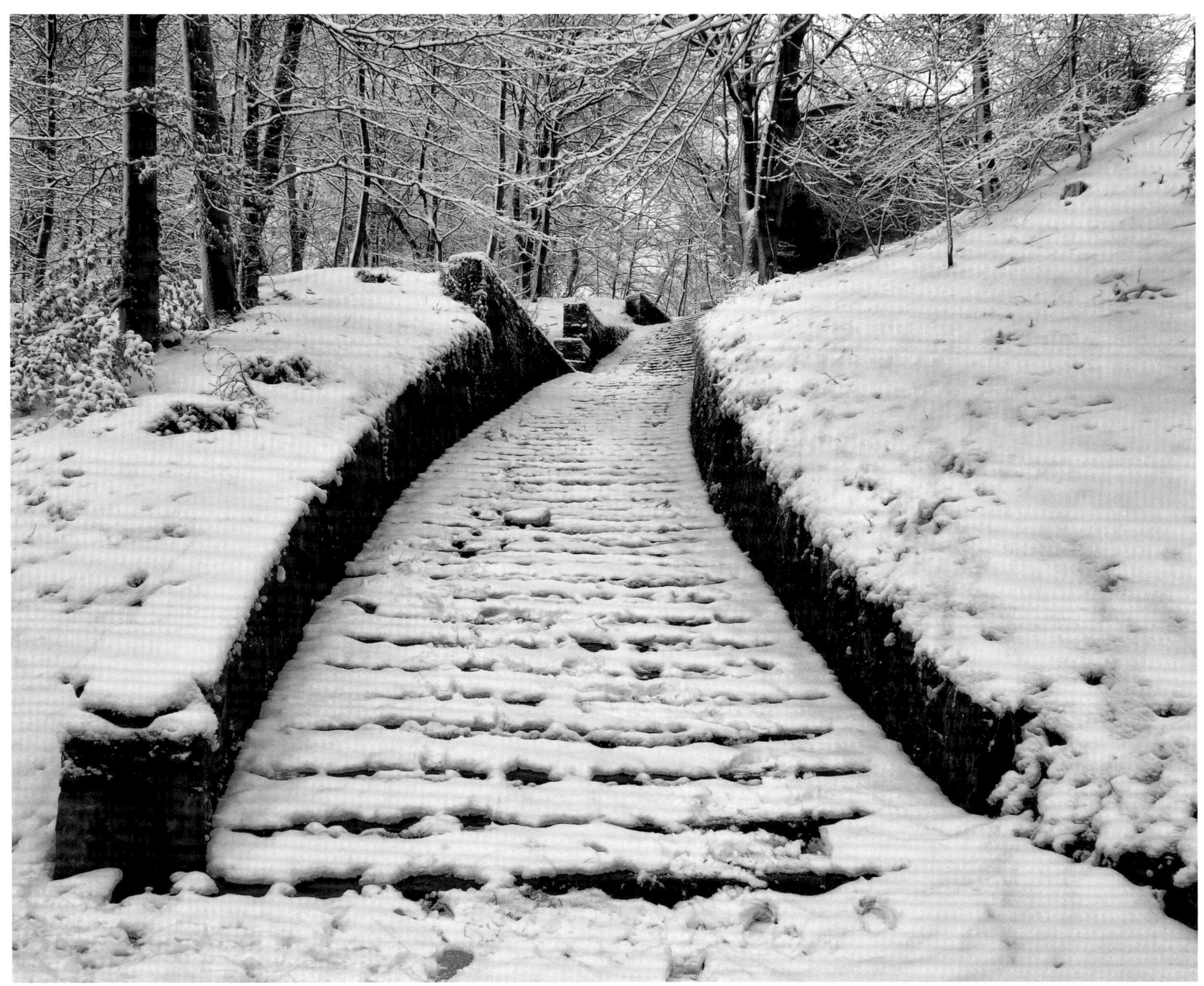

100 Contrast

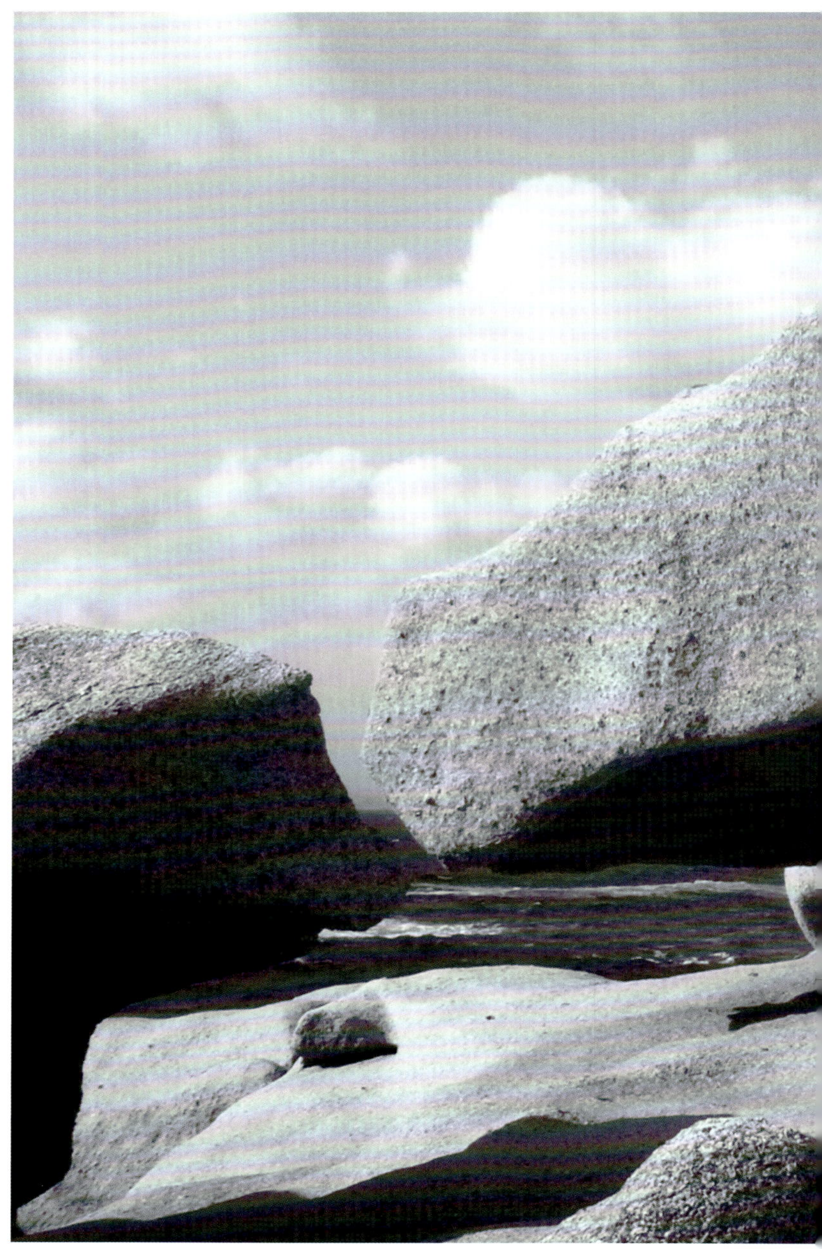

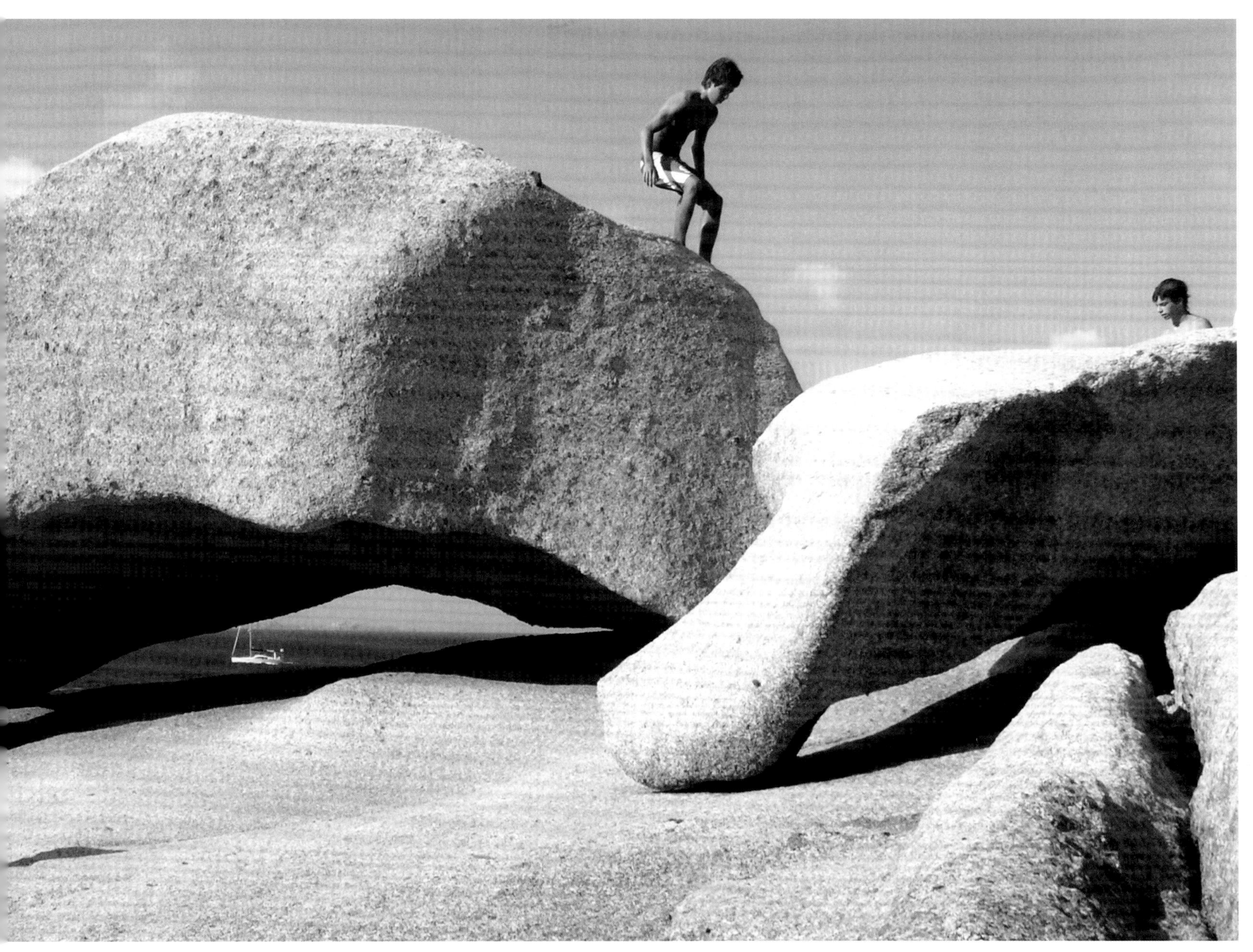

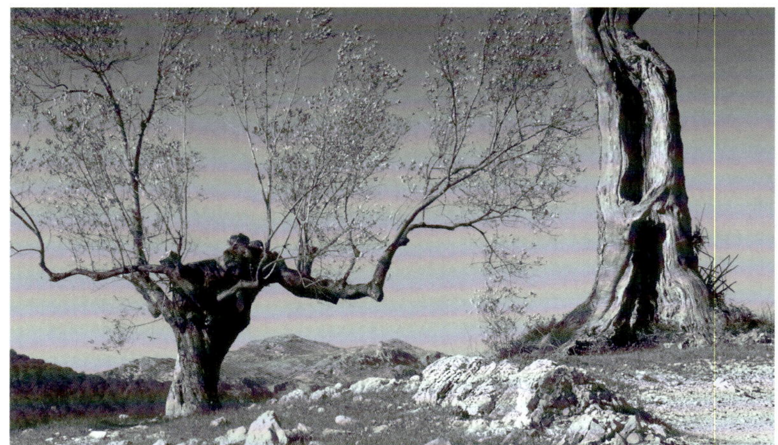

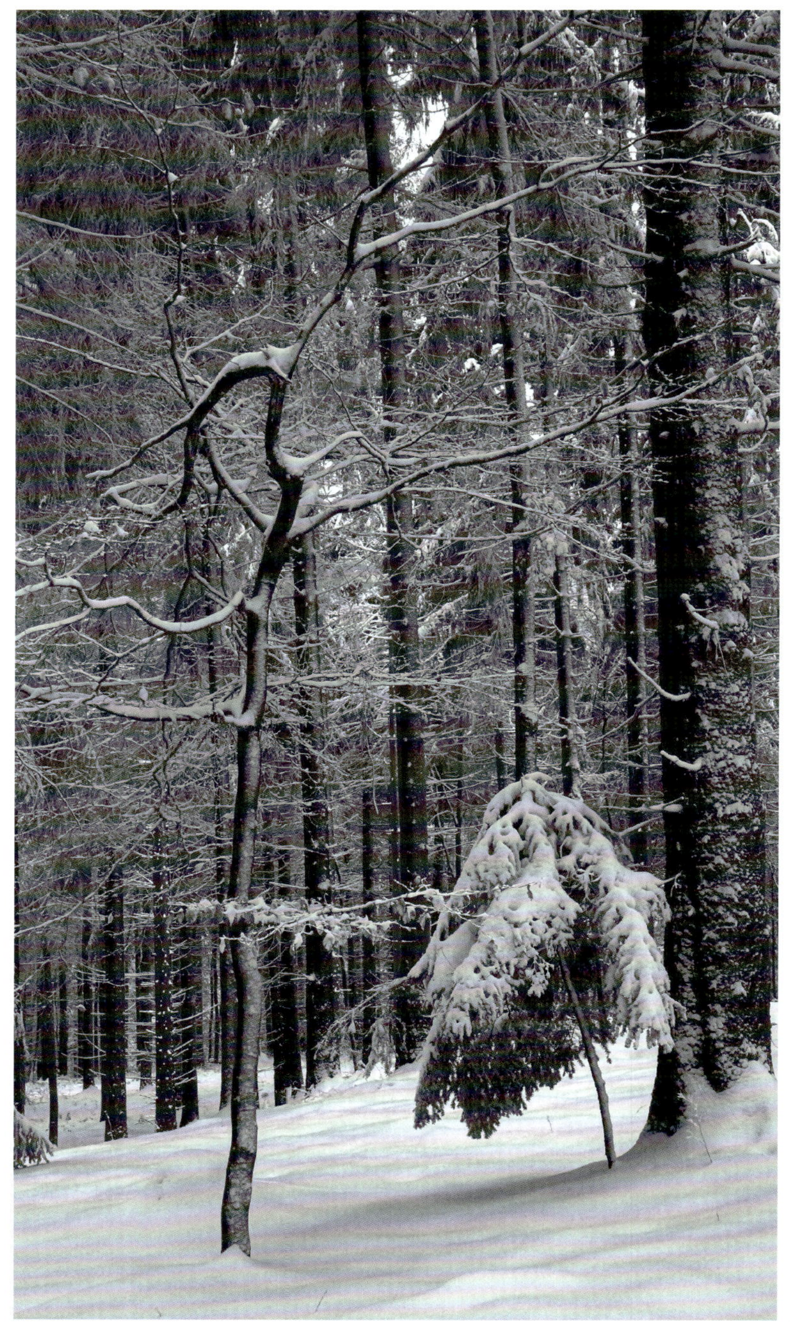

The Big Picture If you keep your eyes peeled while walking through a natural landscape, you will be richly rewarded with a vast diversity of shapes. Any materials that you might need to build fascinating and exciting pictures are readily available in the natural world. These pages reveal different types of trees that distinguish themselves due to their shapes.

The gnarled olive tree with its horizontal branches (top-left) establishes a marked contrast with the narrow, erect trunk standing nearby. The hood-like snowy fir similarly builds a dramatic contrast with the delicate young beech tree next to it (right). The trunk of the willow in the town of Ladenburg on the Neckar River (right-hand page) looks like a sinewy torso in comparison with the hoarfrost-coated trees flanking it on both sides.

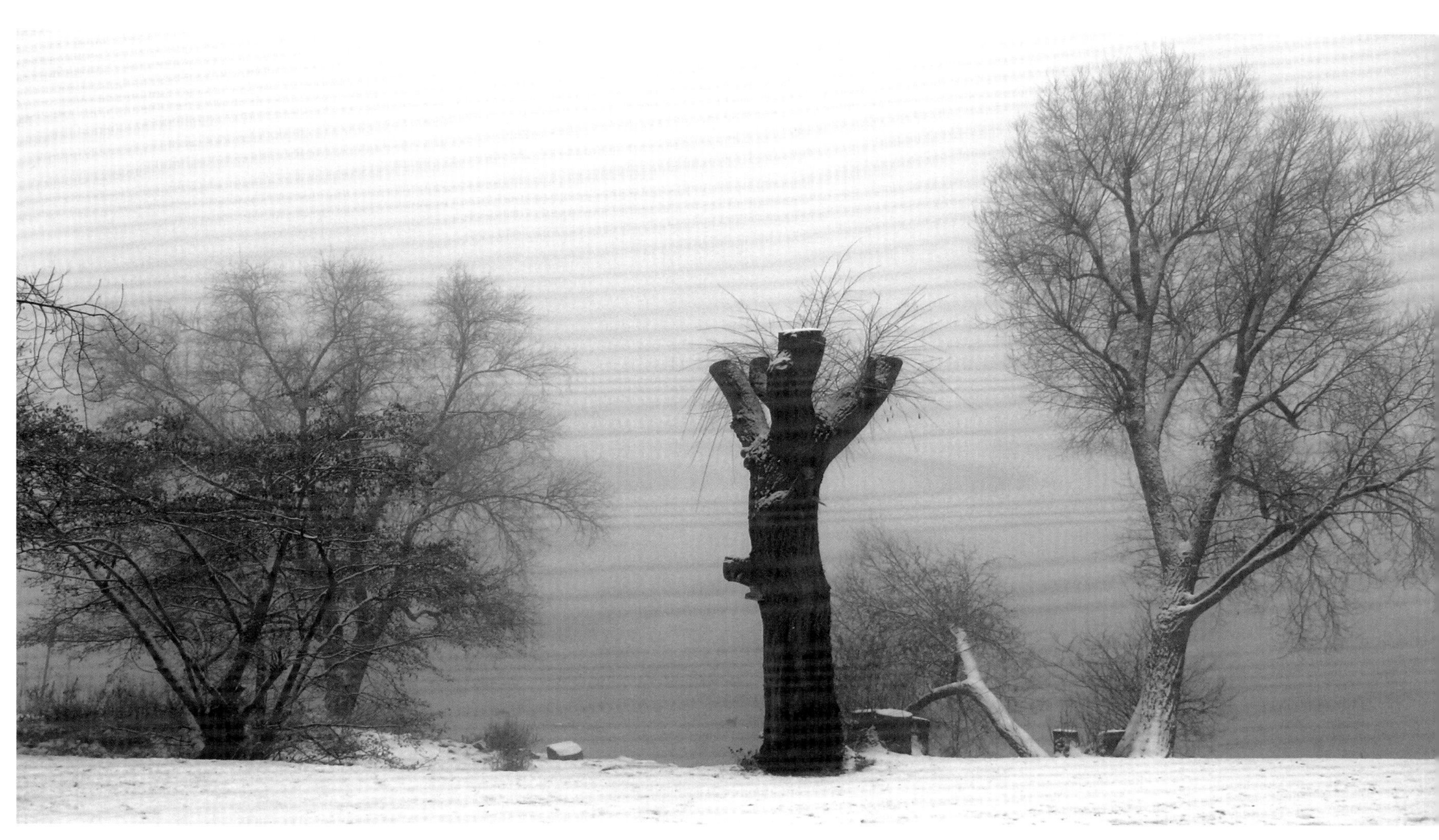

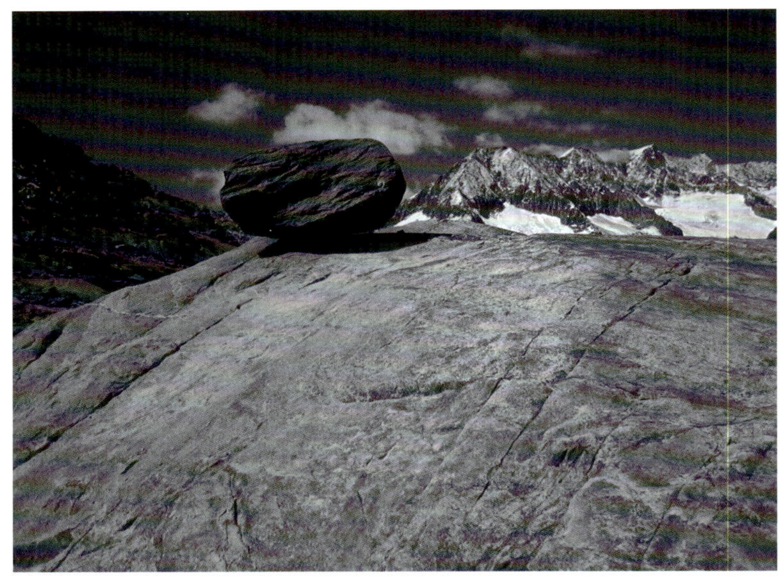

Tip *Keep an eye out for pairs of subjects that differ strikingly from one another and then devise compositions that underscore their visual differences. Some possible options include positioning the contrasting elements diagonally opposite from one another, cropping them in an innovative way, revealing dramatic differences in their surfaces, or playing up varying degrees of brightness.*

Opposites A harmonious photograph can result from the combination of opposites. This statement sounds contradictory, but it is not. A photo is not like a scale that can be balanced only when both sides are at the same height. Decorum in a photograph can be the result of the coexistence of various elements that differ from each other in width, length, shape, orientation, texture, spacing, or brightness.

Juxtaposed visual areas that correspond to the golden ratio tend to create a harmonious effect for viewers. A rough guideline for comparison's sake is 2:3. If you want to play it safe with your compositions, stick to this universal principle of division. Using the grid feature on your camera's display will give you options when composing the relative area sizes in your pictures. However, it's worthwhile to try out contrasts that purposefully deviate from the golden ratio and the classical design principles that stem from this standard.

Contrasts emerge not only from the opposition of similar or similarly shaped objects. The dark boulder that the shrinking Aletsch Glacier deposited on a rock face does in fact create a contrast, but the opposition is not particularly exciting (left). The overall effect of the photograph showing the granite boulders in the north of Sardinia, however, is completely different (right-hand page). The contrast here is not only built through shapes—the opposition also builds a striking substantive contrast between the bizarre animal-like rock formation and the diminutive figure of the woman.

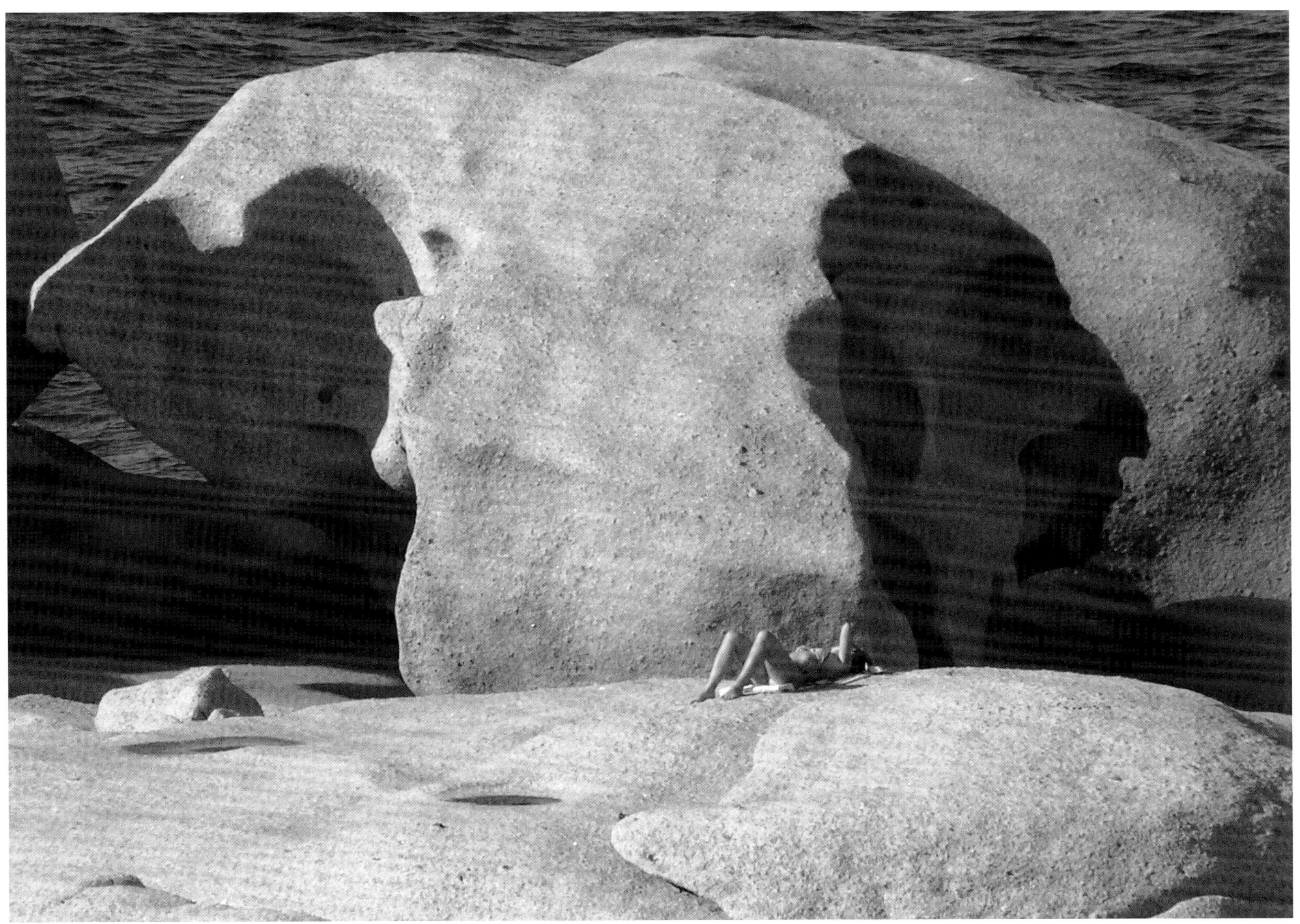

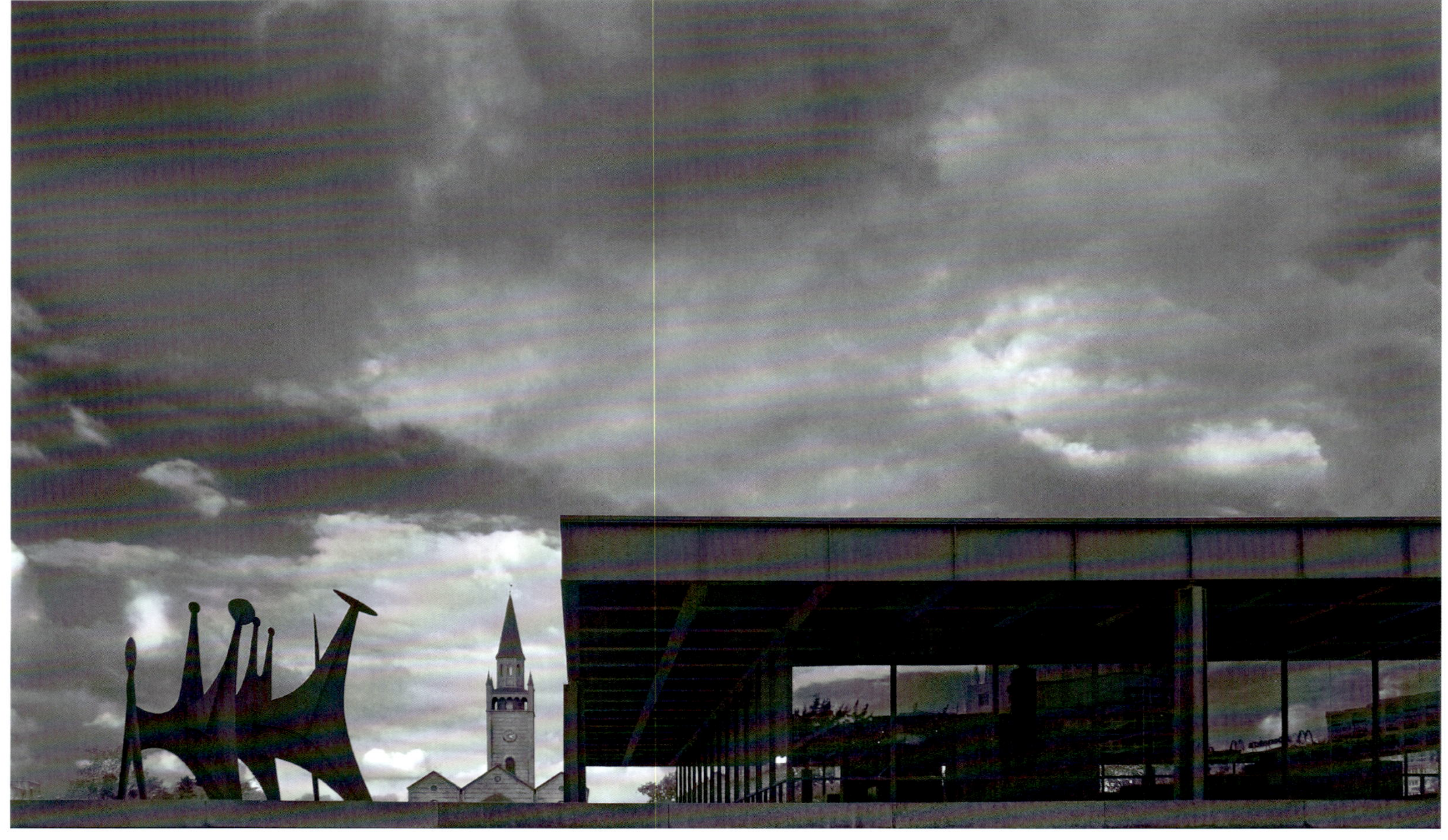

Contrasting Shapes This photograph of the New National Gallery in Berlin presents virtually every example of establishing visual tension through contrasting shapes: round/cornered; pointed/dull; large/small; high/low; more/less; light/dark; straight/bent; horizontal/vertical; narrow/broad; hard/soft; and thick/thin (top).

While the photo in Berlin is teeming with various elements that have different shapes, the picture of the airstream in front of the New York Public Library is focused on fewer shapes. The contrast between the trailer and the regular dividing lines in the architectural façade behind it is the main attraction of the image (right-hand page).

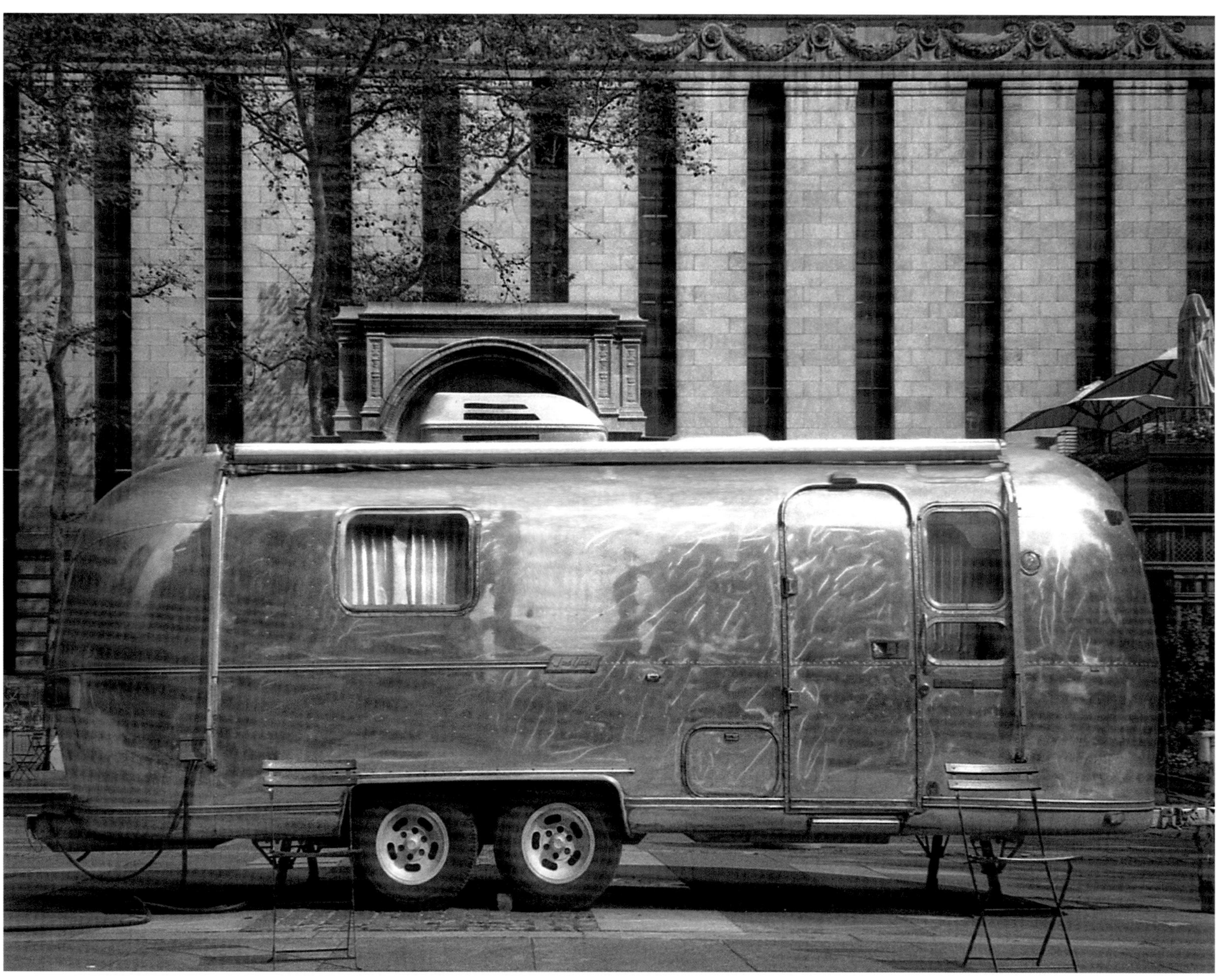

Conspicuous Contrast Circular shapes command a particularly high level of attention when surrounded by shapes with right angles. Just like eyes, circles have a special effect in the graphic arts. When a circle is cropped at the edge of an image, a viewer naturally completes the shape in his or her imagination. A viewer is compelled to follow the entirety of the ring with their gaze. Curved or arched elements also have a very strong effect, as demonstrated here by the photos of segments of the dome atop the Reichstag in Berlin (bottom-right), the view from the roof of the Academy of Arts at Pariser Platz in Berlin (bottom-left), and the curved rows of benches in the spa gardens of Bad Reichenhall (top). The image of stretches of highway in Mannheim reveals the effect of circles spinning into or out of the image area (right-hand page). The photographs on the next pages were taken in the House of Astronomy in Heidelberg (page 110) and the Mercedes-Benz Museum in Stuttgart (page 111).

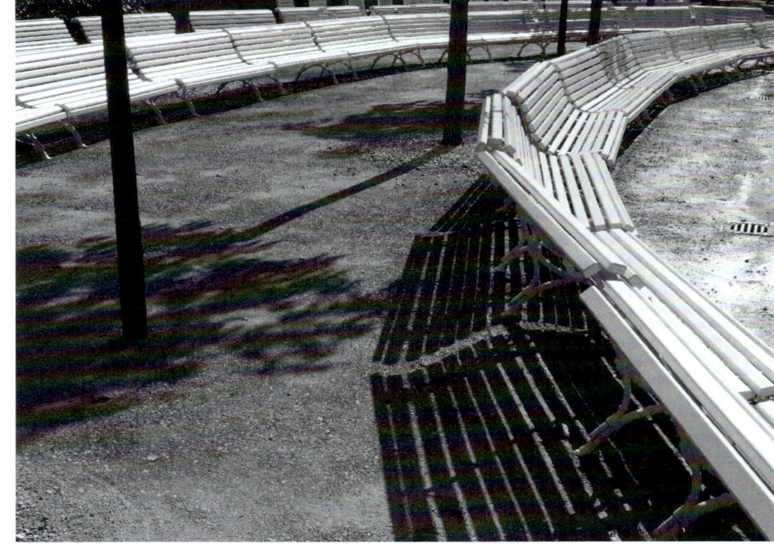

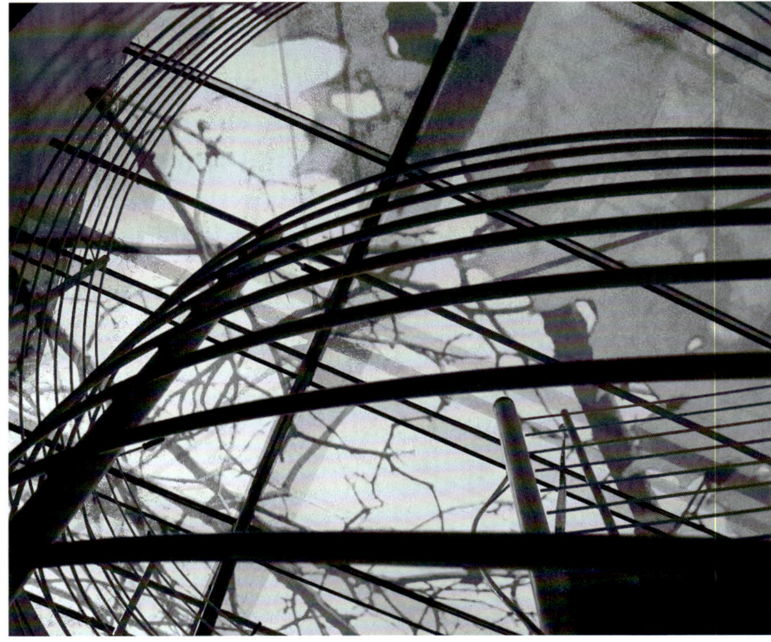

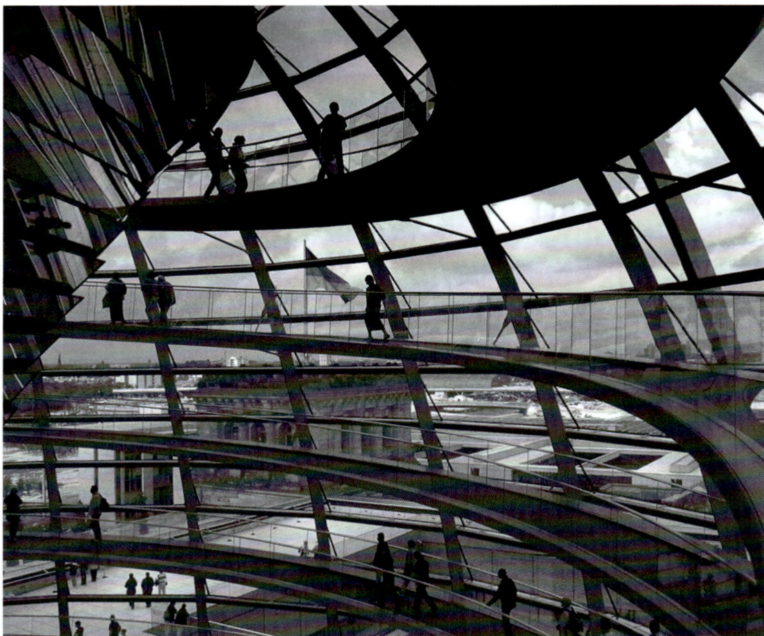

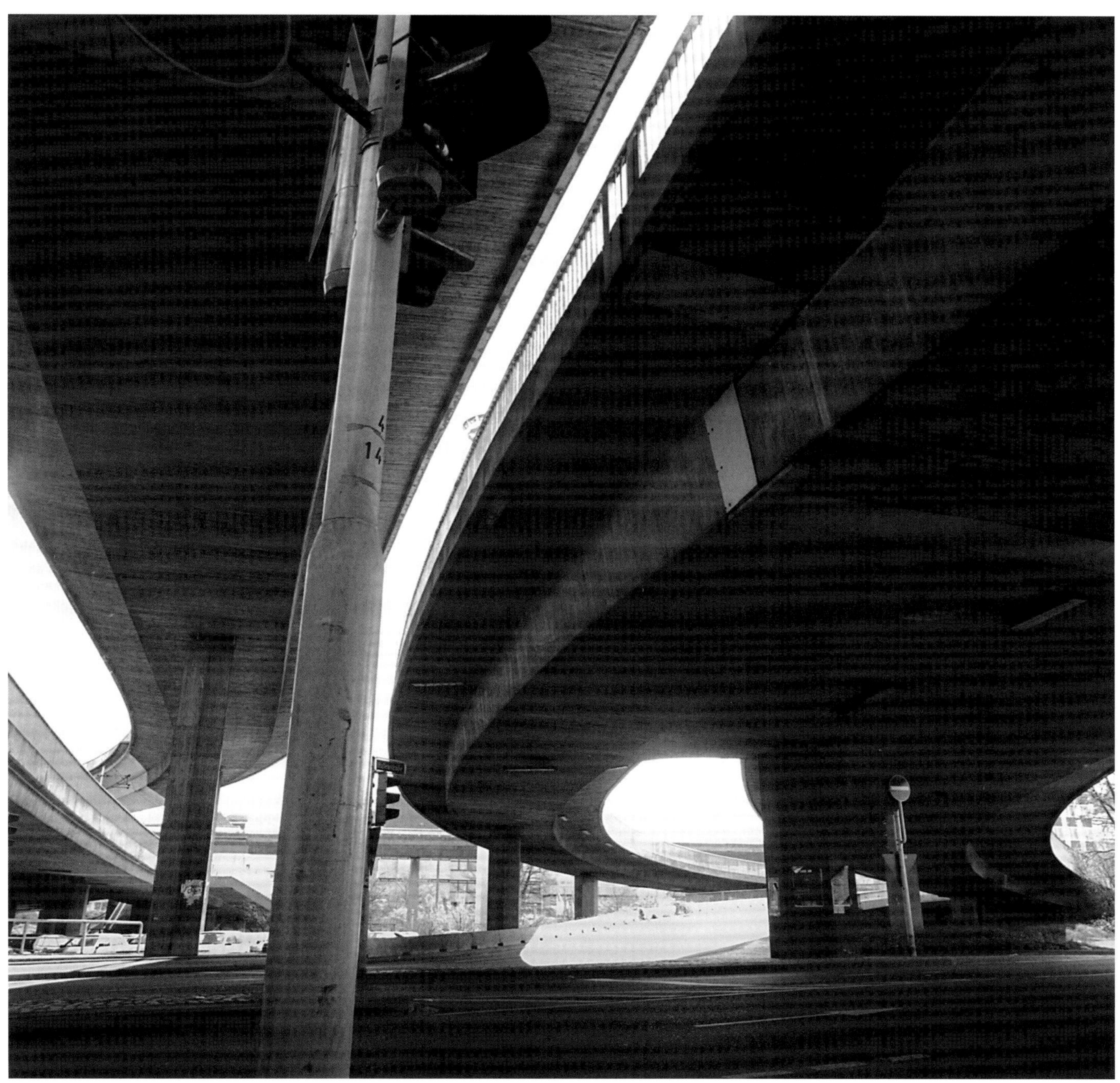

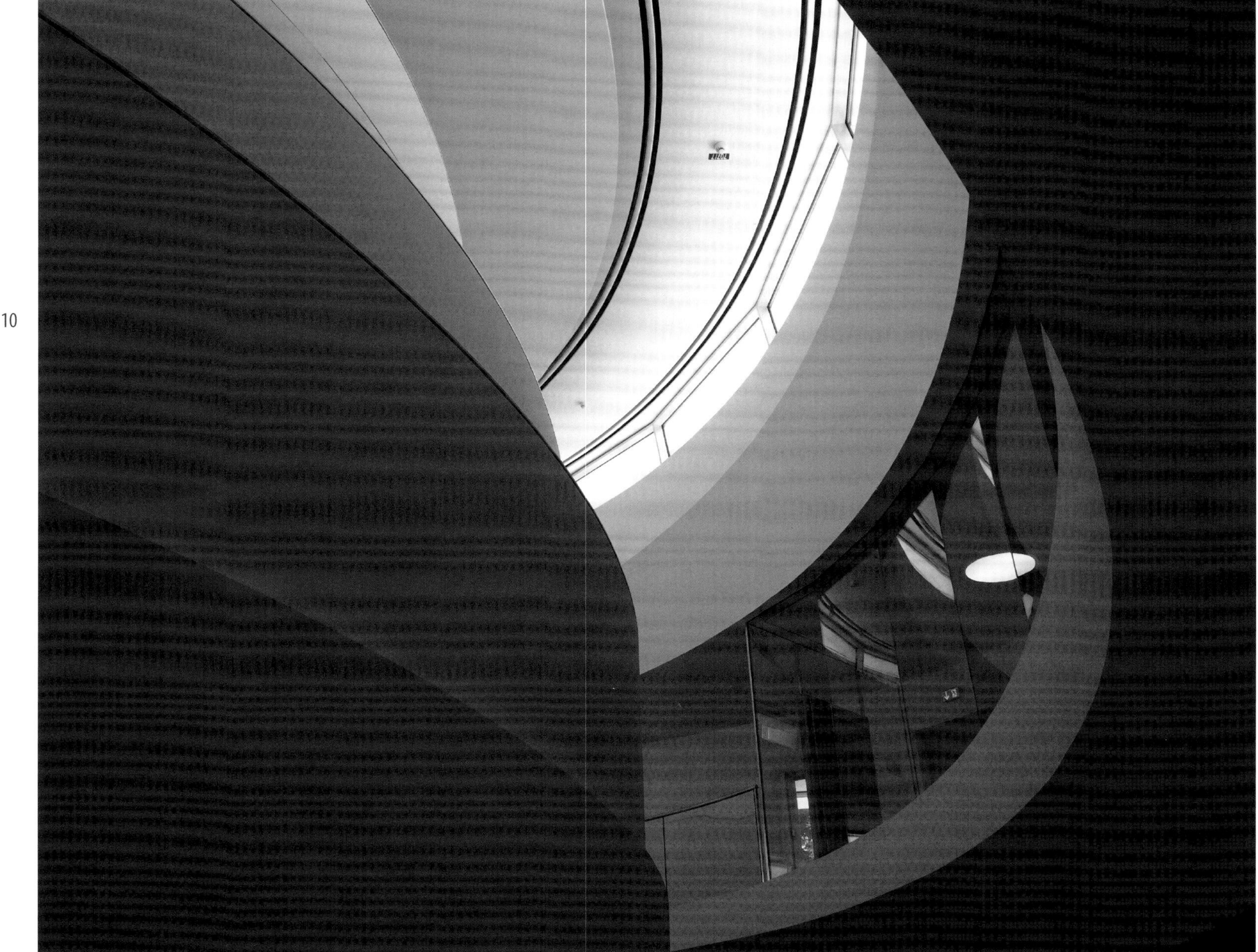

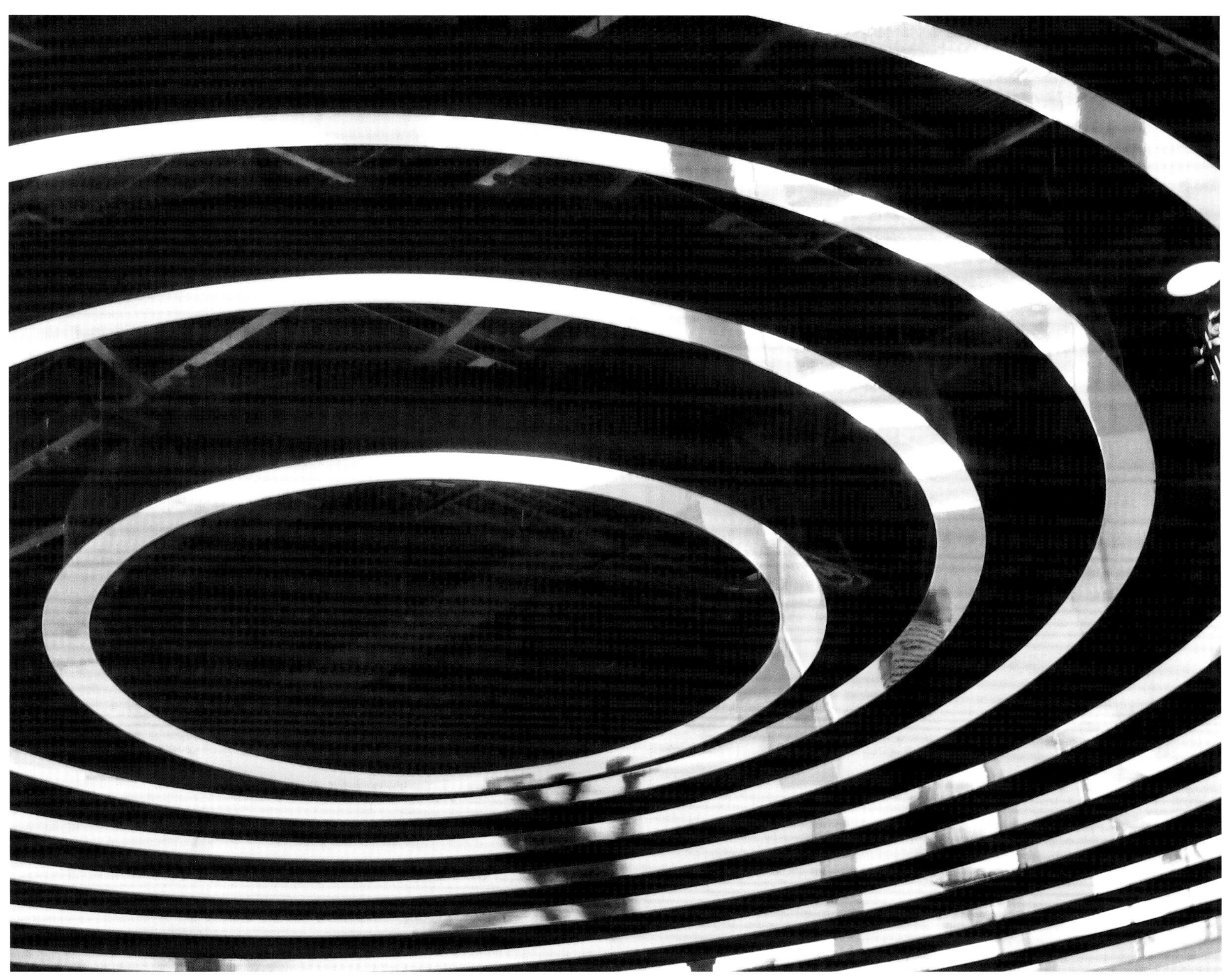

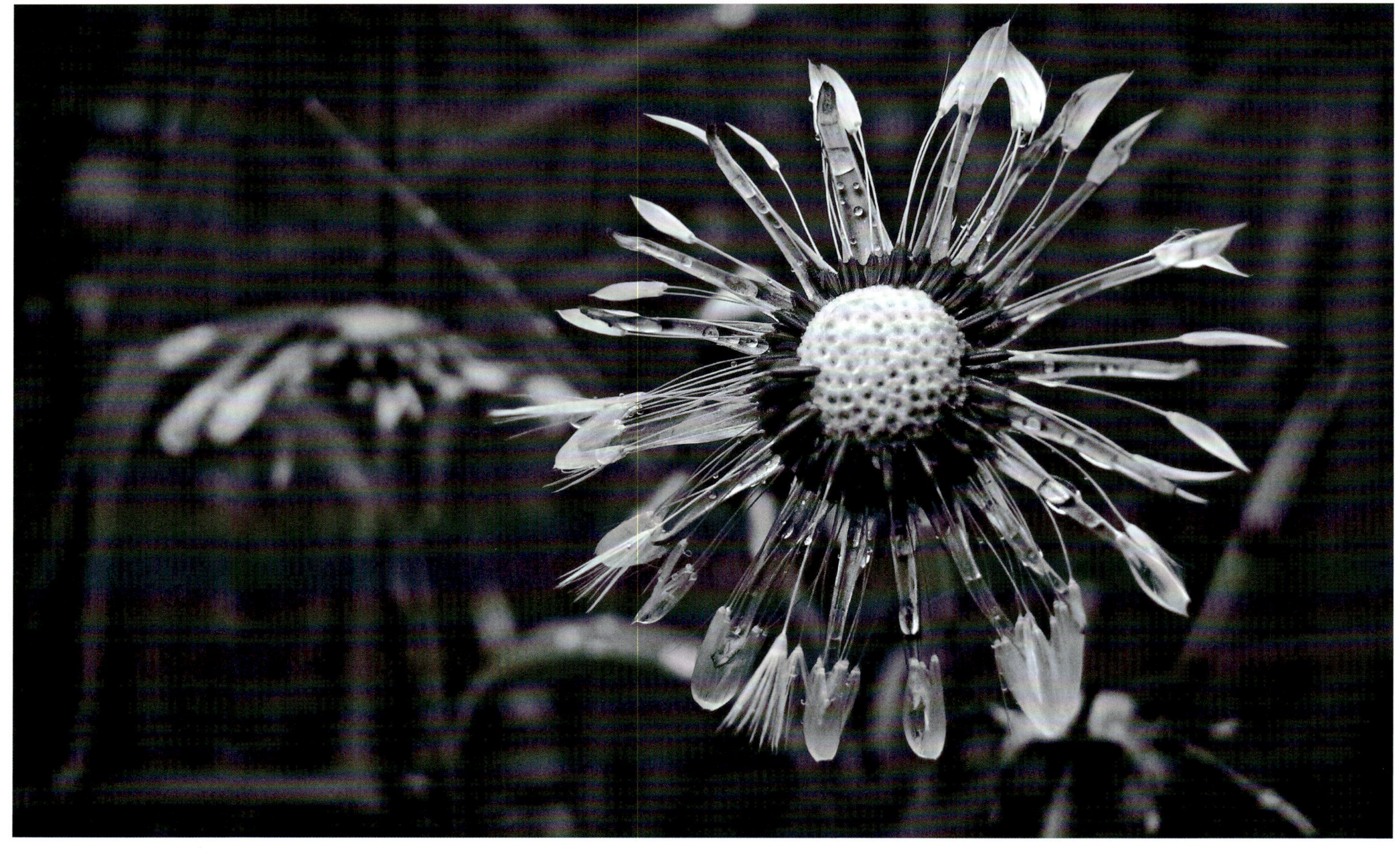

Bull's Eye When a complete circle is captured within the image area, it acts as a solid anchor point. If a circle causes a viewer to associate it with a human eye, then the shape commands his or her attention unwaveringly.

It is not easy to photograph flowers in a way that is not quintessentially common. I discovered this glassy blossom on a rain-soaked meadow in Liguria that reminded me of a wheel of little spatulas (top).

It's hard to believe, but the image of the dandelion (right-hand page) is not a photograph. It was created on a simple scanner! Walter Spagerer, a photographic artist from Mannheim, has used sophisticated technology to develop an aesthetic that is highly difficult to achieve with the optics of a camera. And this is to say nothing of the impressive depth of field that one normally would not expect from a commercial scanner.

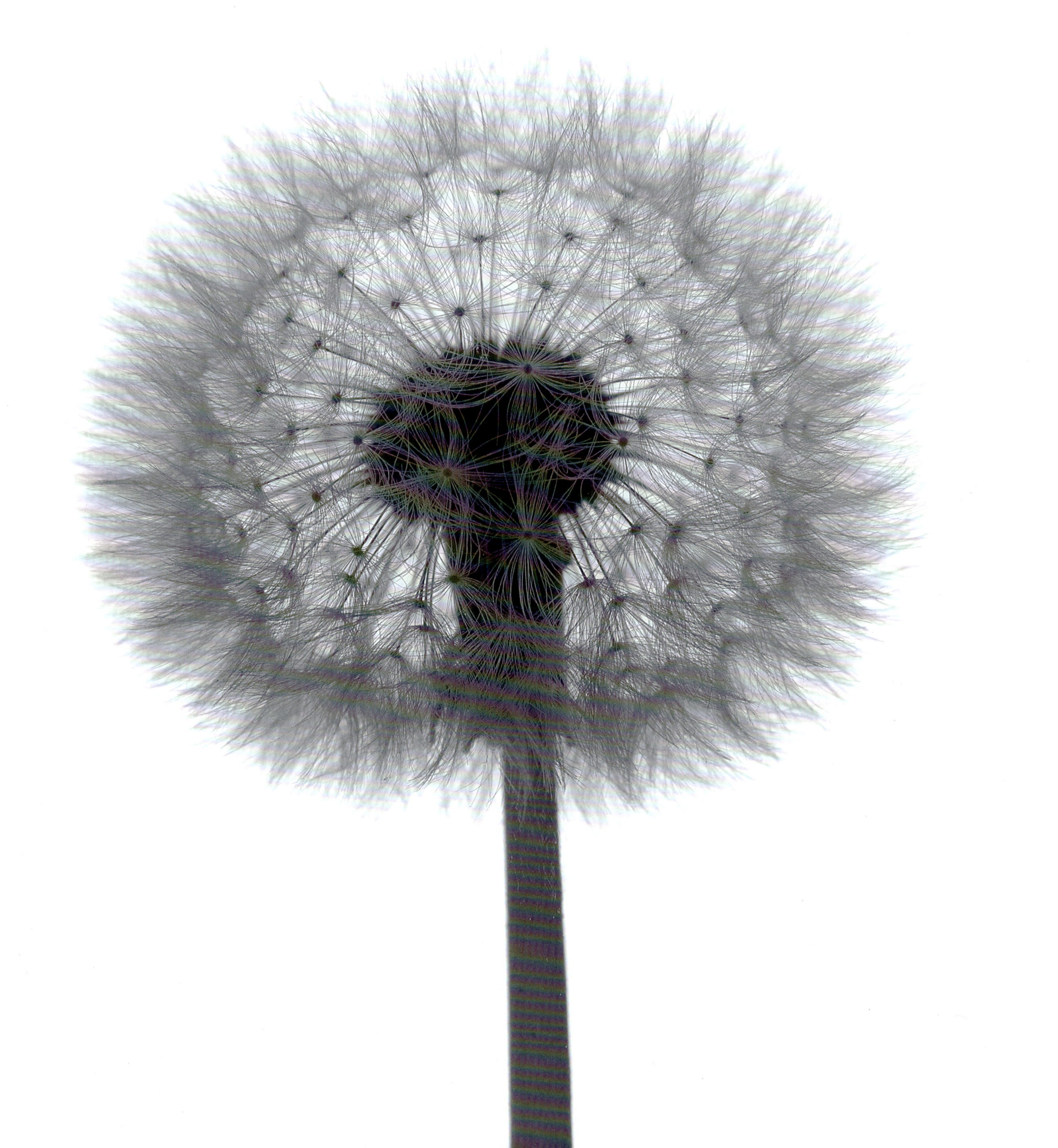

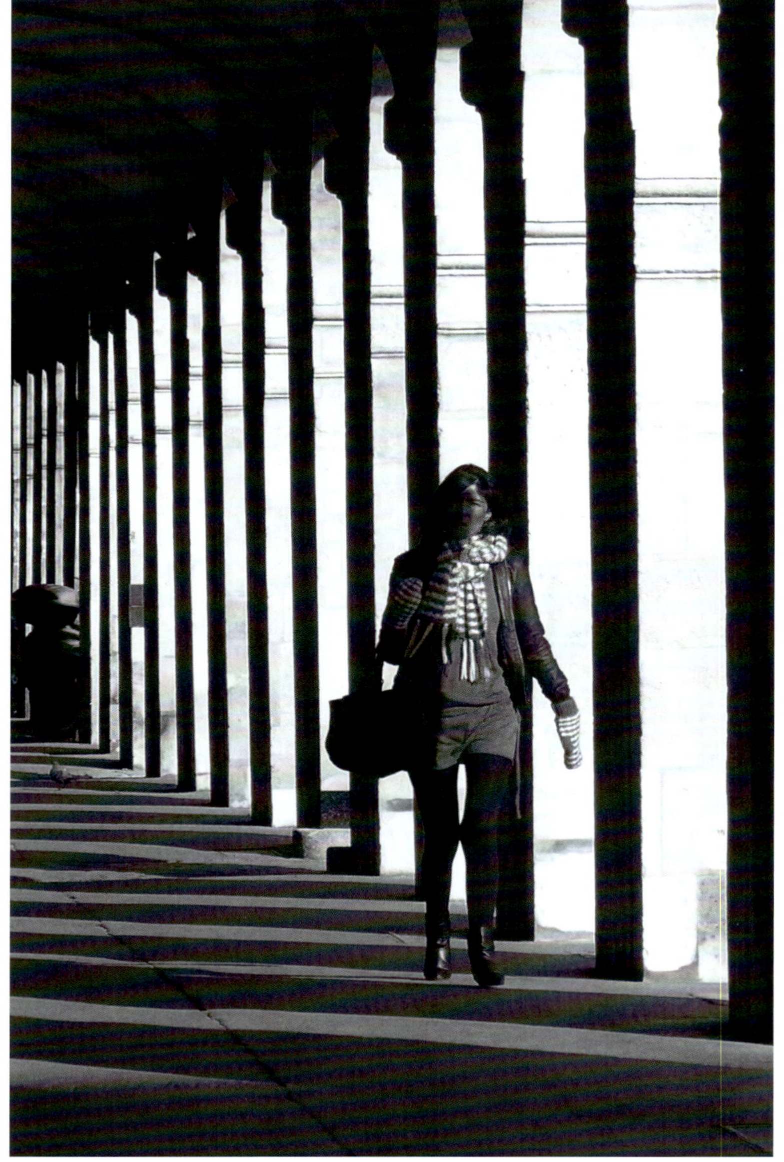

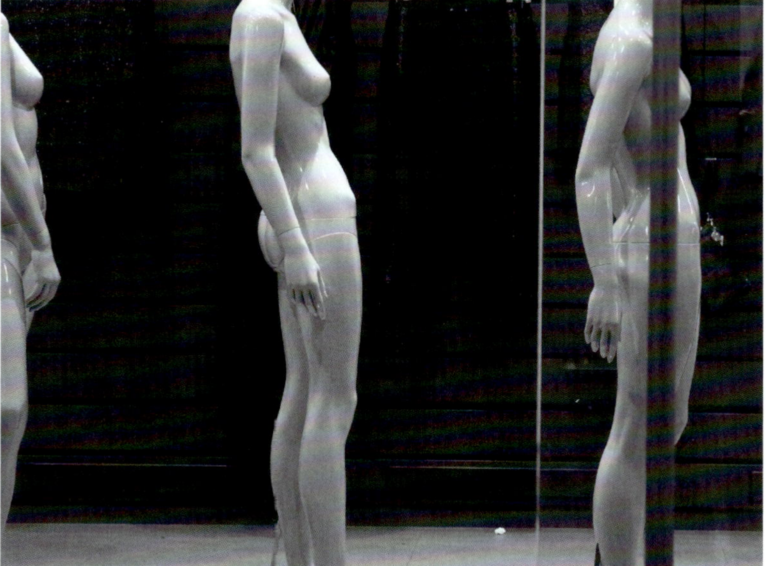

Walkway People have a penchant for uniformity. Neatly spaced sequences can be found at every corner. Our cultural landscape is decorated with static shapes. Lined-up, repeating objects are attractive attention-grabbers when documented within the rectangular area of an image: manicured vineyards, densely planted trees along an avenue, evenly spaced streetlamps, tidy rows of beach chairs, and a parace of mannequins are examples of this concept.
An optical disruption is sometimes needed to break up the monotony of repeating forms. Under the arcade on the Place des Vosges in Paris, a woman disrupts the otherwise steady line of the columns (left). Layering and cropping disrupt the uniformity of the display-window mannequins (top).
An image that departs from the comfort of uniformity can also create an interesting effect; for example, the photo of a walkway in Venice is an example of how a crowd of pedestrians, all heading in different directions, can seem dynamic (right-hand page).

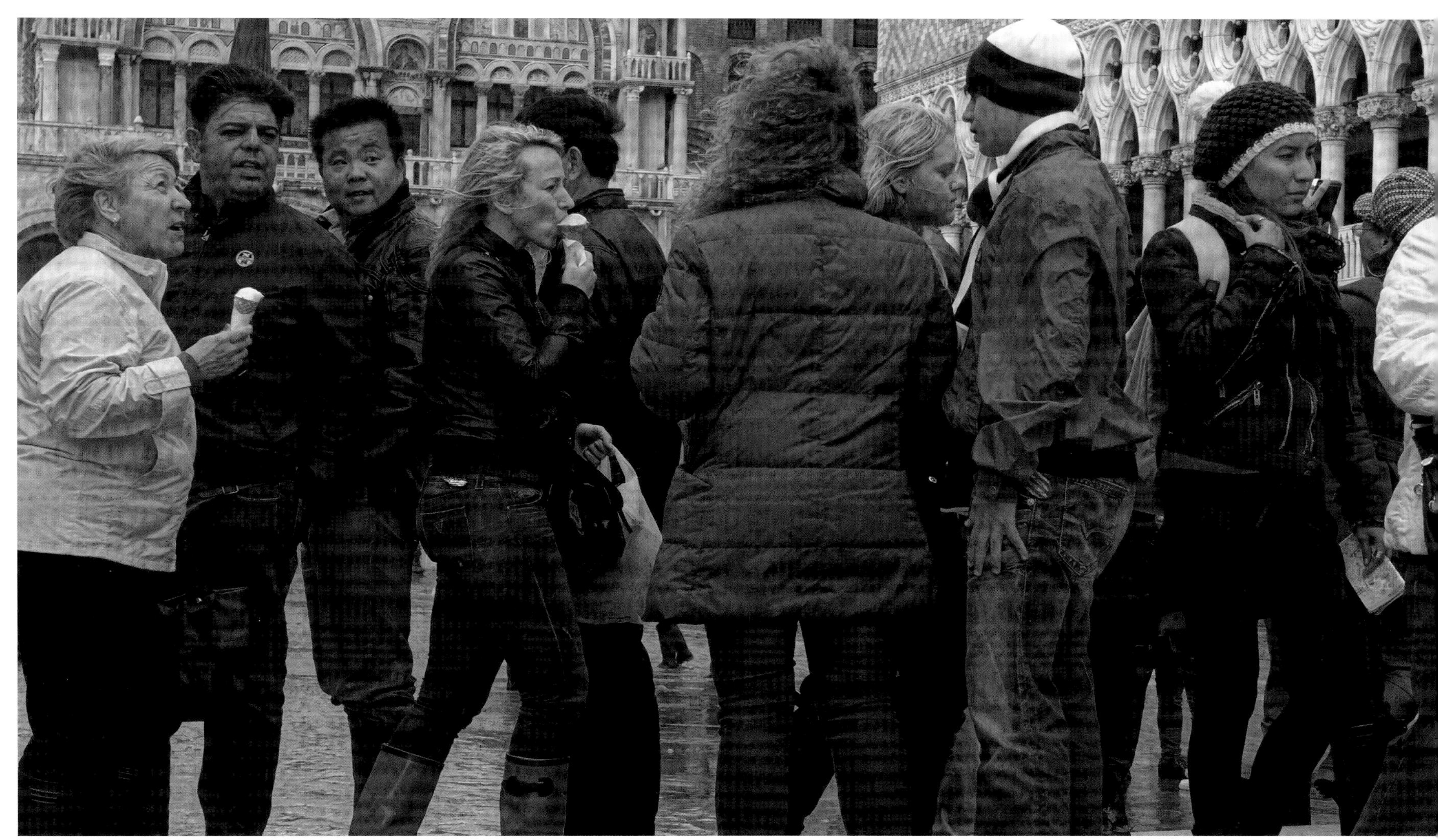

116 Light and Shadow

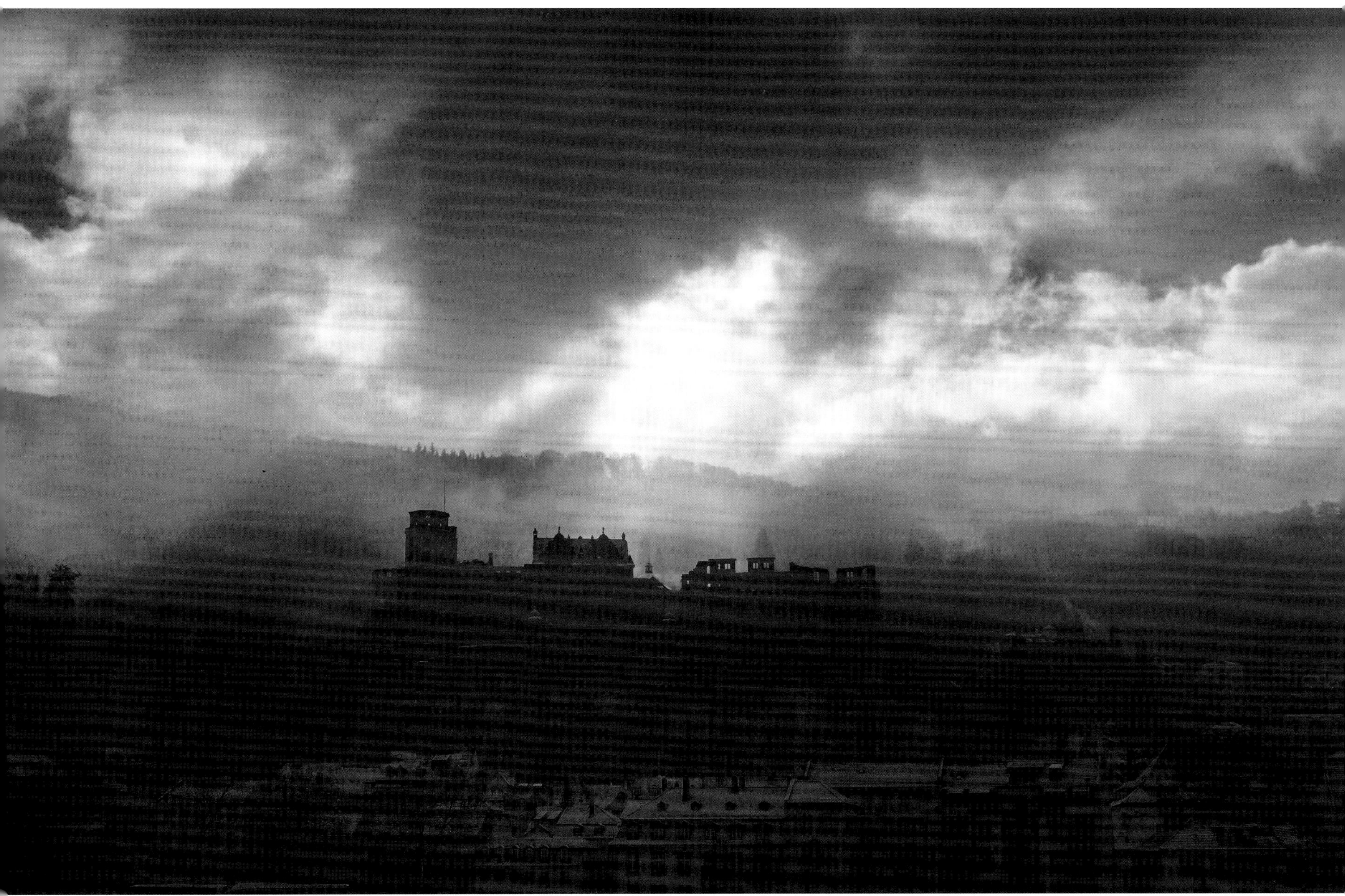

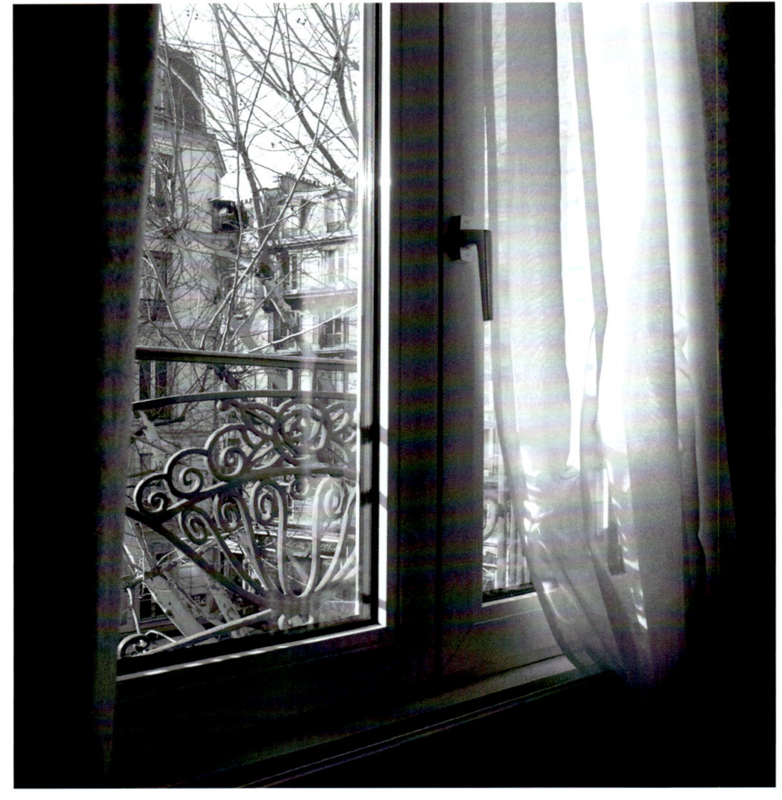

Let the Light In The positive effects of light are well known to everyone. Leo Tolstoy expressed it succinctly: "All the diversity, all the charm, and all the beauty of life are made up of light and shade." Robert Gernhardt—a poet, caricaturist, and painter of the Tuscan countryside—similarly sums up the practice of painting with light in a ballad: "Put some things in the light and watch what the light will do to such things. . . ."

Even today, painters, illustrators, and photographers travel the world in search of regions with particularly attractive lighting. Many artists discover a lighter palette of colors in the southern climes. The light that Max Slevogt found in Egypt on a trip in 1914 must have been a revelation for him, because the pictures he painted in the sun near the pyramids are clearly distinguishable from those he painted up north in the Alps.

The similar way in which light is used in painting and photography has been well documented in exhibitions. Edward Hopper—known for his ability to paint using light—was exhibited alongside photographers whose works illustrated comparable utilizations of lighting. Both forms of art rely on light—and shadow, by necessity—as a quintessential tool.

This photo (left) could be interpreted as an allusion to a painting done by the French impressionist Gustave Caillebotte. The window frame is typical of the Parisian style.

The minute shadows cast by the lamppost and the man near the ocean in Cádiz (right-hand page) reveals the high position of the sun over this city in the south of Spain.

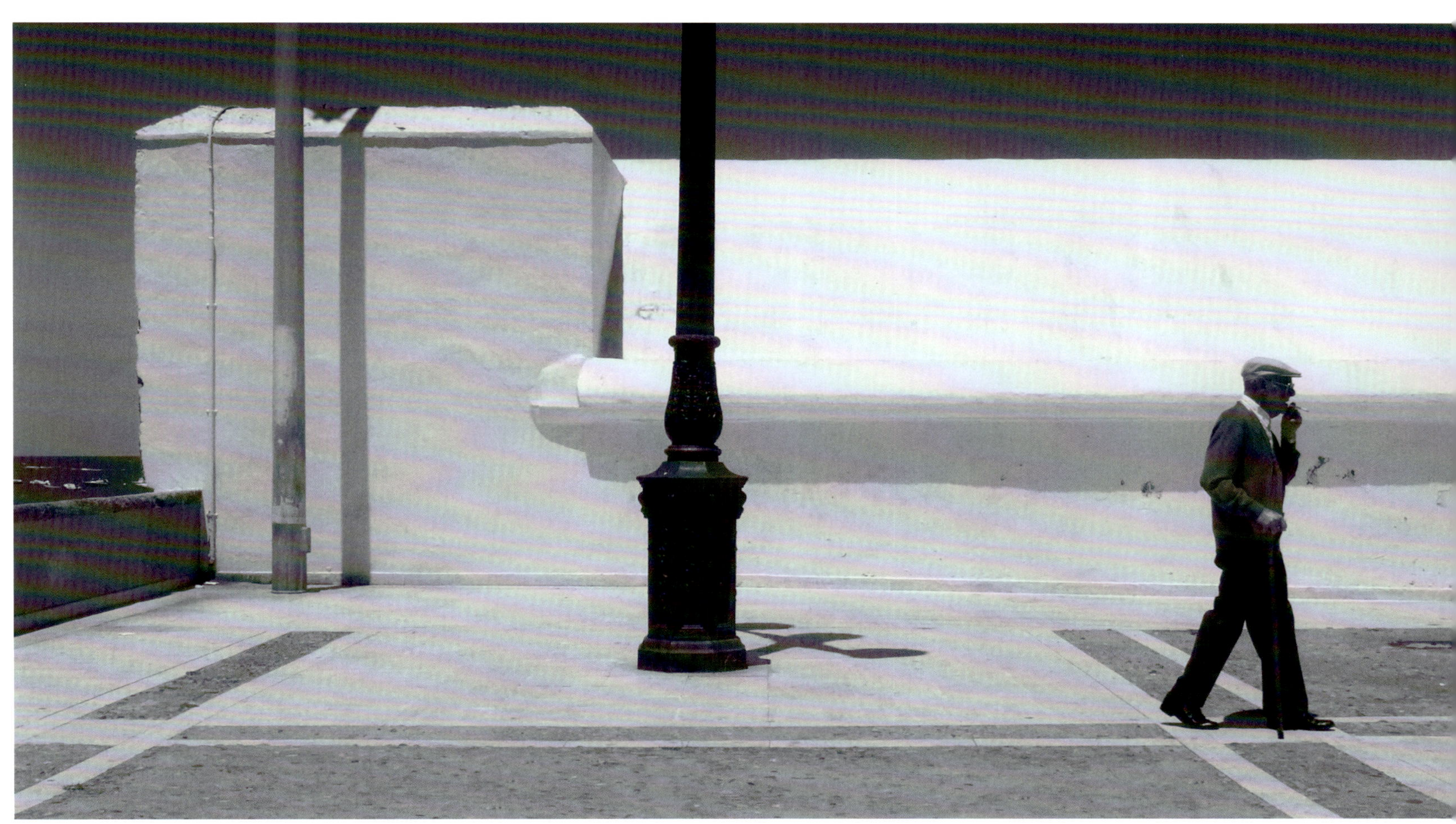

Ice-Cold Warmth Fortune smiles on anyone who has the pleasure of standing above the Aletsch Glacier in Switzerland and gazing out at the mighty river of ice under an immaculately clear sky (top). That's when this spectacle of nature is at its best. Glorious weather for photographers. Really?

Is not a visitor who witnesses the natural spectacle under completely different conditions just as fortunate? Perhaps when low-hanging clouds bear down dramatically on the landscape, allowing for intense pockets of sunlight to shine like spotlights down on freshly fallen snow (bottom-right, bottom-left)?

Areas of shadow and light are spectacular subjects for images—a fact clearly illustrated by the photograph of a snowy trail through the Odenwald (right-hand page). The gray tones of the clouds and sky allow the snow to shine, and a network of intersecting shadows further contributes to the effective composition.

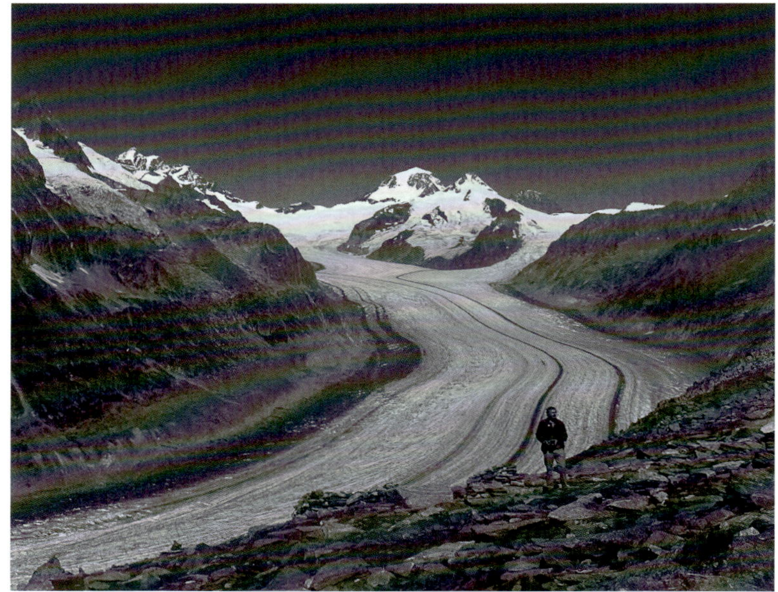

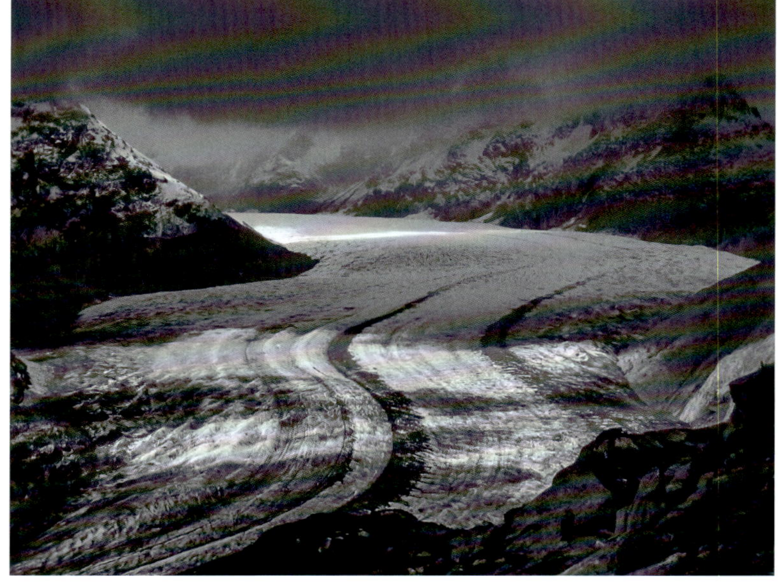

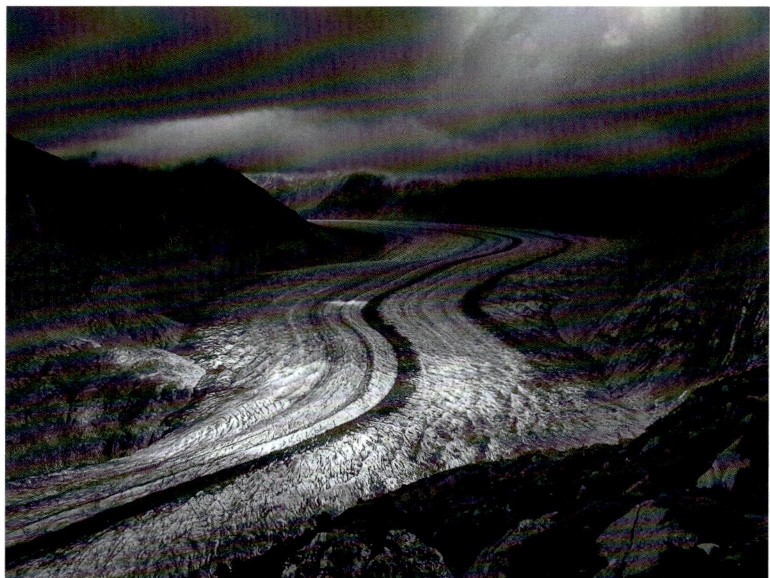

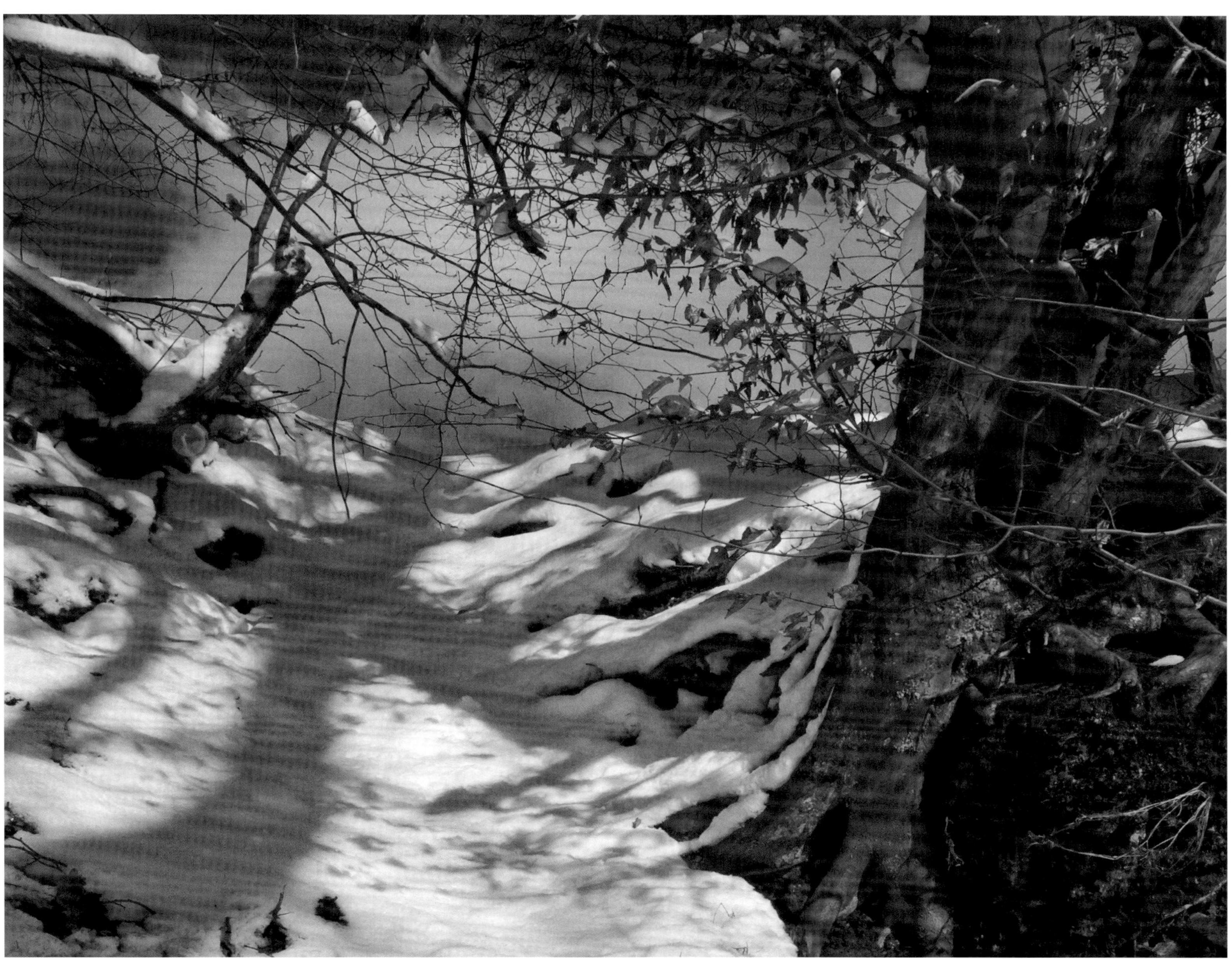

Shadow Begets Light This statement may seem nonsensical at first, but illustrators know that it is not without truth. You have to draw a slew of strokes to achieve the desired effect, especially if the medium you are working with is white. If light is to come alive on the page, it must be engendered with gray tones. The darker the shadows, the brighter the light appears. Rembrandt rendered a work that illustrates this effect beautifully. In 1650 he created a postcard-sized etching of a sea snail. The light effect he created on the shell of the *Conus marmoreus* seems brighter than the paper on which the etching was printed.

Aside from these purely optical effects, light and shadow contrasts can play a principal role in an image's overall composition. The shadows on the charging platform at the Völklingen Ironworks (top) support the central perspective of the composition and contribute to the depth of the scene.

The interplay of light and shadow on the walls of the Academy of Arts, Berlin, during a 2005 closure for renovations (center) takes over the image rather than contributing to its dimensionality. The many diagonal lines produce a tension with the rectangular border of the image area.

The repeating pattern of shadow and light in this alley in the Ligurian town of Taggia (bottom) endows the photo with palpable depth.

The harsh light and the sharply defined shadows disclose that this photograph from the Kalsa Quarter of Palermo (right-hand page) was shot during the middle of the day.

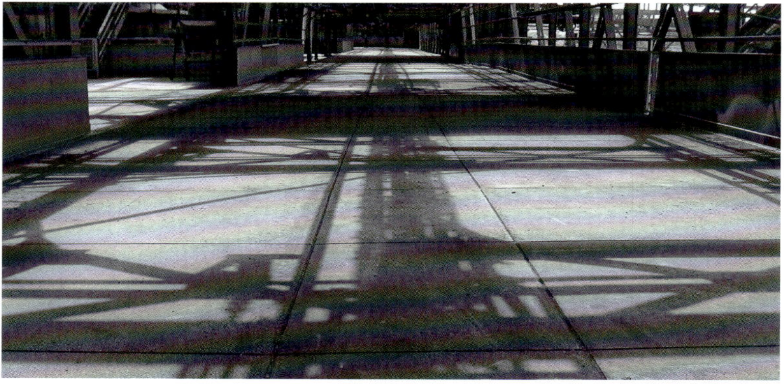

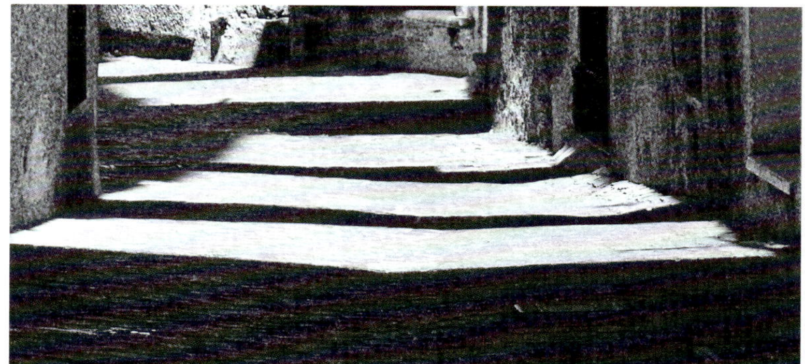

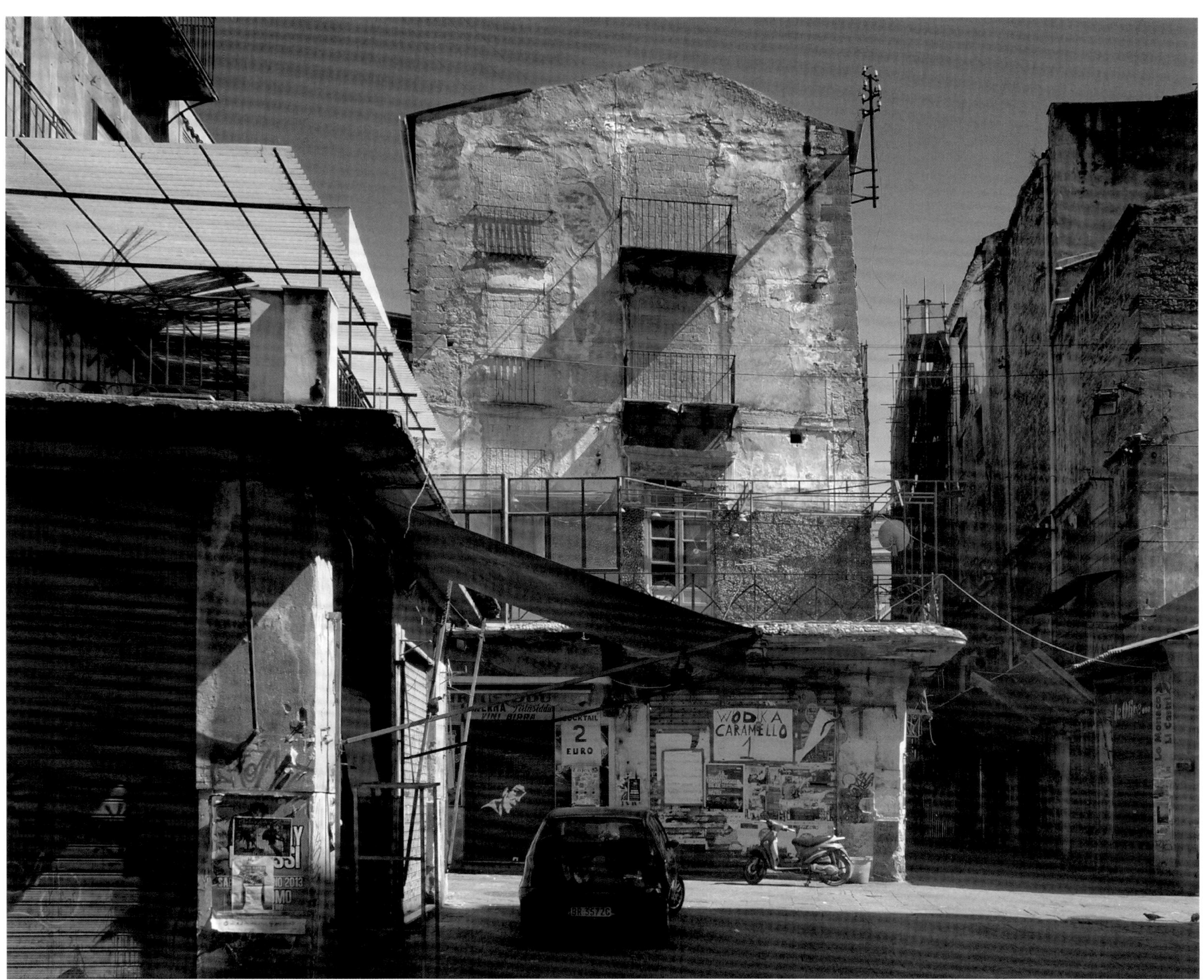
2
EURO
WODKA
CARAMELLO
1

Backlight Directing your camera toward a source of light can be a delightful and approachable task when you know what you are doing. The best method is to press the shutter button halfway down to set the exposure based on the brightest part of the image and then to adjust the camera's direction to obtain your desired image area before actually exposing the photograph. The photograph of the smoker at the Pont des Arts in Paris (top) illustrates a figure with a modest halo effect caused by backlighting. The Institute of France in the background is shrouded in shadow and serves as an important contrast for the main subject.

The pedestrians near the Biblioteque Nationale in Paris are also outlined in a delicate light (right-hand page). The differences in size among the figures and their optimal positioning with respect to one another complement the spatial effect resulting from the composition, which is defined first and foremost by the central perspective.

The contrasts in the photograph of the young man playing soccer in Aspra on Sicily (bottom) are much harsher. When faced with the bright light of the afternoon sun, the camera's automatic exposure mode opted for a tiny aperture, permitting the sky to retain details such as the clouds. The cost of this is the loss of interior detail in the shadows, but this quality is exactly what makes this image so charming. If the details of the figure in the foreground were desirable, fill flash could have been employed.

Tip *A few tools can be used to prevent stray light and flare effects from marring your images. Using a lens hood is the path of least resistance.*

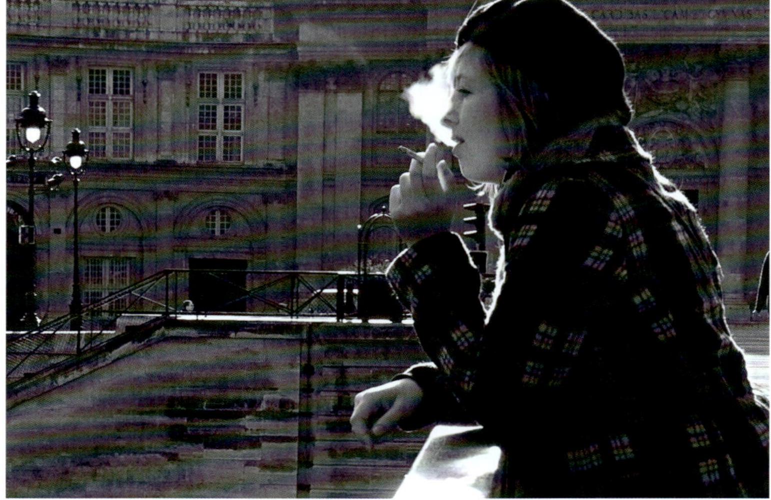

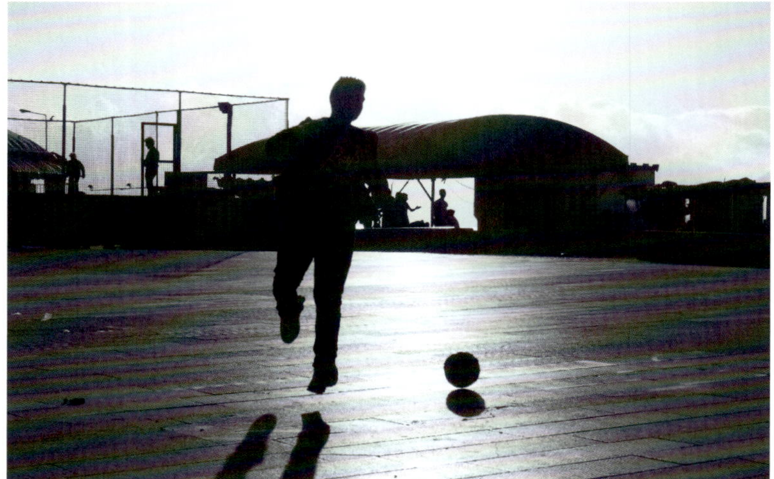

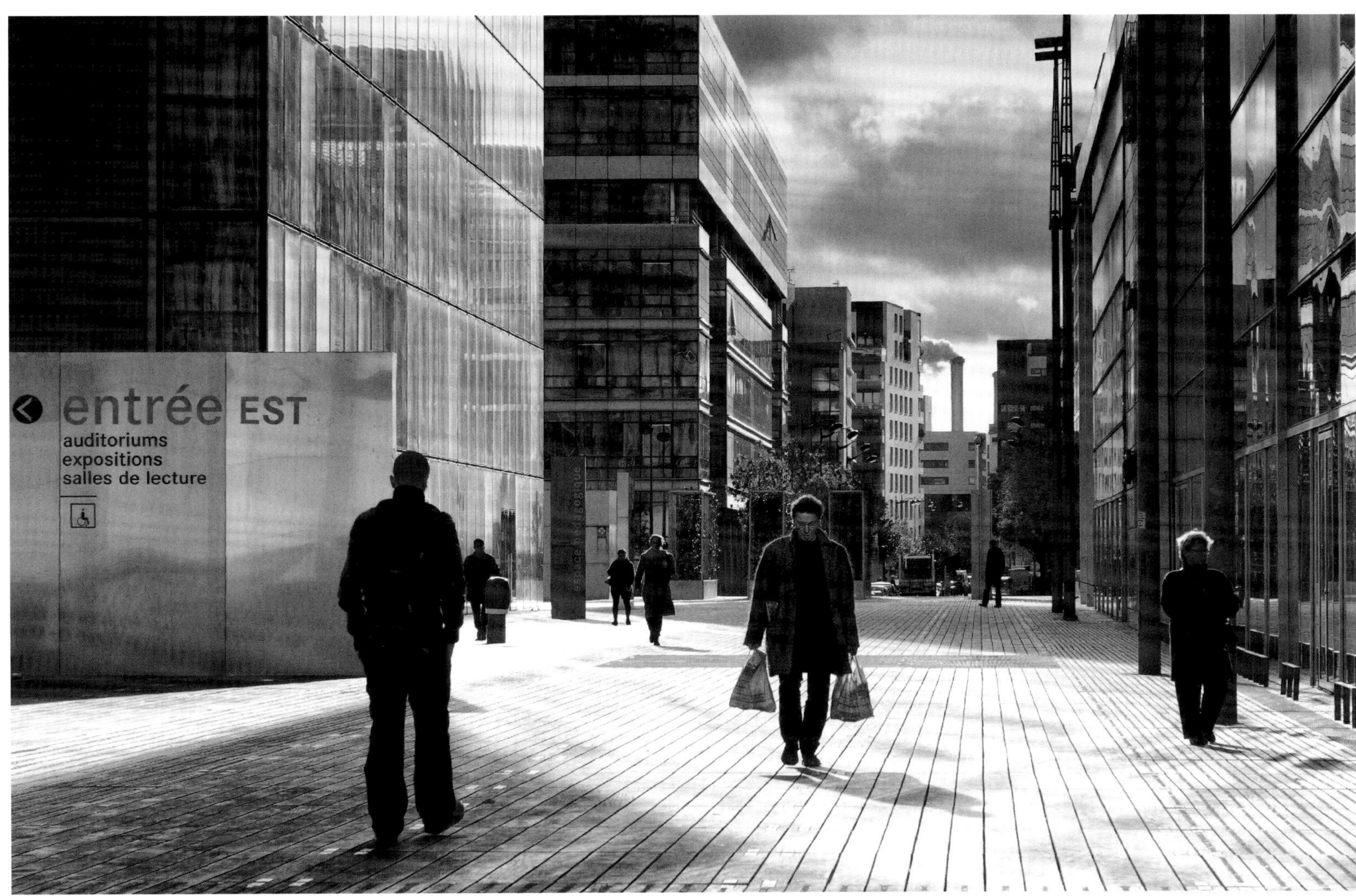
entrée EST
auditoriums
expositions
salles de lecture

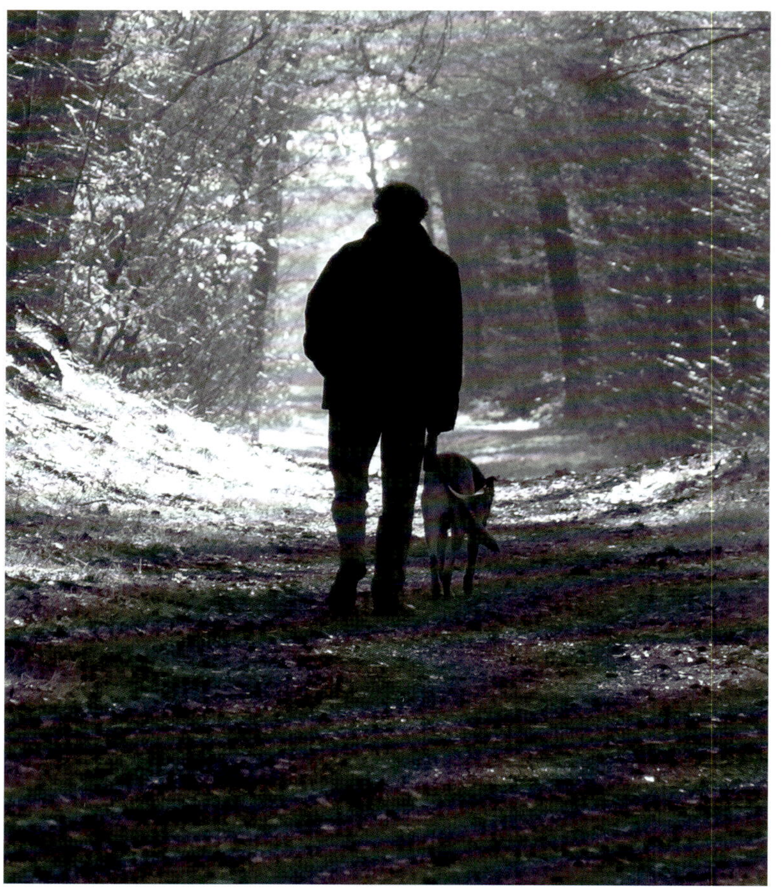

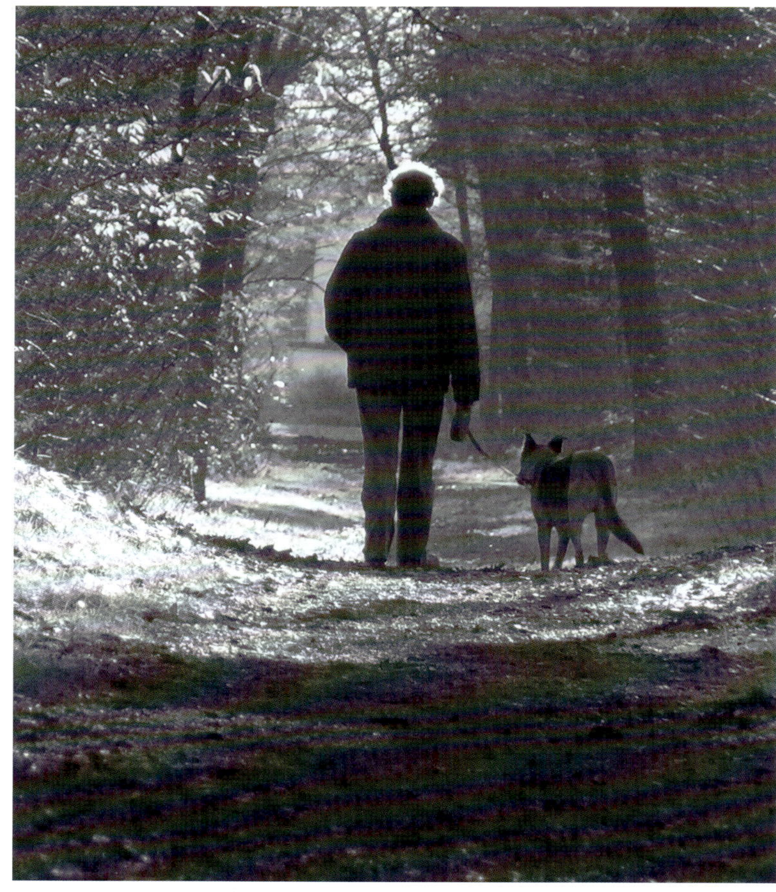

A Subtle Difference These images are of a trail in the Käfertal Forest in Mannheim. The slanted sunlight falling through the trees creates strips of light along the forest floor. The walker and his dog pass rhythmically through areas of shadow and light. The first exposure shows both of them shrouded in shadows, the second shows the man's hair illuminated with backlighting, and the third depicts both subjects as illuminated. Now even the man's clothes and the dog's fur are outlined in a contour of light. Each picture in this series, from left to right, is better than the previous. The differences between them are subtle, but have a huge effect on the overall look and feel of the images.

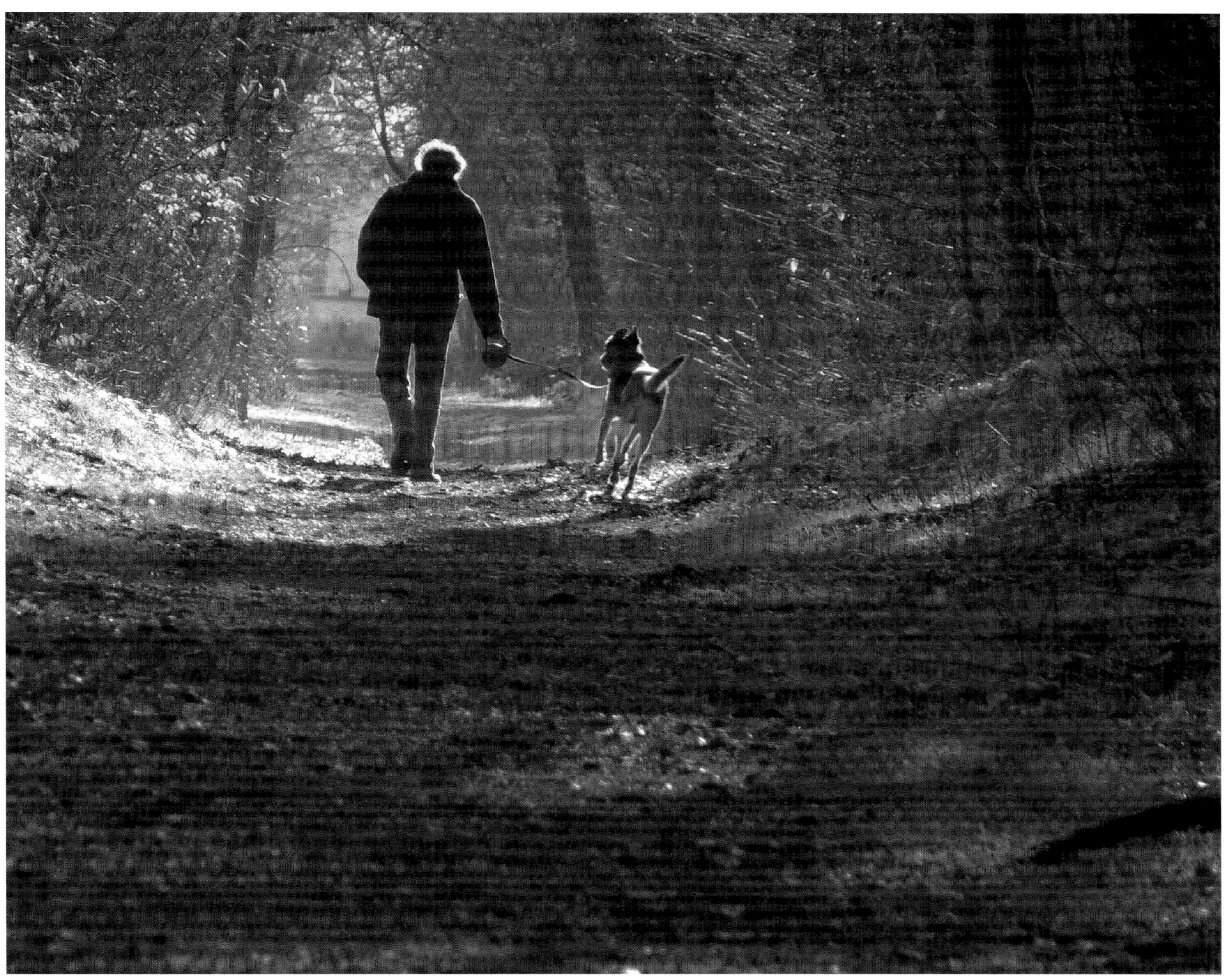

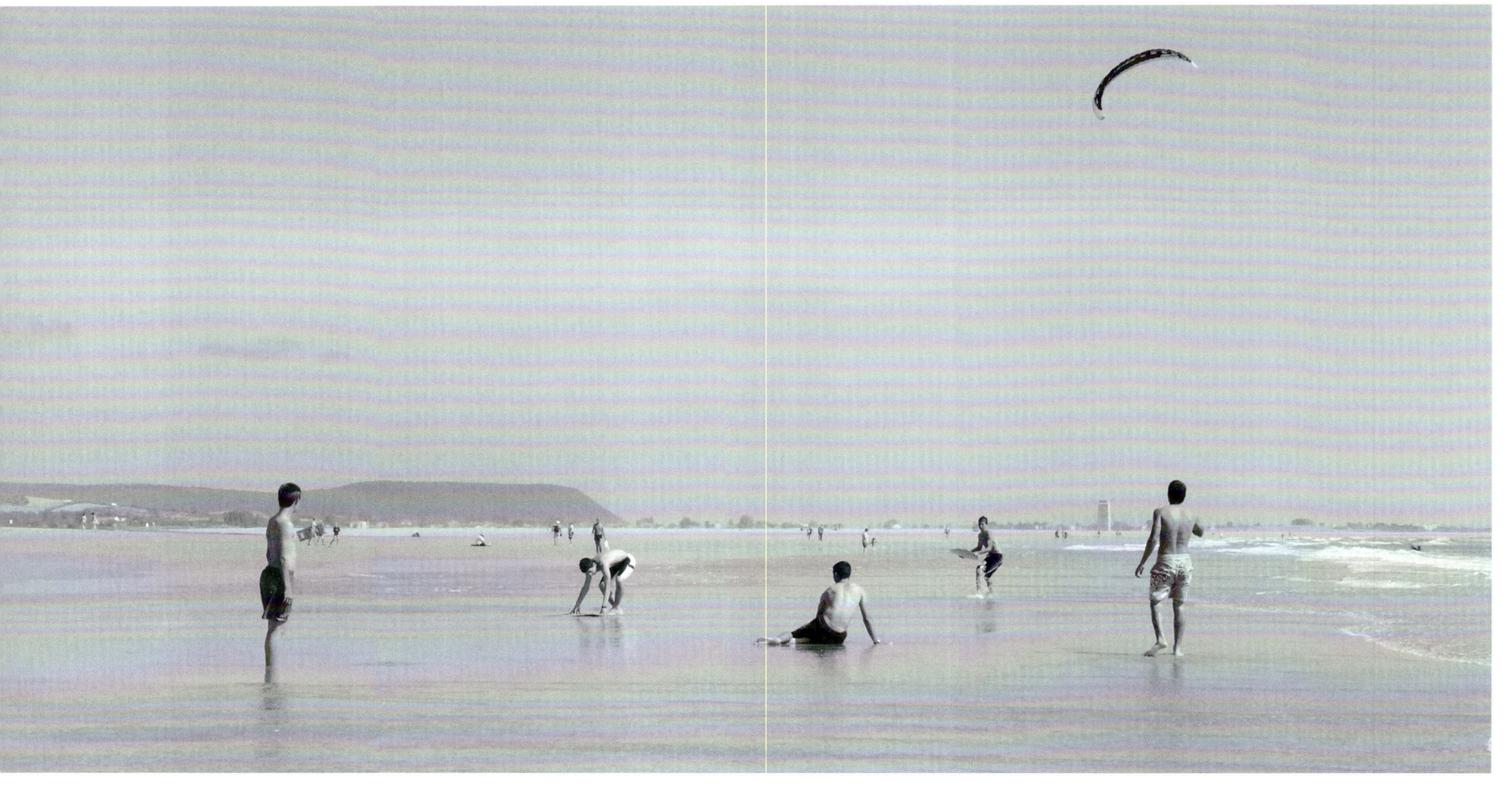

Light Spaces These images are scenes from the beaches near Conil de la Frontera in Andalusia (above) and the French coast (right-side page). The sand reflects the intense summer sun. The farther away the people are from the camera, the more they are enveloped in a fine haze. In both compositions the sky takes up two-thirds of the image area and the horizon line is shifted toward the bottom. The beach in Andalusia is surrounded by hills, groups of trees, sand dunes, and a small hamlet with a tall tower. In contrast, the photograph taken on the French coast does not even feature a visible horizon. The beach seamlessly blends into the sky, creating a seemingly endless area of light. The diminishing size of the human figures provides a structural point of reference for the viewer to interpret the scene.

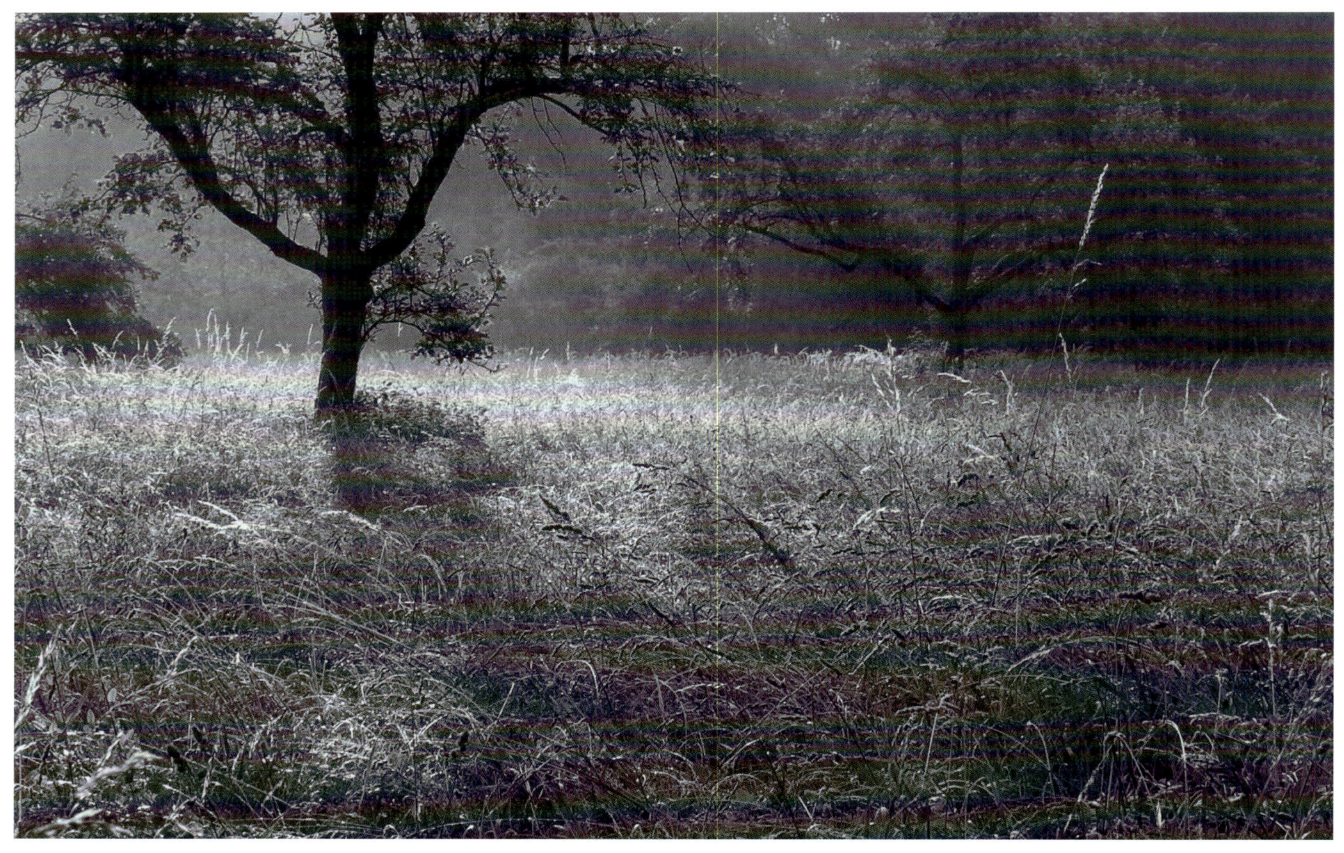

130

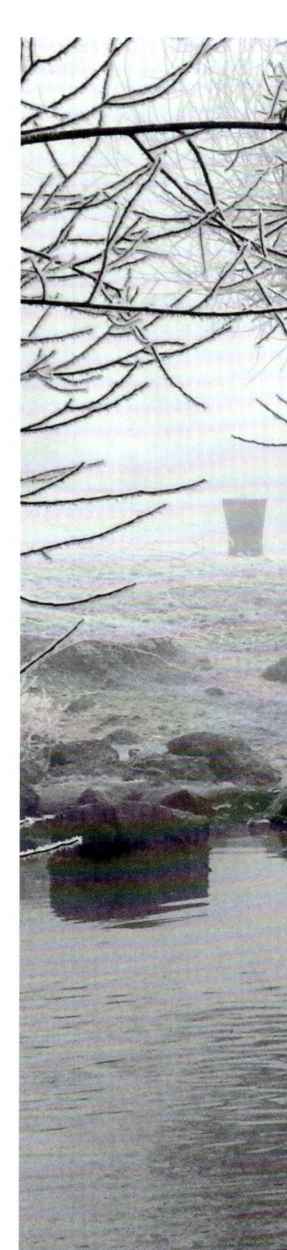

Early Birds Nature photographers tend not to sleep in late. They prefer to work when the day's light is in transition, when haze and fog enshroud the landscape, when the sun casts long shadows, or when fresh-fallen snow is still undisturbed.

The day's first rays of sunlight illuminate the still-dewy grass in a meadow of the Biedensand Nature Reserve on the Rhine (above).

A hoarfrost covers the landscape not far from the Neckarhausen ferry just before the sun breaks through to melt it (right-hand page).

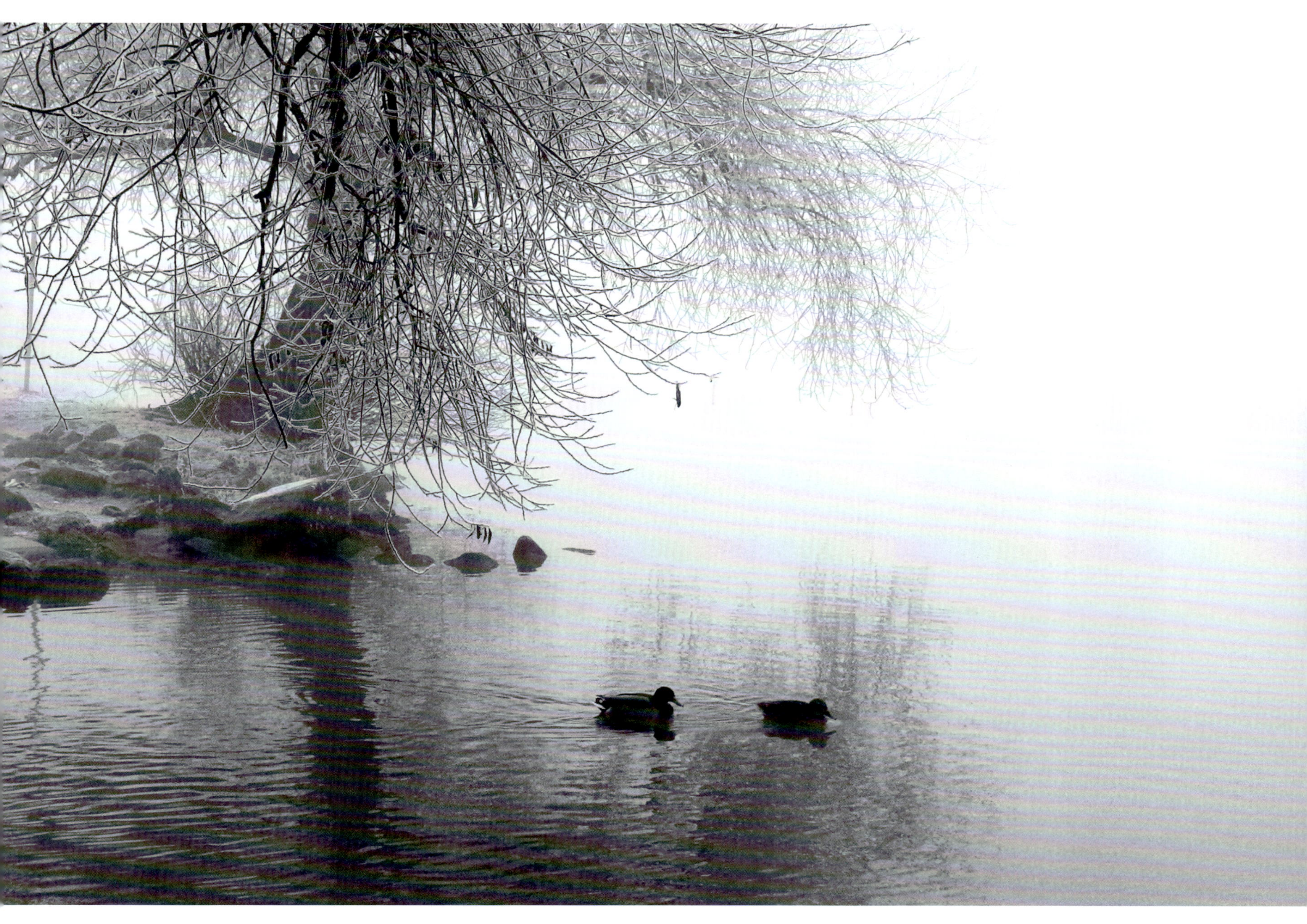

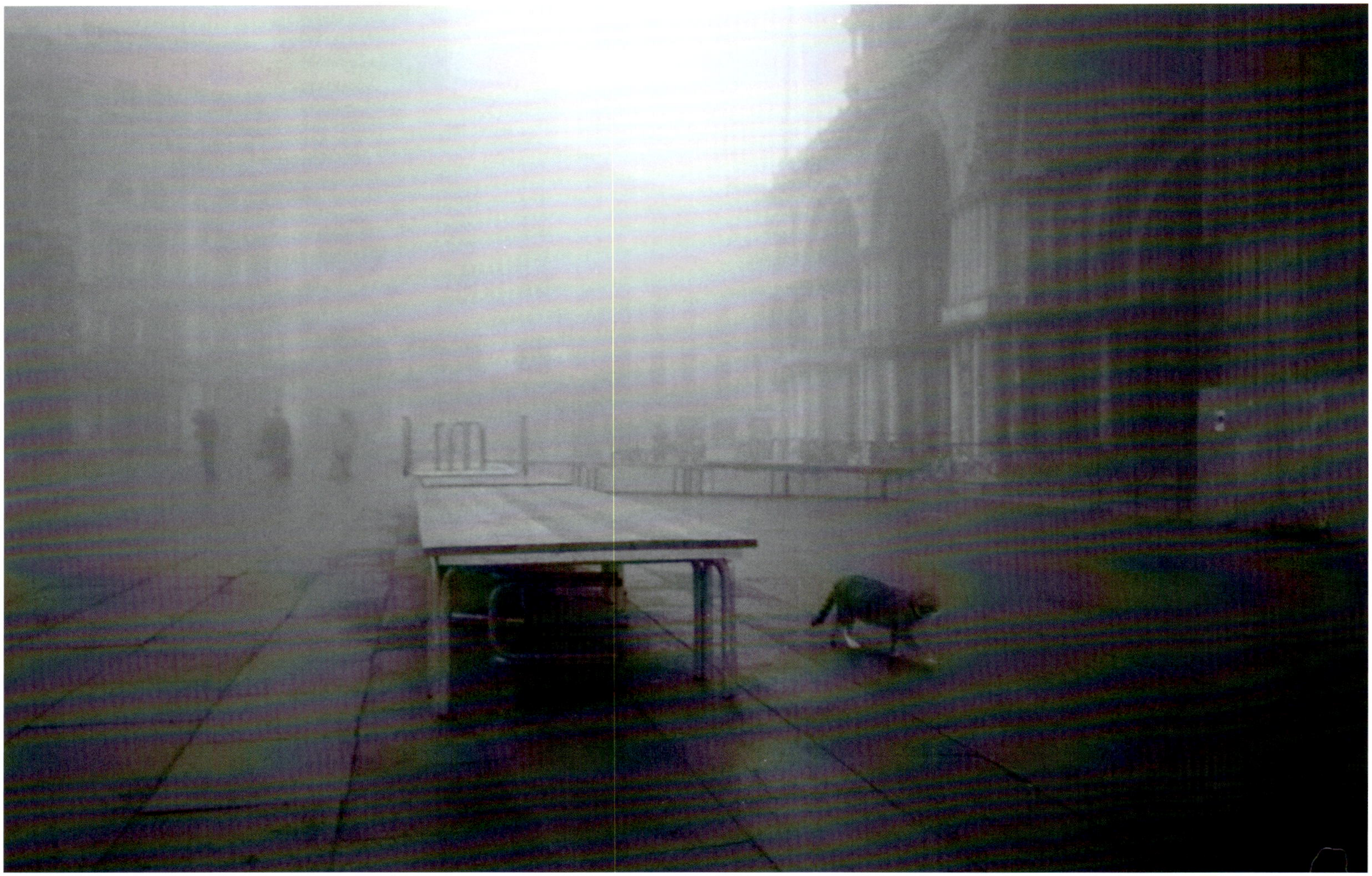

All Weather Poorly illuminated scenes pose no problem for the fast image sensors found in today's digital cameras. A steady hand also obviates the need for a tripod in many cases, which is how these early morning photographs were shot. The left photo was taken in St. Mark's Square in Venice and the right photo was taken n a skiing and sledding zone in the Kohlhof area near Heidelberg.

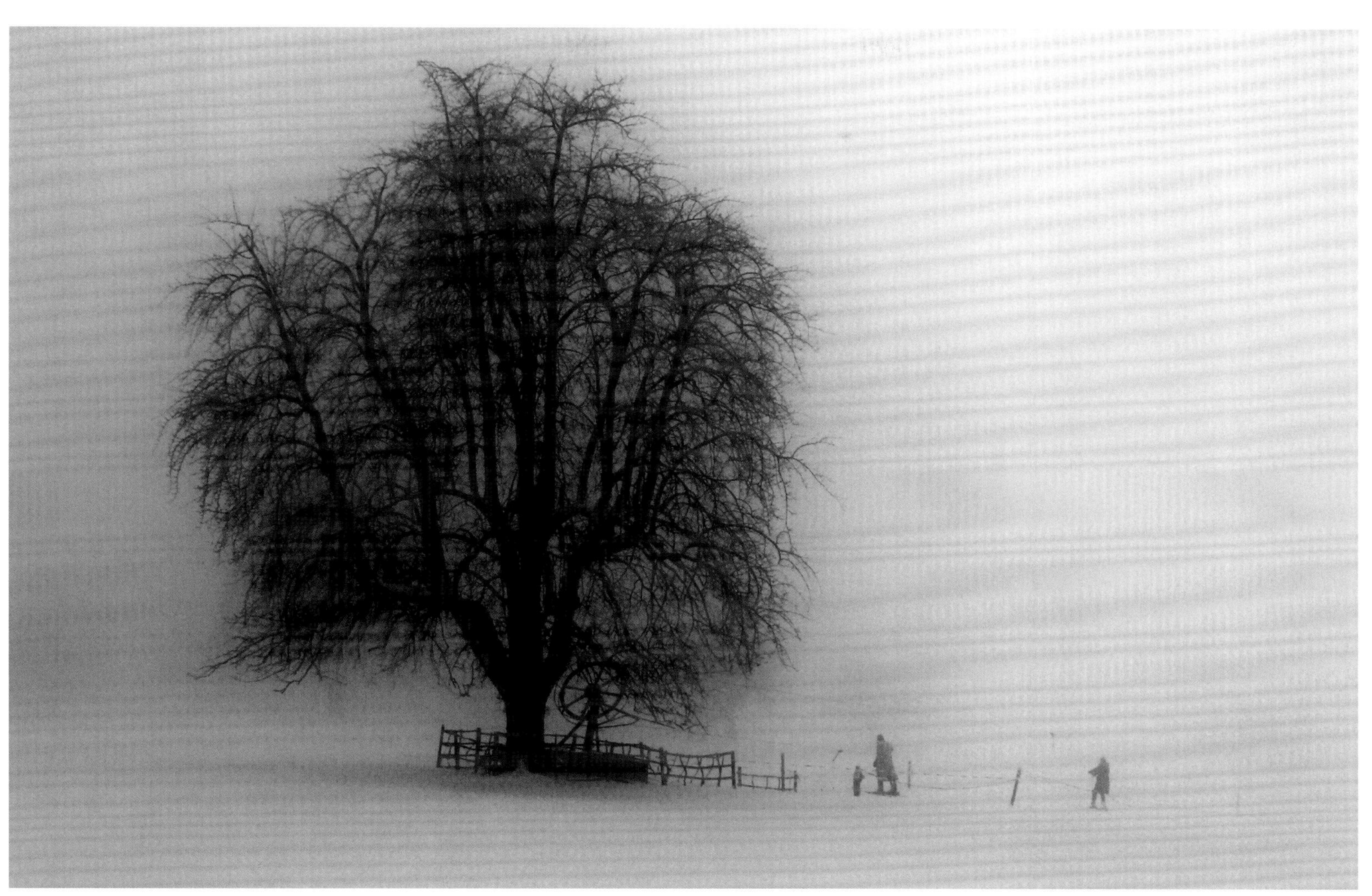

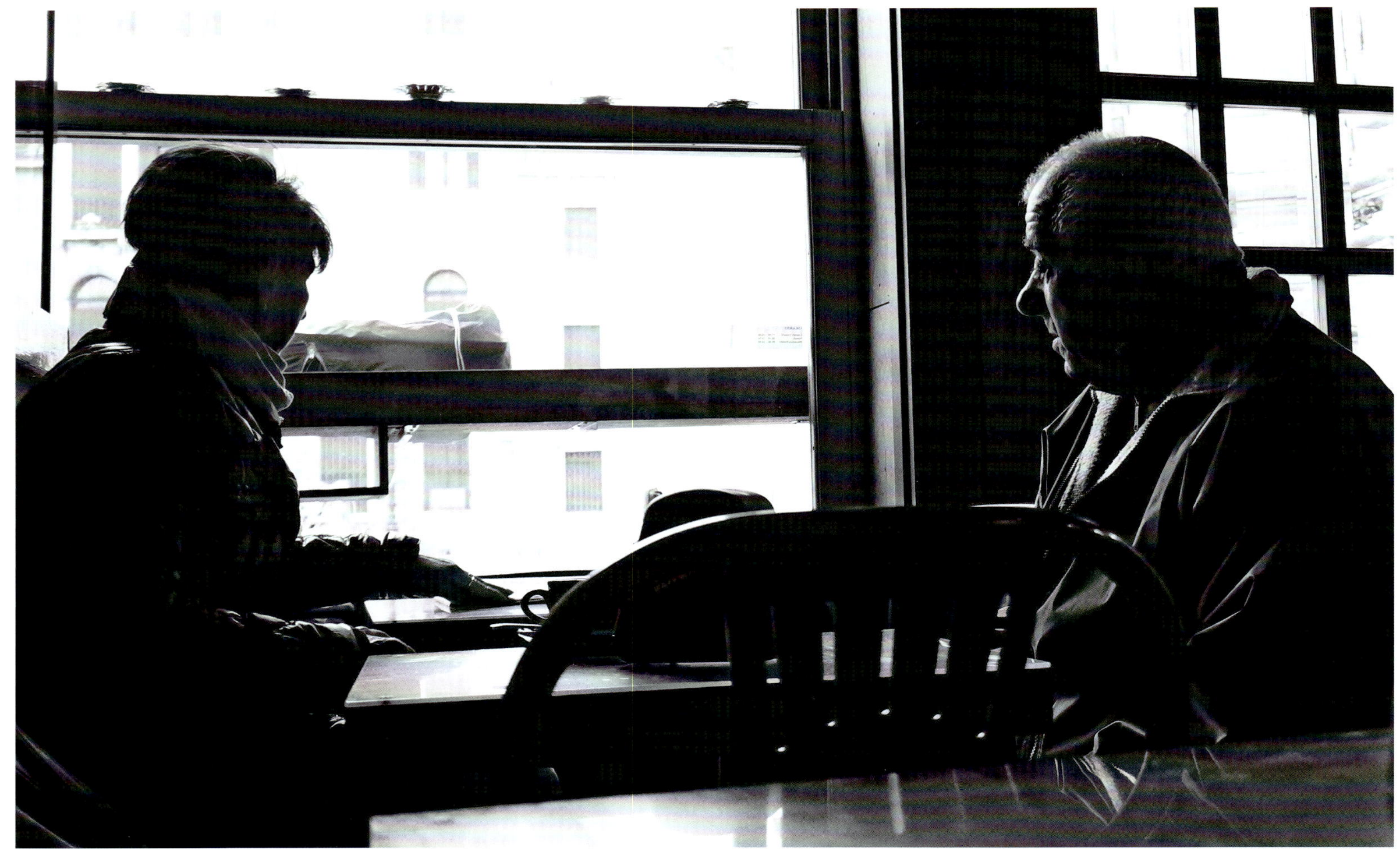

Multiplicity It is difficult to find a photograph that embodies one single principle of design. In almost every case, multiple methods are used simultaneously. Viewers perceive these compositional methods even if they are employed subtly. Neither of these two photos can be reduced to a single principle of design. The prevailing concept for the images is the couple sitting together, though each image begs a different interpretation. Light/dark contrasts, backlighting, formal structures and frameworks, diagonal movements, golden ratios, sequence, and various contrasts of shapes also contribute to the images' compositions. The photographs were taken at a bar in Venice (above) and in the King's Apartment at Kensington Palace in London (right-side page).

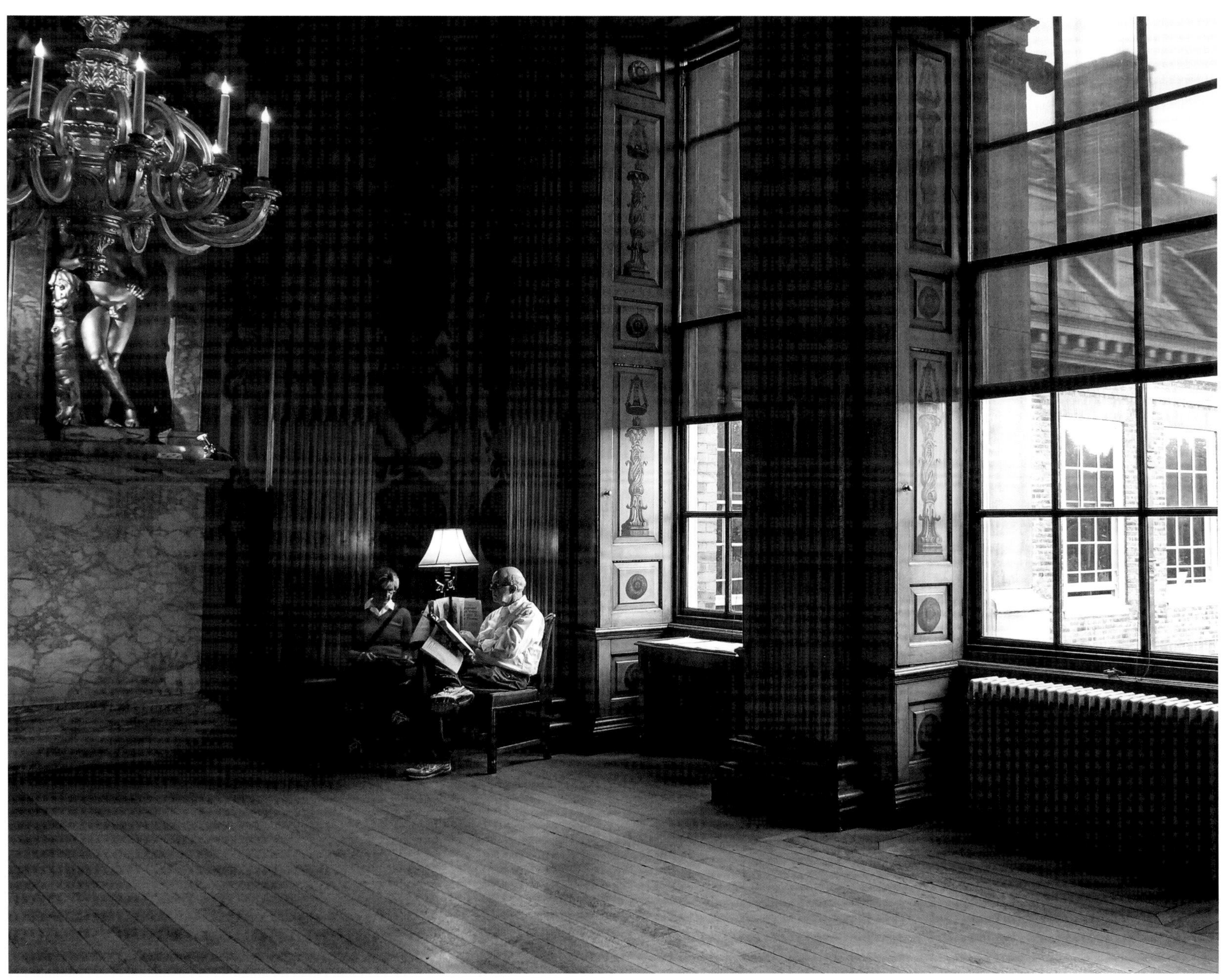

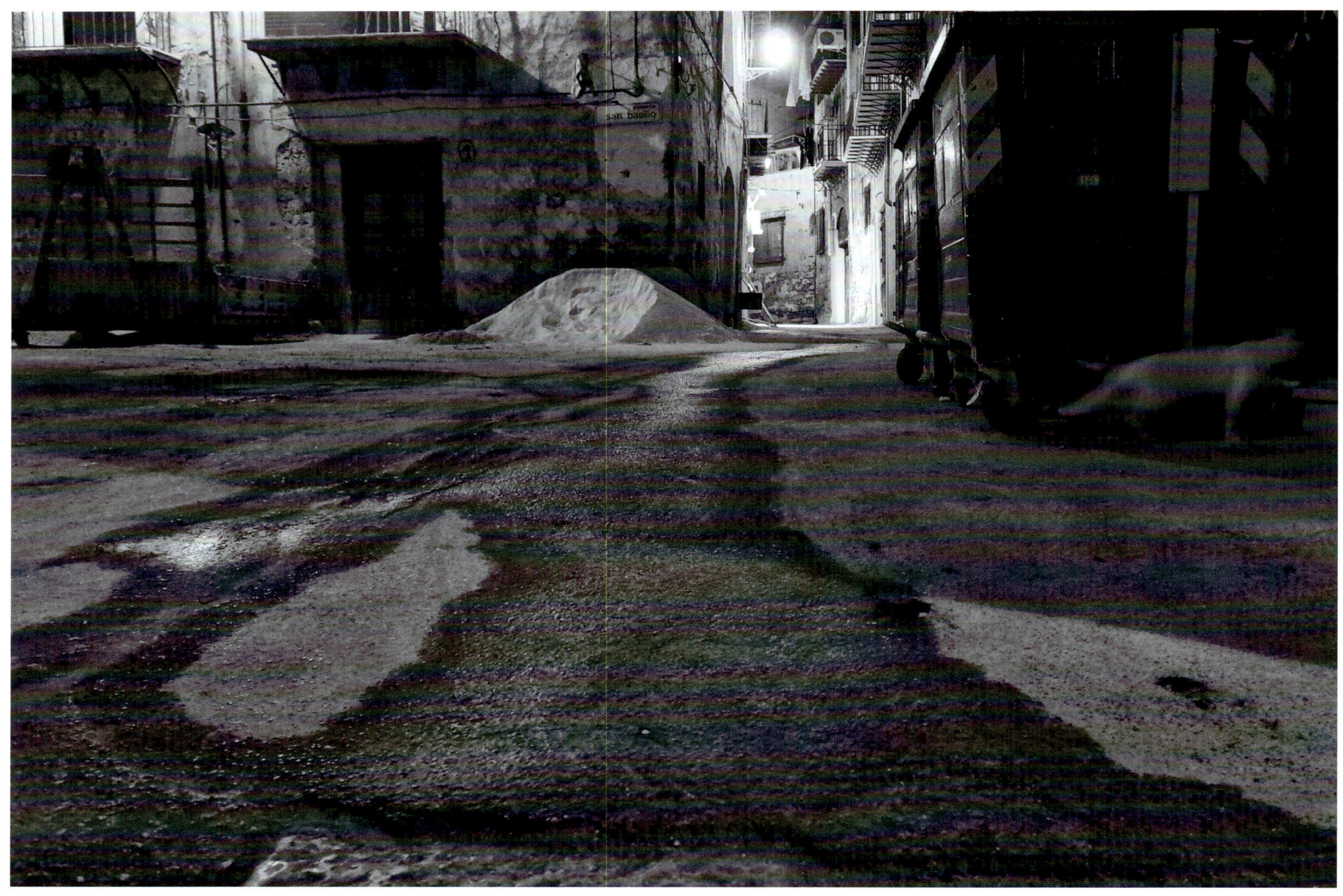

Nighthawks These photographs, taken in the Kalsa Quarter of Palermo (top) and in front of the famous Shakespeare and Company bookstore in Paris (right-hand page), show that motion blur in night exposures is not a problem. On the contrary, blur brings life into these scenes.

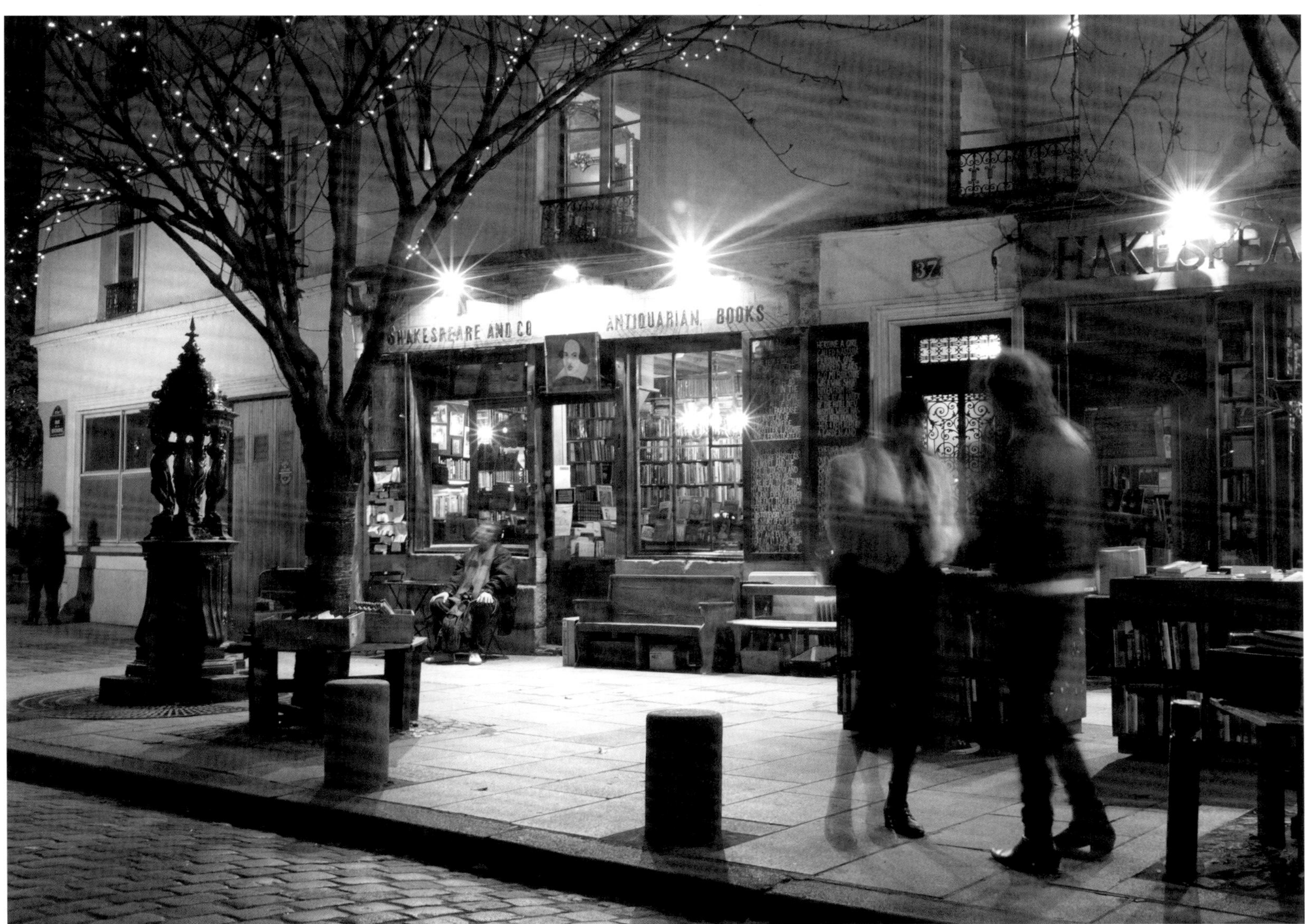
SHAKESPEARE AND CO
ANTIQUARIAN BOOKS
37

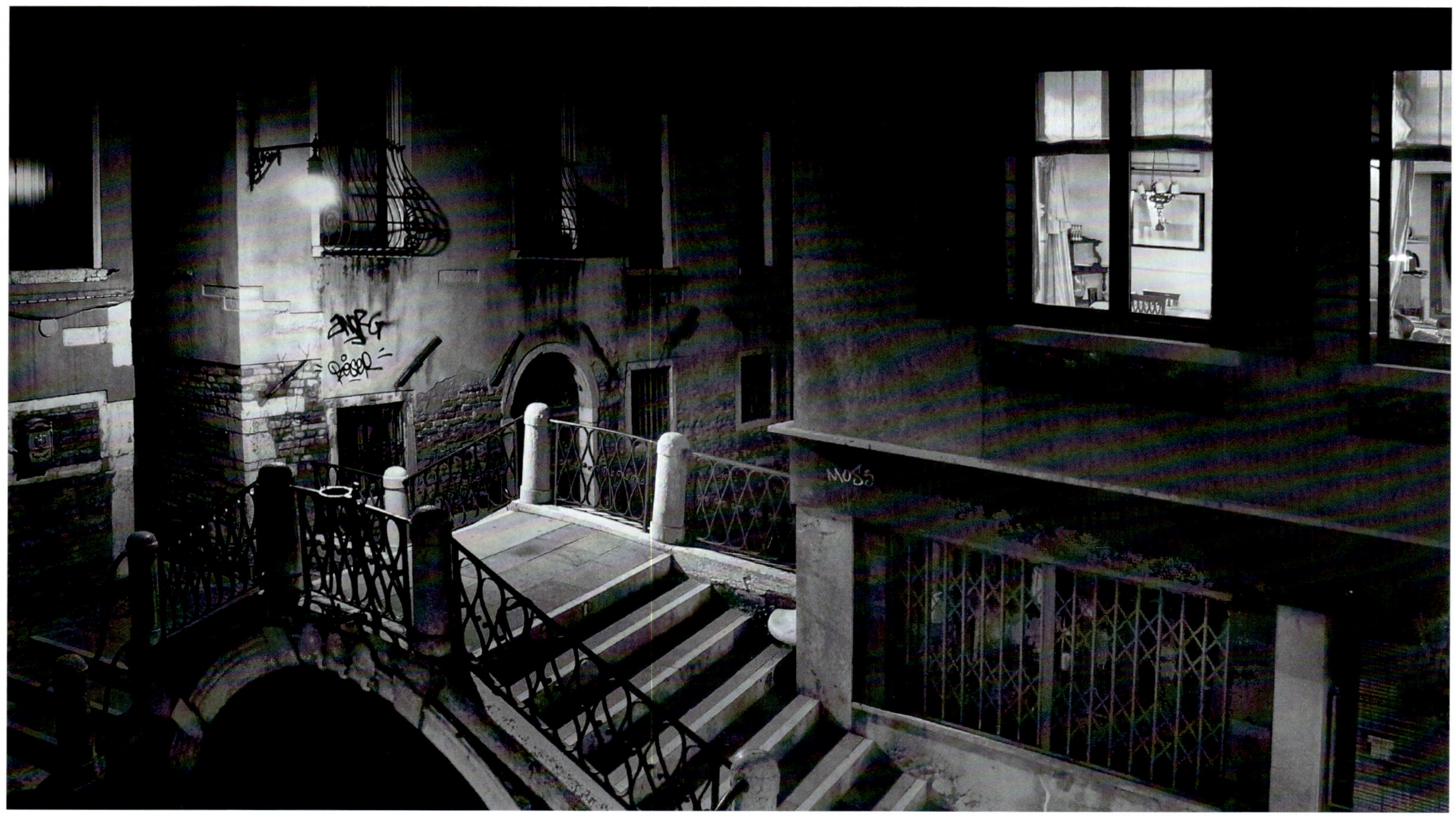

The Dark Side of Light Late night in Venice is a wonderful opportunity to experience the city without the distraction of daytime bustle—and an ideal time to shoot photographs. The sensors in today's digital cameras have no trouble with the poor lighting conditions during these hours. They bring certain details to light that one would not notice with the naked eye. These details are often not visible until the photographs have been viewed at full size on a computer monitor or have been edited. It's important to take several pictures of the same subject for this very reason: you should be able to pick from a pool of options to find an exemplar that is sharp and compositionally sound. I shot these midnight photographs of an olive tree on the island of Crete (page 140) and a snow-covered terrace at the Heidelberg Castle (page 141) nearly blind in the darkness.

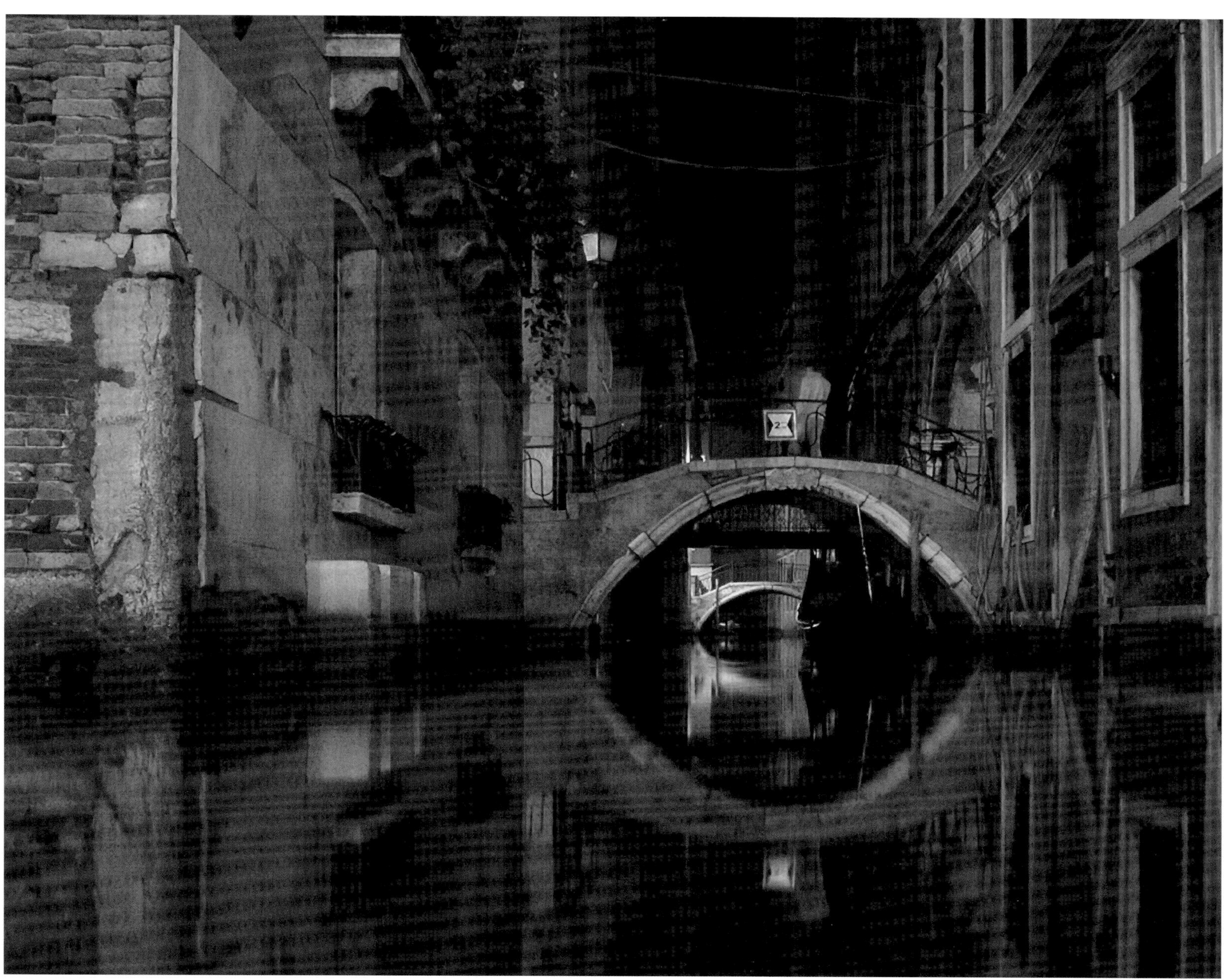

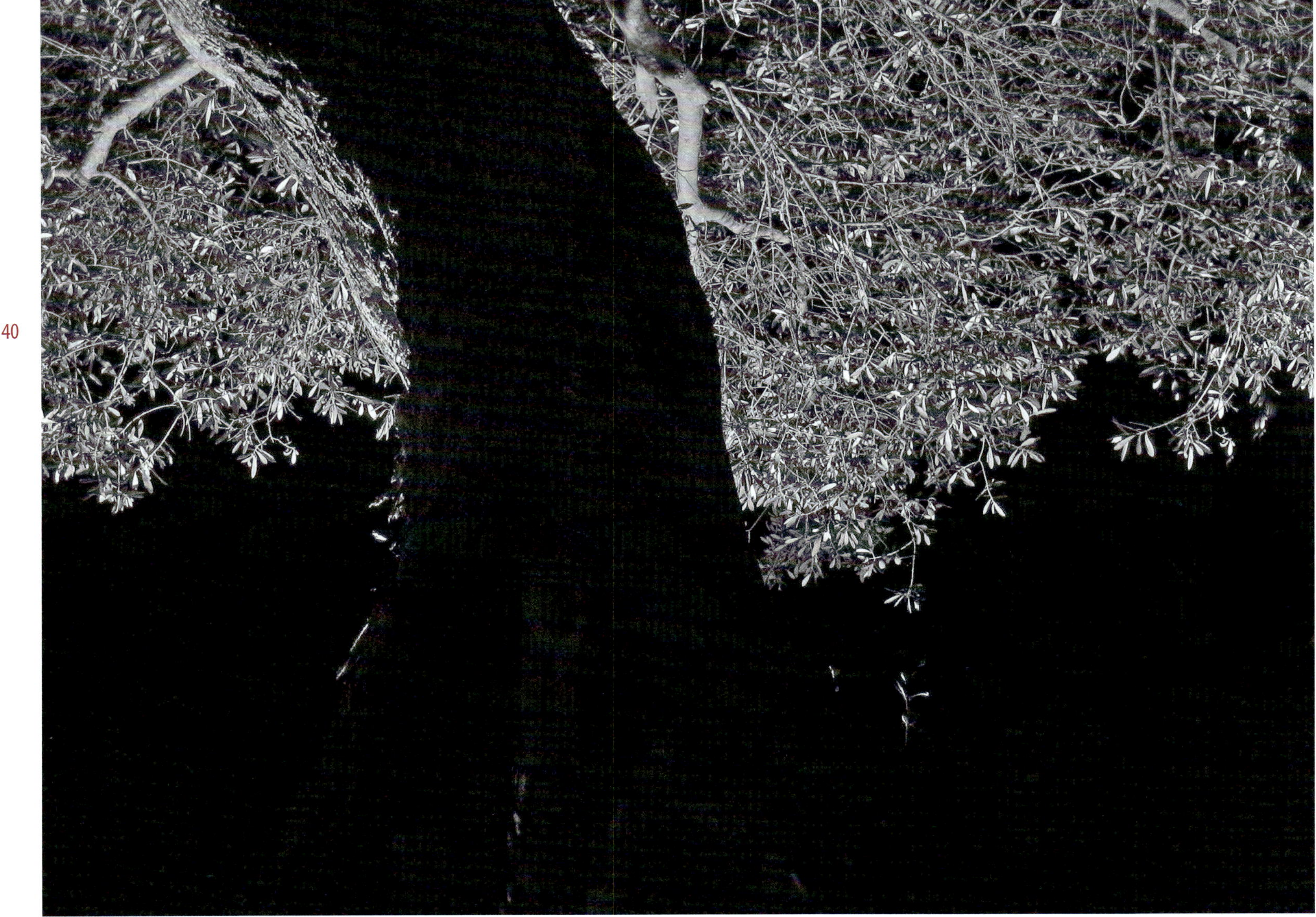

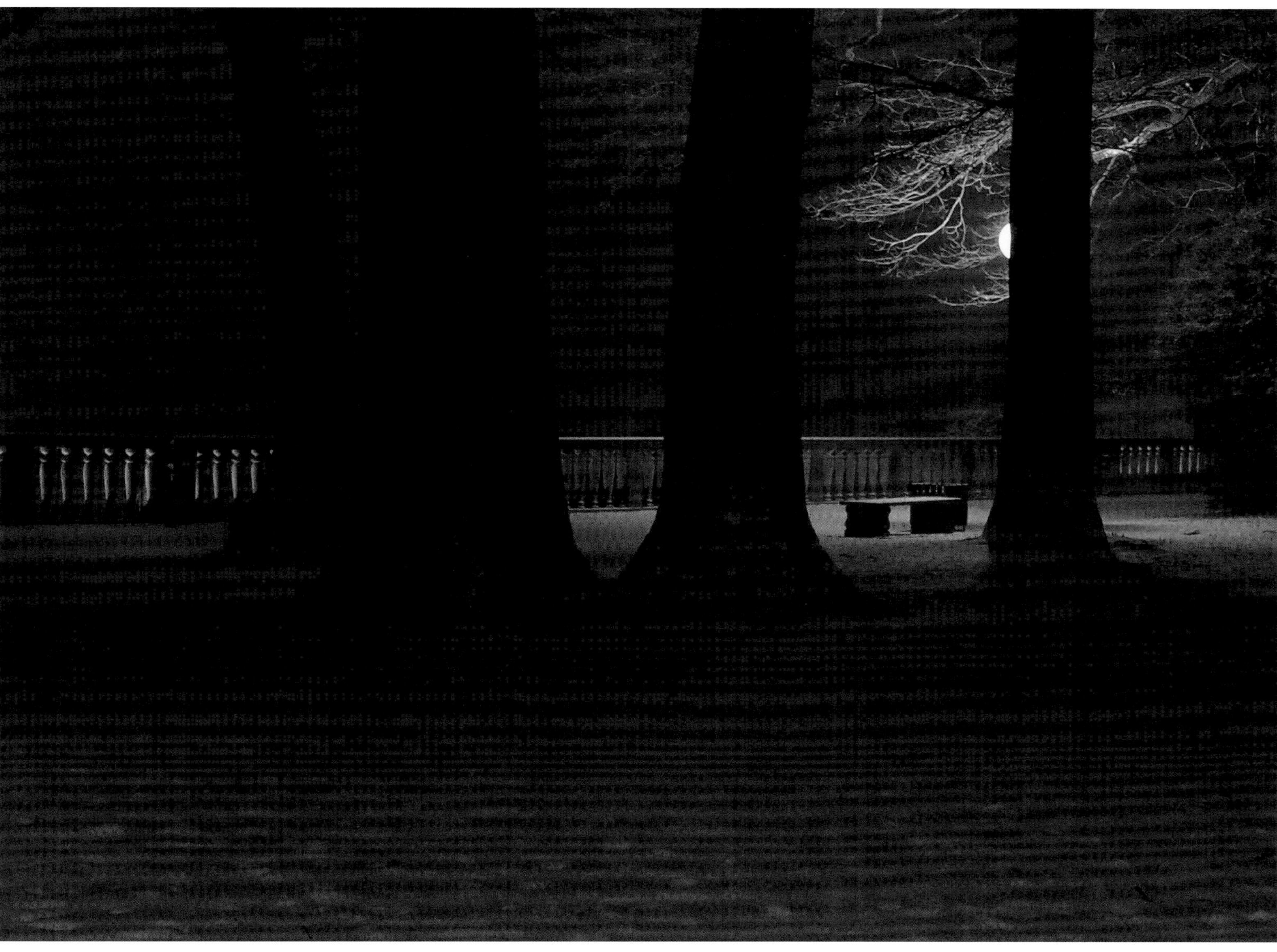

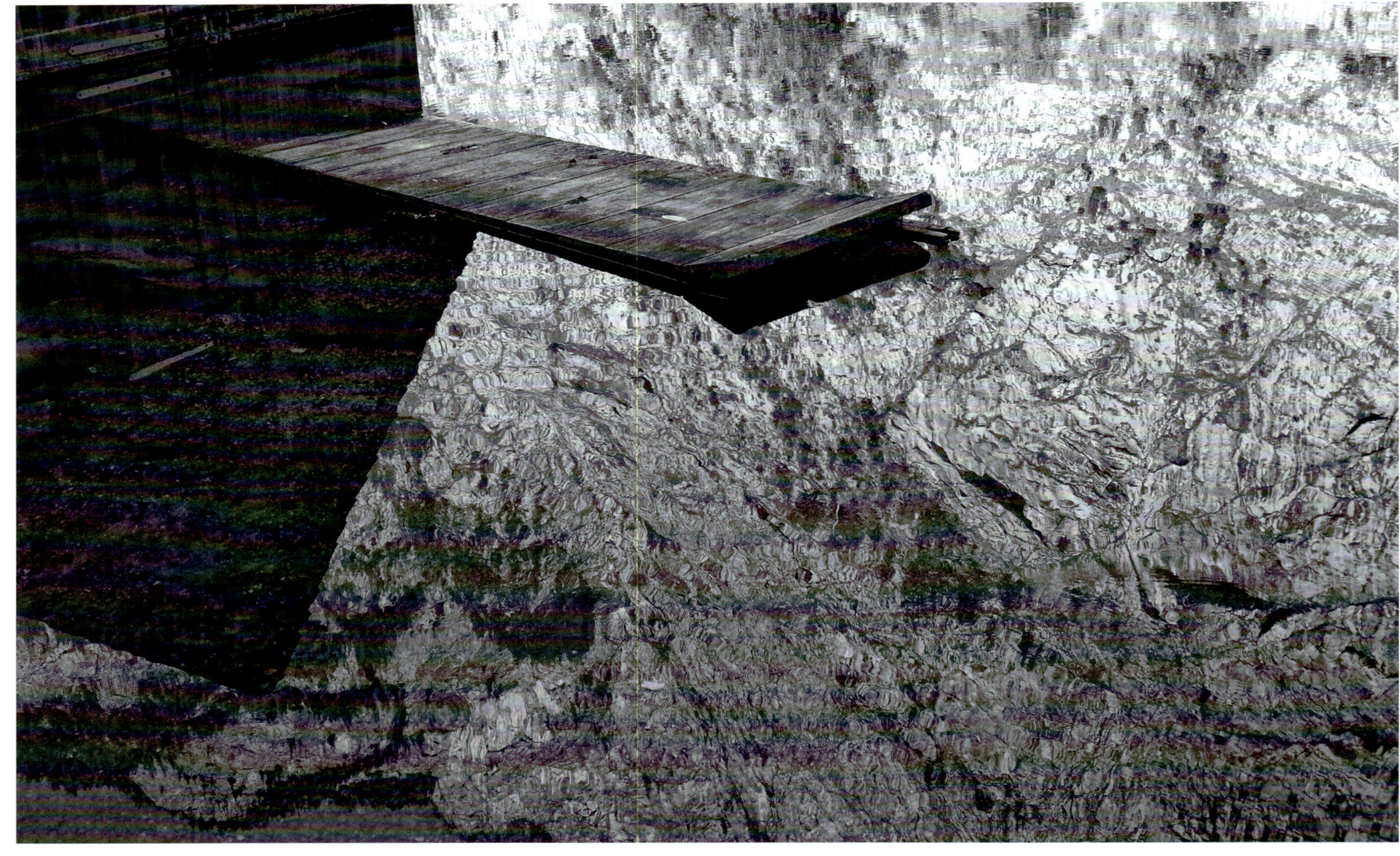

Reflections Due to the reflective quality of water, floating objects can make for particularly rich photographic subjects. This diagonal jetty (top) on the Obersee (near the Königsee) in Bavaria juts across the iridescent texture of the reflected rock wall, which seems to dive into the water.

In contrast, the silhouettes of the reflected leaves on the Lac de la Maix in the Vosges (right-hand page) have a more graphic or formal quality—they serve as a pleasant foil to the floating log that contributes a sense of depth to the photo. Other key compositional elements in the photo include diagonal lines, light-dark contrast, and a compression of visual elements.

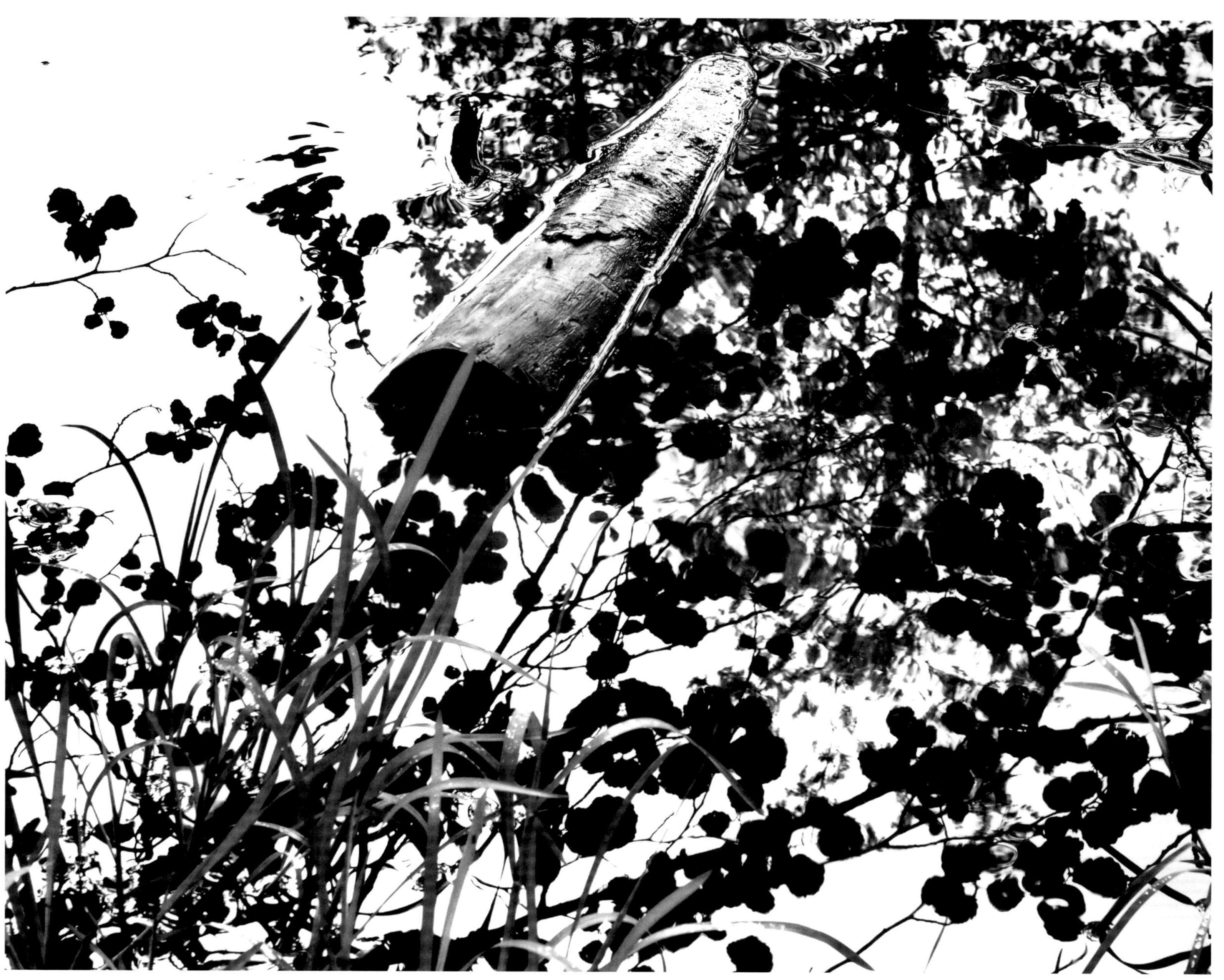

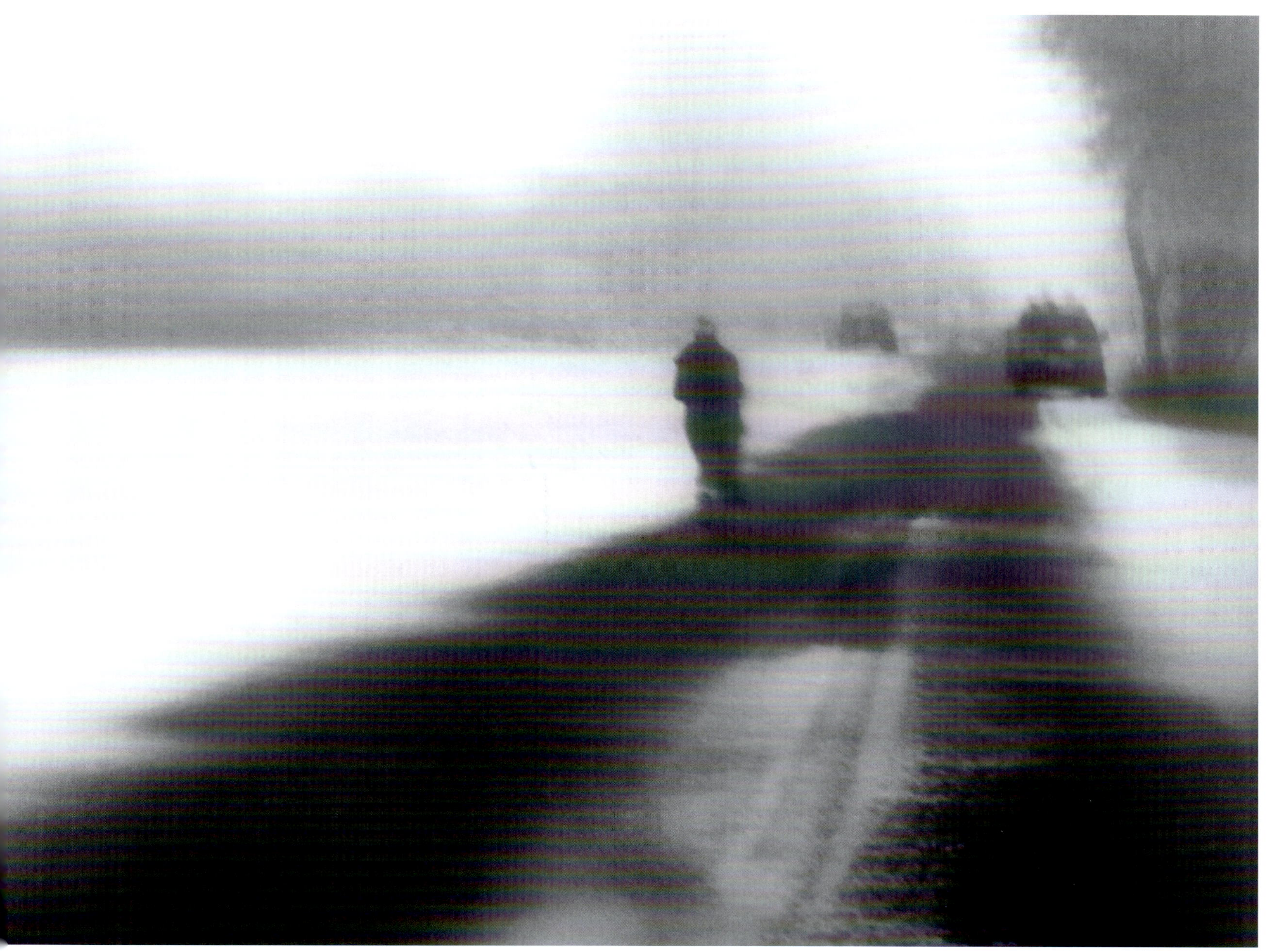

Chance and Intention Holding your camera loosely with an outstretched arm and snapping a photo arbitrarily sometimes produces really exciting results. This method is how I captured the photograph of the jogger (page 145). Within a collection of coincidental photos, there is often one that has real thematic and compositional merit. One need not equate this method with deliberate photographic composition.

It is not easy to create a photograph in Venice that does not resemble a photograph that has been taken many times before. Clichés can be avoided by skipping out on the usual tourist traps and heading off the beaten path with your camera—particularly early in the morning or late at night. Opting to shoot in black-and-white helps to eschew a familiar colorfulness and also tends to suit the character of this extraordinary city (left).

These nighttime photos from Venice were not taken in such a haphazard manner. The rocking gondolas at the Punta della Dogana on Dorsoduro were photographed on a stormy night as the flood waters pushed into the lagoon (right-hand page).

Tip *Take a chance on chance. Release the shutter and see what happens without giving any thought to your camera's settings. And do not delete these spontaneous photos from your memory card without examining them on your computer monitor. You may discover something extraordinary.*

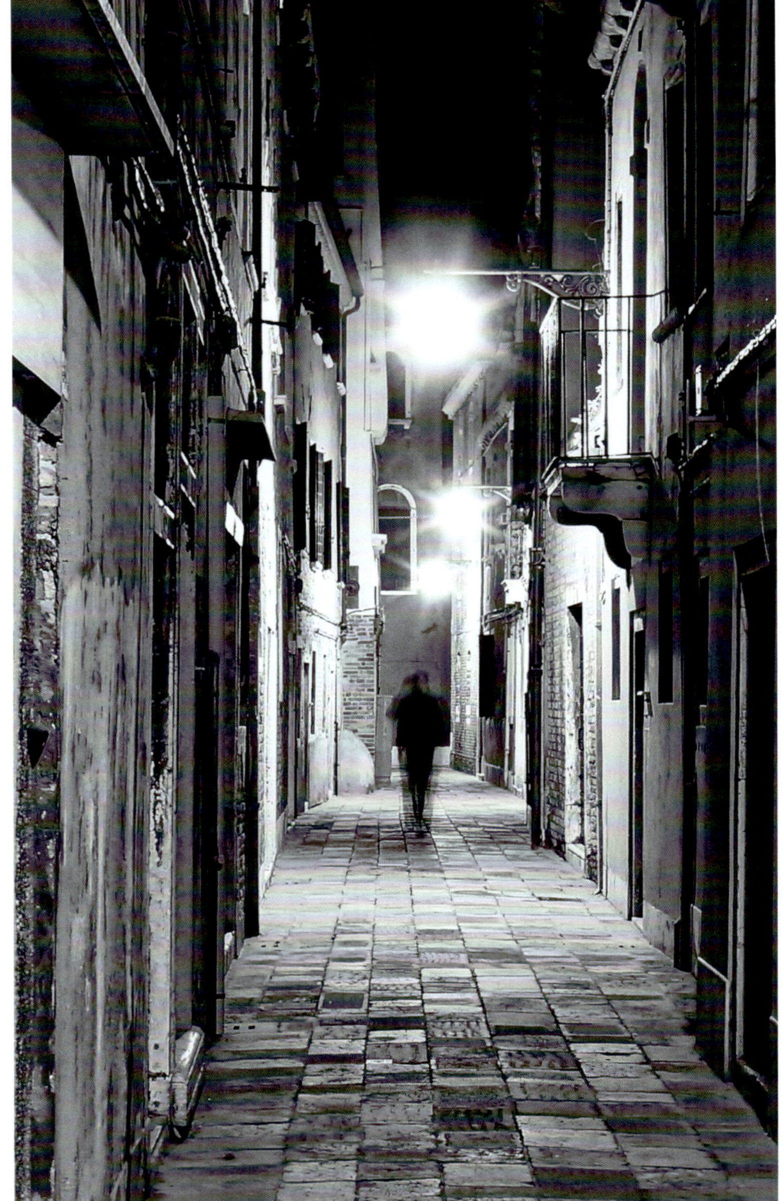

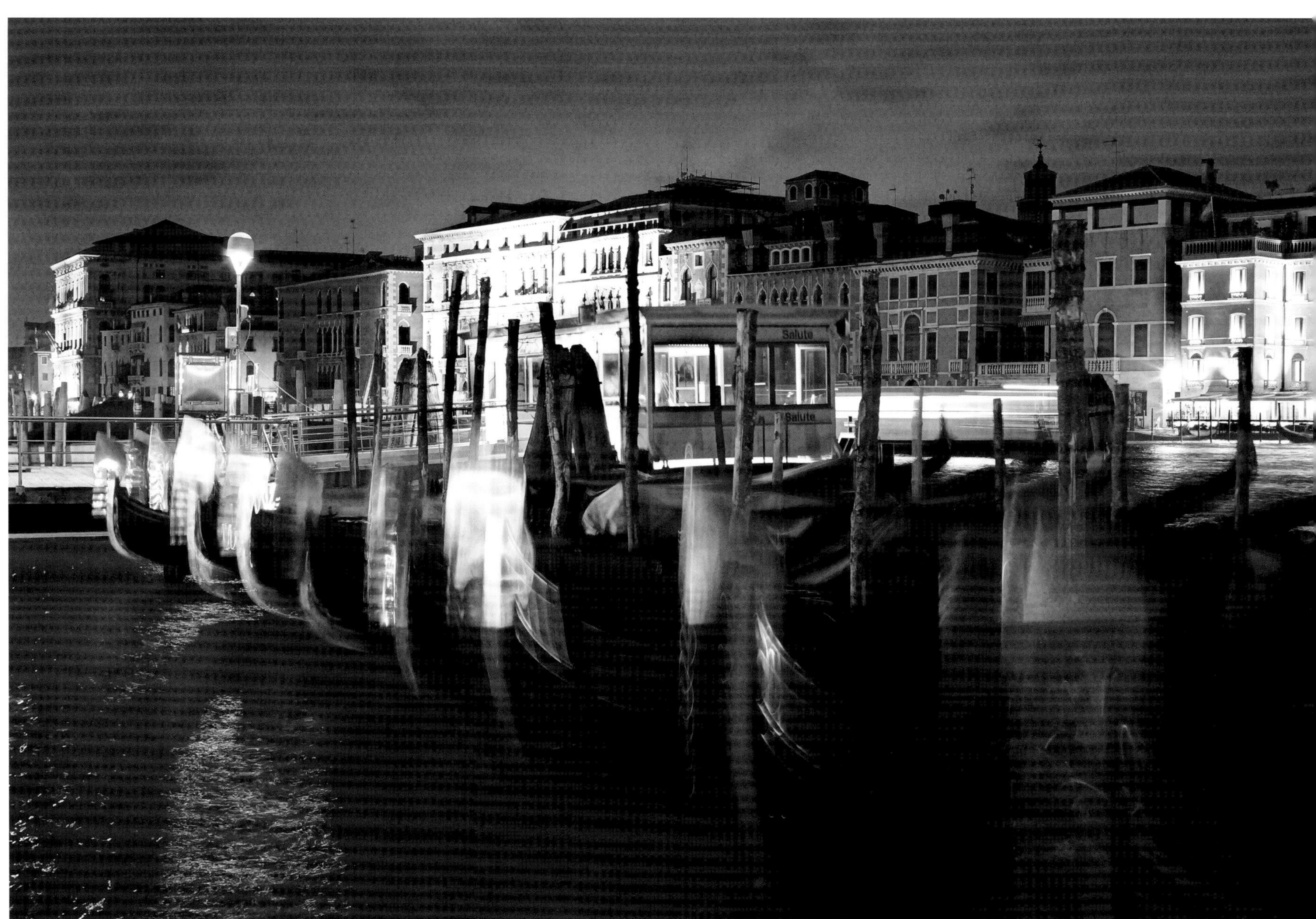
Salute
Salute

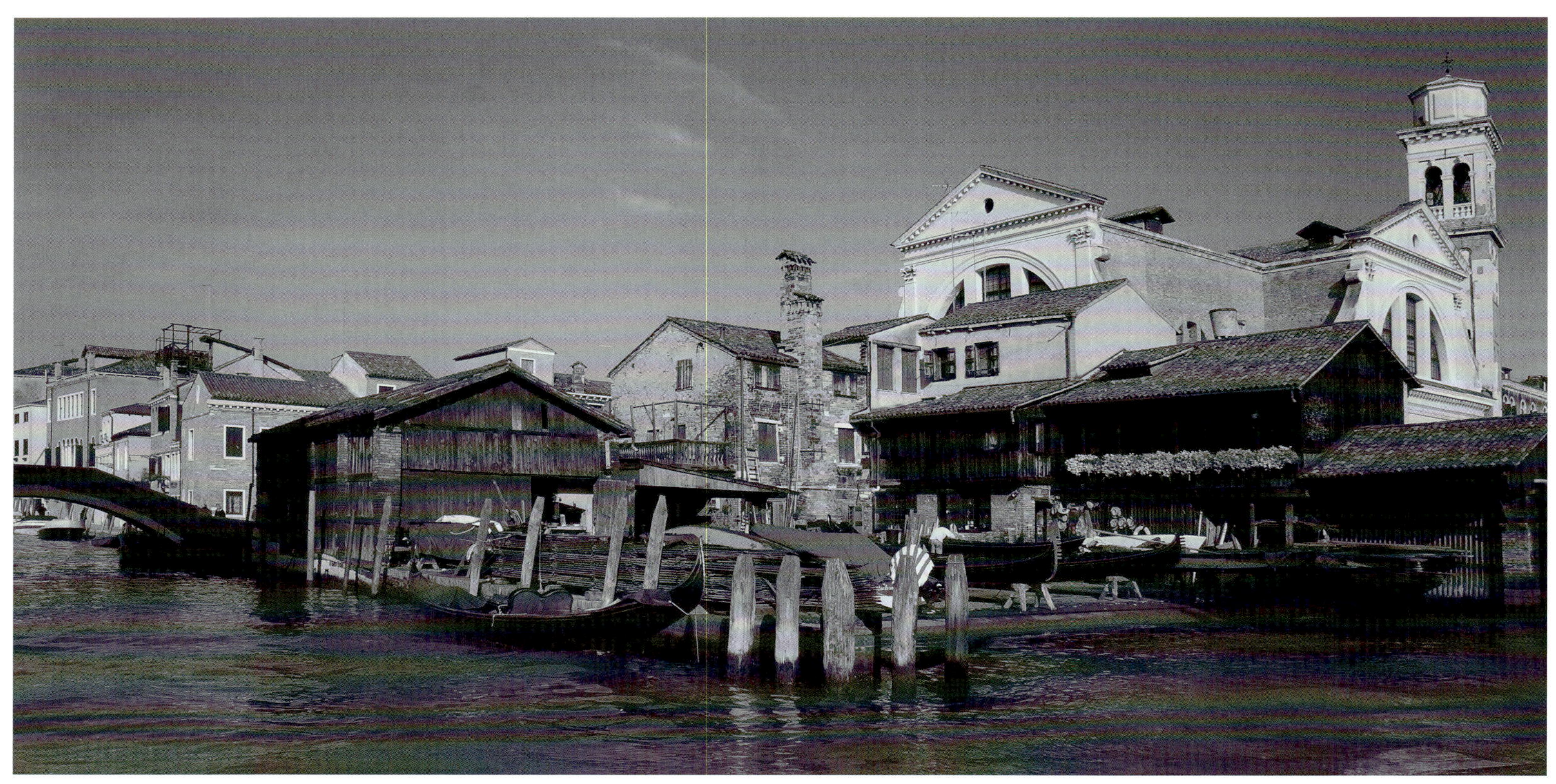

Tip *Do not always wait until distracting elements have moved out of your way. Motion blur can provide a useful dimension to the content and appearance of an image. Use your camera's burst mode for a greater likelihood of success.*

Stillness and Movement The photo of the gondola dock at Rio Trovaso (top) could almost pass for a historical photograph; there are no aspects of the photograph that define it in any particular era. In contrast, the Venetian fire-boat racing by the exact same location (right-hand page) is an object that places the photograph in a particular time. A slow shutter speed produced the obvious motion blur, which adds another layer to the image. The photo suggests how the age-old sites of the city are constantly juxtaposed with the restless bustle of the modern world. Here, content and style form a perfect unity.

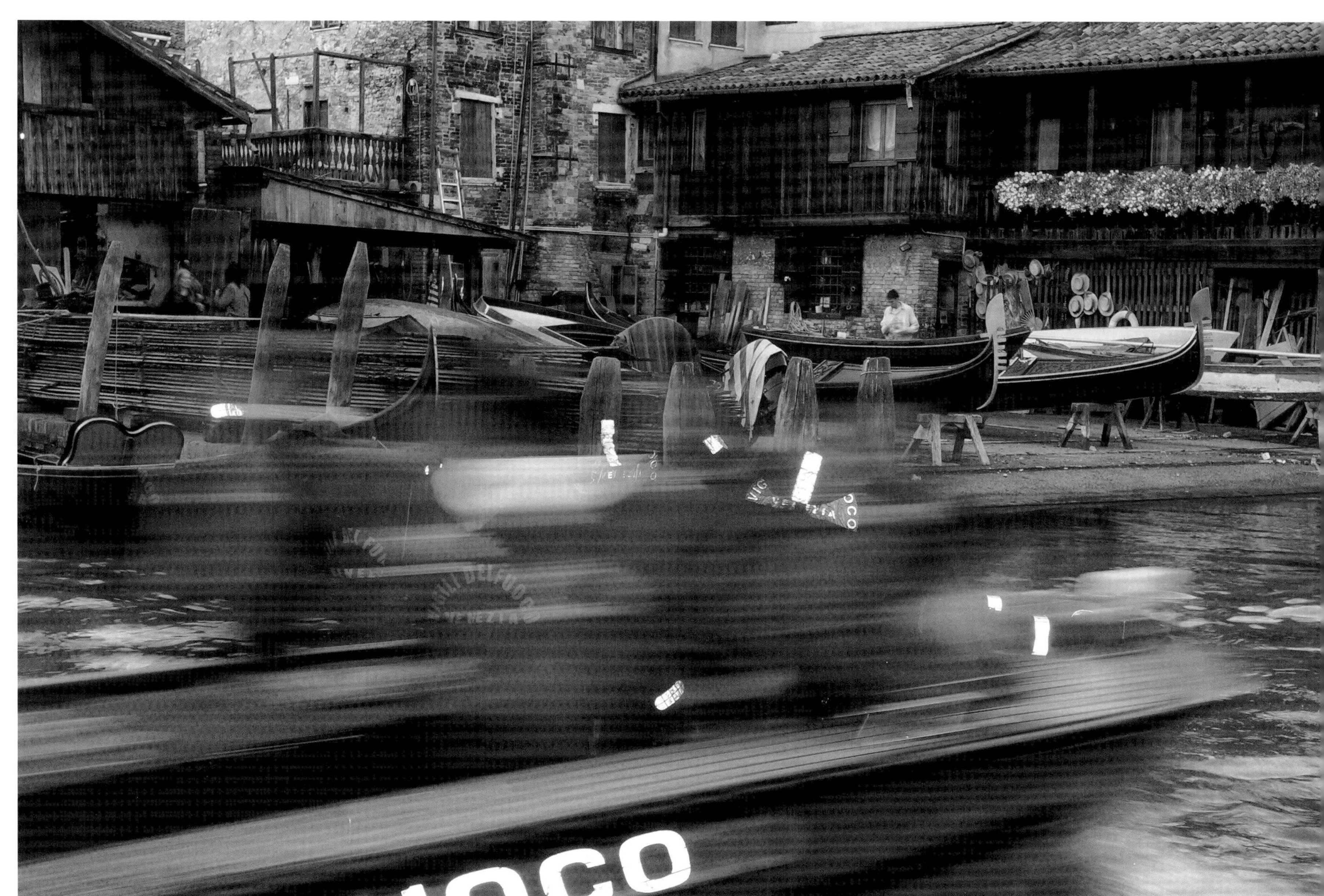
OCO

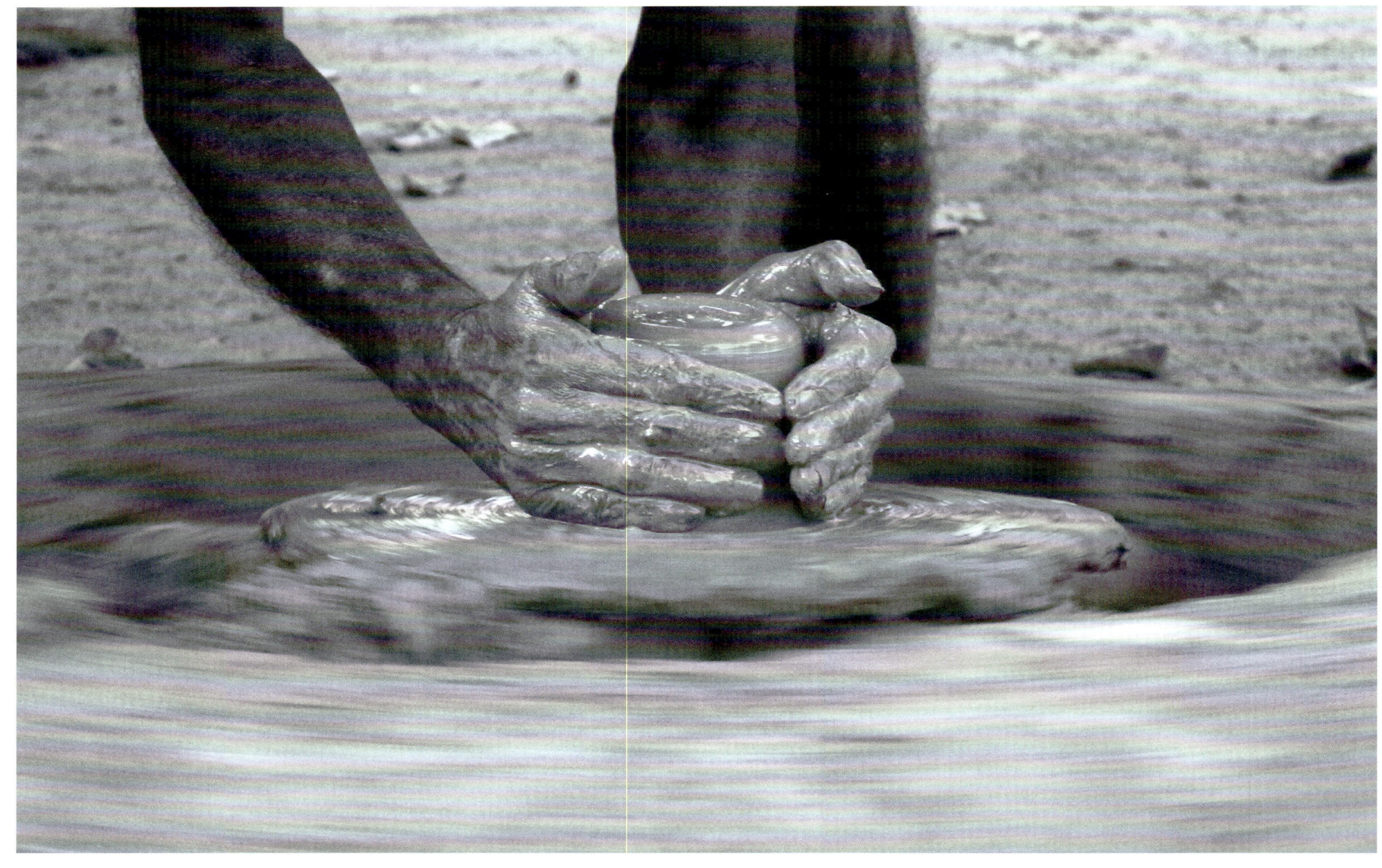

Static and Dynamic A razor-sharp photo is not perfect because of its sharpness any more than a blurry photo is creative art just on account of its distortion. In other words, motion blur is an excellent design tool—when it supports the content of the image. The photo of the potter is a particularly good example. Steady hands are required to shape vessels on the potter's wheel: this is how the quickly rotating clumps of clay end up being balanced. The blurring of the potter's wheel in this image makes all the sense in the world. The blur in the picture of the waiting room at the train station in Munich (right-hand page) visually conveys the ceaseless agitation of this locale, with the few people standing still providing a telling contrast.

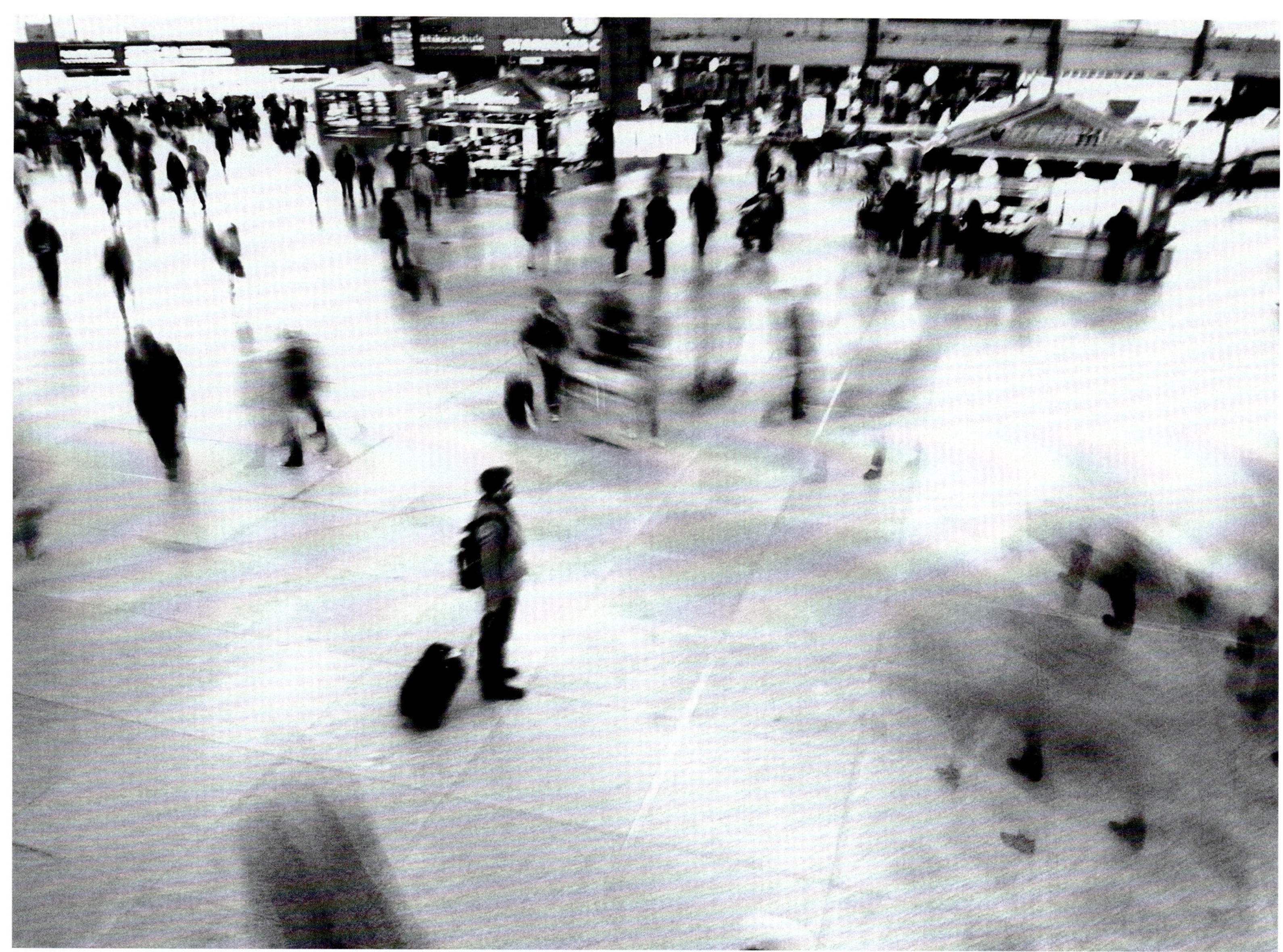

Options The course for the bicycling portion of the Heidelberg triathlon crosses the Old Bridge. These two pictures reveal divergent methods of capturing the same subject. The first option (left) reveals a cyclist who appears relatively sharp in the image. In contrast, his background, including the boy watching the race, falls into blur. This effect arises from panning the camera at approximately the same velocity as the cyclist as he races past. The second option (right-hand page) features a sharp background and a cyclist who appears as a smudge of blur.

The left picture makes the main subject look as though he has been glued to the cobblestones, whereas the right photo tells the story of the race much more dramatically. The right photo also has more to say: the clapping man facing the racers at the edge of the image represents the spectators of the race—and his own racing bike provides clues about the setting of the image. There are various compositional techniques at work in each photo. The truncated cyclists suggest that the figures in both images are speeding into the picture. The bridge railings divide the image areas into a pleasant 2:3 relationship. The boy and the triathlete are positioned in relation to each other, as are the blurred racer and the spectator. While the boy and the cyclist in the left image are facing each other, the cyclist and the spectator in the right image are facing away from each other; however, each pair exemplifies an expression of movement in opposing directions. As on the previous pages, these photos are testaments to the goal of the photographer and the benefits of aligning the content of an image with its composition.

Tip *Many cameras offer various exposure modes designed to suit specific and common situations such as quickly moving objects (e.g., sports, children, etc.). The manual exposure mode (M) allows you to define the aperture and shutter speed yourself, enabling you to invite blur into your images by choosing a long exposure time.*

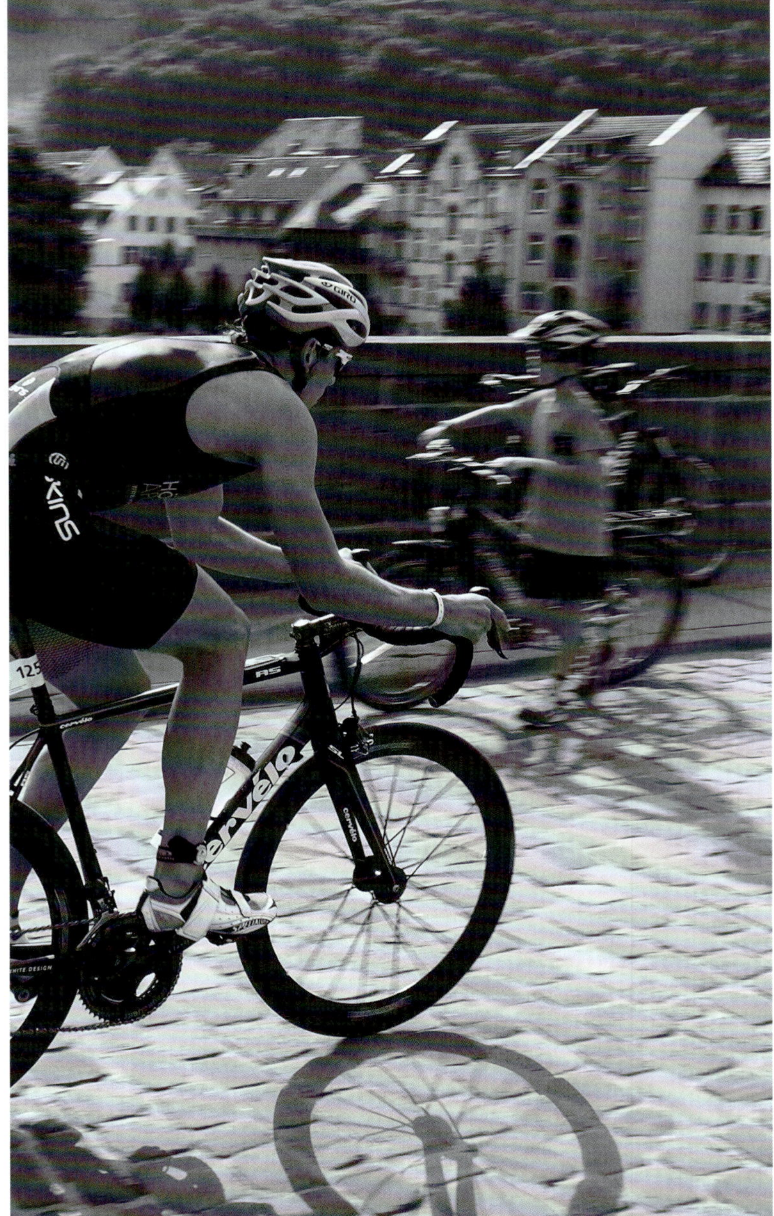

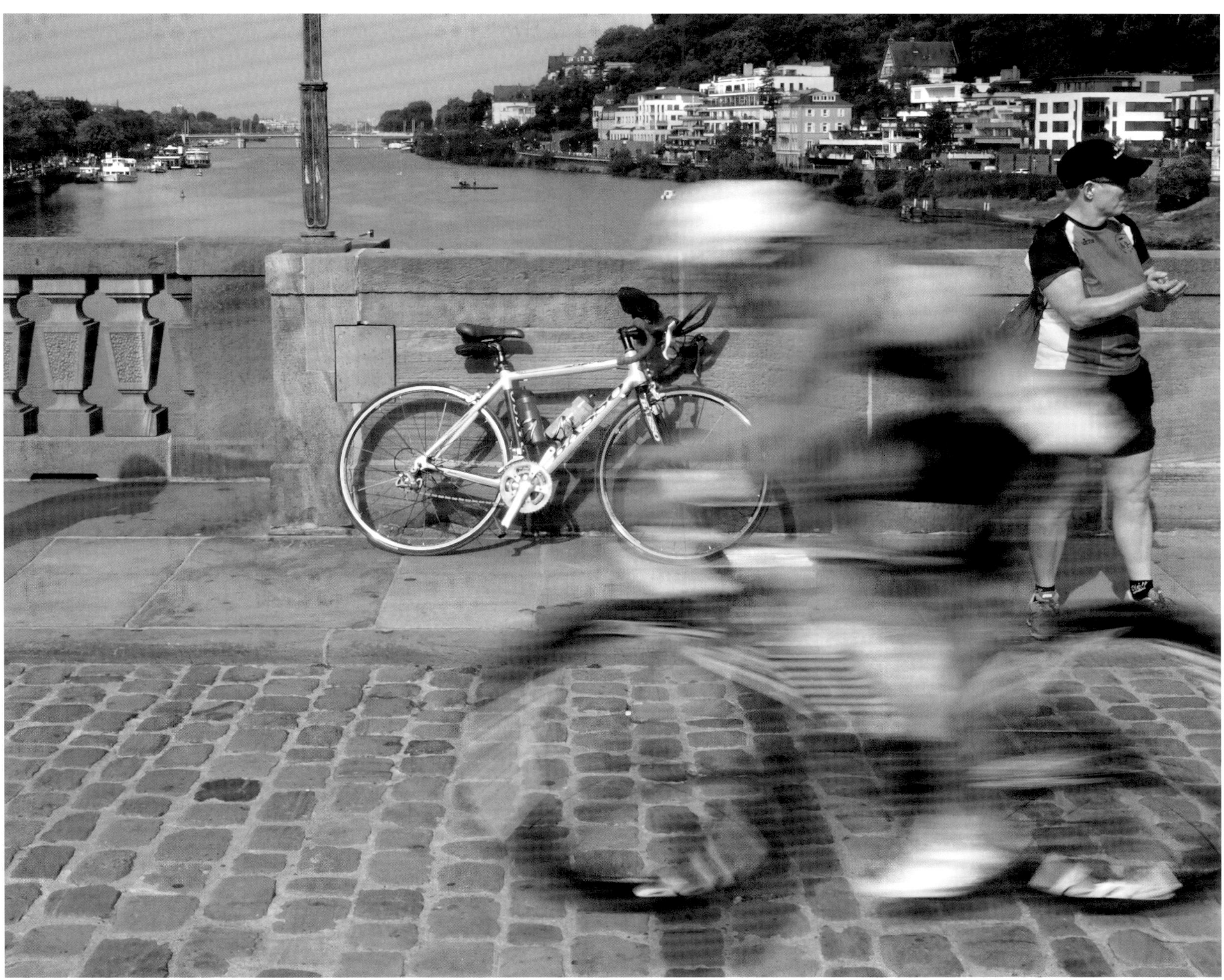

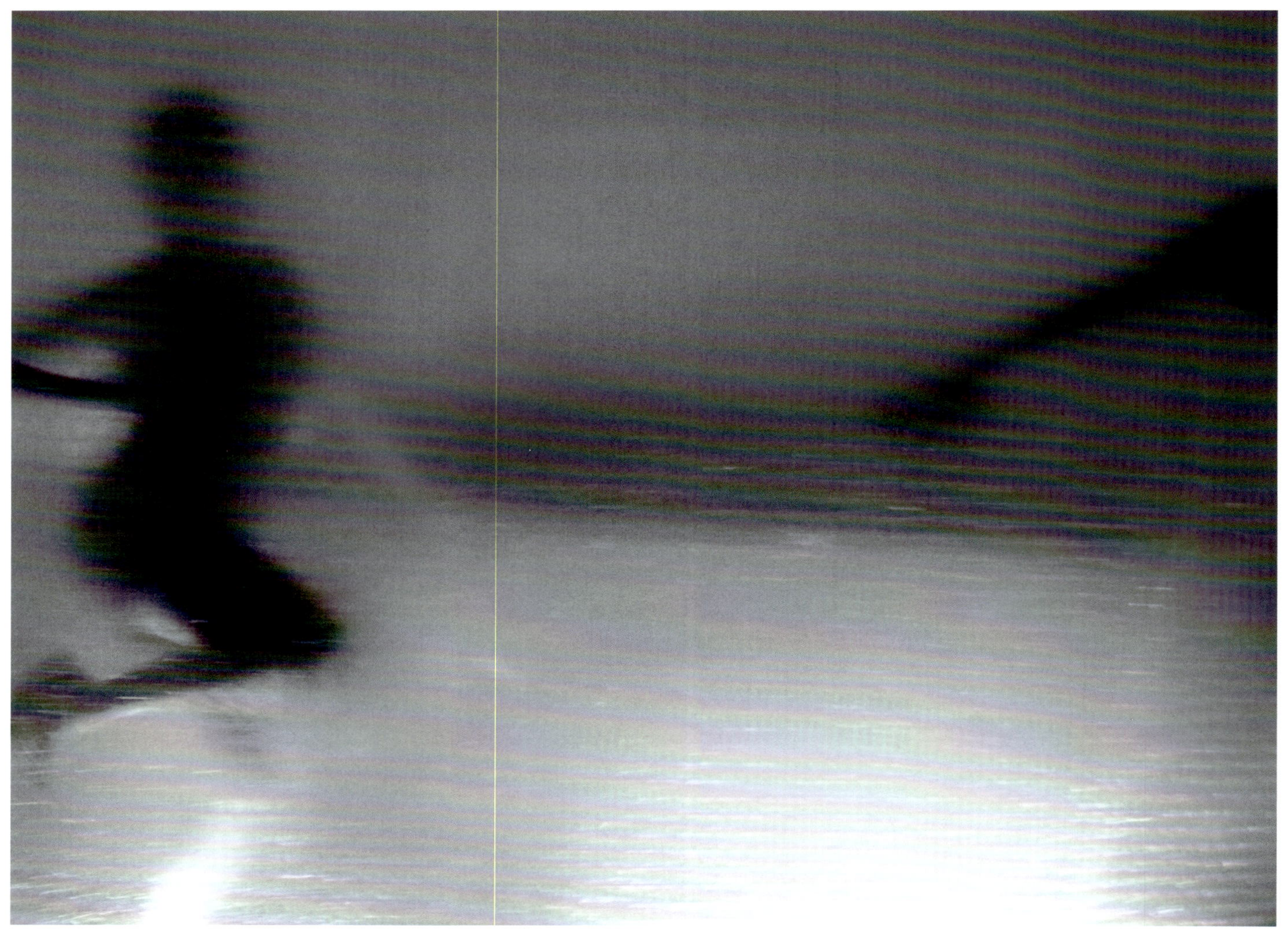

Experiments The left photo is of a performance at the Altes Hallenbad in Heidelberg, and the right photo is of a glass wall in the café at the Tate Gallery of Modern Art in London. The appeal of these photographs is not only due to the blurry effects and the partially transparent materials. The composition, the sense of entering and exiting the image area, the truncations, and the alignment of the visual elements also contribute to their overall effect.

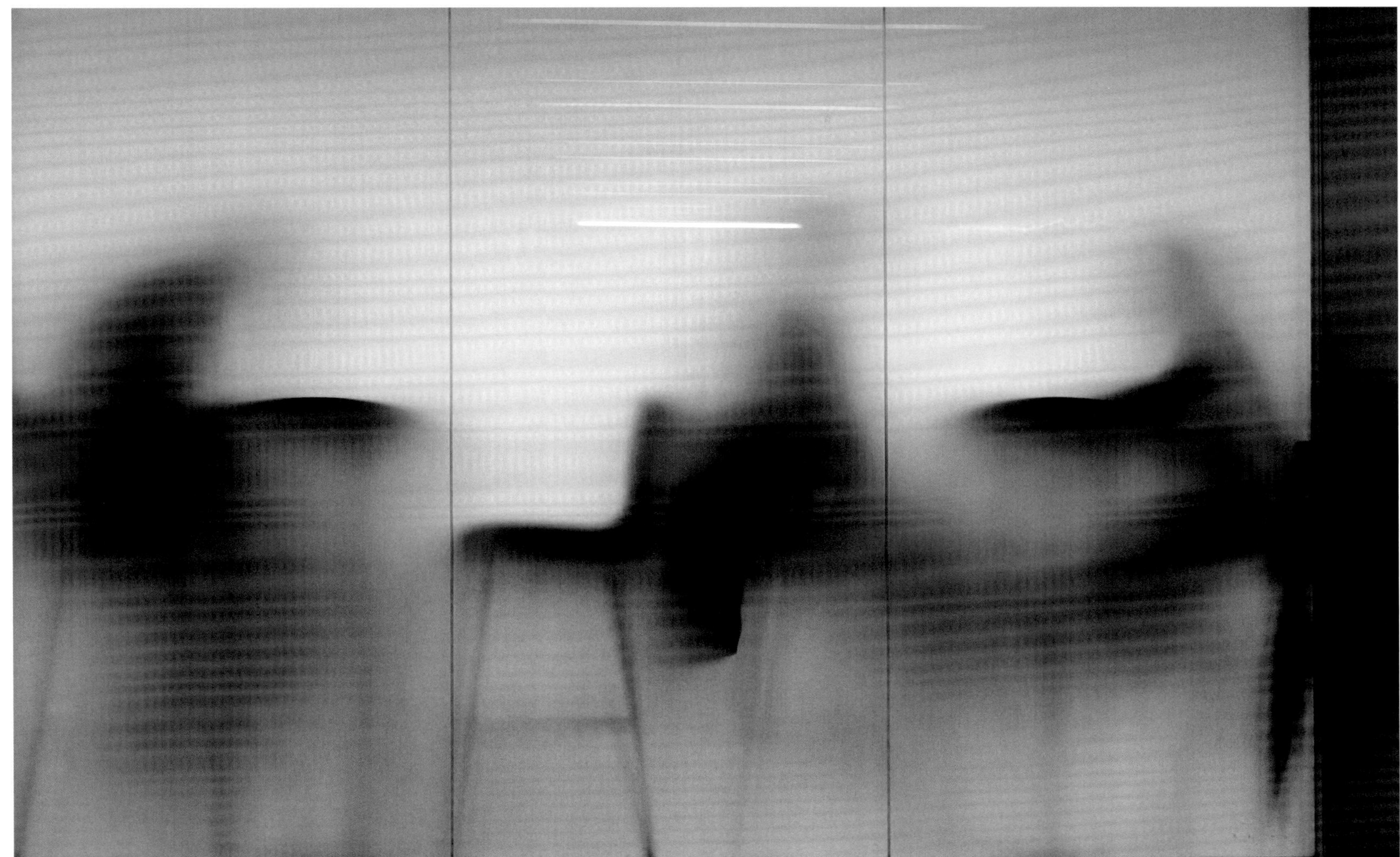

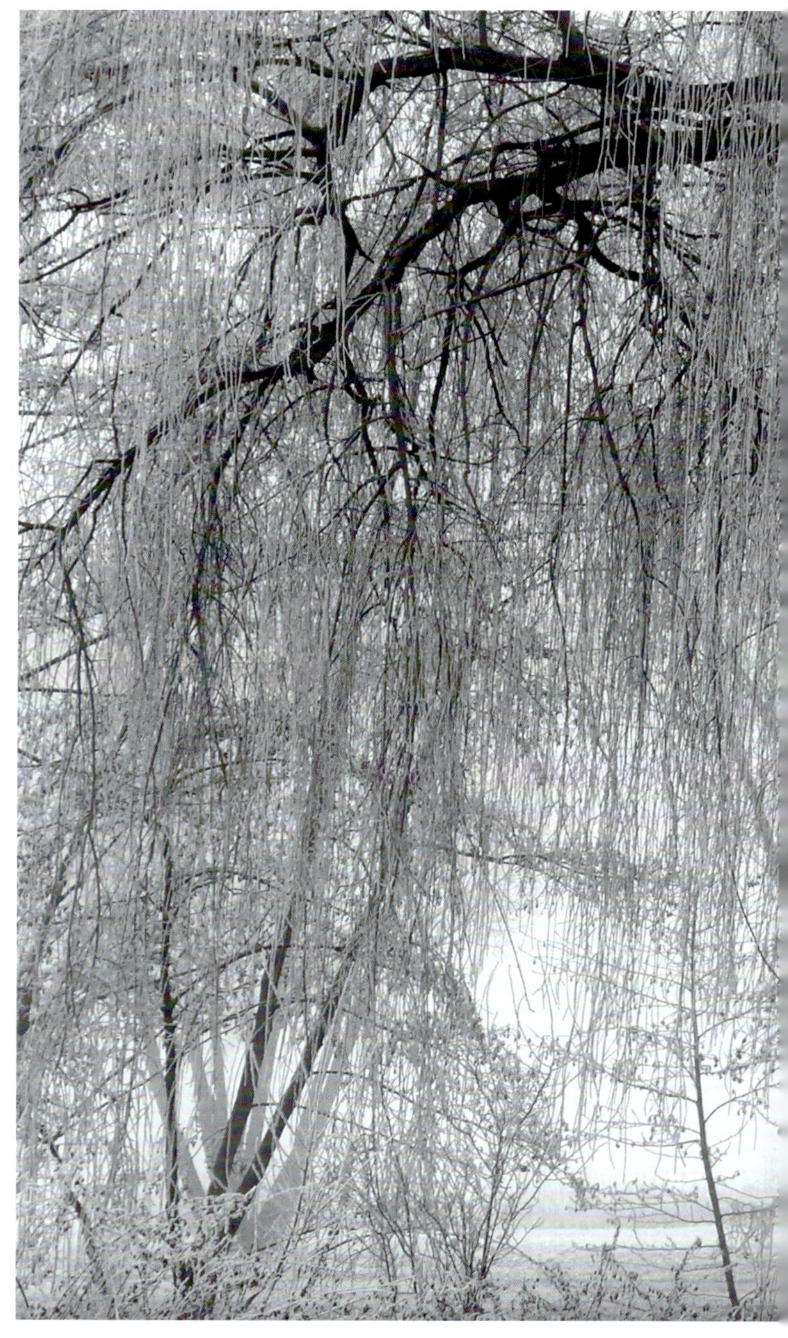

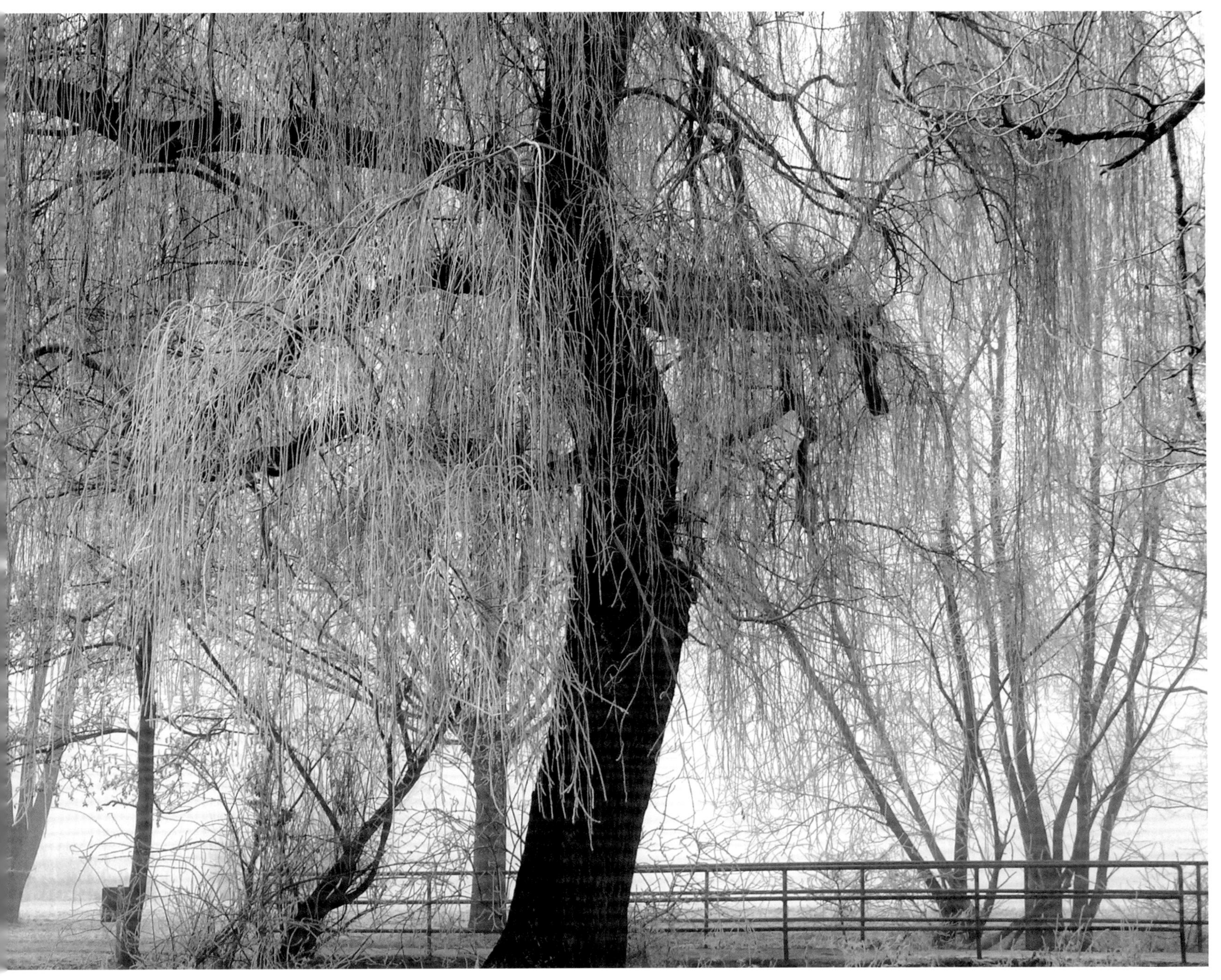

A Universe Identifying and isolating textures amid an abundance of optical impressions is one of the most satisfying tasks for a photographer. You often do not realize the beauty of a texture or pattern until inspecting it through a viewfinder, on the camera's display, or later on a computer monitor. The rows of vines in the Badischen Bergstrasse region of Germany provide a fascinating contrast to the huts and the delicate trees (top). As with other photos in this book, this picture relies on a synthesis of several elements of design: diagonal lines, a contrast arising from small and large objects, varying thicknesses in the pattern, and the graphic effect of the emblematic vines are all highlights of this winter scene.

The patterns in this photo of oats in a field in Liguria (bottom) feel disheveled. The texture of the grain provides an attractive formal contrast with the leaves of the olive trees and their dark branches.

The photo showing an irregular rhythm of grass set against snow (right-hand page) has a completely different feel. The spot-like panicles and the fine wisps of the blades visually evoke the feel of a Japanese ink painting, or the look of a musical score drafted in ink.

The bark of the olive trees (page 160, 161) is as varied as the shapes of the trees themselves. The textures in the trunks cascade through the branches and are wound in an interlocking braid. Only on a second look did I spot the sheep that sought respite from the midday sun at the base of the sinewy trunks. The animal's fur is almost like camouflage against the trees' bark.

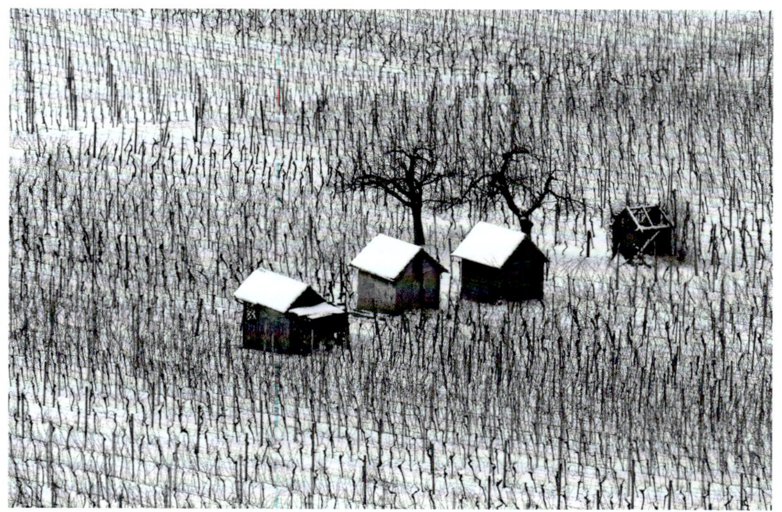

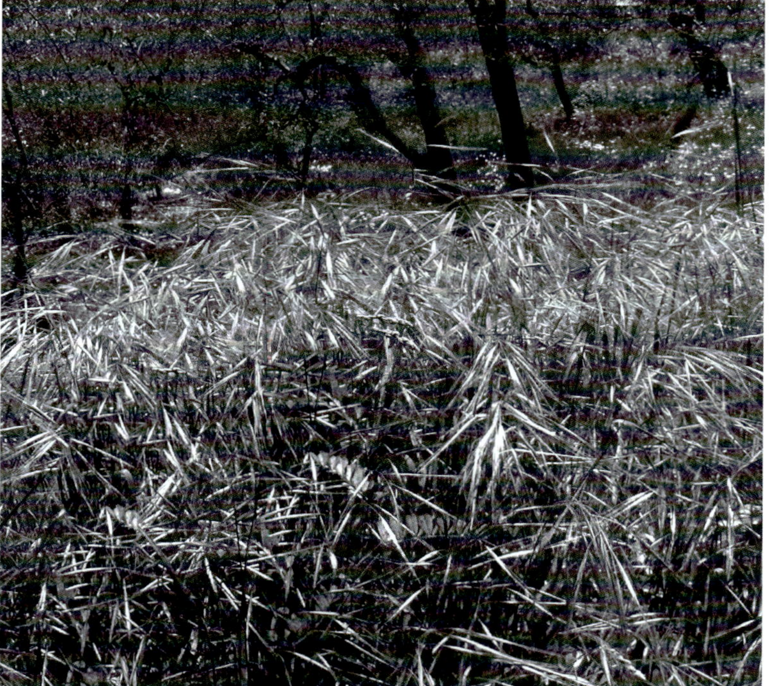

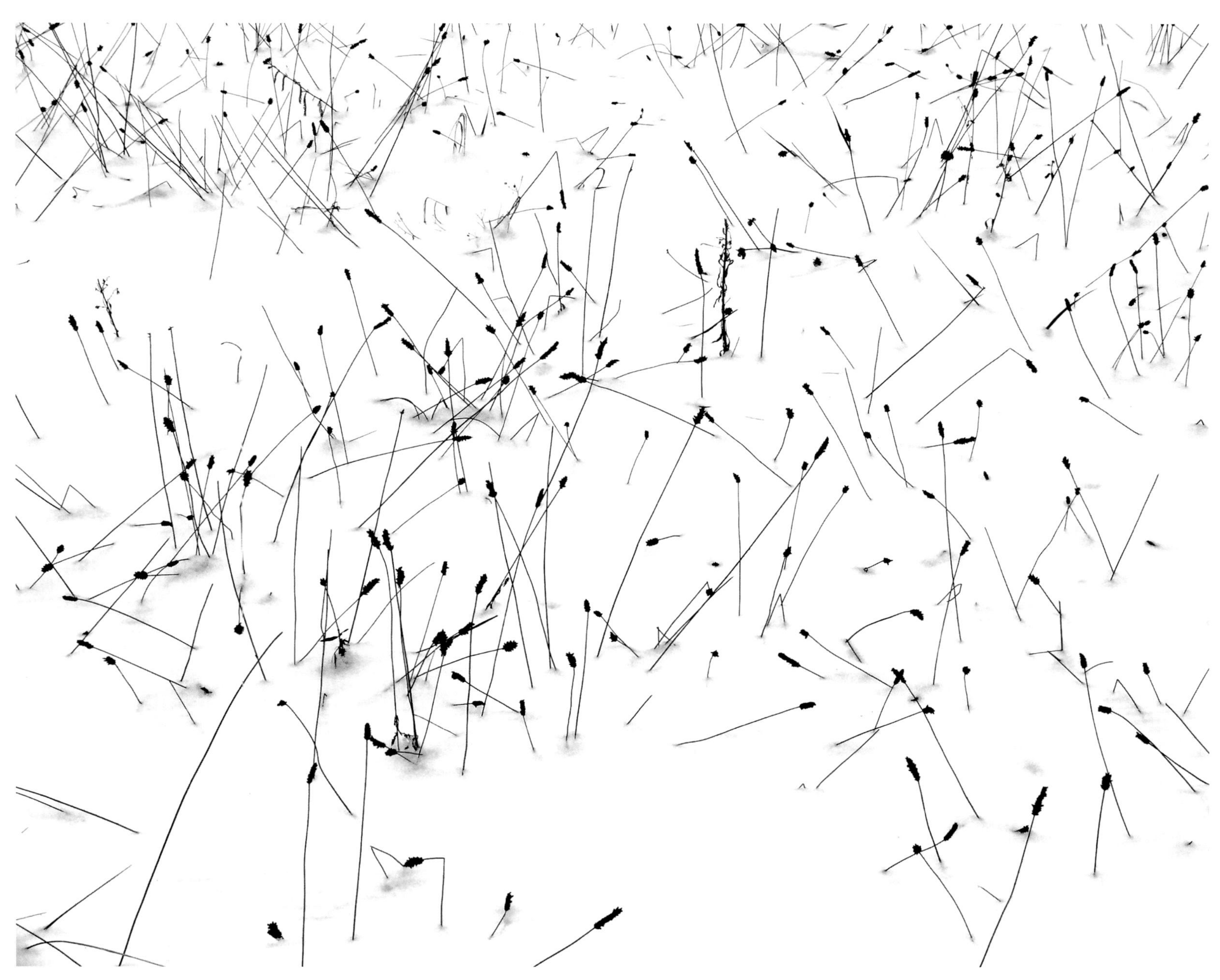

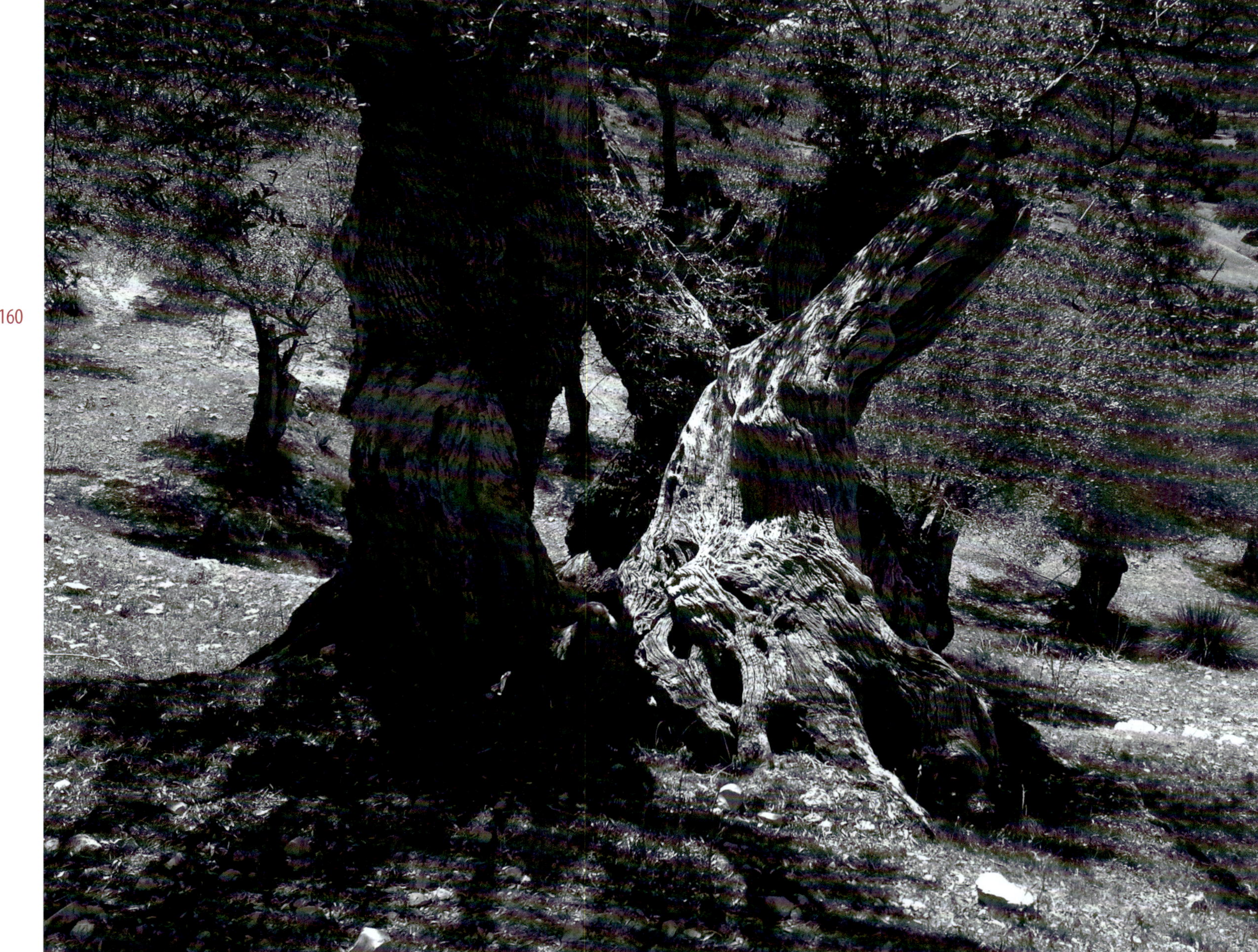

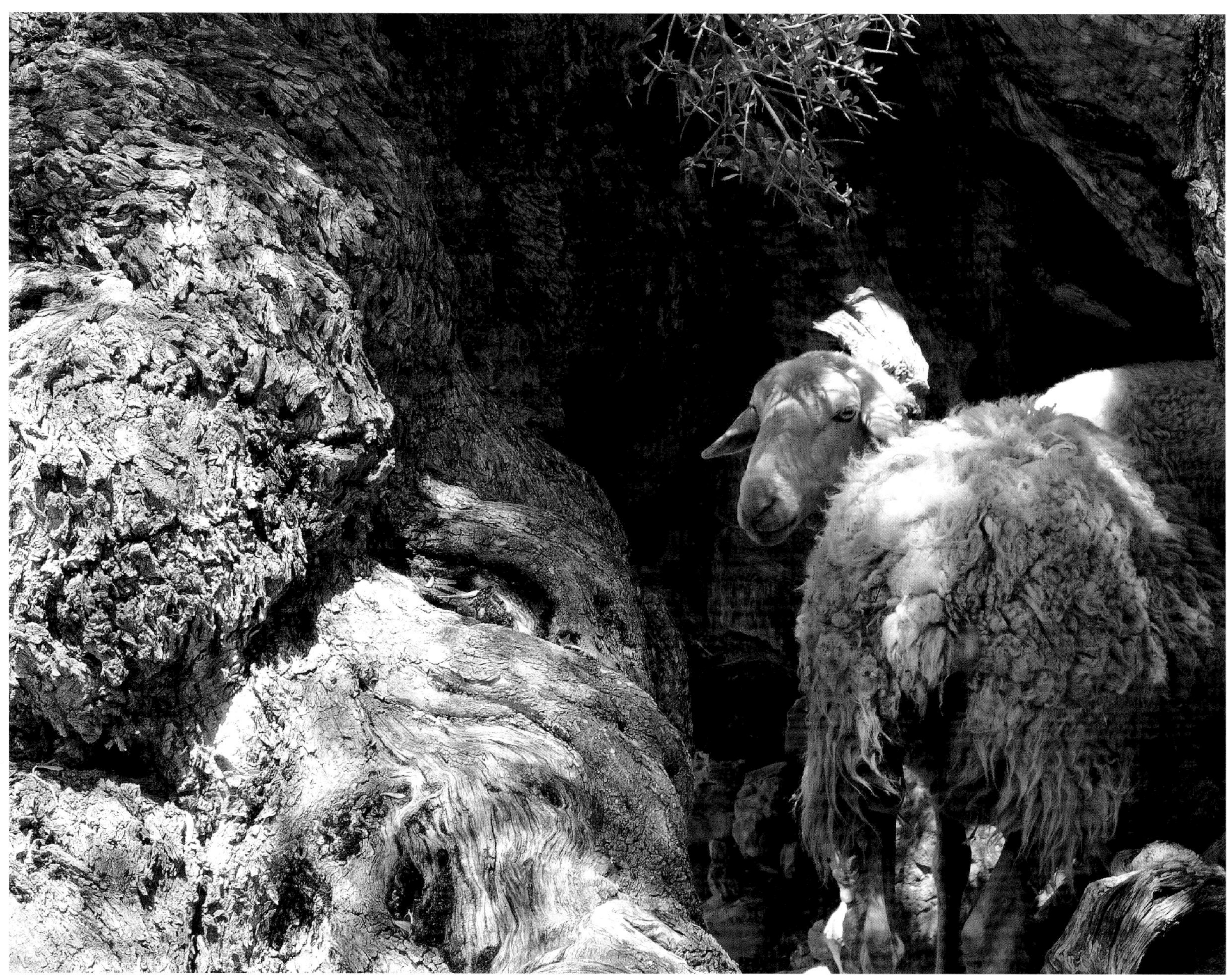

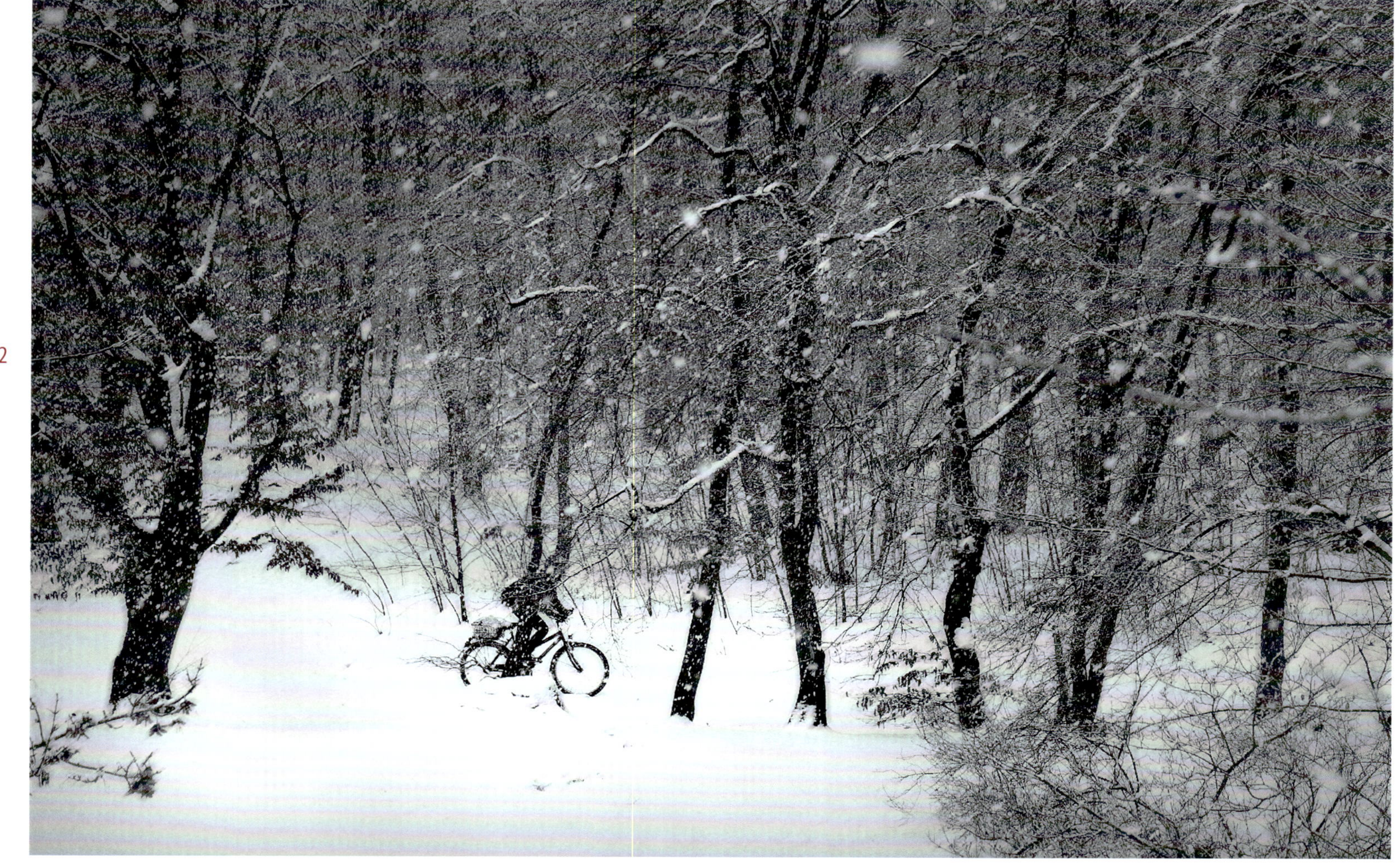

Moving and Stationary On the surface, these wintertime photographs are quite similar. But despite having textures that fill up the entire image area, the two pictures differ in essential ways. The image with the bicyclist keeps the eye from settling in one place. This effect is due to the swirling snowflakes and the way the cyclist leans forward, and accentuated by the rhythm of the trees. In contrast, the bird's-eye view photo of the garden seems utterly frozen. Every detail is fixed in its place. The photo conveys the calm that often occurs after a snowfall.

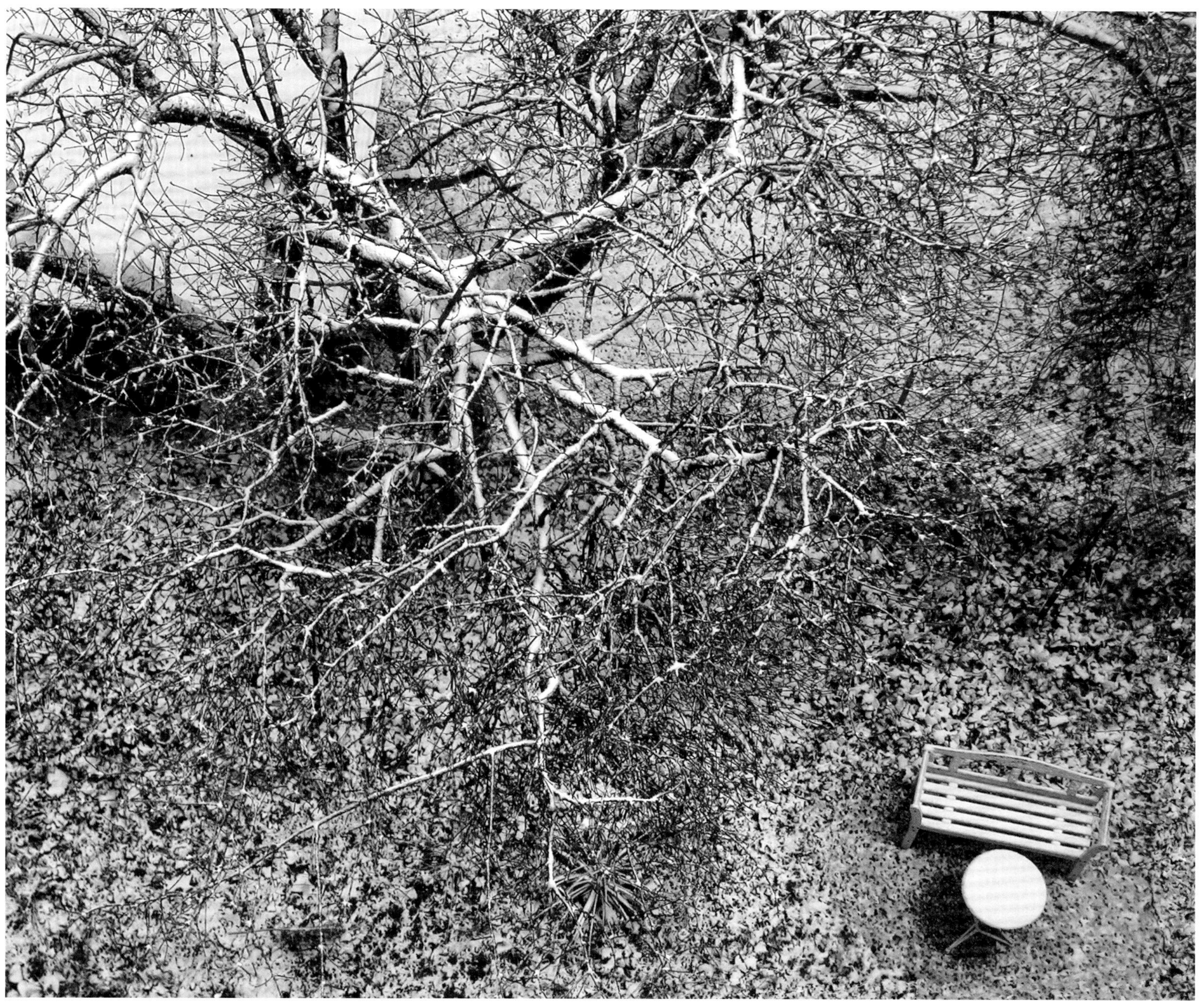

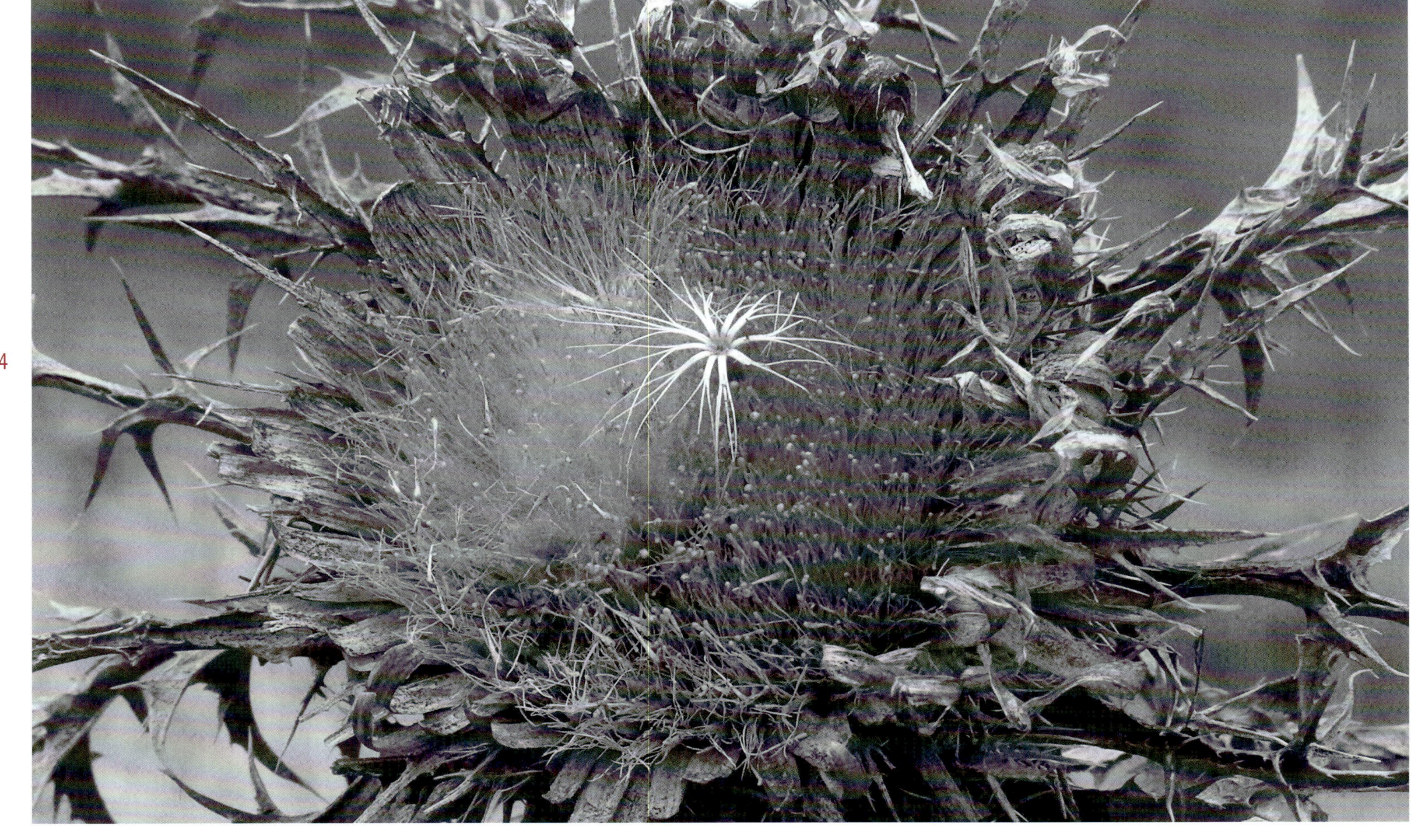

Tip *Test to see if your camera takes good closeup or macro exposures. If it does, use this function to explore a world that is inaccessible to the naked eye.*

Closeup The charm of both of these photos depends on the tension between their main subjects and the rectangular edges of the image area. The silver thistle (above) was shot in Liguria and the ice-covered grass (right-hand page) was shot on the Rhine River near Speyer.

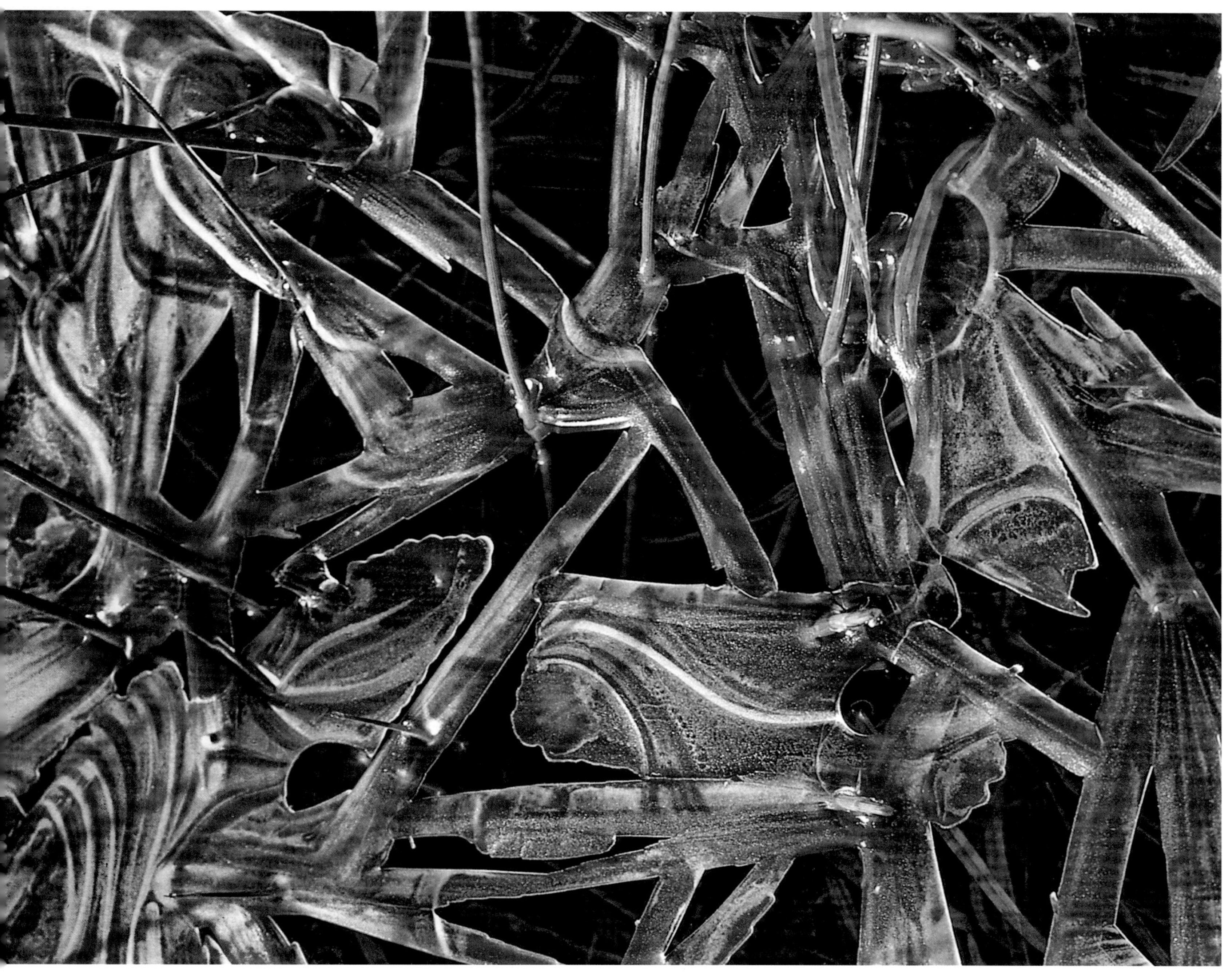

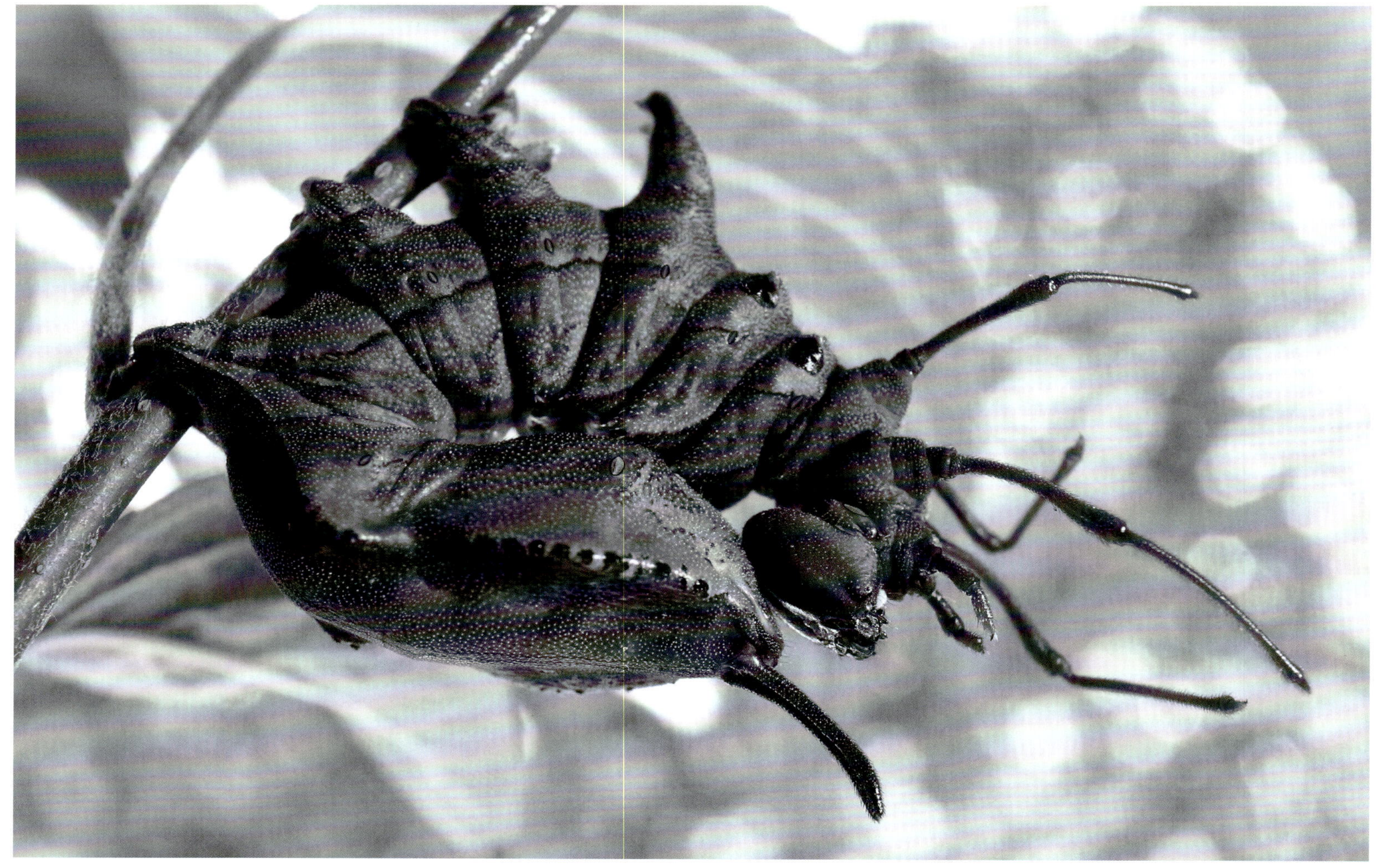

Macrocosm The threatening postures of these caterpillars were captured with a macro lens. Several details were already visible on the camera's display, but the startling sophistication of the moths' crawling bodies came to light only when examining the pictures later on a computer. Both photos were selected from a pool of many based not only on their sharpness, but also on the success of their composition. While the image of the lobster moth caterpillar (top) shows the creature on a light background curled up into an oval, the picture of the winter moth caterpillar (right-hand page) relies on opposing diagonal lines for visual tension.

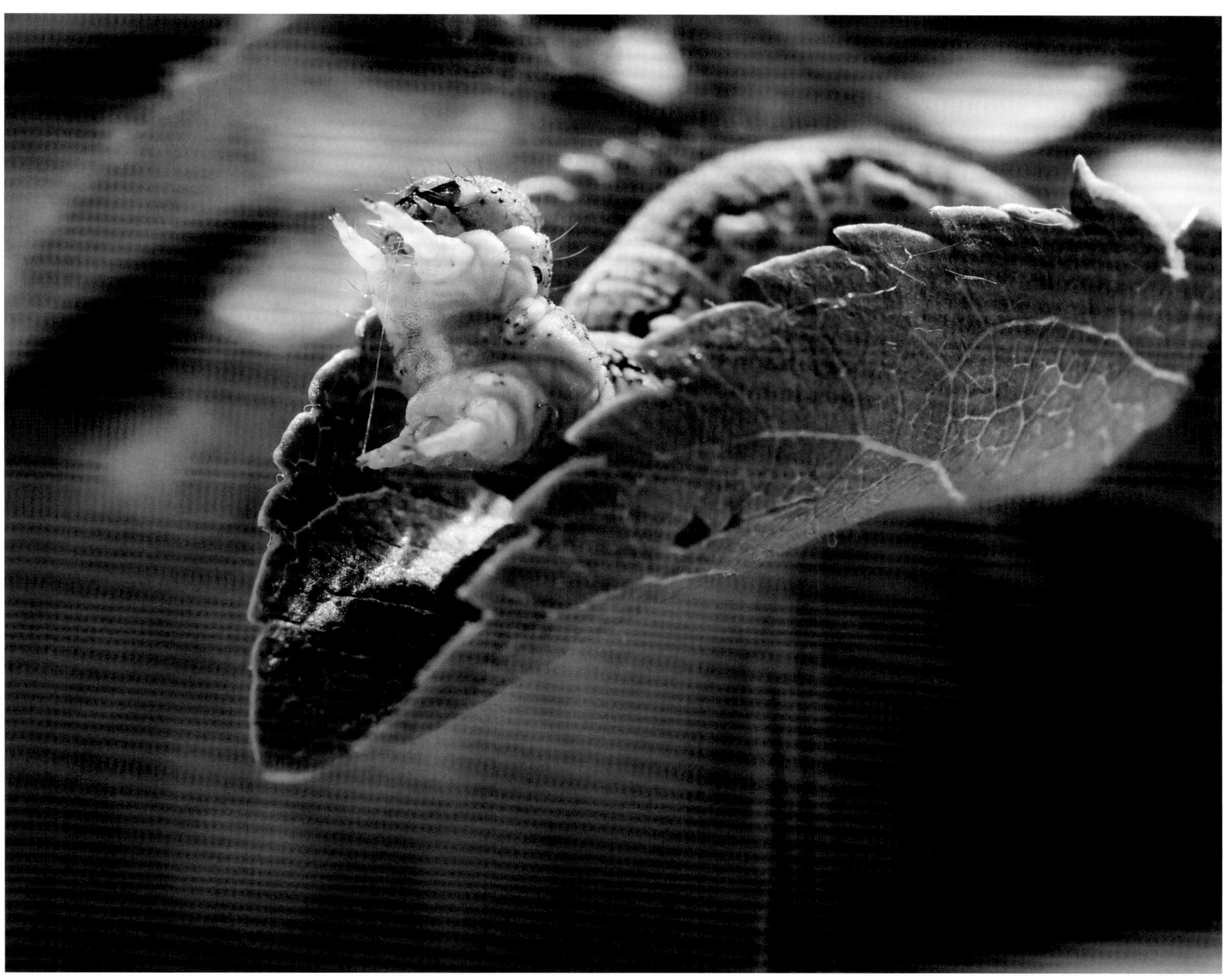

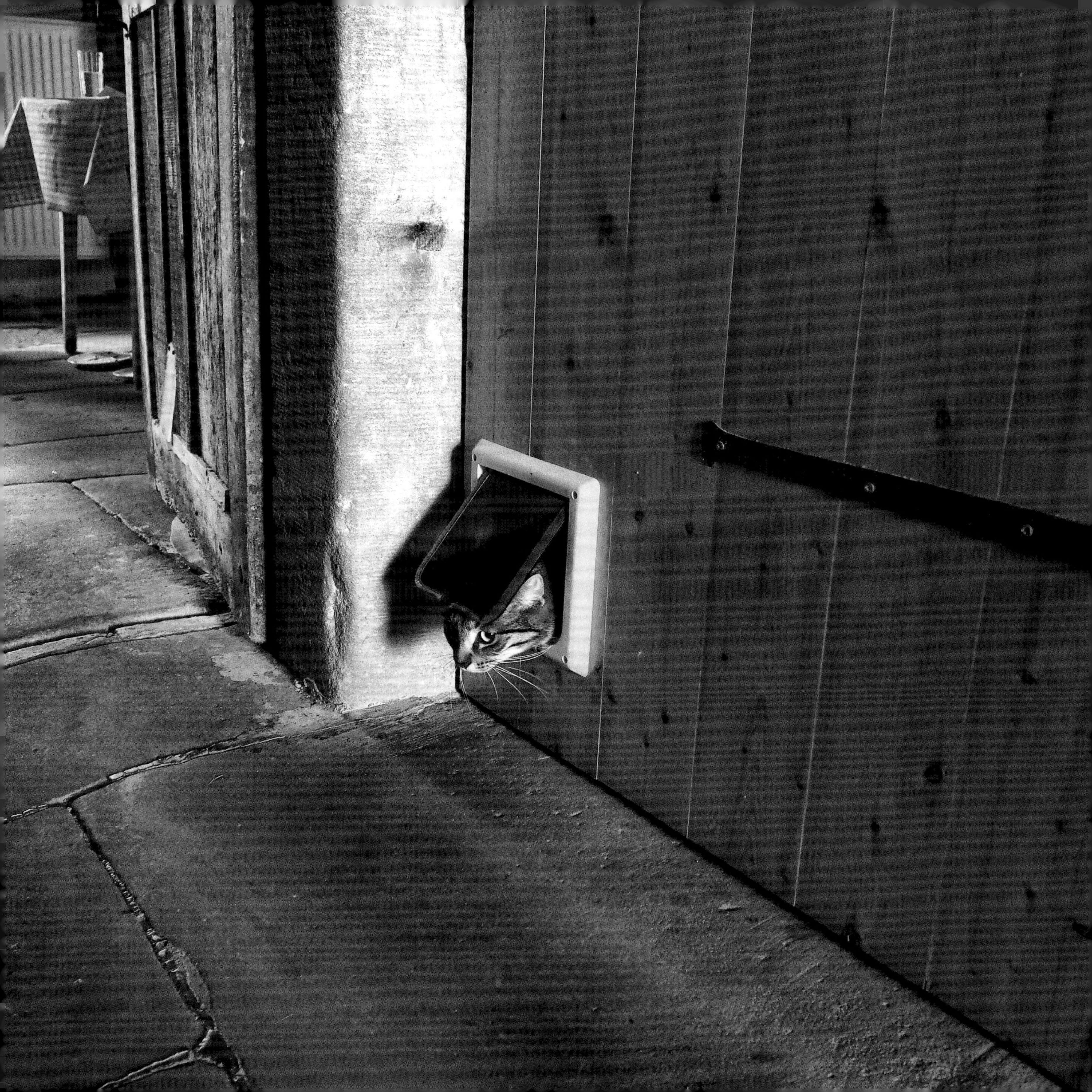

On the Lookout Photographers require a hunter's instinct—not unlike those instincts possessed by some of our favorite subjects: cats make excellent models to follow. Their patience ensures the successful pursuit of a mouse or bird. Patience is necessary for photography: sometimes you have to wait for just the right moment to capture. And patience was exactly the quality I exercised when capturing this domesticated beast at just the right moment (page 169).

Some photos irresistibly invite speech bubbles. The two cows on the Moosfluh above the Aletsch Glacier (top) seem as though they are greeting an exhausted hiker with a casual, "Well, how was it?" The effective composition comprising the flag pole, the rock ledge, and the cow heads was more coincidence than careful planning.

Anyone who has visited the Cimetière Montmartre in Paris will remember the stray cats there. In the bottom photo, one of them decided to rest at the feet of two dogs keeping watch over a gravestone.

Capturing a photo of the nuthatch (right-side page) with a rectangle of light in the background was purely a stroke of luck. The contrasting forms of the arrow-shaped bird and the plump pumpkin gives the image a variety of different shapes and angles.

Tip *Quickly moving subjects make capturing well-composed photos more difficult. One way to deal with this challenge is to use your camera's burst mode. Doing so means you will be able to choose the picture with the best composition from several options.*

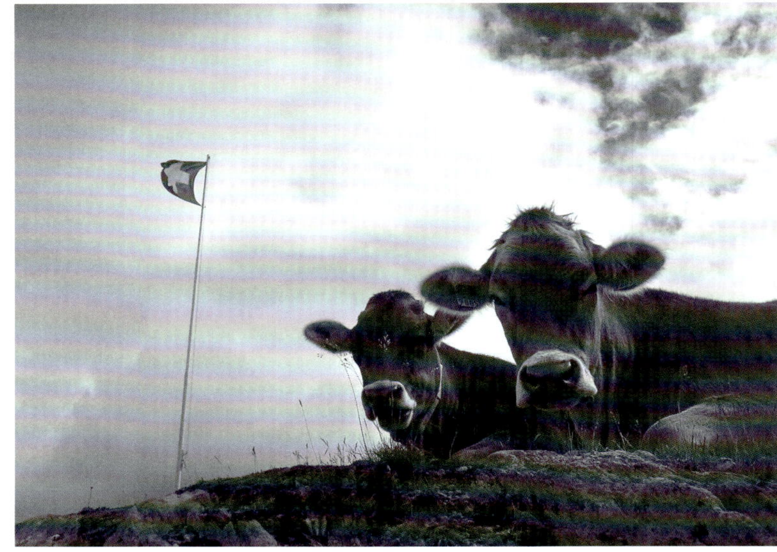

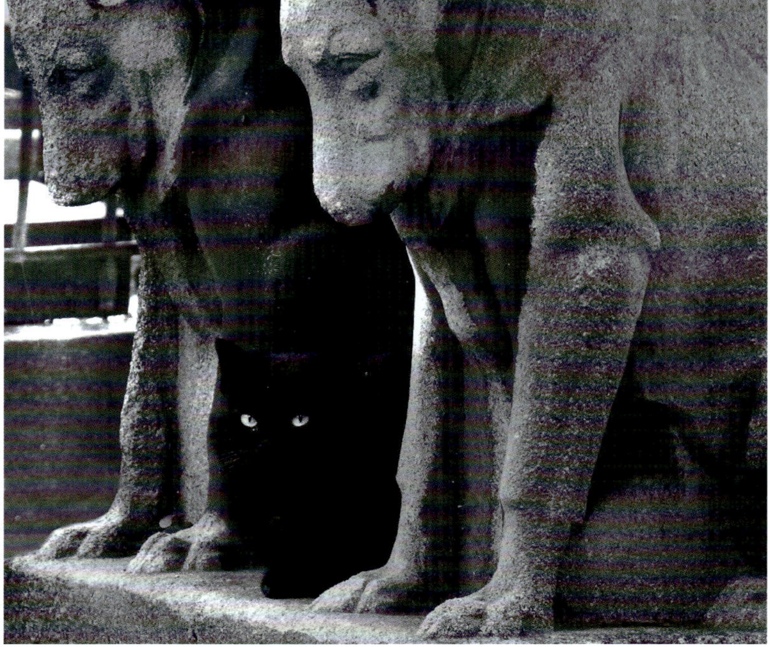

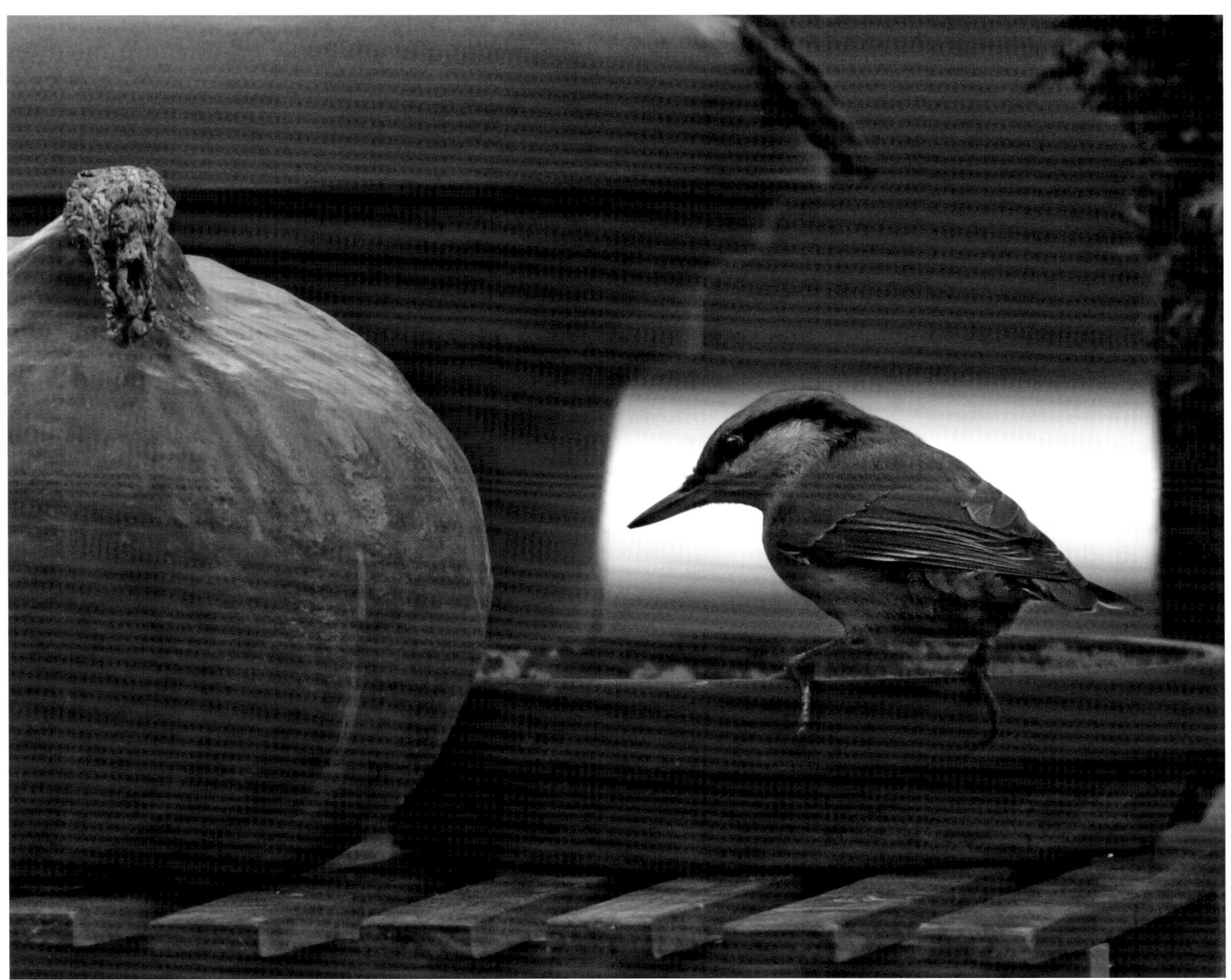

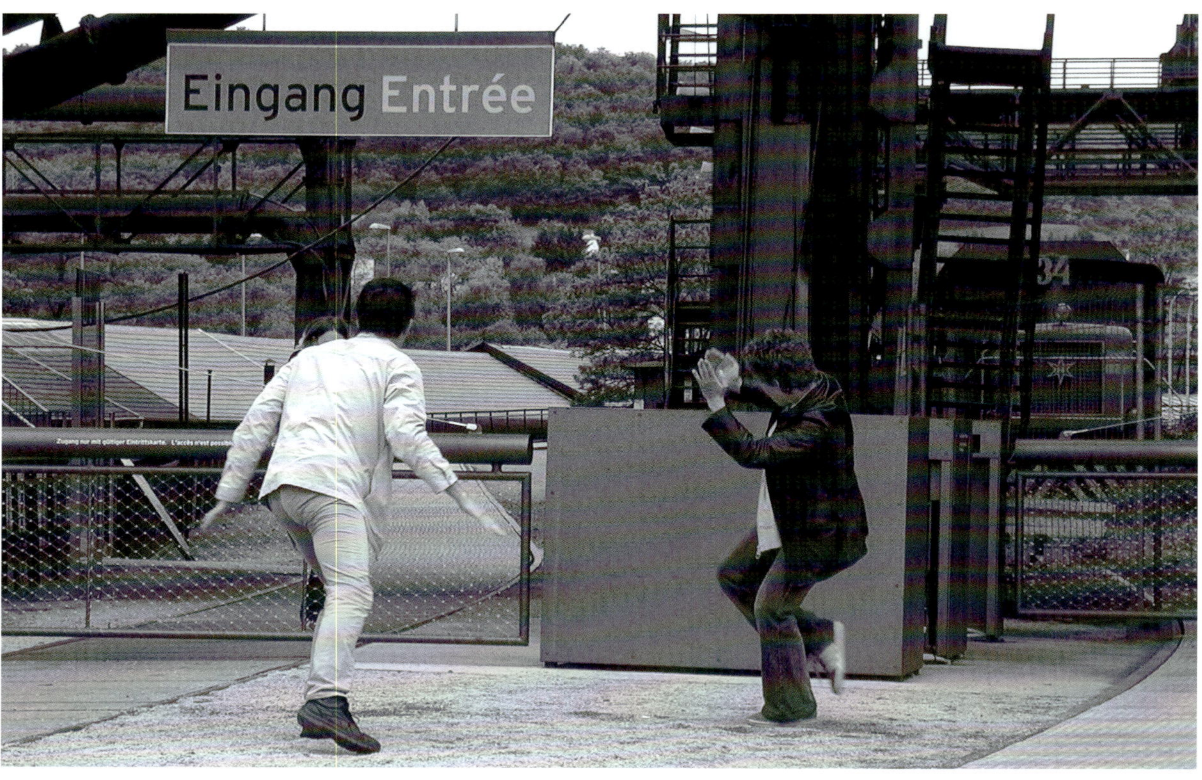

Tip *When you head out intending to take pictures, make sure your camera's battery is fully charged and that you have not left your memory card in your computer. Keeping spare batteries on hand will prevent frustrating situations.*

Windfall Some photos fall into your lap without requiring much work on your part at all. However, an attentive eye, a sense for where to be, a quick reaction time, and some courage naturally help bring these moments about. This entrance to an area of the Völklingen Ironworks, a World Heritage Site, was locked. The two jokers wanted to change that using martial arts (top).
Fat Tuesday in Heidelberg. The photographer anticipated that the chipper ladybug was about to hop from behind the corner (right-hand page). The sign with an arrow for bicyc e traffic is the icing on the cake.

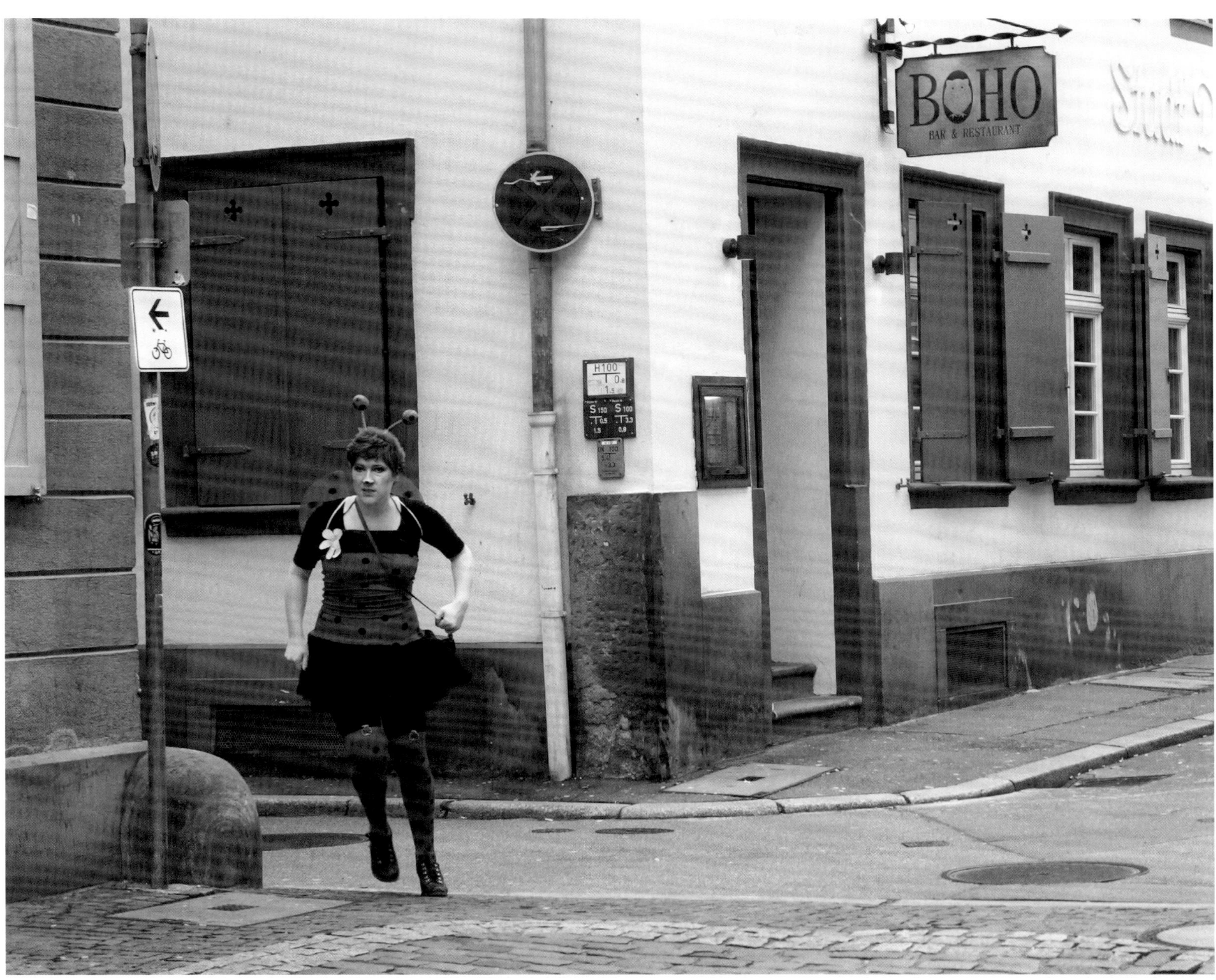
BOHO
BAR & RESTAURANT
H100

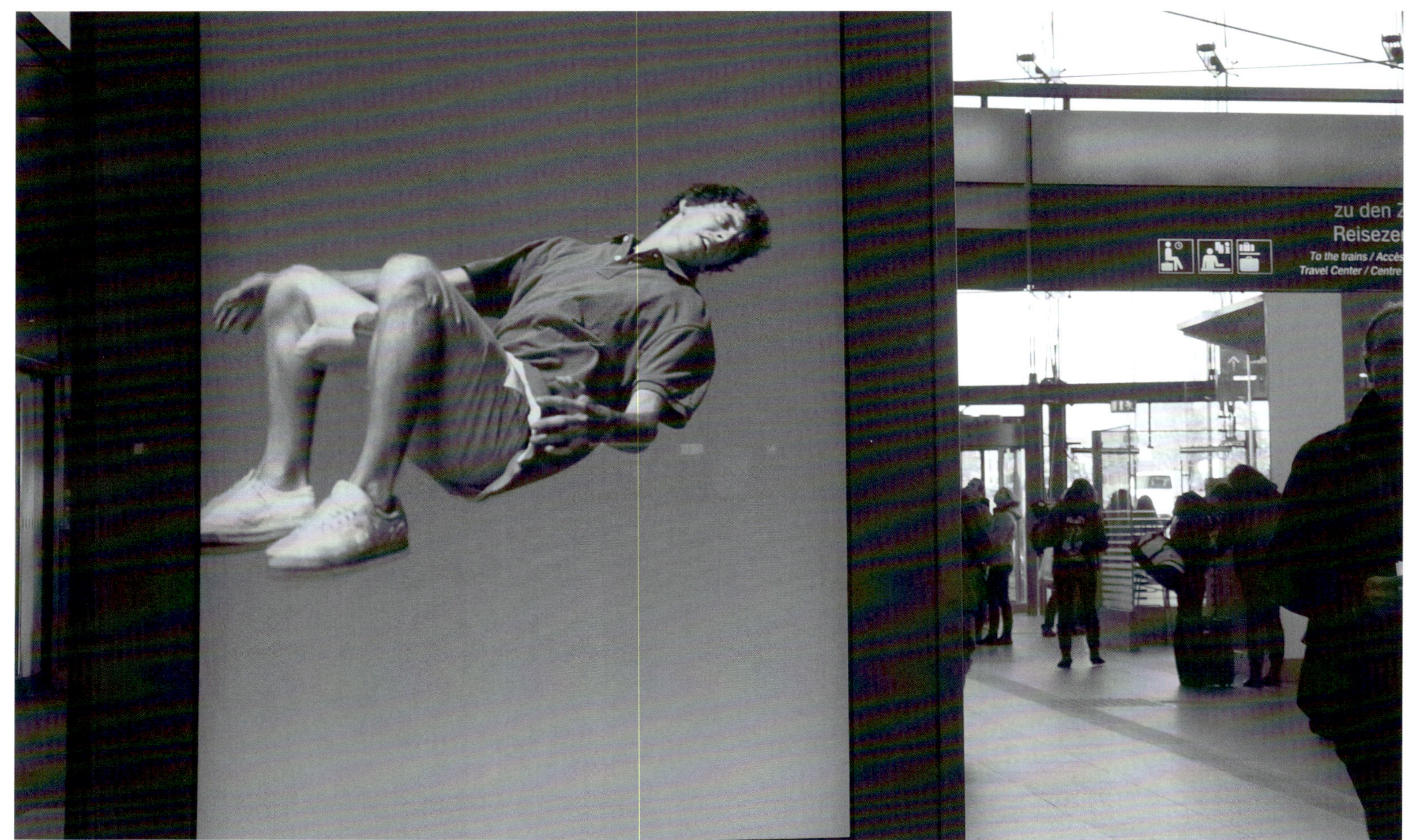

Reflexes These performers were photographed in the main train station in Berlin (top) and on the beach of Conil de la Frontera in Andalusia (right-hand page). In the train station, I watched a performer execute an aerial somersault; I was able to work patiently and wait for him to repeat the somersault to get my desired picture. The picture on the beach was another story: I had to act in the blink of an eye—and with a great deal of good luck—to capture the image at just the right moment.

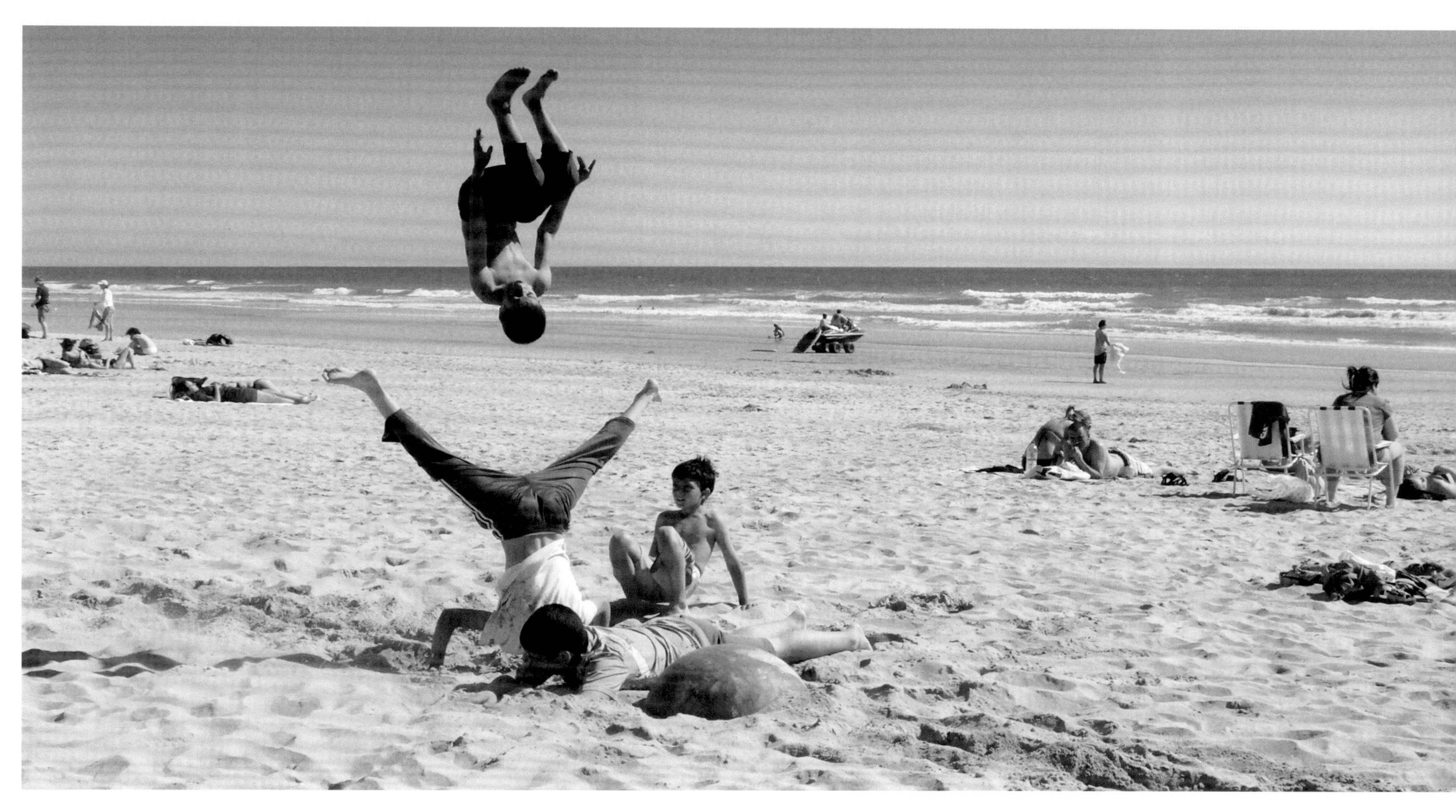

Dialogue Depicting two people engaged in conversation is a classic subject for the visual arts. Many factors affect the quality of such a composition, including the intensity of the interaction, eye contact, the closeness of the exchange (perhaps underscored by a deliberate crop), and the orientation of the figures. These variables determine whether such a photo will be boring or exciting.

The gaze and posture of the salesman at the bird market on the Île de la Cité in Paris is expressive (bottom). His counterpart seems interested, but he clearly has not made a decision yet.

The eye contact between the boy and the caged canary beyond his reach is touching (top).

A mixture of enthusiasm, caution, and vigilance can be seen in the face of the man on the Piazza San Marco in Venice (right-hand page).

All three photos rely heavily on a diagonal connection between the subjects, which accounts for a large part of the tension within the rectangular image area of each.

Tip *Candid snapshots of people who know you are taking their picture are no longer candid. Asking permission to photograph them in advance defeats the purpose. In general, you can tell whether a photograph has been staged. This issue is an unsolved problem that can be addressed only with empathy and intuition.*

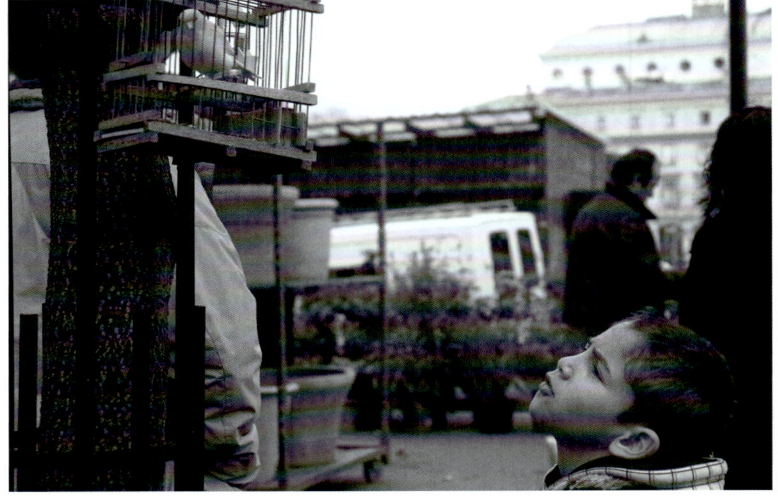

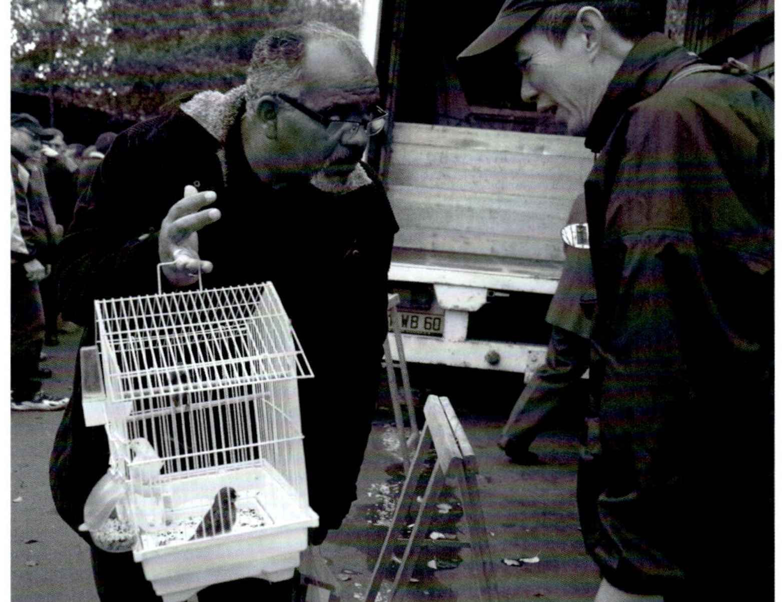

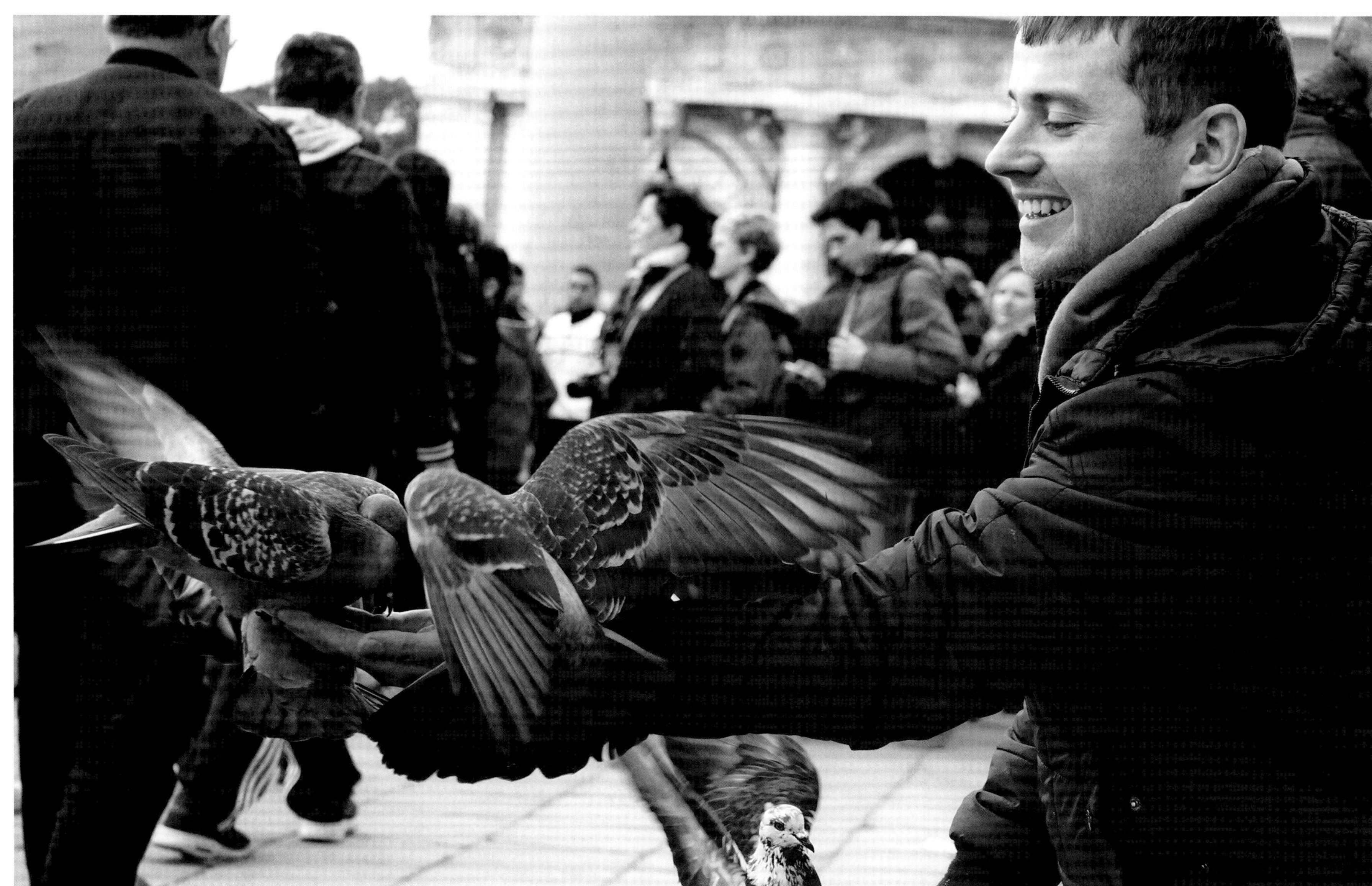

Pairs Conversations can take place between much more than just people sitting at a table or animals playing with one another. Visual pairs can be made of the most incongruous of neighbors.

The pair in the top image is comprised of the house in Bettmeralp and the cloud that seems to shine a spotlight on it. Nature's poetry.

Dialogues can arise between objects that seem to have nothing to do with one another but nevertheless resemble each other in their shapes, as is the case with the tumbleweed and the cloud (bottom-right).

The cyclist and the gracefully curved tree have no formal similarity (bottom-left). But the juxtaposition of a stationary object and a mobile shape create a

sort of visual conversation.

What could the Father Rhine statue (right-hand page) in the gardens of the Schwetzingen Palace be thinking as he gazes out at the empty white bench? That is up to your imagination.

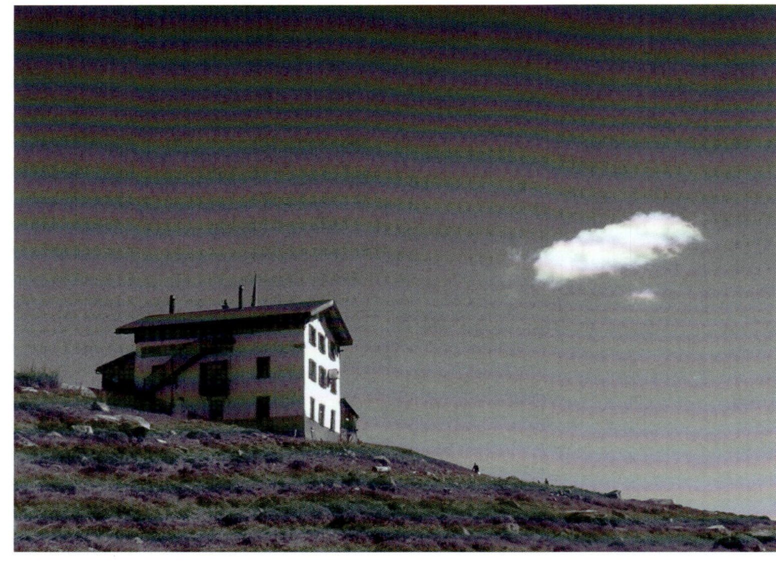

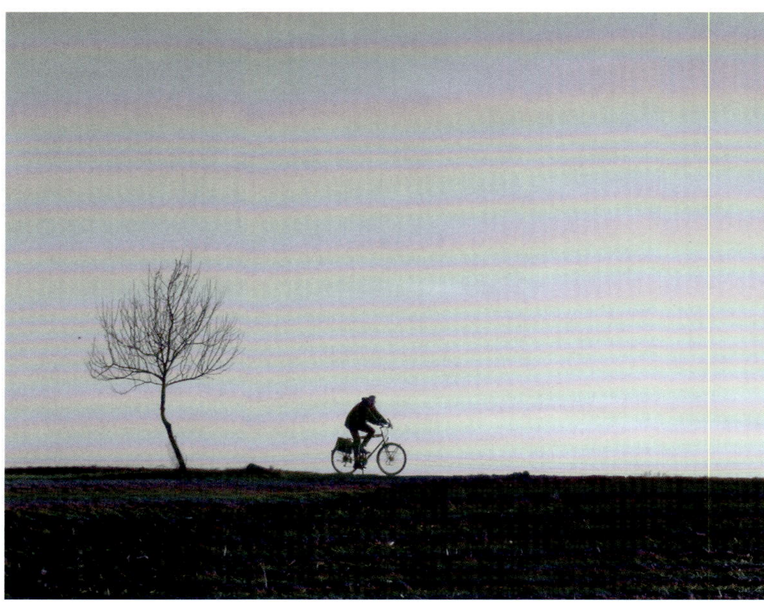

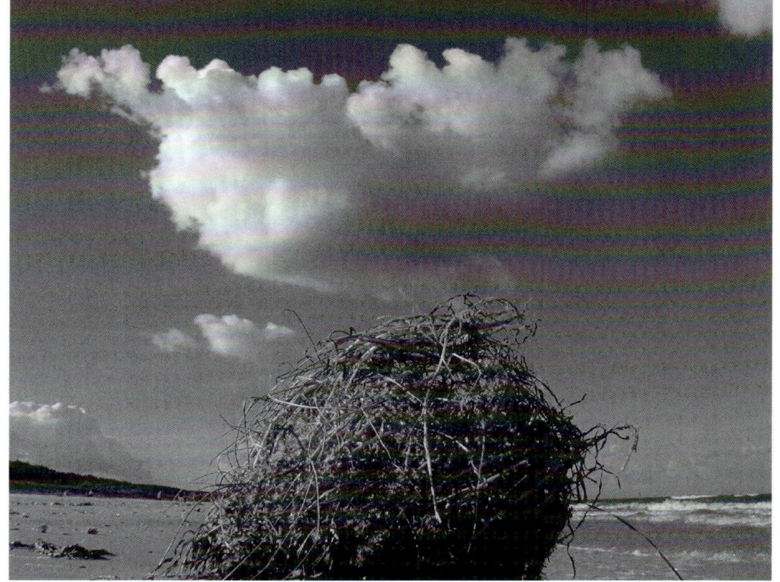

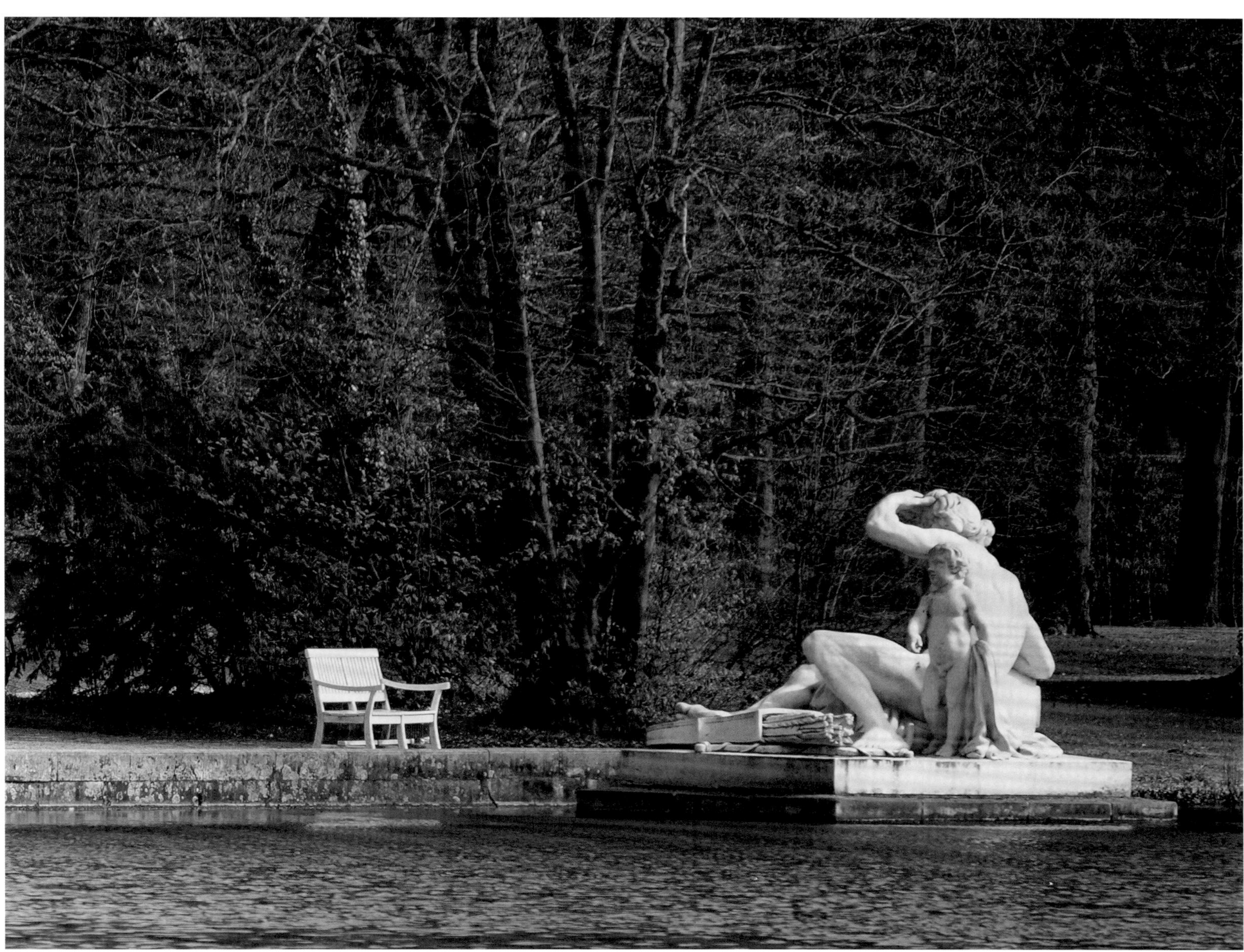

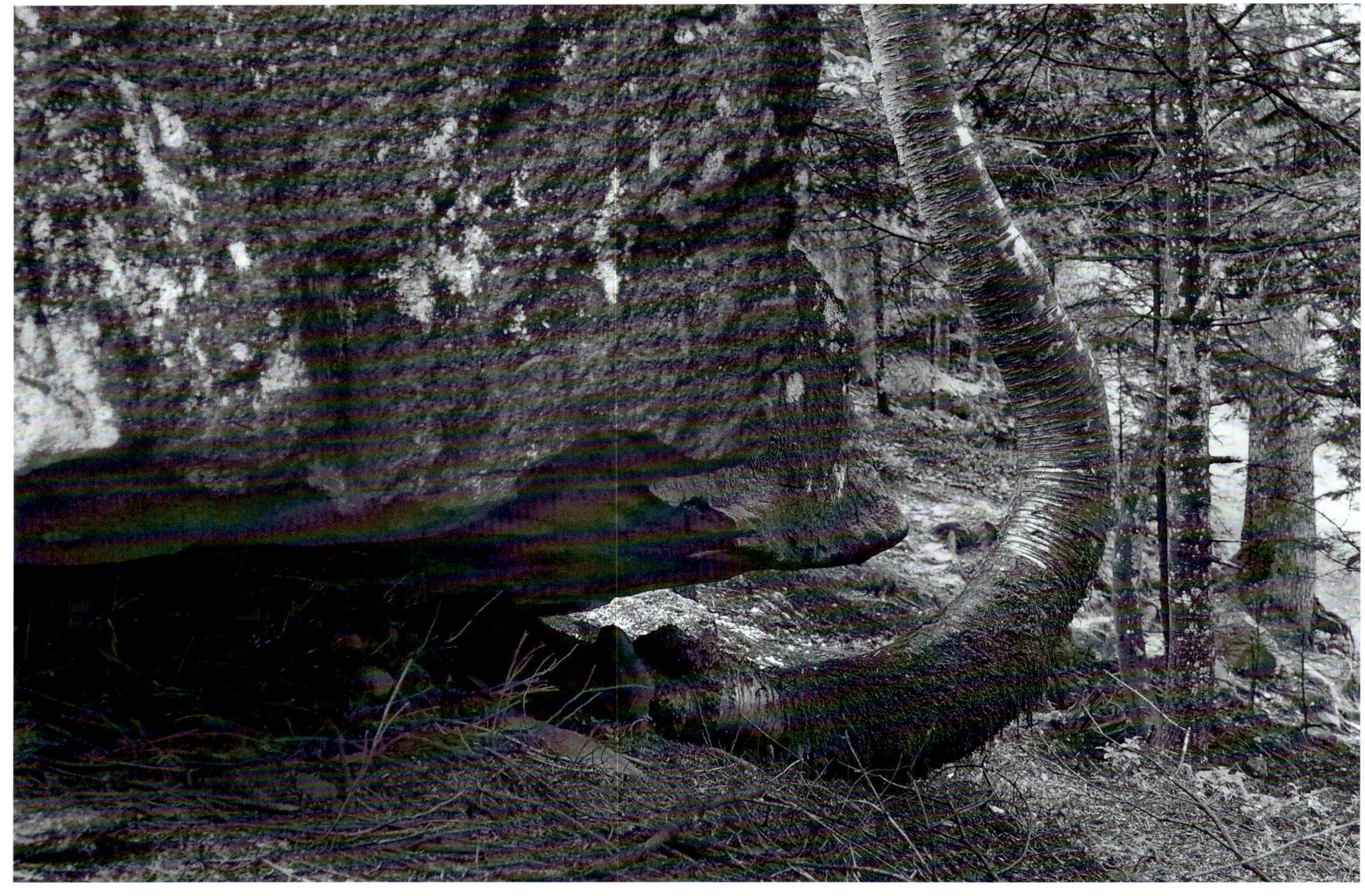

Eyes Peeled It is just like hunting for mushrooms. You always wonder why your basket is still empty while others' seem to be overflowing with the most beautiful of bounties. But sometimes it happens the other way around, too: everyone wears blinders at some time. I am convinced that it is possible to train yourself to look for subjects. Regular attention to works of art can help you improve your sensibility for quality. Learning by seeing also hones your ability to understand and use compositional design principles. The tree growing around a boulder (top) and the beech's elephant-like foot (right-hand page) are both picture-worthy subjects noticed with attentive eyes.

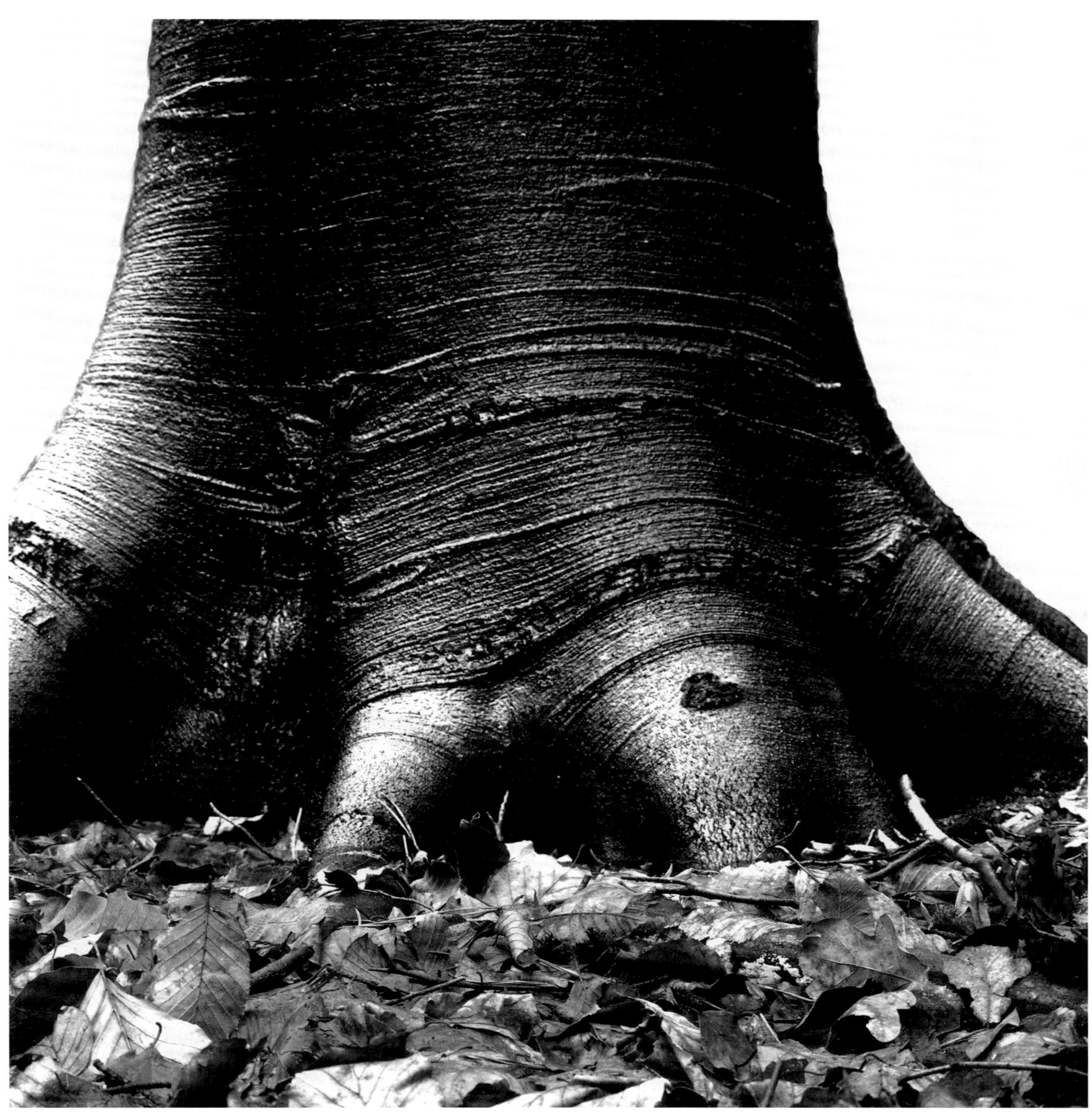

Thanks My friend Walter Spagerer is owed tremendous thanks. I have long benefited from his immense photographic knowledge and ability. My publisher, Gerhard Rossbach, and his colleagues, have earned many special thanks for their helpful and competent handling of my book. I am delighted that my daughter, Julia, was able to assist with the layout of the book. My wife, Ursula, played a key role in this project, and not only because she created the type of environment necessary for an undertaking of this kind, spanning several months. Many of my photographs were taken on our travels together and many are the direct result of her watchful eye. Her photos can be found on pages 2, 3, 24, 25, 35, 76, 77, 84, 85, 92, 121, 123, 135, 155, and 184. Photos by Walter Spagerer can be found on pages 11, 20 (bottom), 91, 109, 113, 118, 129, 151, 162, and 181. Thanks to Arlette Paresys for the images on pages 66 and 150 as well as to Bärbel Mattauch for the image on page 1. Hans Dorenburg is pictured on the cover of the book in the act of drawing on location. Thanks to him and to everyone else for permission to reproduce their likenesses.

I created the remaining photographic works. I shot them over the years with a variety of film and digital cameras of varying quality. Today I predominantly use an Olympus OM-D.

In an effort to portray the art of composition as a widely applicable discipline that is universal to all types of visual arts, I have alluded to several artists and their works at various places in the book to serve as examples. Because there are many ways to access these images today, I have opted not to include reproductions of them in this book.

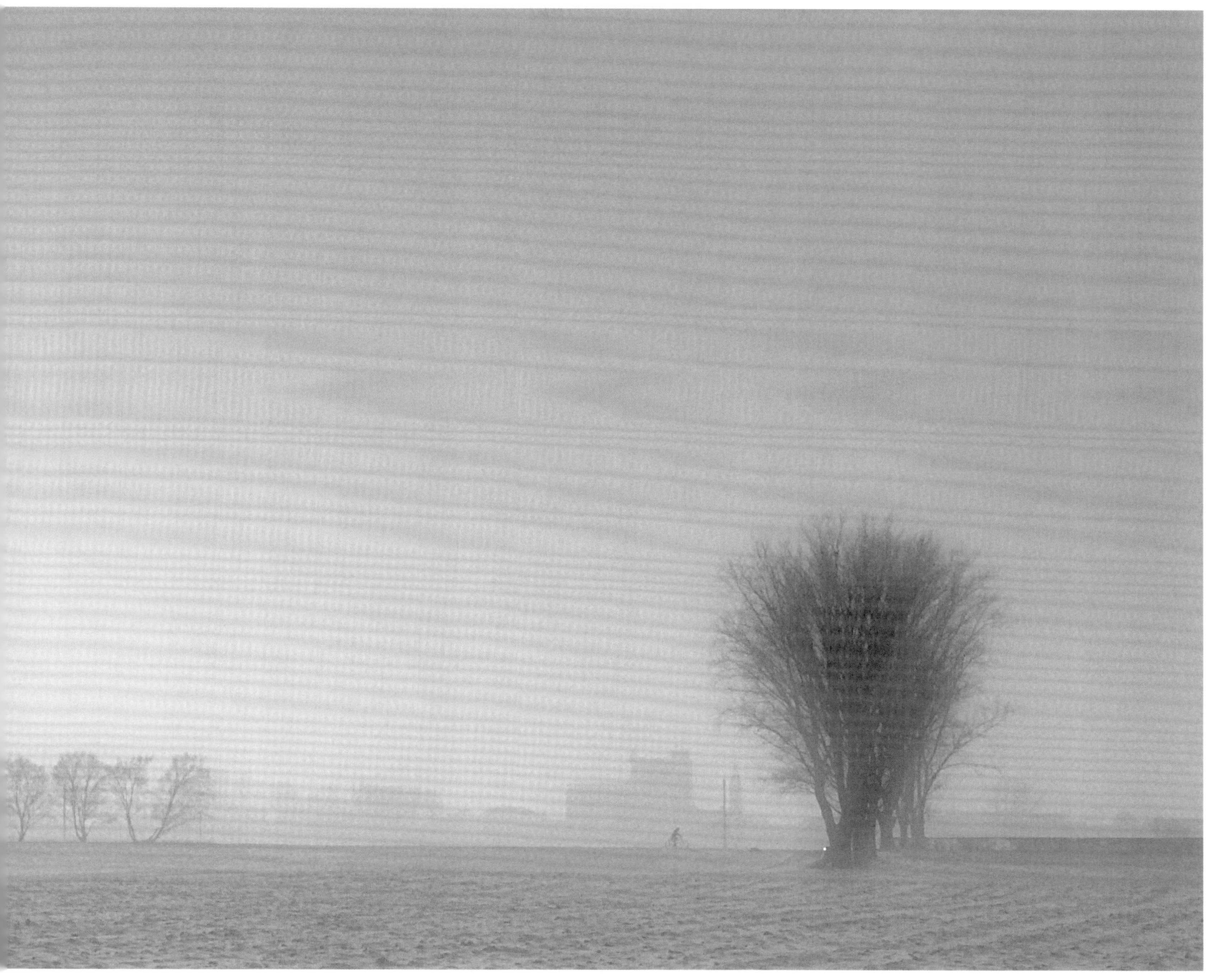

184

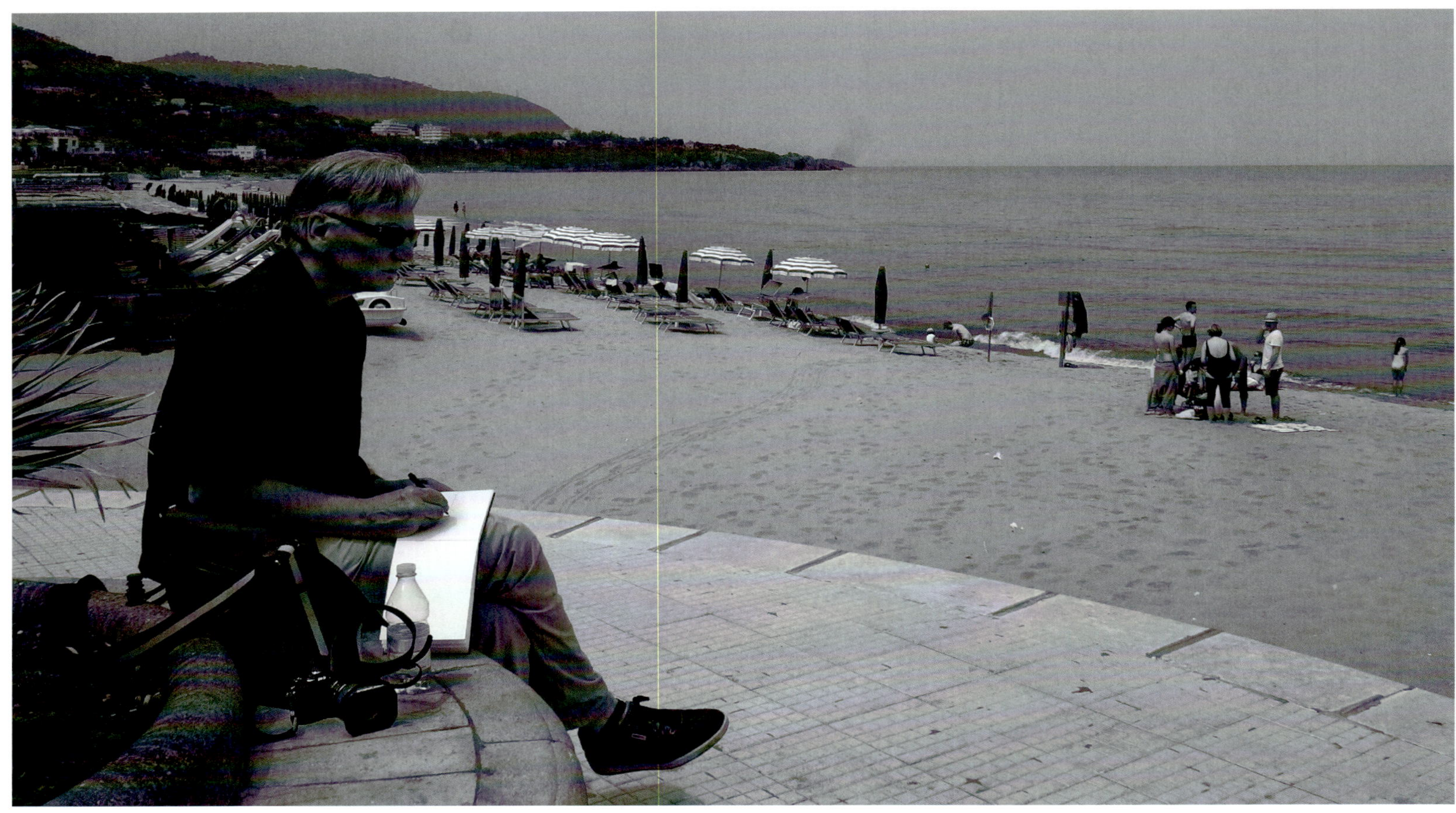

The Author Albrecht Rissler started to draw as a child—and has never stopped. Drawing has played a key role in his development as a window dresser and later as a poster artist and a freelance graphic designer. He studied pedagogy and taught art and technical subjects for 10 years at various schools. In 1980 he founded an illustration studio and worked for a number of book and magazine publishers. In 1988 Albrecht Rissler was hired as a professor of drawing and illustration at the University of Applied Sciences, Mainz. The subject of image composition—often informed by photography—is a key topic in his courses on illustration and in his publications. He has published two other books, on drawing: *Zeichnen. Unterwegs mit Stift und Skizzenbuch* in 1995 and *Zeichnen in der Natur* in 2012.

Albrecht Rissler

Project Editor: Maggie Yates
Translator: David Schlesinger
Copyeditor: Denise J. Iest
Layout: Julia Rissler, Albrecht Rissler, Friederike Diefenbacher-Keita
Cover Design: Helmut Kraus, www.exclam.de
Printer: Friesens Corporation
Printed in Canada

ISBN 978-1-937538-56-9

1st Edition 2014

Rocky Nook Inc.
802 East Cota St., 3rd Floor
Santa Barbara, CA 93103
www.rockynook.com

Title of the German original: Komposition
ISBN 978-3-86490-141-6

Library of Congress Cataloging-in-Publication Data

Rissler, Albrecht.
Photographic composition : principles of image design / by Albrecht Rissler. -- 1st edition.
pages cm
Includes bibliographical references and index.
ISBN 978-1-937538-56-9 (softcover : alk. paper)
1. Composition (Photography) I. Title.
TR179.R57 2014
770.1--dc23
2014017567

Distributed by O'Reilly Media
1005 Gravenstein Highway North
Sebastopol, CA 95472